# From Grading to Classification

# China's Path to Education Modernization

Zhenguo Yuan

*General Editor*

Vol. 3

Xu Guoqing

# From Grading to Classification

## The Reform and Development Path of Vocational Education

PETER LANG
Lausanne • Berlin • Bruxelles • Chennai • New York • Oxford

**Library of Congress Cataloging-in-Publication Control Number:** 2022002056

Bibliographic information published by the **Deutsche Nationalbibliothek.**
**The German National Library** lists this publication in the German National Bibliography; detailed bibliographic data is available on the Internet at http://dnb.d-nb.de.

Cover design by Peter Lang Group AG

This translation project was funded by the Chinese Fund for the Humanities and Social Sciences.
The 1st book of this series actually has the funding information.

ISBN 9781433169304 (hardback)
ISBN 9781433195969 (ebook)
ISBN 9781433195976 (epub)
DOI 10.3726/b15939

Original title: 从分等到分类—职业教育改革发展之路
Xu Guoqing.

Published by Peter Lang Publishing Inc., New York, USA
info@peterlang.com - www.peterlang.com



This publication has been peer reviewed.

# Table of Contents

# List of Figures

# List of Tables

# General Preface to *China's Path to Education Modernization*

## Comprehensively Deepen Reform and Accelerate the Realization of Education Modernization

In December 1978, the Third Plenary Session of the 11th CPC Central Committee determined the ideological line of emancipating the mind and seeking truth from facts, and made major decisions on reform and opening-up. Since reform and opening-up, China's economy has maintained sustained growth for 40 years; the GDP per capita has leapt from the 171st to the 70th[1] position in the world; the GDP has jumped from the 9th to the 2nd postion[2]; the rate of contribution to the world economy has increased from 3.05% in 1978 to 31.53%[3] in 2016. This is a miracle not only in Chinese history but also in world history.

China's education is an important part of this miracle and also a significant impetus for its creation. The gross enrollment rate for preschool education in China has increased from 12.62% in 1981 to 77.4% in 2016, exceeding the average level of medium- and high-income countries by 5 percentage points; the consolidation rate for nine-year compulsory education reached 93.4% in 2016, surpassing the average level of high-income countries; the gross enrollment rate for secondary education increased from 39.56% in 1981 to 87.5% in 2016, 5 percentage points higher than the average level of medium- and high-income countries; the gross enrollment rate of higher education has increased from 1.6% in

1981 to 42.7% in 2016, above the average of medium- and high-income countries by 6 percentage points. At the same time, China's PISA performance and university development have done quite well, revealing a considerable improvement in the quality of China's education.

The development of education has brought about significant changes in China's human resource structure. The average years of schooling for the population aged 16–59 has risen from less than 5 years in 1981 to 10.35 in 2016; the proportion of the population with college degrees or above has increased from 0.58% in 1982 to 12.44%[4] in 2015. The number of China's expected years of education in 1990 was 8.8, ranking 119th in the world; it increased to 13.5 years in 2015, and the world ranking rose to 83rd.[5] China has transformed from a country with a large population into one with huge human resources, and is striding towards a country powerful in human resources day by day.

The academic world has taken an increasingly keen interest in revealing the successful experiences and reasons for China's reform and opening-up, and Chinese scholars also feel obligated to do so. John King Fairbank (1907–1991), a famous American research scholar on China studies, published *The United States and China* 70 years ago. This was the first monograph in which a comparison between China and the United States had been conducted by a Western scholar. In this book, Fairbank said that China was undergoing a modernization movement, and its most fundamental feature was the determination to abandon all the traditions and institutions of China, and think of all Western civilizations and institutions, including language, as a counterpart. As a result, China's modernization can be considered as a process of the West's constant impact on China and China's constant responses to the West. The "Impact-Response Model" had been the consensus among Western scholars on China's upcoming modernization road for a long time.[6] However, in 1991, he said in *China: A New History*, which was published two days before his death that: "After 50 years of experience and observation, I found that China's modernization is probably not a result of impact-response, but a result of an inherent revolution and development impulse."[7]

Ronald H. Coase (1910–2013), a Nobel Prize winner in economics, published *How China Became Capitalist*, a book co-authored with his assistant Wang Ning at the age of 102. In this book, he said: "China is highly successful and her development will carry on. However, the development of China's economy can not be explained by traditional Western economics. The success of China's reform is an unexpected consequence of human behavior."[8]

The world is pluralistic. There is not only one path to modernization, nor a standard road. The successful practices of China and its education modernization have proved that there are many paths to and forms of modernization, as thoroughly demonstrated by China's successful modernization to the world.

## Education Modernization Is the Consistent Theme of Chinese Educational Reform and Opening-Up

Practice shows that the history of Chinese educational reform and development since reform and opening-up is about exploring and striving for educational modernization, and progressing in the modernization of socialist education with Chinese characteristics.

In 1983, Deng Xiaoping wrote an inscription for Beijing Jingshan School, "Gear education to the needs of modernization, the world and the future." This reflected the Chinese people's aspirations and determinations to develop education, and established the ideological foundation and strategic direction for the reform and development of Chinese education.

The *Decision of the CPC Central Committee on the Reform of the Education System* in 1985 clarified the monumental mission of socialist education modernization: "Not only must we let go of our efforts to improve existing talent, but also greatly enhance the whole Party's understanding of education. Gear education to the needs of modernization, the world and the future, in order to massively prepare new qualified talented people of all kinds at all levels who can adhere to the socialist direction for the economic and social development of our country in the 1990s and the beginning of the next century."

In 1993, the CPC Central Committee and the State Council issued *Outline of China's Education Reform and Development*, which further clarified the target of Chinese education reform and development: "After decades of endeavor, we will establish a more mature and perfect socialist education system and realize education modernization."

In July 2010, *Outline of the National Medium- and Long-Term Education Reform and Development Plan (2010–2020)* clearly stated: "By 2020, we will basically realize education modernization, form a learning society, and become one of the countries powerful in human resources." The *Outline* requires us to prepare human resources ahead of time for the basic realization of education modernization in China.

In 2017, the 19th CPC National Congress emphasized once again: "Building a country powerful in education is the foundation project for the great rejuvenation of the Chinese nation. We must give priority to education, expedite education modernization and develop education that people are satisfied with." The 19th CPC National Congress report further underlined how urgent it was to achieve education modernization.

In a word, education modernization has always been the consistent theme and head-line banner of Chinese educational reform and development, and has become the ideal pursuit and spiritual impetus for bringing together all the forces of China to develop education as a priority. It has not only guaranteed human resources and intellectual support for the modernization of industry, agriculture, national defense, science, and technology, but has also had a decisive significance in building a prosperous, democratic, civilized, harmonious, and beautiful modern socialist country.

## The Deepening of Reform and Opening-Up Is a Powerful Engine for Education Modernization

Chinese education modernization has always been accompanied by reform and opening-up. Education modernization has established the overall direction for education reform and development. Reform and opening-up has not only provided a powerful impetus for the realization of education modernization, but also laid out the basic path for the rapid advancement of education modernization in China.

In 1977, China restored the policy of the entrance examinations for higher education and sent students aboard, signaling China's reform and opening-up. Since then, education reform has gradually been launched and deepened in the context of reform and opening-up throughout the country. Through bringing order out of chaos from 1977 to 1985, the full-scale launching from 1985 to 1993, the comprehensive deepening from 1993 to 2010, and the promotion of comprehensive education reform since 2010, China has created a brand new model of socialist education modernization with Chinese characteristics.

**Emancipating the mind and bringing order out of chaos in the period 1977–1985.** Since the late 1950s, education was not given its due important position for a long time, and worse still, it was frequently impacted by previous political movements due to the focus of the Party's work not being toward economic construction, and that the Party was influenced by the "Left" ideology of "making class struggle as the central task." The "Cultural Revolution" pushed this kind of "Left" error to the extreme by denying knowledge and eliminating education, thus seriously destroying the course of education and severely devastating masses of teaching fellows. This not only impeded the growth of a whole generation but also widened the gap between the education of China and the developed countries which had already shrunk in many aspects. Since the Third Plenary Session of the Eleventh CPC Central Committee (1978) when the leadership began bringing order out of chaos, the Party Central Committee made a series of new judgments and decisions on education, which contributed to the resumption of Chinese education on the path of vigorous development.

**The full-scale launch of education reform from 1985 to 1993.** Rome was not built in one day. In the initial stages of reform and opening-up, the misconception of despising education, knowledge, and talented people still prevailed; the "Left" influence on education was not completely eliminated; the situation that education could not meet the demands for socialist modernization was not fundamentally turned around. The backwardness of Chinese education and the disadvantages of the education system became more prominent when faced with China's opening-up to the outside world and invigorating the domestic economy, as well as the all-round development of reconstructing the economic system and the rise of a new world-wide technological revolution. In particular, with regard to the supervision of administrative authorities over education, relevant government departments exercised overbroad and rigid administration of schools, especially institutions of higher education, and caused schools at all levels to lose proper vigor; at the same time, government departments didn't well manage what they should have. In terms of the education structure, basic education was weak; the number of schools was insufficient; the quality was unsatisfactory; and qualified teachers and necessary equipment were seriously lacking. Vocational and technical education, which was urgently needed for economic construction, was not properly developed; the proportions of specialties, disciplines, and school levels within higher education were out of balance. At the same time, outdated curriculum, rigid and single teaching methods, and serious neglect of practice were prevalent in schools at all levels, which could not meet the demands for economic and social development to different degrees and lagged behind the current development of science and culture. Therefore, the *Decision of the CPC Central Committee on the Reform of the Education System* pointed out: "We must carry out systematic reform of the education system in order to fundamentally change this situation." The *Decision* also established the basic policy that "education serves socialist construction, and socialist construction relies on education." That is, we should start with the reform of the education system, concentrate on streamlining administration and delegating government powers as well as expanding schools' autonomy, and reform the labor and personnel system accordingly, so as to significantly improve the consciousness and ability of education at all levels to actively adapt to the multiple needs of economic and social development.

**The comprehensive deepening of education reform from 1993 to 2010.** During this period, after bringing order out of chaos and the gradual development of various educational reforms, nine-year compulsory education began to be implemented in a planned way and by stages; vocational and technical education was developed to a considerable extent; higher education was developed rapidly and initially established a system with various levels, forms, and disciplines. Various forms of adult education and ethnic education developed greatly; the management system with county-level governments as the main management body in basic rural education achieved remarkable results. However, China's education was still relatively backward on the whole, and it still failed to adapt to the demands of accelerating reform and opening-up and modernized construction; the strategic position of education was not yet fully implemented in practice; investment in education was insufficient; teachers were underpaid and the conditions for operating schools were poor; educational theory, teaching content, and methods were separated from reality to varying degrees; obvious weak links existed in school ideological and political work; and the education management system and operational mechanism seemed to be relatively rigid. Therefore, the 14th CPC National Congress clearly stated that "we must put education in a strategic position to prioritise its development and strive to improve the ideological, moral, scientific and cultural level of the whole nation. This is the fundamental plan for achieving China's modernization." In order to implement this major strategic deployment, the CPC Central Committee and the State Council issued *Outline of China's Education Reform and Development*. It first proposed "the proportion of financial education expenditure (including the appropriations for education at all levels, extra charges of urban and rural education funds, funds for holding and establishing primary and secondary schools by enterprises, and tax reduction and exemption of school-based industries) shall account for 4% of the GDP by the end of this century," and decided that "the reform of the education system should adopt comprehensively coordinated and step-by-step approaches, speed up the pace, reform the over-broad and rigid administration within the system, and initially establish a new education system which is compatible with the reform of the socialist market economic system, political system, and scientific and technological system." The promulgation of this pragmatic document has promoted Chinese education to a new stage of being internationalized, lifelong, and diversified.

**Education entered a new stage of comprehensive reform since 2010.** After more than 30 years of hard work, China's education system has been enhanced gradually, and education levels have improved continuously. In the first decade of the 21st century, free compulsory education in urban and rural areas was fully achieved; vocational education has developed rapidly; higher education has entered the popularized stage; and educational equity has taken a major step forward. However, faced with the new situation of further development of economic globalization, rapid progress of science and technology and increasingly fierce competition for a talented workforce, and new demands created by economic upgrading and social transformation for education, Chinese education is still confronted with a series of major challenges and many fierce contradictions. These are manifest as the concept of education is relatively backward; the content and methods are relatively outdated; the schoolwork burden for primary and middle school students is too heavy; and quality-oriented education is difficult to promote; students are poorly equipped to adapt to the demands of society, take up an occupation, and start a business; innovative, practical, and competent talented people are in extremely short supply; the educational system and mechanisms are not perfect; schools lack operating vitality; the educational structure and overall arrangements are not reasonable; the development of education between urban and rural areas and different regions is unbalanced; the development of education in poverty-stricken areas and ethnic areas is relatively lagging; education lacks enough investment and the strategic position of giving priority to the development of education has not yet been fully implemented. Therefore, it is necessary to deepen the comprehensive reform of education, especially the reform in key areas and key links, make it our fundamental task to foster character and civic virtue, take reform and innovation as a powerful driving force and give strategic priority to the promotion and improvement of education fairness and quality, focus on the reform of the examination and enrolling system and the separation of management and evaluation from personnel management, and concentrate on the cultivation of an innovative, competent, practical, and international workforce. In this regard, the paper, *Outline of the National Medium- and Long-Term Education Reform and Development Plan (2010–2020)* promulgated by the CPC Central Committee and the State Council in 2010 set forth a comprehensive deployment strategy, and thus started a new journey of transiting from a big education country to a strong education country and achieving corresponding development.

## The New Era Has Opened Up a Brighter Future for Education Modernization

In 2017, the 19th CPC National Congress was successfully held, which ushered in a new era of socialism with Chinese characteristics. The Congress made a historical judgment that the principal contradiction facing Chinese society has evolved between unbalanced and inadequate development and the people's ever-growing needs for a better life, and proposed a two-stage goal to strive for: in the first stage from 2020 to 2035, we will build on the foundation created by the moderately prosperous society with a further 15 years of hard work to see that socialist modernization is basically realized; in the second stage from 2035 to the middle of the 21st century, we will, building on having basically achieved modernization, work hard for a further 15 years and develop China into a great modern socialist country that is prosperous, strong, democratic, culturally advanced, harmonious, and beautiful.

Talent is the key and education is the foundation for the future development of China and the great rejuvenation of the Chinese nation. If a country wants to become strong, it must strengthen its education first. The 19th CPC National Congress report clearly stated that strengthening education is fundamental to our pursuit of national rejuvenation and emphasized that we must give priority to education, speed up its modernization, and develop education that people are satisfied with. This has established a new orientation, proposed a new target, and pointed out a new path for Chinese education reform and development in the new era. From 2035 and even to 2050, we must adhere to deepening education reform in all areas; resolutely get rid of all outdated thinking and ideas and all institutional impediments; break through the blockades of vested interests and draw on the achievements of other civilizations; respect the principles of education and the maturing of talent; make greater efforts to optimize the structure and layout of education; take greater steps in education fairness and quality improvement; take more effective measures to stimulate educational vitality; systematically innovate student training models; comprehensively improve the supply capacity of individualized, diversified, and high-quality education services; insist on the path of socialist education with Chinese characteristics; and continuously modernize the governance system and governance capacity of education.

## Sum Up Experiences, Look to the Future and Connect with the World

Tremendous changes have taken place in Chinese education over the past 40 years of reform and opening-up, which have improved the well-rounded development of all our people, enhanced the composite national strength, and benefited millions of people. Reviewing the historical process of China's educational reform and opening-up, analyzing the solutions to various complicated challenges in various important historical periods, summarizing the successful experiences of education, profoundly understanding the regular characteristics behind the phenomenon, all play an irreplaceable role in enriching and developing our theoretical system, sticking to the path and strengthening our confidence in socialist education with Chinese characteristics. To this end, we have organized and compiled *China's Path to Education Modernization: A Research Series Commemorating the 40th Anniversary of Reform and Opening-Up*, and listed it as the key research project in Shanghai social science "40 Years of Reform and Opening-Up." This series, guided by the modernization of socialist education with Chinese characteristics, takes the historical process and major events as its basis and framework. It can be divided into 10 volumes. We have made systematic attempts to summarize the achievements and experiences of all forms of educational theoretical innovation, institutional innovation, policy innovation, and the forward movement of educational development at all levels, and made due efforts to build a socialist educational theoretical system and discourse system with Chinese characteristics.

The task of theoretical research is not only to know the world but more importantly to transform it. The ultimate target of understanding the principles is to guide practice. China's education has completed the transition from a weak education country to a big education country. It is a more formidable task and greater cause to stride forward from a big education country to a strong education country. Faced with overwhelming information, network and data, and a future full of uncertainties, only by deepening our understanding of the principles of education and strengthening our understanding of the maturing of talent can we carry forward our cause and forge ahead into the future, speed up the pace of education modernization, develop education which is more equitable, of higher-quality and more vigorous, and forge ahead along the right path of socialism with Chinese characteristics.

The achievements of Chinese education not only benefit the Chinese people but also contribute to the innovation of education in the world. There is no path or model that can be copied and imitated blindly to realize the modernization of education. Over the past 40 years of China's education reform and opening-up, by actively learning from the world's advanced concepts and successful experiences, adhering to and respecting the principles of education, and sticking to developing education by taking root in China, we have successfully opened up a path of achieving education modernization in a progressive way in a country with an enormous population, uneven development, and low overall development level. Summarizing the course of education reform and opening-up over the past 40 years can not only provide the world with Chinese experiences and Chinese wisdom for the realization of education modernization, but also help to accelerate

China's education modernization, bring China closer to the center of the world arena, and continuously make greater contributions to mankind.

Yuan Zhenguo, chief editor of the series
May 2018

## Notes

1 Data source: United Nations Statistics Division (https://unstats.un.org). The statistical measuring standard is GDP per capita (current U.S. dollar), of which 187 countries were included in 1978 and 212 countries were included in 2016. The data related to China in this chapter does not include the Hong Kong Special Administrative Region of China, the Macao Special Administrative Region of China, and the Taiwan region of China, unless otherwise stated.
2 Data source: United Nations Statistics Division (https://unstats.un.org). The statistical measuring standard is GDP per capita (current U.S. dollar), of which 187 countries were included in 1978 and 212 countries were included in 2016.
3 Data source: World Bank Database (https://data.worldbank.org.cn/indicator). The statistical measuring standard is GDP (the U.S. dollar was a constant price in 2010), and is calculated according to "China's contribution rate to world economic growth = China's GDP growth / world GDP increment *100%."
4 Data source: The Bulletin of the National Bureau of Statistics of the People's Republic of China on the main data of the 1982 census (http://www.stats.gov.cn/tjsj/tjgb/rkpcgb/qgrkpcgb/200204/t20020404_30318.html), the bulletin on a national 1% population sample survey in 2015 (http://www.stats.gov.cn/tjsj/zxfb/201604/t20160420_1346151.html).
5 Data source: the related education (year) by United Nations Development Programme (http://hdr.undp.org/en/data#) the number of countries with data statistics was 172 in 1990 and 191 in 2015.
6 John King Fairbank: The United States and China (the fourth edition), World Affairs Press, 2000 edition, pp. 132–134; p. 451.
7 Author: John King Fairbank, translator: Xue Xuan, China: A New History, Cheng Chung Book Co., Ltd, 2001 edition, pp. 492–493.
8 Author: Ronald H. Coase,Wang Ning, translator: Xu Yao, Li Zhemin, How China Became Capitalist, China CITIC Press, 2013 edition, pp. 1, 206–210.

# Foreword

The tremendous economic and social changes over the past 40 years of reform and opening-up have provided a seedbed for the historic achievements in the development of vocational education in China. In 1985, the paper, *Decision of the CPC Central Committee on the Reform of the Education System* gave vocational education its status as "half the sky" in secondary education and ushered in a new era for its development. The development of vocational education over the past 40 years can be divided into three phases: That is, the restoration and development phase of secondary vocational education in the 1980s, the phase of stability and consolidation in the 1990s, and the phase of strengthening the system and comprehensively deepening foundations since the 21st century. From starting everything from scratch in the 1980s to the intense hard work in the 1990s, and then to the scientific development in the 21st century, vocational education has come through a crucial historical period. It has developed more systemically and deeply than any other period in history.

It is the core mission and logical for vocational education to pursue an equal status with general education, construct an independent vocational education system, and realize the modernization of vocational education in this period. The fundamental aim is to enable people to equally treat and truly accept vocational education, so that vocational education can fully contribute toward economic and social development. Over the past 40 years of reform and opening-up, without the vigorous development of vocational education, we could not cultivate a large number of skilled people required for economic development; worse still, much of society would be unproductive due to a lack of skills, and this would constitute a heavy burden on economic development.

The primary achievement of vocational education development in the past 40 years is the establishment of its national strategic position, of which the basic premise is to recognize the value of skilled workers. From the beginning of reform and opening-up to the end of the 20th century, vocational education suffered hardships, combined with the shortage of highly skilled workers faced by China's industrial upgrading in the early 21st century. The two factors aroused a lively discussion on the social status of skilled workers in society, and established the concept that "skilled people are also valued as professionals," thus promoting the establishment of the strategic position of vocational education at the state level. This established an important foundation principle for policy formation of an exemplary vocational education system in the 21st century.

With the support of powerful national policies, vocational education has made breakthroughs in every field. First, the vocational education system has basically taken shape. From the recovery of secondary vocational education in the 1980s to the large-scale development of higher vocational education in the early 21st century, and then to the transition to undergraduate education since 2010, China has firstly established a modern vocational education system, which constitutes secondary vocational education, higher vocational education, and technology-applied undergraduate education and maintains various internal communication channels. Second, development of fundamental requirements and resources for construction have been fully carried out and great breakthroughs have been made, including some important breakthroughs in school-enterprise cooperation; the adjustment of professional structure is relatively successful as a whole, and the capacity of the service industry in vocational colleges has improved by a large margin; the model of student training and curriculum reform has been thoroughly developed; faulty development has overcome the basic allocation and competency of teachers; and some successful pilot cases have emerged in the reform of a modern apprenticeship system. Vocational education has begun to be gradually established as a valued education type.

At present, China's vocational education has entered a new era. The main challenges faced by vocational education in the new era were: to further consolidate the status of vocational education and accomplish each connection smoothly; to establish a national institutional platform for school-enterprise cooperation; to set up a scientific assessment system in order to analyze labor demand for industrial development; to build national professional teaching standards for vocational education; to establish a standardized and systematic training system for vocational education teachers; and to enhance the top-level design and advance the implementation of a modern apprenticeship system.

# List of Abbreviations

Asia-Pacific Economic Cooperation (APEC)
Beijing Tourism Group (BTG)
Bundesinstitut für Berufsbildung (BIBB)
Bundesministerium für Bildung und Forschung (BMBF)
Canada-China College Linkage Program (CCCLP)
Canadian International Development Assistance (CIDA)
Cataloging In Publication (CIP)
China Railway High-speed (CRH)
Communist Party of China (CPC)
Competency-Based Education (CBE)
Computer Numerical Control (CNC)
Deutscher Industrie- und Handelskammertag (DIHK)
Developing a Curriculum (DACUM)
European Union (EU)
Gross Domestic Product (GDP)
Intellectual Property Protection (IPR)
International Labour Organization (ILO)
International Network on Innovative Apprenticeship (INAP)
International Standard Book Number (ISBN)
International Standard Industrial Classification (ISIC)

Master of Education (M.Ed.)
Ministry of Education (MOE)
Ministry of Finance (MOF)
Ministry of Human Resources and Social Security (MOHRSS)
National Development and Reform Commission (NDRC)
National Education Technology Plan (NETP)
National Society for the Promotion of Industrial Education (NSPIE)
National Vocational Qualification System (NVQ)
People's Republic of China (PRC)
Programme for International Student Assessment (PISA)
Shanghai Sipo Polytechnic (SHSIPO)
Sports Utility Vehicle (SUV)
Standing Conference of Ministers of Education and Cultural Affairs of the Länder in the Federal Republic of Germany (KMK)
State Development Planning Commission (SDPC)
State Economic and Trade Commission (SETC)
Suzhou Industrial Park Institute of Vocational Technology (SIPIVT)
Technical and Vocational Education and Training (TVET)
The Ministry of Commerce of the People's Republic of China (MOFCOM)
United Nations Educational, Scientific and Cultural Organization (UNESCO)
United Nations Industrial Development Organization (UNIDO)
Unmanned Aerial Vehicle (UAV)
World Trade Organization (WTO)

# Introduction

The 40 years of reform and opening-up was not only a period of world-shaking change in China's economy and society, but also a period of historical achievement in China's vocational education. China's GDP was 74.4127 trillion yuan in 2016, while it was only 0.3645 trillion yuan in 1978, an increase of 204 times in 38 years. More importantly, China's economic model was successfully transformed from a planned economy to a socialist market economy with Chinese characteristics over the past 40 years. Amidst such significant change, the demand for developing vocational education has increased while simultaneously a solid material foundation for its development has emerged. Vocational education began from scratch in the 1980s, moved to an intense work period in the 1990s, and finally to the scientific development stage in the 21st century, constantly developing through these crucial historical periods. It is significant to systematically tease out the developmental history of vocational education during this period and summarize the accomplishments and uncover the crucial problems that exist so as to determine the development goals and strategies for the next stage.

# 1. Phases and Achievements of Vocational Education over the 40 Years of Reform and Opening-Up

Over the past 40 years since reform and opening-up, vocational education has developed simultaneously along the two dimensions: scale and conceptualization. By combining the two dimensions, we can divide the development of vocational education over the past 40 years into three phases. That is, the restoration and development phase of secondary vocational education in the 1980s, the phase of stabilization and consolidation in the 1990s, and the phase of building an innovative system based on firm principles since the 21st century.

## 1.1. The Restoration and Development Phase of Secondary Vocational Education in the 1980s

The foremost mission of vocational education was to comprehensively restore secondary vocational education in the 1980s. Of course, this doesn't mean higher vocational education was completely absent during this period. As a matter of fact, during the 20 years from the initial stage of reform and opening-up to the all-around development of secondary vocational education in the late 20th century, we also made some attempts to develop higher vocational education in China, such as operating vocational colleges and five-year junior colleges. Moreover, as early as in 1985, the paper, *Decision of the Central Committee of the CPC on the Reform of the Education System* propounded the requirements for building a vocational education system. However, the scale of higher vocational education was very small during this period and the primary task was to restore and develop secondary vocational education. Furthermore, the restoration and development of secondary vocational education principally lay in massively increasing its scale, and the idea of putting basic principles in a prominent position had not yet been realized because of the onerous task of scale restoration and development.

During the "Cultural Revolution," secondary vocational education suffered grave damage due to the prejudice of the "Gang of Four" against vocational education. In 1978, the number of students in secondary vocational schools only accounted for 7.6% of the total number in senior high school, and the structure of secondary education was seriously unbalanced. The Party and state leaders were acutely conscious of the demand for skilled people during the period of rapid economic development after reform and opening-up. Meanwhile, the severely unbalanced secondary education was neither successful in attracting students nor meeting the needs of society for diversified skilled workers. At the first national education conference, which was held after dismantling the influence of the "Gang of Four" in 1978, the Minister of Education, Liu Xiyao proposed the requirements for adjusting, rectifying, and enhancing common senior high schools while also vigorously developing vocational education as the main theme of the report. Since then, secondary vocational education began to gradually recover. After developing for several years, the paper, *Decision of the Central Committee of the CPC on the Reform of the Education System* in 1985 clarified the requirements for adjusting the structure of secondary education and vigorously developing vocational and technical education. The goal was to "spare no effort to equalize the entrants in various vocational and technical education schools at the senior high school level in most regions to that of common senior high schools in 5 years or so."[1] This proportional requirement is still in use today and extended to higher education, which requires higher vocational education to have approximately the same enrollment scale as common higher education.

During this period, the restoration and development of secondary vocational education, in addition to continuing to operate secondary specialized schools and technical training schools, has also developed a new form of secondary vocational education, namely vocational high schools, which developed from agriculture high schools of the past. Because vocational high schools did not have the special operational policies that secondary vocational schools and technical schools had, they suffered many hardships during the development stage. Nevertheless, they still made undeniable contributions to the restoration and development of secondary vocational education. This was because its enrollment rates were close to secondary vocational schools most of the time, and it was a relatively important force among the three types of secondary vocational schools.

After more than 10 years of restoration and development, China's secondary vocational education has gradually grown on a considerable scale. The 1991 paper, *Decision of the State Council on Vigorously Developing Vocational and Technical Education* (No. 55 [1991] from the State Council) declared that new student enrollment of various secondary vocational and technical schools had achieved approximately the same-size ratio with ordinary high schools, and that the single structure of secondary education had clearly changed. In the 1990s, the enrollment scale of secondary vocational education was stable overall and the enrollment ratio even exceeded that of ordinary high schools in some years. In 1997, for example, the enrollment of secondary vocational schools accounted for 56.2% of that in senior high schools.

## 1.2. The Phase of Stable Scale and Establishing the Initial Foundations for Vocational Education in the 1990s

The goal that the number of enrollments in secondary vocational education should be "roughly equal" to that of common high school education was basically accomplished, and it ushered in the phase of a relatively stable period. Hence, vocational education began to probe how to promote the best-practice content and foundations for optimal school operation. However, the construction level of vocational education was still relatively low at the time, especially as the related theoretical research was still lagging behind. As a result, the consolidation of basic principles and structures failed to make significant progress on the whole. It was based on this consideration that we call this phase the initial phase of developing the content and substance based on firm principles. Accordingly, the development of vocational education in the 1990s can be described as a connecting stage between the 1980s and the 21st century. However, stabilization does not signify inaction or insignificance, and stabilization always precedes the breakthroughs of the future.

The development of the educational structural foundations for vocational education in this period was mainly embodied in curriculum reform and faculty development.

### 1.2.1. Curriculum Reform and Its Achievements

Curriculum reform mainly refers to pilot competency-based curriculum reform in some regions of a few provinces and cities. In 1985, the directive, *Decision of the Central Committee of the CPC on the Reform of the Education System* indicated the problems in vocational education curriculum at that time. Namely, "much of the curriculum content was outdated; the teaching methods were rigid; teaching practice was not considered; the major setup was too narrow, deviating from the demands of economic and social development and lagging behind the development of contemporary science and culture to different degrees." All these can be considered as chronic illnesses of vocational education curriculum. However, the description of curriculum problems in vocational education was only on the anecdotal level, which lacked a deep understanding of the essence of the problems and failed to find an effective way to solve them. The "CBE" curriculum model (competence-based education curriculum model) was propagated in the United States, Canada, and other countries in the late 1980s, which provided at least a technical solution to these problems.

The "CBE" curriculum model advocates that the curriculum should be determined by enterprise and that the specific method is to develop a curriculum based on job task analysis tables created by enterprise technical experts. This was completely revolutionary compared to the original discipline-based curriculum and, at that time, its introduction placed vocational education scholars in an entirely new world, in which they could actively carry out pilot projects. Shanghai and Jiangsu were the places which carried out in-depth pilots. In 1996, Shanghai launched the "10181" project, to complete curriculum reform and compilation of model teaching materials for 10 common required courses, to complete 18 kinds of teaching materials for typical majors and types of work in 5 years, and to basically form a secondary vocational curriculum and teaching material system, which reflected the characteristics of China, Shanghai, and the era in about 10 years. Although these attempts at curriculum reform failed to materialize into a fundamental reversal of the curriculum model at the practical level, it indeed made strict use of job task analysis methods for curriculum development. Curriculum developers employed some enterprise technical professionals to develop competency modules according to the requirements of developing "CBE" curriculum and formed some DACUM tables. Due to the lack of deep understanding of how "CBE" curriculum development technology can link up with the original curriculum models in China, the curriculum reform ultimately failed to be carried out in depth because it did not know how to transform the results of task analysis into the curriculum.

While "CBE" curriculum reform made progress, it was also questioned by some scholars. Mr. Huang Kexiao, for example, had always claimed that the discipline curriculum model should not be ignored in vocational education, and a "pluralistic integrated curriculum model" should be implemented. He especially put forward the construction of a technical discipline curriculum. He even tried to explain the implications of retaining a technical discipline curriculum but failed. Mr. Jiang Naiping proposed the curriculum model of "broad basis, flexible modules," which did not completely deny the "CBE" curriculum model. The content of the "flexible modules" was the competency-based curriculum. However, he added "broad basis" to this foundation and tried to remedy the problems with the "CBE" curriculum model. These proposals were valuable, as they emphasized that systematically learning technology theory was precisely the point of cultivating vocational education in China.

### 1.2.2. Faculty Development and Achievements

In terms of faculty development, the rapid expansion of secondary vocational education in the 1980s gave rise to an acute shortage of teaching staff. Through various approaches and efforts, the overall situation of teaching staff improved significantly in the 1990s. Statistically, the number of full-time teachers in secondary specialized schools and vocational high schools at the end of 1996 was 204,300 and 268,500, respectively, throughout the country, an increase of 9,559 and 13,600 over those in 1985. The total number of full-time teachers in the three types of secondary vocational schools increased rapidly in the late 1990s, reaching 761,100 in 1999.

The main achievement of vocational education faculty development in this period was the relatively well-established vocational and technical standard education. There were two ways to do this: one was to independently establish vocational and technical education colleges and the other was to set up vocational and technical normal schools on the basis of existing colleges.

The first independent vocational and technical normal colleges were established in 1979, namely the Tianjin Technician Normal College (now the Tianjin University of Technology and Education) and the Jilin Technician Normal College (now the Jilin Engineering Normal University). The former began enrolling students in 1980, while the latter began in 1979. From 1979 to 1988, eleven independent vocational and technical normal colleges were established in China. By 2000, there were eight independent vocational and technical normal colleges throughout China. These independently established vocational and technical normal colleges put a high value on exploring the features of how to cultivate vocational education students, especially their practical skills. In order to highlight this feature, these schools not only established skill training centers but also recruited students from secondary vocational schools. Therefore, the students they cultivated were well received by vocational schools.

The other approach was to set up vocational and technical normal colleges within the existing universities. In the late 1980s and early 1990s, the State Education Commission (now Ministry of Education (MOE) of the PRC successively approved eight universities, including Tianjin University, Zhejiang University, Hebei Normal University College of Career Technology, Tongji University, Southeast University, Xi'an Jiaotong University, Hunan Agricultural University, and Sichuan University, to establish vocational and technical normal colleges or rural vocational education teacher training centers to cultivate vocational faculty by relying on the tremendous strength of these well-established universities. Today, the vocational and technical normal colleges in some universities still maintain and operate well, while some have been abolished. In addition to these eight universities, some local universities have also established vocational and technical normal colleges, such as the Vocational and Technical Education College in Guangxi Normal University and Yunnan Normal University, etc.

Another important achievement for the development of vocational education in the 1990s was the promulgation of *Vocational Education Law of the People's*

*Republic of China* in 1996, which filled the void in the legislation on vocational education. The *Law* is broad in content, and defines the important aspects of vocational education. However, due to the lack of specific mandatory regulations, it failed to play a distinct role in resolving practical problems.

### 1.3. The Phase of the Initially Formed System and Comprehensively Deepening Structural Foundations since the 21st Century

The turn of the century in the 20th and 21st centuries is another important turning point for the development of vocational education in China. In 2002, the State Council convoked the conference on national vocational education and promulgated the *Decision of the State Council on Vigorously Promoting the Reform and Development of Vocational Education.* In 2005, a national conference on vocational education was held and the *Decision of the State Council on Vigorously Developing Vocational and Technical Education* was issued. This kind of high-standard vocational education conference was held twice within such a short period of time, which not only showed that the Party and the state attached great importance to the development of vocational education, but also demonstrated that vocational education suffered a major crisis at that time. Whether vocational education could survive this crisis was of great importance to its future. Fortunately, with concentrated efforts implementing a series of positive measures, vocational education survived the difficulties and ushered in the glory of today.

There were two kinds of factors of great concern in vocational education by the state: one was negative and the other was positive. The negative factor was that the reform of the labor and personnel system had greatly diminished the attractiveness of secondary specialized schools and technical training schools. The expansion of higher education made it easier to attend colleges and universities and increasingly junior middle school graduates chose regular senior secondary schools. The combination of these negative factors led to the sharp decline in enrollments in secondary vocational education. Although the two documents issued by the State Council in 2002 and 2005 were rich in content, the core purpose of their release was to require all sectors of society to attach importance to vocational education and stabilize the enrollment numbers in secondary vocational education. As for the positive factor, there was an increasing demand for the industrial transformation from labor-intensive and resource-intensive to technology-intensive in order to realize industrial upgrading, which was fueled by China's industrial development after over 20 years of rapid growth. Industrial upgrading required highly skilled workers. However, highly skilled workers only accounted for a very small proportion of the Chinese population at that time, and it was difficult to find highly skilled people even with the lure of high salaries. This phenomenon was also brought into the public focus.

The combination of the two factors firstly triggered the discussion of the concept of denomination, of which the essential question is how to consider the status of skilled workers and whether they can be called professionals ("talents" in Chinese idiom). This is because only those who graduated from secondary technical schools or above could be called "professionals" in China's personnel system in the past. At that time, China's industry was generally at the initial stage of development, and there was no condition to provide superior wages for skilled workers, which objectively led to the low status of skilled professionals.

The result of this great discussion is that people have become increasingly open to the concept that "skilled workers are also professionals," and the strategic position of vocational education was established at the national level. This laid an important conceptual and policy foundation for the formation of the splendid history of vocational education in the 21st century.

This is the period when the glorious history of vocational education took shape. Of course, it can be attributed to the demands that MOE proposed for vocational education according to industrial development and a series of important and timely development measures launched by MOE. History once again proved that active development is the best means of resolving a crisis. The achievements of this period can be summarized into two aspects: the initial formation of the vocational education system and the comprehensive construction of its content and substance.

In terms of system formation, China initially established a modern vocational education system, which consists of secondary vocational education, higher vocational education, and applied technology undergraduate education and multiple communication channels within them. Although the system still has many problems, such as the blocked internal communication channels and loose connections with the outside, it is a remarkable historical achievement to reach this standard. Few countries or regions in the world can implement vocational education at the three levels of secondary education, postsecondary education and undergraduate education. In most cases, vocational education is mainly implemented at the secondary education level, such as in Germany; or mainly implemented at the higher education level, such as in the United States; or secondary vocational education will be obviously weakened when it is upgraded to higher vocational education, such as Taiwan in China. The basic construction conditions of vocational colleges made remarkable progress during this period. Thanks to the large increase of educational expenditure, a great number of vocational colleges with excellent infrastructure have emerged. As a result, the image of vocational education has distinctly changed in society.

In terms of content and substance construction based on firm educational principles, a large number of new concepts emerged during this period, such as school-enterprise cooperation, professional structure adjustment, student training models and curriculum reform, double-quality faculty development, a modern apprenticeship system, etc. The content and substance of educational principles was comprehensively developed in this period, and corresponding reform measures made great breakthroughs in the development of the fundamental content and substance of vocational education.

1. School-enterprise cooperation has made significant breakthroughs in some areas. Although it is difficult to carry out school-enterprise cooperation, great breakthroughs have been made in some areas where industries are relatively mature and some successful cases have emerged at the college level. For most vocational colleges, school-enterprise cooperation has become a normal practice in school operations.
2. The capacity of developing the service industry for vocational colleges has been greatly improved. At the national level, several large-scale adjustments of specialty categories better reflected the new demand for skilled professionals in industrial development. At the level of vocational colleges, the concept that "develop service industry, set up specialties according to market requirements" has deeply taken root; many labor-demand analysis research reports have emerged; the market consciousness of specialty setting in vocational colleges has been generally strengthened; specialty setting is generally identical with the market in general.
3. The student cultivating model and curriculum reform have been deepened to a great extent. Most vocational colleges have set up diversified training models within school-enterprise cooperation. For example, some vocational colleges arrange for students to study in enterprises in the form of substituted work experience and some introduce enterprise masters to teach in schools. As a whole, students' practical learning opportunities have been greatly extended. The curriculum reform has had obvious effects. The idea that determined curriculum reform in this period mainly included the systematic course of work process, project courses, etc. The common goal was to develop the curriculum on the basis of workplace-ability demand. Although we still have problems such as how to implement the newly developed curriculum into classrooms and how to construct the national governance system of the curriculum at the macro level in practice, the theory and development methods of the advanced vocational education curriculum in the world are deeply understood and accepted in vocational

educational circles. Moreover, we have obtained a large number of successful reform cases at the local level because we are increasingly adept at developing curriculum.

4. Faculty construction has achieved significant results. The most prominent achievement is the dramatic increase in the number of teachers and decline in the student-to-teacher ratio of under 20:1. Teachers' educational background has also been greatly improved. Many people with master's and doctor's degrees work as teachers in vocational colleges, which improves the basic quality of teachers in vocational colleges. Although it is still a challenge to cultivate double-quality teachers, teacher's education and teaching ability have been greatly improved through various cultivation channels.
5. Modern apprenticeship reform has achieved initial success. Modern apprenticeship reform has not been launched for long, and has failed to achieve remarkable practical results. Nevertheless, there are still some successful pilot cases.

## 2. Main Features of the Development of Vocational Education over the 40 Years of Reform and Opening-Up

There is a fundamental difference in the development of vocational education between the past 40 years of reform and opening-up and any other previous historical stage. This is not only because that the earth-shaking changes in China's economy and society have provided a great need and solid conditions for the development of vocational education, but also that vocational education in this period started from a completely different point. That is, to pursue the construction of a complete vocational education system, namely, systematic development. The conceptual foundation of such kind of development presents a completely different pattern, compared with the scattered experiments before the reform and opening-up of vocational education and the partial developments from the beginning of the new China to before reform and opening-up. This concept is embodied in the directive, *Decision of the Central Committee of the CPC on the Reform of the Education System* in 1985: "Gradually establish a vocational and technical education system from elementary to advanced level which is industry-supported, well-structured and compatible with common education."[2] Looking back at the 40-year history of reform and opening-up, we can see that vocational education is basically advancing in this direction.

Compared with the past, the development of vocational education in this period has a prominent feature. That is, much development was carried out with the support of scientific research. So it can be called scientific development. The actual manifestation is that a large number of institutions specialized in vocational education research have emerged and a large number of colleges and universities have established master and doctor pilots in vocational and technical education to cultivate senior researchers in the field of vocational and technical education. The East China Normal University was the first one to establish a specialized vocational and technical pedagogy research institute and degree programs. Vocational education researchers have also extensively participated in the decision-making and reform practice of vocational education, which has greatly strengthened the theoretical support for the development of vocational education and enhanced the development of vocational education in many sophisticated ways. For example, the curriculum reform of vocational education is a highly professional reform that cannot be carried out through experience alone. Since the 1990s, a large number of scholars have focused on vocational education curriculum research in China. They have not only enabled Chinese vocational education circles to learn about the latest achievements in vocational education curriculum research in western countries, but also proposed many vocational theory and practice models that suit the national conditions of China. These models have played an important role in improving the quality of vocational education.

The combination of systematic development and scientific development can be called the modernization of China's vocational education, which includes the modernization of the system and the modernization of the content. The system is to content what skin is to fur. Both are two inseparable aspects of one thing. To achieve modernization is the valuable core pursuit of China's vocational education over the past 40 years of reform and opening-up, thus it is the main logical thread to interpret the development history of China's vocational education in the past 40 years. Consequently, in vocational education, although "modernization" did not officially appear in the form of a "modern vocational education system" until in the *Decision of the State Council on Vigorously Developing the Reform and Development of Vocational Education* in 2002, the consciousness of building a modern vocational education came into being at the beginning of reform and opening-up and lasted throughout the entire period.

What is the purpose of building a complete vocational education system? What is the aim of realizing the scientific development of vocational education? There is a common voice at the heart of vocational education colleagues, that is, to transform the vocational education from a kind of low-level education into an education that has specific functions for economic, social, and individual development and on the basis of extensive requirements; to make the relationship between it and other types of education more equal rather than hierarchal. This book adopts the concept of "from grading to classification" to express this desire of vocational education colleagues. Up to this day, every aspect of vocational education has made tremendous progress. Now comes to the question: are we getting closer to this goal, or is it indicating that other things need to be considered? Objectively speaking, with the improvement of the vocational education system and the enhancement of its quality, people have accepted vocational education more and more. However, vocational education is still far from the goal of "establishment" acceptance. It seems that many factors affecting the status of vocational education come from outside of vocational education. Constructing an employment system that is compatible with the current model of China becomes the fundamental need to address the demand for highly skilled people for economic development.

## 3. The Challenges and Thoughts for Developing Vocational Education in the New Era

Since the beginning of the 21st century, vocational education has made distinct progress in both system construction and content development, though, it still confronts many extremely difficult problems. The 19th National Congress of the CPC put forward the view that "socialism with Chinese characteristics has crossed the threshold into a new era." The proposal of this concept shows that we are at a critical stage of historical development and at an important turning point. The basic feature of economic development is that "China's economy has been transitioning from a phase of rapid growth to a stage of high-quality development. This is a pivotal stage for transforming our growth model, improving our economic structure, and fostering new drivers for growth. It is imperative that we develop a modernized economy. This is both an urgent requirement for getting us smoothly through this critical transition and a strategic goal for China's development." The mission of vocational education is to provide a large number of high-quality skilled people for industrial upgrading and provide strong support for the balanced development of society. In order to accomplish this mission and develop vocational education in this new era, we should continue to deepen reform and build a more mature modern vocational education system in the following ways.

### 3.1. System Construction Should Further Consolidate the Status of Vocational Education and Smooth Various Cohesive Relationships

Since the initial formation of China's vocational education system, China continued to emphasize the strategic position of vocational education. However, the position of vocational education is not stable, and retrogression even arises in vocational education. For example, in recent years, there have been some declines in enrollment in secondary vocational education in some provinces and cities. Whether secondary vocational education is still needed and what scale of secondary vocational education is needed has become a hot topic at the moment. Although various cohesive relationships in the vocational education system have been built, the channels are still not broad enough and the internal communication is not very smooth.

### 3.2. School-Enterprise Cooperation Needs to Build a National Institutional Platform

Instability is also the prominent problem that school-enterprise cooperation currently faces. The cooperation is carried out between vocational colleges and enterprises; the state does not have a systematic school-enterprise cooperation platform; whether vocational colleges can set up a school-enterprise cooperation relationship is determined by how local enterprises depend on vocational colleges in terms of the demand for skilled people. Consequently, it is very tough to promote the school-enterprise cooperation. Moreover, even the established school-enterprise cooperation relationships are extremely unstable and operate for a relatively short duration of time. The next major problem to be resolved is how to establish a stable school-enterprise cooperation mechanism through state intervention. Furthermore, the current cooperation is still at a relatively low level, and it needs to be refined so that school-enterprise cooperation in cultivating talent can be fully improved.

### 3.3. The Analysis of Industrial Demand for Talented People Needs to Be Scientific

There have been many reports on the industrial demand for trained people. Some are released by the education administrative departments and various associations, and some are carried out on major establishment and curriculum development by vocational colleges. Much research effort has been put forth, but the effect is not conspicuous. The primary reason is that it is a highly scientific work to analyze the industrial demand for workers, and researchers without professional training are unqualified for this task. Therefore, it is necessary to establish specialized research institutions at national, provincial, and municipal levels to study this issue in the future. This will not only lighten the burden of school operations for vocational colleges and make major setup more scientific, but also improve the management of labor employment in a more scientific way.

## 3.4. Curriculum Construction Should Concentrate on Exploiting National Professional Teaching Standards

Professional teaching standards are the foundation for the operation of the vocational education teaching system, which have extremely great strategic importance in standardizing vocational college teaching, deepening curriculum construction, and improving the overall teaching quality. The development of national professional teaching standards is involved in transforming the governance model of the teaching operation system in China. Standardizing vocational education teaching content has become the common trend in western developed countries since the 1990s. China has lagged behind western countries for decades in this process and needs to catch up with as little delay as possible.

## 3.5. The Key of Faculty Construction Is to Establish a Teacher Cultivating System

Only with a standardized and systematic vocational education teacher cultivating system can we continuously acquire first-class vocational education teachers and make it possible to construct modern vocational education. If we do not have such a system and always adopt piecemeal methods to hurriedly resolve teachers' insufficient capacity, then we won't succeed in education modernization. In the past few decades, China has tried to build multiple paths to cultivate vocational education teachers. Some have been weakened and strengthened and some are still working. What we need to solve in the future is to integrate these paths into one system and specify the functions of each link horizontally and vertically in order to make vocational education teacher cultivation transform from piecemeal projects to institutionalized standards.

## 3.6. The Promotion of a Modern Apprenticeship System Requires Systematic Design

Although there are some successful cases of modern apprenticeship schemes, they cannot be generalized because their success often comes with special conditions.

As a very complicated personnel cultivating model, the successful construction of a modern apprenticeship scheme firstly involves a very sophisticated institutional system, such as the system to motivate the enthusiasm of enterprises and teachers to teach apprentices; to stimulate apprentices' enthusiasm to thoroughly learn research skills; to check the effect of cultivating apprentices so as to estimate the input effectiveness; to guarantee the relative stability of the master-apprentice team; how to safeguard the stability of apprenticeship funding; to resolve various contradictions while implementing apprenticeships, etc. Furthermore, the modern apprenticeship system is not a single-level apprenticeship model, and it contains multiple levels in itself. How to position the relationships of modern apprenticeship at all levels is also an issue that needs to be studied in depth. Only by doing well to develop these top-level concepts can we effectively construct a modern apprenticeship scheme.

The solutions to the problems mentioned above still lie within the realm of vocational education. However, the problem of vocational education often links together with economic, social, and even political issues. Only by comprehensively and progressively deepening the reform from these perspectives can we fundamentally resolve these problems in the development of vocational education. One of the core issues is to realize occupational equality, including improving the working environment of skilled workers such as earnings, promotion opportunities, working conditions, etc., and implement appropriate restrictions on the behaviors of enterprises as market entities. This involves the essential issue of "how to position the market economy pattern in China."

## Notes

1 The Central Committee of the CPC: Decision of the Central Committee of the CPC on the Reform of the Education System, 1985.
2 The Central Committee of the Communist Party of China: Decision of the Central Committee of the CPC on the Reform of the Education System, 1985.

CHAPTER ONE

# Adjusting the Structure of Secondary Education

From the establishment of the new nation to the beginning of the reform and opening-up period, China's school vocational education at first developed very slowly with the main path for cultivating skill-oriented workers being apprenticeships in factories at that time. This path propped up the basic requirements of new China's economic development needs for skilled workers. "New apprenticeship schemes were gradually established in whole industries and various places around 1963 and later became the method of cultivating a reserve of technical workers with the largest scale and largest number."[1] The political environment had a tremendously destructive effect on the development of school vocational education before the reform and opening-up period. Because of the prejudice of the "Gang of Four" against vocational education, many vocational schools were closed and this brought the development of school vocational education almost to the verge of collapse. "During the 'Cultural Revolution', all kinds of vocational education in China suffered unprecedented catastrophes: schools were closed down; school buildings were occupied; teams were scattered and people's minds were in turmoil. In 1969, technical schools were almost devastated and only 32,000 students were left in secondary technical schools"[2]; in 1978, secondary vocational school students only accounted for 7.6% of the total number of high school students.[3] With the comprehensive development of economic construction since reform and opening-up, the Party and the State quickly realized the great significance of developing vocational education. The introduction of some important documents has pushed China's vocational education into a new era of development. We have come to increasingly realize its great significance and profound influence when looking back at the 40-year history.

Figure 1.1 The Gate of Guangxi Transport School

## Part 1 The Fermentation of the Idea of Structural Reform in Secondary Education

It is universally accepted that the revitalization of vocational education started in the late 1970s. However, Li Lintian, the former director of the Department of Secondary Specialized Education in MOE, once proposed that the restoration of vocational and technical education may date back to 1971. At that time, because of the "suspension of classes for the revolution" and the lack of technical talent, relevant ministries and commissions of the State Council and representatives of each province and city attending the 1971 Education Work Conference strongly urged the restoration and development of specialized secondary schools and technical schools. This proposal was supported by Premier Zhou Enlai, and specialized secondary education and technical education achieved great progress in 1971. By 1976, it had surpassed the highest levels attained in 1965 before the Cultural Revolution.[4]

It is worth deeply acknowledging the efforts made by people in the 1970s for the restoration and improvement of vocational education in an extremely complicated political environment. However, we still need to further investigate the two stages: "regaining the past" and "creating the future." The restoration of vocational education during this period was put forward after people realized the problems caused by the serious damage to the former vocational education system. It was not a new plan for the future development of vocational education. However, after reform and opening-up, the development of vocational education was not simply to restore the former vocational education, but to profoundly transform China's education system. That's to say, it specified that vocational education was a significant component of China's educational structure, and its scale should be roughly equivalent to that of general education. This orientation is of great significance because it established the basic developmental framework of vocational education for the next few decades. In addition, after reform and opening-up, the institutional environment for the development of vocational education had also undergone fundamental changes and the core change was the diversion of the economic model from a planned economy to a market-oriented economy. This change made the institutional environment for the development of vocational education much more complicated, brought about a large number of new problems, and greatly modified the tasks of development. For example, the problems confronted by school-enterprise cooperation during the market-oriented economy stage are completely different from those during the stage of the planned economy stage. In the problem-solving process, a large number of new vocational education theories and practice patterns emerged and they have brought about a completely different form of vocational education in China. Nowadays, this new form of vocational education is called modern vocational education. Therefore, the development of modern vocational education should be defined as beginning at the end of 1970s, namely, after the formal proposal of reform and opening-up.

The basic framework for the development of vocational education since reform and opening-up 40 years ago was ultimately validated by the directive, *Decision of the Central Committee of the CPC on the Reform of the Education System,* promulgated in 1985. However, the important educational ideas contained in this document have undergone a distillation process, which may date back to the First National Education Work Conference held by MOE in April 1978, after the downfall of the "Gang of Four." It was during this conference that the "structural reform of secondary education" was proposed for the first time. At that time, the structural adjustment of secondary education was related to two issues. First, the backward vocational education in the past led to workers' relatively low level in education and skill in the initial stage of reform and opening-up. "The third census data show that, by July 1, 1982, the overwhelming majority of non-agricultural workers were illiterate, semi-illiterate, with primary and junior high school education level; the proportion was as high as 72%."[5] The proportion of agricultural workers was obviously much higher. "By the end of 1984, nearly half of all production workers in the units under state ownership and collective ownership were primary workers at or below the third level, accounting for about 49.2%; the proportion would reach 55.1% if apprentices with lower skill levels were added."[6] The qualities of skilled workers could hardly meet the demand of economic development for skilled people. Second was the problem of how to help thousands of people across such a narrow footbridge. The severe imbalance in the structure of secondary education made admission to universities the only path for people to acquire professional knowledge and skills. This would make the college entrance examination competition extremely fierce considering that the resources of higher education were very limited at that time. Furthermore, many educational factors, which were not beneficial to the physical and mental development of students, may stem from this. This was also disadvantageous for the students with diverse abilities to obtain a suitable path for their success.

During the conference in 1978, former Minister of Education, Liu Xiyao, stated in the theme of the report: "While adjusting, rectifying and improving regular senior high schools, we must vigorously develop various forms of rural secondary schools, secondary specialized schools and technical schools, implement a part-work (or part-time farm work) and part-study system in most schools and significantly increase the proportion of these schools over the entire secondary education."[7] This idea was endorsed by Deng Xiaoping. Around 1978, Deng Xiaoping came back to the central leadership position and consecutively visited North America and Western European countries. He looked into the economic and social development of the developed countries and their internal motives with acute eyesight, and seriously speculated about the direction and path of China's development. It was also during this conference that Deng Xiaoping, on behalf of the Central Committee, stressed that the proportion of agricultural middle schools, secondary specialized schools, and technical schools should be increased in order to meet the requirements of socialist economic construction. "Deng Xiaoping's speech at the National Education Work Conference in 1978 can be considered as the trigger for the pilot work for the structural reform of secondary education."[8]

During the Second Session of the Fifth National People's Congress from June 18 to July 1, 1979, Hua Guofeng put forward the requirements for the development of vocational education: "Secondary vocational schools must implement various kinds of secondary vocational education in a planned way. This is not only an urgent requirement for socialist construction in various respects, but also conducive to solving the employment problem of a large number of high school graduates." "We must set aside some funds to operate labor service enterprises in large- and medium-sized cities nationwide and organize all unemployed people for employment training and labor services through multiple forms."[9]

From April 1 to 5, 1980, MOE held a national working conference on secondary specialized education in Beijing, with the purpose of studying the developmental tasks of secondary specialized education in the new era. Vice Premier Fang Yi attended this conference. On May 8 and 22, 1980, the Secretariat of the Central Committee discussed the paper, *Outline of the Report on Educational Work* submitted by the Party Group of MOE and the explanations made by the Minister of Education Jiang Nanxiang and proposed that "in order to reform the education system, we should develop vocational schools and secondary specialized schools; improve the educational and technical levels of workers."[10] Subsequently on September 27, 1980, MOE and the State Labor Bureau (now MOHRSS) reported to the State Council on the issues related to the structural reform of secondary education. The CPC Central Committee and the State Council made a prompt response! On October 7, 1980, the State Council forwarded the *Report on the Structural Reform of Secondary Education* by MOE and the State Labor Bureau in the form of document No.252 [1980] from the State Council. And the following day, on October 8, 1980, the State Council approved and forwarded the *Summary of the National Conference on Secondary Specialized Education by MOE* in the form of document No.258 [1980] from the State Council. From all these, we can see how much attention Party and state leaders attached to the structural adjustment of secondary education and the vigorous development of vocational education, and how imperative this task was at that time. The *Report on the Structural Reform of Secondary Education* "solved many critical issues that affected the long-term development of China's vocational and technical education, and laid a solid foundation for the *Decision of the Central Committee of the CPC on the Reform of the Education System* in 1985."[11]

After this conference, many other important conferences were also held to discuss the development of vocational education. For example, from November 30 to December 13, 1981, the Fourth Session of the Fifth National People's Congress put forward: "In terms of secondary education, we should gradually transform the circumstance that there were too many regular senior high schools and too few vocational middle schools, actively develop secondary specialized schools and cultivate a large number of skilled workers and intermediate-level professionals, in order to benefit labor employment and improve the cultural, technical and political level of the staff corps."[12] In addition, the Party's 12th National Congress held on September 6, 1982, required the strengthening of secondary specialized education;

the Fifth Session of the Fifth National People's Congress, held from November 26 to December 10, 1982, called for the continual reform of the structure of secondary education; the First Session of the Sixth National People's Congress held from June 6 to 21, 1983, requested that the number of students in vocational high schools should account for 40% of the total number of senior high school students.[13] State-level conferences were so frequently held for issues concerning the development of vocational education, which indicated that the development of vocational education was a highly ranked concern by the state at that time. This laid the ideological foundation for the release of the historically significant document *Decision of the Central Committee of the CPC on the Reform of the Education System.*

## Part 2 New Student Enrollments of Vocational and Technical Schools Should Be Equivalent to That of Regular Senior High Schools

The directive *Decision of the Central Committee of the CPC on the Reform of the Education System* ultimately determined, in the form of a state edict, to vigorously develop vocational education and make new student enrollments of secondary specialized education account for 50% of that of secondary education. It was an extremely important document, which was released during a critical historical period. This document was discussed at the National Education Working Conference from May 15 to 20, 1985, and was published on May 27, 1985. People from various circles reached a consensus on the important position that *Decision of the Central Committee of the CPC on the Reform of the Education System* has had in the contemporary history of Chinese education. It is generally identified as the starting point of China's comprehensive educational reform in the new era. This is especially true for vocational education, because it is this document that opened up new prospects for the development of vocational education. As commented by people, "the *Decision of the Central Committee of the CPC on the Reform of the Education System* was the most important framework document which guided the development of China's vocational and technical education over the past 2 decades. All subsequent documents about the development of vocational and technical education are constituted on the basis of it."[14] This comment is not overstated at all, and its significance is comparable to the U.S. *Smith-Hughes Act.*

The *Decision of the Central Committee of the CPC on the Reform of the Education System* is brief in length and highly concise and simple in words, which points directly at the core issues of education and proposes straightforward policies and measures. It clarifies the purpose and theme from the very beginning: "The education system reform is fundamentally designed to improve the quality of the nation, to bring forth more talent and bring forth better talent."[15] In the first part of this document, it is specified that "education must serve the interests of socialist construction, which in return should rely on education. The magnificent task of socialist modernization requires us not only use and strive to improve the existing talent, but also to greatly improve the Party's understanding of education and point towards modernization, the world and the future, so as to extensively prepare all kinds of new qualified talented people at all levels who can adhere to the socialist orientation for China's economic and social development in the 1990s and the initial period of the next century. It also requires us to bring up hundreds of millions of well-educated, technical and skilled workers in various professions such as industry, agriculture, commerce, etc.; to create tens of millions of factory directors, managers, engineers, agronomists, economists, accountants, statisticians and other economic and technical staff who have modern technology and business management knowledge as well as the operational ability." This document is composed of five parts. The third part focused on "adjusting the structure of secondary education and vigorously developing vocational and technical education," which specially elaborates on the basic concepts, policies, and measures for the development of vocational education. It is proposed in the document that "socialist modernization not only requires advanced science and technology experts, but also urgently needs millions of middle and junior technicians, managers, technicians and other urban-rural workers who have received good vocational and technical education. Without such an army consisting of labor and technicians, advanced technology and advanced equipment cannot become a real social productive force."[16] In terms of developmental goals, the document explicitly proposes: "Endeavour to make new student enrollment of senior high vocational and technical schools in most areas equal to that of regular senior schools in about five years, and reverse the current unbalanced structure of secondary education."[17]

*Decision of the Central Committee of the CPC on the Reform of the Education System* has had widespread influence in all walks of life since it was promulgated. People wrote articles to explain their understandings of the *Decision of the Central Committee of the CPC on the Reform of the Education System* from different angles one after another. East China Normal University organized a group of experts to write papers. The results were published in the *Journal of East China Normal University (Educational Sciences)*. Three of the 17 articles were devoted to discussions of vocational education. Thus, we can see that people attached considerable importance to the development of vocational education and the adjustment of secondary education at that time. Dai Yufang said in *Develop Vocational Education and Propel*

*Economic Development* that "it is undeniable that our era is a time of technological and systematic invention and innovation. Among them, invention and innovation, or the speed of technological development, are largely determined by the number of 'capable people' engaged in actual work, as evidenced by the fact that the economic growth rate over the past few decades has become increasingly dependent on the speed of technological development. Now that technological development depends on technical personnel, vocational and technical education becomes a prerequisite for accelerating national economic development."[18] In *Establishing Vocational and Technical Education System as Soon as Possible*, Ying Junfeng mainly discussed the problem that the path is obstructed for specialized and technical expertise to grow. "There is often no way for a technical school graduate, who has been assigned to work in a factory and then obtained the title of intermediate technical worker, to make improvement in his work; the path is also obstructed for a secondary specialized school graduate, who has gone to work and obtained the technician title, to grow somewhat in the original direction. The only way is to change his job category and go to a staff position or to full-time university if he wants to improve." He believed that vocational and technical education is not systematic in itself, which obstructs channels for graduates' further study and makes them lose hope for the future. Thus, it is an important factor that impedes the development of vocational education.[19]

Of course, this document is not perfect, and we can even say that it has deficiencies in its explanations about the specific policies of the development of vocational education. Some very important issues are not clearly stated in this document. For example, there is no clear requirement on how to fund the urgent development of vocational education. Thus, it posed great difficulties for the development of vocational education, especially the development of vocational high schools. Of course, the document does not purport to propose any arrangements for funding. This is possible because the problems could not be solved when the policies were formulated. Besides, this document does not contain many concepts that we are very acquainted with now, such as industry-academy cooperation, curriculum reform, amalgamation of general and vocational education and the connection of secondary and higher vocational education, let alone concepts like internationalization and informatization. Some measures were impeded in the subsequent implementation, such as developing vocational technology normal institutions. The number of such institutions has been gradually reduced from 11 at its peak to only a few by changing their names and merging them. Like many other laws and documents that have exerted great influences in history, though it is not perfect and the language is extremely simple, we can certainly see that it "lays the foundation for the development of modern vocational education." This great significance comes from the following two aspects:

## 1. Designating "Half the Sky" Position to Vocational Education in China's Educational Structure

China's first educational system, namely, the Ren-Yin Educational System, incorporated vocational education into the formal education system. In this educational system, "from the horizontal view, there are simple industrial schools parallel to higher elementary schools; medium industrial schools and normal schools parallel to middle schools; official schools, higher industrial schools and normal schools parallel to higher schools."[20] After the establishment of the new nation, the government attached great importance to the development of vocational education, and placed the development of vocational education in an extremely important position during the first national education work conference in 1949. It clearly proposed that "secondary schools shall mainly develop toward secondary specialized schools and cultivate large quantities of intermediate construction cadres."[21] However later, vocational education stalled as influenced by the "Gang of Four." During the ten-year "Cultural Revolution," over 2 million fewer students graduated from secondary specialized schools.[22] And the students trained by the schools did not really reach the level of secondary specialized education. There is no doubt that other types of education also suffered great losses. The task of developing vocational education was also written into the *Constitution of the People's Republic of China*. Article 19 of the *Constitution* stipulates that "the state establishes and administers schools of various types, popularizes compulsory primary education and promotes secondary, vocational and higher education as well as preschool education."

However, what had a significant impact on the subsequent development of vocational education was not only the supporting idea of "vigorously developing vocational education," but also the *Decision of the Central Committee of the CPC on the Reform of the Education System* which clearly stipulated: vocational education should be divided equally with general education in enrollment rates, and is the key factor in support of the development of vocational education. This is because, if we do not explicitly propose the ratio of 50% and only put forward our desire to vigorously develop vocational education, then it will be difficult to guarantee the development of vocational education. Does 10% indicate vigorous development? What about 30%? Without a definition, "vigorous development" would be empty talk. With the ratio of 50%, we will have a clear goal to pursue, and local governments can have clear development tasks to accomplish. Only when vocational education reaches a certain scale can we build an internal system, and thus truly becomes a distinctive and valued type of education rather than a gathering place for those students who are continually eliminated from general education.

However, the previous education systems and documents, no matter how much they emphasized the importance of developing vocational education, few explicitly proposed the specific ratio required for vocational school enrollments. The Sixth National People's Congress once recommended that the required number of students in vocational high schools should reach 40% of the total students in high schools. Unfortunately, this ratio failed to become a strict guide for the development of vocational education. The previous *Report on the Structural Reform of Secondary Education* has no relevant statement concerning that. The most powerful expression that can be found is: "the reform of secondary education structure mainly refers to reforming the senior high education: in order to adapt senior high education to the requirements of socialist modernization, we should implement the policy of developing general education with vocational and technical education simultaneously, developing full-time schools together with part-work and part-study schools and spare-time schools, and developing schools run by the state together with schools run by business departments, factories and mines, and people's communes at the same time. The educational undertakings in the county should orient toward the rural areas and serve various infrastructure projects in rural areas. All trades and professions should be encouraged to establish a wide range of vocational (technical) schools in urban and rural areas. Some regular senior high schools can be appropriately converted into vocational (technical) schools, vocational middle schools, and agricultural middle schools. By adjustment and reform, the ratio of students in various vocational (technical) schools to that of the overall higher secondary education should be greatly improved."[23] Sun Zhenhan was one of the document contributors and the Deputy Director of the Department of Vocational and Technical Education of the State Education Commission. According to his recollection, the first draft of *Decision of the Central Committee of the CPC on the Reform of the Education System* stipulated that the proportion should be 70%, with reference to the German "enrollment ratio of general high school to secondary vocational school." However, this proportion met widespread local resistance, and was compromised to 50% later, which was probably a result of the average of 70% and the actual ratio of 30% at that time.[24]

By sorting through the documents that once had a great influence on the development of vocational education, we can further see that the ratio of 50% had a profound impact on the development of vocational education (see Table 1.1). All these documents, almost without exception, specified the ratio of students enrolled in general education to those enrolled in vocational education, or explicitly referred to the number of students enrolled in vocational schools. Over the past 30 years, one of the key indicators for MOE to evaluate the development of local vocational education is to see whether the ratio of students enrolled in secondary vocational schools has reached the bottom line of 50%. Once lower than this ratio, the vocational educational policy makers would make a judgment that vocational education had suffered a decline, and then take effective measures to increase the ratio. "The enrollment ratio of regular high schools to secondary vocational schools" has become the basis for people to consider the development situation of vocational education. At present, the systematic structure of vocational education is once again undergoing profound changes. Under current circumstances, a lively debate has been held by people about whether it is necessary to maintain the number of secondary vocational education enrollments at 50%. This ratio may need to be redefined. However, no matter how much to actually change the enrollment ratio of secondary vocational education, the requirement that "the enrollment ratio of secondary vocational education must be determined" has enjoyed popular support. This is because people have fully realized that "vigorous development" without an explicit ratio is not very effective after experiencing this phase of history.

Table 1.1 Expressions about the "enrollment scale ratio of regular high school to secondary vocational school" in important documents since 1985

| Document Names | Related Statements |
|---|---|
| *Outline of China's Education Reform and Development* (No.3 [1993] from the CPC Central Committee) | 1. The number of students in senior high vocational and technical schools has increased greatly. Junior and senior high school graduates who fail to enter a higher school generally receive vocational and technical training for different years. This enables the incoming labor force in urban and rural areas to receive necessary vocational and technical pre-employment training.<br>2. By 2000, the proportion of new student enrolments in various secondary vocational schools and the total enrolments to the number of students at high school stage should be maintained at around 60% nationwide; the proportion of the number of cities that have popularized high school education shall reach 70%. |
| *The Ninth Five-Year Plan for China's Educational Development and the Development Outline by 2010* (No.45 [1996] from the Planning Department of State Education Committee) | Vocational education focuses on the post-junior middle school period and is divided into three levels: post-primary school period, post-junior middle school period and post-senior high school periods. The total enrolments in various senior high vocational schools shall reach 12.75 million, with an increase of 3.357 million over that in 1995 and an annual growth rate of 6.3%. The proportion of total enrolments in various senior high vocational schools nationwide to that of the whole senior high school has increased to about 60%. |

(*Continued*)

Table 1.1 Continued

| Document Names | Related Statements |
|---|---|
| *Action Plan for Education Rejuvenation for the 21st Century* (MOE, December 24, 1998) | Continue to implement the diversion of post-junior middle education and actively develop secondary vocational education from the actual situation of each place. The existing proportion of senior high vocational education and general education should be maintained in an effort to meet the goals proposed by the *Outline of China's Education Reform and Development.* |
| *Decision of the State Council on Vigorously Promoting Vocational Education Reform and Development* (No.16 [2002] from the State Council) | Secondary vocational education should be the focus; the proportion of secondary vocational education to regular high school education should be roughly the same; the scale of higher vocational education should be enlarged. Vocational schools and vocational training institutions should further adapt to economic and social development and the demands of the labor market, enhance their ability to develop independently, improve school conditions, and comprehensively improve education quality and efficiency. During the 10th Five-Year Plan period, vocational education shall provide the society with over 22 million secondary vocational school graduates and more than 8 million higher vocational school graduates. |
| *Decision of the State Council on Vigorously Developing Vocational Education* (No.35 [2005] from the State Council) | By 2010, the enrollment scale of secondary vocational education shall reach 8 million, which is roughly the same as that of regular high schools. The enrollment scale of higher vocational education shall account for more than half of that of higher education. During the Eleventh Five-Year Plan period, more than 25 million secondary vocational school graduates and more than 11 million higher vocational college graduates shall be sent to work in the community. With the further development of various forms of vocational training, hundreds of millions of urban and rural workers are cultivated every year, thus worker qualities are demonstrably improved. The conditions of operating vocational education have been generally improved; teaching staff construction has been further strengthened; the quality and efficiency have been significantly enhanced. |
| *Outline of the National Medium- and Long-Term Education Reform and Development Plan (2010–2020)* | Reasonably determine the enrollment ratio of regular high school and secondary vocational school according to the requirements of economic and social development and keep the overall enrollments of regular high schools roughly the same as that of secondary vocational school in the near future. |

Table 1.1 Continued

| Document Names | Related Statements |
|---|---|
| *Decision of the State Council on Accelerating the Development of Modern Vocational Education* (No.19 [2014] from the State Council) | The structure and scale are more reasonable. Keep the overall enrolment scale of secondary vocational school roughly equivalent to that of regular high school; make sure the enrolment scale of higher vocational education accounts for more than half of that of higher education and the overall education structure is more reasonable. By 2020, the number of students in secondary vocational schools will reach 23.5 million; the number of junior vocational college students will reach 14.8 million; and the number of undergraduate vocational school students will reach a certain scale. The continuing education of employees shall reach 350 million. |
| *Construction of Modern Vocational Education System (2014–2020)* | 1. Secondary vocational education plays a fundamental role in the modern vocational education system, which can provide basic knowledge, techniques and skill education for junior and senior high school graduates and cultivate skilled personnel. Secondary vocational education is the focus of vocational education, and the overall enrollments of regular high school shall be maintained roughly equal to that of secondary vocational schools.<br>2. The scale of higher vocational education shall account for more than half of higher education, and undergraduate vocational education shall achieve a certain scale. |
| *The Thirteenth Five-Year Plan for China's Educational Development* (No.4 [2017] from the State Council) | Consolidate and improve the level of secondary vocational education. Carry out vocational education at the stage of compulsory education. Keep the enrollment scale of regular high school roughly equivalent to that of secondary vocational education and develop high school education by focusing on secondary vocational education in the central and western regions. Strengthen the basic capacity or the building of secondary vocational education, concentrate on improving the basic conditions for operating schools in poverty-stricken areas and weak secondary vocational schools. Adjust and optimize resource allocation, and co-ordinate a group of secondary vocational schools as a whole. Establish a comprehensive enrollment system and a unified enrollment platform between secondary vocational schools and regular high schools, and expand the regional scope and enrollment scale of high-quality secondary vocational schools. |

Although all the documents above continue to emphasize that the ratio of vocational education enrollments should be equivalent to that of general education, we can still see the vast differences in the requirements of the ratio from these specific documents. Since the release of *Decision of the State Council on Vigorously Promoting Vocational Education Reform and Development* in 2002, the statements have become more direct and explicit. This reflects people's growing demand for the continual maintenance of the ratio after the sharp decline in the scale of secondary vocational education, which occurred at the turn of the 20th and 21st centuries.

## 2. Take the Transformation of the Underlying Attitudes as the Logical Starting Point of the Development of Vocational Education in China

The second major significance of this document is that it sets out from the transformation of attitudes toward vocational schools and work roles and proposes the necessity of vigorously developing vocational education and systematically cultivating technicians, skilled workers, and first-line managers. This starting point strikes at the most pivotal issues in the development of vocational education. The key reason why our society does not attach importance to vocational education is that people do not consider skilled workers as professionals deep down in their hearts; most people are still stuck in the traditional perspective that only those engaged in complicated intellectual work are professionals and those skilled workers are absolutely not professionals because their work is considered simple. Since they are not professionals, it is difficult to truly acknowledge the value of their labor and carefully carry out planning regarding their education. In all countries that attach importance to vocational education, skilled workers have a very high status. Establishing the status of skilled workers is the logical starting point for the development of vocational education. This issue is explicitly discussed in the subsequent chapter of this book. As history indicates this problem is far from solved; the contradiction between the ideal and reality has always existed and even intensified, which has become a critical factor seriously complicating the development of vocational education in China.

It was fairly difficult for people to have such understandings at that time. This is because, on the one hand, this concept needs to be built on people's in-depth insight into the knowledge and capacity structure of skilled workers, and on the other hand, it is confronted with a distorted perspective that is brought about by favoring college students selected after the recovery of the college entrance examination. This kind of distorted perspective did not arouse great interest in the society except in the vocational education field. Few people could appreciate its profound implication from this perspective and more people were just excited about re-establishing the status of intellectuals. It can be clearly seen from the writings of some authors at that time: "Talented people are the key to the success of socialist modernization. The fundamental task of education system reform is to cultivate qualified personnel. All this, in the final analysis, comes down to the future and destiny of the country."[25] "The primary task of scientifically educating people is to liberate intelligence. Only when we try our best to achieve extraordinary improvement for normal teenagers and children can we expect to reach advanced world levels in modern science and technology within a few decades."[26] In this regard, the document also sharply points out: "The issues of vocational and technical education have been emphasized for many years, and the situation has not really been opened up. The important reason lies in the deficiency of due requirements for political, cultural and technical preparation of the employed for a long time, and the deep-rooted stereotypical ideas of despising vocational and technical education left over from history."[27] Therefore, Meng Guangping, former director of the Department of Vocational and Technical Education of the State Education Commission, believed that structural adjustment of education and vigorous development of vocational education is not just a process of transformation in schools, but also of changes in educational thinking. The core is to thoroughly realize technical and skilled workers are also professionals and fully recognize the importance of developing vocational education for the construction of contemporary society.

## Part 3 Development of Secondary Vocational Education under the Educational Structure Adjustment Policies

Under the guidance of the education structure adjustment policies, vocational education has entered a stage of rapid development and the unbalanced structure of secondary education has been reversed. We can use three sentences to summarize the development of vocational education from 1978 to 1998. The reason why 1998 is selected as the boundary of analysis is that a very significant event happened in 1998, namely, the repeal of the special policy that the state assigned jobs for secondary technical school graduates in a unified way and the three categories of secondary vocational schools began to converge. This policy had an important impact on the subsequent developmental path of vocational education: the unbalanced secondary education structure has been fundamentally reversed; the internal development of secondary vocational education is extremely uneven; and the development of secondary vocational education benefits from the strong promotion of the government.

## 1. The Structural Imbalance of Secondary Education Has Been Fundamentally Reversed

The period from 1978 to 1998 was a golden epoch for the development of secondary vocational education in China. Since then, with the profound transformation of China's current social and economic structures, this period is gone forever. That is the reason why the older generation of vocational education leaders, scholars, and researchers has always been fascinated by the thriving development of vocational schools during that period.

By the end of 1981, the number of schools and students in regular high schools nationwide had begun to decrease sharply, while vocational schools had developed rapidly in that year. Statistically, the number of students in vocational middle schools (classes) and vocational schools reached 213,000 throughout the country; the number of students in agricultural middle schools reached 268,000, accounting for 23.8% of the total number of students in high schools. This fundamentally changed the simplified structure of secondary education. In 1983, there were 5,481 vocational schools nationwide, with 1.22 million students (including 4,073 agricultural schools and 680,000 students). According to statistics from 8 provinces and cities, there were nearly 400 majors and professional courses taught in vocational schools nationwide.[28] This situation was fundamentally reversed in the 1990s. In 1991, *Decision of the State Council on Vigorously Developing Vocational and Technical Education* (No.55 [1991] from the State Council) announced: "By the end of 1990, various vocational and technical schools have grown to more than 16,000, with over 6 million students; at the same time, more than 2,100 employment training centers have been established nationwide, and more than 900,000 unemployed people are enrolled every year; the new student enrollment of various senior high school vocational and technical schools is almost the same as that of regular senior high schools; the simplified education structure has changed a lot."[29] In 1993, the *Outline of China's Education Reform and Development* further proclaimed: "Vocational and technical education has been developed to a considerable extent. New student enrolments at secondary vocational and technical schools and the number of students in high schools have exceeded 50%, which has changed the simplified structure of secondary education."[30] It even proposed that "by 2000, the proportion of new student enrollment in various secondary vocational schools and the total enrolment of the number of students at the high school stage should be maintained at around 60% nationwide; the proportion of the number of cities that have popularized high school education shall reach

70%."[31] In 1995, the number of students in regular secondary vocational schools (namely, secondary specialized schools, technical schools, and vocational high schools) reached 9,393,000, with an increase of 55.3% over 1990 and an annual growth rate of 9.2%. There were 7,131,600 students in regular senior high schools, 41,500 fewer than that in 1990. The proportion of students in various vocational schools compared to that of the whole senior high school increased from 45.7% in 1990 to 56.8%, with an increase of 11.1%.[32]

The development of various secondary vocational schools nationwide from 1978 to 1999 is shown in Tables 1.2 and 1.3.

Table 1.2 Number of various secondary vocational schools, regular senior high schools, and students nationwide from 1978 to 1999

| | Unit: 10,000 People | | | | | | | | | |
|---|---|---|---|---|---|---|---|---|---|---|
| | Secondary Technical School | | Secondary Normal School | | Vocational Middle School | | Technical School | | Regular Senior High School | |
| School Type Year | Number of Schools | Number of Students | Number of Schools | Number of Students | Number of Schools | Number of Students | Number of Schools | Number of Students | Number of Schools | Number of Students |
| 1978 | 1,714 | 52.92 | 1,046 | 35.99 | ... | ... | 2,013 | 38.19 | 49,215 | 1,553.08 |
| 1979 | 1,980 | 71.41 | 1,053 | 48.44 | ... | ... | 2,933 | 63.99 | 40,289 | 1,292.00 |
| 1980 | 2,052 | 76.12 | 1,017 | 48.21 | 3,314 | 45.36 | 3,305 | 70.03 | 31,300 | 969.79 |
| 1981 | 2,170 | 63.2 | 962 | 43.69 | 2,655 | 48.08 | 3,669 | 67.92 | 24,447 | 714.98 |
| 1982 | 2,168 | 62.8 | 908 | 41.13 | 3,104 | 70.35 | 3,367 | 51.19 | 20,874 | 640.05 |
| 1983 | 2,229 | 68.84 | 861 | 45.48 | 5,481 | 22.01 | 3,443 | 52.52 | 18,577 | 670.98 |
| 1984 | 2,293 | 81.12 | 1,008 | 51.13 | 7,002 | 74.48 | 3,465 | 62.76 | 17,847 | 689.81 |
| 1985 | 2,529 | 101.29 | 1,028 | 55.81 | 8,070 | 229.57 | 3,548 | 74.17 | 17,318 | 741.13 |
| 1986 | 2,741 | 114.59 | 1,041 | 61.13 | 8,187 | 256.00 | 3,765 | 89.20 | 17,111 | 773.37 |
| 1987 | 2,854 | 122.26 | 1,059 | 65.12 | 8,381 | 267.61 | 3,952 | 103.10 | 16,930 | 773.73 |
| 1988 | 2,957 | 136.82 | 1,065 | 68.34 | 8,954 | 279.31 | 3,996 | 116.08 | 16,524 | 745.98 |
| 1989 | 2,940 | 149.29 | 1,044 | 68.46 | 9,173 | 282.27 | 4,102 | 126.70 | 16,050 | 716.12 |
| 1990 | 2,956 | 156.71 | 1,026 | 67.73 | 9,164 | 295.01 | 4,184 | 133.17 | 15,678 | 717.31 |
| 1991 | 2,977 | 161.60 | 948 | 66.14 | 9,572 | 315.55 | 4,269 | 142.21 | 15,243 | 722.85 |
| 1992 | 2,984 | 174.28 | 919 | 66.56 | 9,860 | 342.76 | 4,392 | 155.60 | 14,850 | 704.89 |
| 1993 | 3,046 | 209.83 | 918 | 72.20 | 9,985 | 362.59 | 4,477 | 173.90 | 14,380 | 656.91 |
| 1994 | 3,093 | 241.40 | 894 | 78.39 | 102,017 | 405.61 | 4,430 | 187.09 | 14,241 | 664.80 |
| 1995 | 3,152 | 287.36 | 897 | 84.8 | 10,147 | 448.32 | 4,507 | 188.59 | 13,991 | 713.16 |
| 1996 | 3,206 | 334.78 | 893 | 88.00 | 10,049 | 473.27 | 4,467 | 191.81 | 13,875 | 769.25 |
| 1997 | 3,147 | 424.98 | 815 | 90.52 | 9,693 | 533.91 | 4,395 | 193.10 | 13,880 | 850.07 |
| 1998 | 3,234 | 405.97 | 875 | 92.11 | 10,074 | 541.62 | 4,362 | 181.30 | 13,948 | 938.00 |
| 1999 | 3,147 | 424.98 | 815 | 90.52 | 9,639 | 533.92 | 4,098 | 156.05 | 14,127 | 1,049.71 |

Note: 1. "..." indicates that statistics are deficient in this item; 2. In order to compare, some data about regular senior high school development are listed in the figure. (Data source: *Educational Statistics Yearbook of China;* being processed)

Table 1.3 The ratio of senior high school new student enrollment to the total number of high school students in main years

| (%) | | | | | | |
|---|---|---|---|---|---|---|
| | | | Secondary Vocational School | | | |
| Year | Total | Regular Senior High School | Subtotal | Secondary Technical School | Technical School | Vocational Senior High School |
| 1965 | 100.0 | 48.2 | 51.8 | 19.5 | 3.7 | 28.6 |
| 1980 | 100.0 | 81.1 | 18.9 | 10.4 | 5.8 | 2.7 |
| 1985 | 100.0 | 64.1 | 35.9 | 13.6 | 6.4 | 15.9 |
| 1990 | 100.0 | 54.3 | 45.7 | 17.0 | 10.0 | 18.7 |
| 1997 | 100.0 | 43.8 | 56.2 | 24.0 | 10.0 | 22.2 |
| 1998 | 100.0 | 45.0 | 55.0 | 23.9 | 9.3 | 21.8 |
| 1999 | 100.0 | 47.9 | 52.1 | 23.5 | 8.3 | 20.3 |
| 2000 | 100.0 | 53.5 | 46.5 | 21.8 | 6.2 | 18.5 |
| 2001 | 100.0 | 59.1 | 40.9 | 19.2 | 5.7 | 16.0 |
| 2002 | 100.0 | 61.9 | 38.1 | 16.8 | 5.6 | 15.7 |
| 2003 | 100.0 | 63.1 | 36.9 | 16.1 | 6.2 | 14.6 |
| 2004 | 100.0 | 63.0 | 37.0 | 15.7 | 6.6 | 14.7 |

(Data source: calculated according to relevant data in the *Educational Statistics Yearbook of China*)

## 2. The Extremely Unbalanced Development within Secondary Vocational Education

The overall scale of vocational education has developed quickly; however, great differences exist between the different types of vocational schools within vocational education. Before reform and opening-up, secondary vocational schools consisted of secondary specialized schools, technical schools, and agricultural senior high schools; after reform and opening-up, the concept of agricultural senior high schools was expanded to vocational senior high schools. The three types of schools were different in that: secondary specialized schools were mainly operated by industry or state authorities, and graduates were employed as cadres and their job allocation was institutionally protected. Technical schools were mainly operated by labor departments or industry enterprises, and graduates were employed as workers and their employment was guaranteed. Vocational middle schools developed most rapidly, with the education administrative department as its competent department. The training objective was to combine secondary and technical schools; however, neither the source of capital nor the employment of graduates was guaranteed.

From the administration affiliation of the three types of schools and relevant supportive policies regarding school operations, we can see that secondary specialized schools were the easiest to develop, followed by technical schools, and vocational secondary schools were extremely difficult to develop. Secondary specialized schools had a very high status at the time. Due to the small number of college enrollments at that time, the number of students in undergraduate and junior colleges was only 1.208 million in 1983.[33] However, with the comprehensive restoration and development of the economy, professionals in all walks of life were extremely scarce, and thus secondary specialized schools became an important channel to quickly acquire professional qualifications. With this background, relevant ministries and commissions attached great importance to secondary specialized schools, and often reserved the best places for such schools; they also provided strong financial support. Technical schools were mainly operated by enterprises and labor departments, but some were operated by industry authorities. The enterprises that could operate technical schools were all enterprises with relatively strong financial resources. The technical schools operated by industry authorities could enjoy the same treatment as secondary specialized schools. Therefore, the conditions for operating technical training schools were also advantageous at that time. For example, the average cost of students in secondary specialized schools and technical schools directed by the Ministry of Railways in the 1980s was more than 2,000 yuan.[34] These kinds of financial conditions are beyond the reach of many vocational schools nowadays. Secondary specialized schools and technical schools were also in charge of assigning graduates' jobs when they graduated, and this made them more attractive. As a matter of fact, there was a common phenomenon in the 1980s, that the best-performing junior high school graduates often tended to consider entering secondary specialized schools as their top priority, followed by key senior high schools.

The education administrative department is the organizer of vocational middle schools. However, when the education administrative department takes charge of vocational education, it neither has the solid financial strength as the economic authorities and state-owned enterprise, nor takes charge of employment indicators as does the labor department. Under such circumstances, you can imagine how difficult it is to operate a vocational middle school. Operating many forms of schools, through multiple efforts, using a multiple-channel approach and with multiple financing, were all policies that had been considered in secondary vocational schools. Since the government can't afford the costs of vocational schools or provide employment indicators, then it had to give vocational middle schools the freedom to develop independently in the market economy. Many principals had not only developed the skills to acquire funding, but also the ability to earn a profit.

Setting up stores and developing school-operating enterprises are important ways for many vocational schools to obtain the funds required for school operations. Some places, such as Dalian, also introduced the policy of "who chooses the person for a job, pays." That is, the employers who hire the graduates are required to pay the education administrative department.[35]

When East China Normal University organized scholars to write about the experiences they had in studying *Decision of the Central Committee of the CPC on the Reform of the Education System*, Li Liping described this problem in-depth. She said in the *Vocational Middle School Should Have Its Reasonable Position*: In 1984, the number of enrolled students in secondary vocational schools, technical schools, and vocational secondary schools in Shanghai accounted for 52.4% of the total enrollments in senior high schools, and the number of enrolled students in vocational secondary schools reached 45.4% in the three types of schools, thus becoming an important constituent part of secondary vocational education system. Objectively, secondary specialized schools and technical schools have been studying the experience of school operations from the former Soviet Union in the 1950s for 30 years, and have formed their own models. However, vocational schools are still in the exploratory stage. At the same time, secondary specialized schools and technical schools have relatively reliable financial resources and have the advantage over vocational middle schools in terms of teachers, teaching materials, equipment, and internship places. However, the key lies in the subjective factors, which are mainly reflected in the training objectives, the enrollment and assignment system. "According to the current division of labor, secondary specialized schools concentrate on cultivating technicians; technical schools center on cultivating skilled workers, while the graduates of vocational middle schools are not perfectly classifiable. They are not viewed as true technicians and they are considered to have secondary school education background when calculating out labor statistics. Furthermore, it is hard to consider them as 'workers', at least not as skilled workers who graduate from technical schools. Therefore, society does not recognize their qualifications either."[36] In terms of the enrollment system, assignment system and stipend system, they are not treated equally with secondary specialized schools, technical schools, and vocational middle schools. In terms of enrollment, the order of applying for college is secondary specialized school, technical school, and vocational middle school in sequence. Specialized school and technical school students not only have no need to pay tuition fees, but also have scholarships for the entire duration. However, vocational middle school students do not have scholarships, and they have to pay tuition fees. The difference in their job assignments is even greater. All the students in secondary specialized schools and technical schools are assigned jobs without considering their performance, while vocational middle school students will not be assigned a job. Sometimes in order to reflect the principle of "no assignment" in vocational middle schools, some people will have to stay behind even though they can be assigned to work.

Vocational middle schools were transformed from regular senior high schools that were weak in operating schools from the very beginning. In addition, during the subsequent process of school operations, they had no funding, no equipment, and no graduate prospects. The State Council issued a document in 1980 which stipulated the financing channels for vocational education; however, the amount was often small when it was implemented locally. The student funding standard of vocational schools was not implemented until the dispatch by MOF, MOE, and MOHRSS in 2015, which requested that "all localities should establish and perfect the student funding allocation system for secondary vocational schools by the end of 2016, and actively adopt effective measures coordinated with financial resources to continuously improve the level of student funding and gradually establish a dynamic adjustment mechanism for student funding allocation standards in the following years."[37] Therefore, they failed to attain a good reputation. By 1998, after serious difficulties occurred in operating schools for secondary specialized schools and technical schools, vocational secondary schools became the main force for vocational education due to policy changes, and the poor social image of vocational middle schools inevitably fell on the whole for vocational education. This undoubtedly added great resistance for vocational education to become a viable type of education.

It can be said that the low social status of vocational education nowadays is largely related to the badly planned developmental path and inadequate policy support after the determination of vigorously developing vocational secondary schools in the past. The subsequent development of higher vocational education continues to repeat this conceptualization, which had led to the widespread low social status of higher vocational education. Today, the development of applied technology in undergraduate education is still repeating these policies. Given the circumstances of operating schools with such extreme difficulties, although many vocational middle school principals have mastered the skill of "bronze head and iron mouth," this burden should not be borne by them alone. They learned to raise funds through various channels and even run their own companies and enterprises during this process; however, this should not be the over-riding concern of market-oriented vocational education. Vocational school principals spend too much energy raising funds, and this has a negative impact on the development of vocational education. That is, principals rarely paid enough attention to the internal development of schools; the principal's role of "in charge of external affairs" became a normalized role that was defined over time while deputy principals became responsible for internal affairs. This kind of management structure affects the fundamental requirements and structural development of vocational schools.

## 3. The Development of Secondary Vocational Education Benefits from Strong Government Promotion

Whether secondary specialized schools or technical schools have achieved rapid development due to more favorable conditions, or vocational middle schools have expanded their scale because principals tenaciously overcame all kinds of difficulties, these achievements are essentially due to the strong promotion of the government. Actually, in the development process, secondary specialized schools and technical schools have unquestionably received much governmental support. Although the development conditions are difficult, vocational schools have obtained a lot of support from local governments, and some support has been very strong. The *Decision of the Central Committee of the CPC on the Reform of the Education System* is a national document in itself. When identifying it as the beginning of the construction of modern vocational education in China, we have already acknowledged that China's vocational education has developed under the strong promotion of government.

The biggest advantage of government's strong promotion lies in that it can promote vocational education's rapid development in a short period of time. For our country, where the school vocational education is still at a very weak stage and the huge demand for skilled workers has formed a huge gap due to rapid economic development, it is very important for us to rapidly develop vocational education through the strong governmental promotion and quickly compensate for the "skill deficit" caused by the "Cultural Revolution." Without the government's strong promotion to push the rapid development of vocational education in our country, the subsequent economic miracle would have been difficult to obtain; moreover, it would also lead to an incalculable social problem. This is because the government would have to deal with a large number of young people who cannot go to college and have no skills. This could have become a terrible social problem. If this problem arose, then all the economic achievements obtained long since the reform and opening-up would have possibly been swallowed up by various job-guaranteeing requirements. From this perspective, the Party and State made a very far-sighted decision to adjust the educational structure at that time. However, in the vocational education system formed under the strong promotion of the government, there is also a congenital defect, that is, the lack of sufficiently numerous links to society, especially connections with enterprises. As a matter of fact, this is one of the most important issues that our vocational education is confronted with at present. This problem can be solved easily in a planned economy. It is not a big problem under the conditions of the secondary specialized schools run by industry authorities or technical schools run by enterprises. However, this problem will be very serious if the management authority of vocational education is completely controlled by the education administrative department.

In fact, China's development of vocational education has sustained this path since modern times. Unlike Western vocational education born out of the guild apprenticeship program, China's vocational education has been promoted by external forces and transplanted from Western countries in the form of school vocational education from the very beginning. The Westernization Movement promoted the rise of industrial education and a number of new vocational schools came into being. Pioneers such as Huang Yanpei and Tao Xingzhi promoted the further development of China's vocational education through school vocational education. After the establishment of the new nation, China borrowed vocational educational models from the Soviet Union and established secondary specialized schools and technical schools. However, while introducing Western vocational education school models, China only acknowledged the form of school vocational education and failed to realize that their school vocational education was born out of the guild apprenticeship system and had a profound industrial background. This led to the incomplete state of China's vocational education. Although China once had traditional apprenticeships, our modern vocational education is disconnected from traditional Chinese apprenticeships. The differences in the evolution of development have determined that China's vocational education system is confronted with many problems that do not exist in Western countries at all. It has become the main historical mission for China's vocational education to truly entrench itself in China's industrial background and construct a modern vocational education system with Chinese characteristics.

To establish multiple links with enterprises is the breakthrough point for vocational education to shift from a low-level education to a viable type of education in people's minds. This is true in countries with successful vocational education such as Switzerland and Germany. One of the important reasons why their vocational education is well received by students and their parents is that students can gain access to an attractive apprentice salary while studying and can have a good job after graduation. If they want to go to a school of a higher grade, they have a completely smooth path to follow. How can such vocational education be unpopular? These advantages acquired by vocational education require the support of enterprises. Therefore, the key breakthrough point for vocational education to transform from "grading" to "classification" is to develop vocational education in accordance with its own rules. It is in this sense that we can say China's vocational education is striding forward a modern vocational education. This is because "how to promote industry-academy cooperation" has become the core issue for the development of vocational education since 1998 when some special investments and employment policies that were owned by vocational education were abandoned.

## Notes

1 Wang Xing: The Social Construction of Skill Formation—A Sociology Approach to the Evolving Trajectory of the Apprenticeship in China Factories, Social Sciences Academic Press (China), 2014, p. 274.
2 Yang Jintu: Rise and Fall of Vocational Education and Replacement of Old and New Educational Thinking—A Hundred Years of Vocational Education Review, Research in Educational Development, Vol. 24, No. 2, 2004.
3 Lin Dan: The Illusion and Truth of the Distorted Educational Policies, Teaching and Administration, No. 6, 2004.
4 Vocational and Technical Education: 20 Years of Review and Witnessing, 1999, p. 2.
5 Wang Xing: The Social Construction of Skill Formation—A Sociology Approach to the Evolving Trajectory of the Apprenticeship in China Factories, Social Sciences Academic Press (China), 2014, p. 281.
6 Wang Xing: The Social Construction of Skill Formation—A Sociology Approach to the Evolving Trajectory of the Apprenticeship in China Factories, Social Sciences Academic Press (China), 2014, pp. 282–283.
7 Liu Xiyao: Report at the National Conference on Education (Abstract), 1978.
8 Vocational and Technical Education: 20 Years of Review and Witnessing, 1999, p. 2.
9 Yang Jintu: Major Changes in 30 Years—Overview of the Important Issues in Vocational Education in China in 1979–2008 (Volume I), Educational Science Publishing House, 2011, p. 67.
10 Yang Jintu: Major Changes in 30 Years—Overview of the Important Issues in Vocational Education in China in 1979–2008 (Volume I), Educational Science Publishing House, 2011, p. 68.
11 Vocational and Technical Education: 20 Years of Review and Witnessing, 1999, p. 7.
12 Yang Jintu: Major Changes in 30 Years—Overview of the Important Issues in Vocational Education in China in 1979–2008 (Volume I), Educational Science Publishing House, 2011, p. 69.
13 Same as the above footnote.
14 Vocational and Technical Education: Review and Witness in the Past 20 Years, 1999, p. 10.
15 CPC Central Committee: Decision of the Central Committee of the CPC on the Reform of the Education System, 1985.
16 Same as the above footnote.
17 Same as the above footnote.
18 Guo Yushi, Zhang Tianfei, etc., Notes about the "Decision of the Central Committee of the CPC on the Reform of the Education System," Journal of East China Normal University (Educational Sciences), No. 3, 1985.

19 Same as the above footnote.
20 Sun Peiqing: History of Chinese Education, East China Normal University Press, 1992, p. 575.
21 Dong Cuncai: Encyclopedia of China (on Education), Encyclopedia of China Publishing House, 1985, p. 553.
22 Dong Cuncai: Encyclopedia of China (on Education), Encyclopedia of China Publishing House, 1985, p. 556.
23 MOE, MOHRSS (former State Labor Bureau): Report on the Structural Reform of Secondary Education, 1980.
24 Vocational and Technical Education: 20 Years of Review and Witnessing, 1999.
25 Tan Zhaopeng: Some Experience about Studying "Decision of the CPC Central Committee on Reform of the Education System," Educational Review, No. 4, 1985.
26 Tan Zhaopeng: Some Experience about Studying "Decision of the CPC Central Committee on Reform of the Education System," Educational Review, No. 4, 1985, p. 39.
27 CPC Central Committee: Decision of the CPC Central Committee on Reform of the Education System, Educational Review, 1985.
28 Dong Cuncai: Encyclopedia of China (on Education), Encyclopedia of China Publishing House, 1985, p. 553.
29 State Council: Decision of the State Council on Vigorously Developing Vocational and Technical Education, 1991.
30 The CPC Central Committee, the State Council: Outline of China's Education Reform and Development, 1993.
31 Same as the above footnote.
32 The State Education Committee: The Ninth Five-Year Plan for China's Educational Development and the Development Outline by 2010, 1996.
33 Dong Cuncai: Encyclopedia of China (on Education), Encyclopedia of China Publishing House, 1985, p. 558.
34 Vocational and Technical Education: 20 Years of Review and Witnessing, 1999, p. 28.
35 Vocational and Technical Education: 20 Years of Review and Witnessing, 1999, p. 30.
36 Guo Yushi, Zhang Tianfei, etc., Notes about the "Decision of the Central Committee of the CPC on the Reform of the Education System," Journal of East China Normal University (Educational Sciences), No. 3, 1985.
37 MOF, MOE, MOHRSS: Guidance Opinions on Establishing and Perfecting the Average Allocation System for Secondary Vocational School Students by MOF, MOE and MOHRSS, 2015.

CHAPTER TWO

# Building a Scientific Concept of Talent

The achievements in the development of secondary vocational education during the past 20 years from 1978 to 1998 are worthy of acknowledgment. The number of enrollments in vocational schools has been equivalent to or even higher than that of regular senior high schools for a quite long period of time, which is unprecedented in Chinese history. Therefore, this achievement is of historic significance. It has created a brand-new pattern of developing vocational education in China, made the acceptance of vocational education widely ingrained in people's minds and laid a solid foundation for the construction of modern vocational education in China. However, does this indicate that China's vocational education has continued on a track of steady development since then? Is vocational education truly established as a legitimate and desirable type of education? The difficult development of vocational education over these 20 years shows that the reality is much more complicated than the ideal. A major event at the turn of the 20th and 21st centuries has poured cold water on the general optimism of the vocational education community. That is, the developing trend of vocational education in China has turned steeply downward and the enrollments of secondary vocational schools have fallen sharply. This occurrence has pushed China's vocational education to step into an important historical transitional period. On the one hand, it has reminded the Chinese people that there is still a long way to go before China's vocational education truly becomes an accepted and desirable type of education. On the other hand, it also has activated the vocational education circle to think deeply about the problems existing in the development of vocational education in China, thus bringing about a profound transformation in vocational education. As a result of this transformation, vocational education has deepened its contact network with all sectors of the society, especially with industry and pushed vocational education a giant step toward truly becoming a distinct and important type of education. The key link is the recognition of the value of skilled graduates, that is, the explicit proposal that "skilled workers are also professionals."

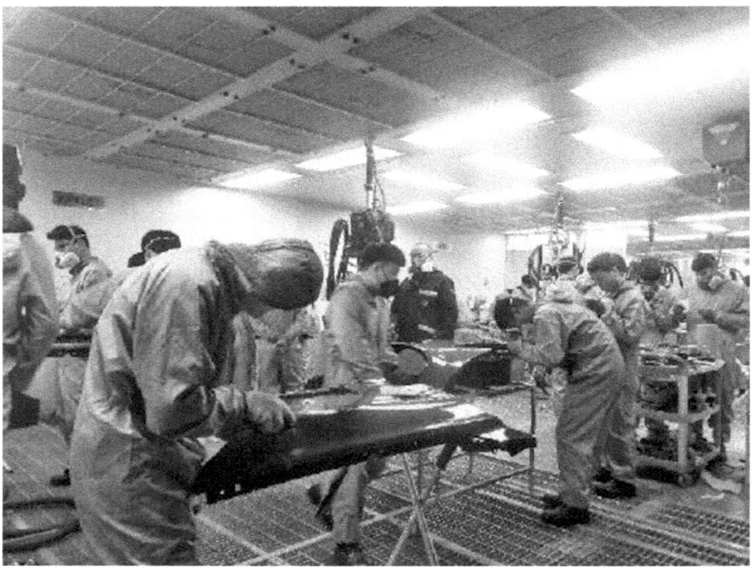

Figure 2.1 Automobile maintenance majors are practicing their coating skills

## Part 1 The Urgent Discussion on Attitudes to Skilled Workers Brought on by the Sharp Decline in the Enrollments of Secondary Vocational Schools at the Turn of the 20th and 21st Centuries

The sharp decline in the enrollments of secondary vocational schools at the turn of the 20th and the 21st centuries should be analyzed as a major event in the development of vocational education. It is a transition point for China's vocational education to truly transform from a planned economy era to a market-oriented era. In addition to some apparent reasons, there are actually some more profound institutional reasons for this.

## 1. The Sharp Decline in New Student Enrollments in Secondary Vocational Schools at the Turn of the 20th and 21st Centuries

In 1995, the new student enrollments of secondary vocational schools accounted for 57.4% of the total enrollments at the senior high school stage,[1] reaching a historic peak. Since then, it started to decline rapidly, and the proportion slipped to 46.5% in 2000. In 2001, it fell even lower to 41.8%, far below 50%. This is the most noteworthy decline in the enrollments of secondary vocational education the turn of the 20th and 21st centuries. This event caused great concern at that time, as it famously broke through the basic principle that "the enrollment scale ratio of general high school should be equivalent to that of secondary vocational school," aroused heated discussion in vocational education circles and stimulated the introduction of a series of policies aimed at containment of the slump. In 2005, MOE proposed that China's secondary vocational education should increase new student enrollments by 1 million every year. It was determined that the enrollment number of secondary vocational education in 2007 would be roughly the same as that of regular high schools, namely, back to the level before the sharp decline. Supported by this policy, the decline in the enrollments of secondary vocational education has been brought under control. However, its impact was very far-reaching.

Seemingly, the primary reasons for the sharp decline in the new student enrollments of secondary vocational schools are as follows:

### 1.1. Structural Reform of the Enrollment System for Secondary Vocational Education

"1998 was undoubtedly a historic year for more than 4,000 medium-sized secondary specialized schools in China. From this year on, the secure jobs that people used to get through secondary vocational education were completely smashed and replaced by having to pay for schooling without job assignment, becoming an integral component of the enrollment system."[2] In the past, secondary specialized school education was favored by people, and the enrollment system was the key reason for that. People would not only be assigned to jobs after graduating from secondary specialized schools, but also become "cadres." All these held great attraction for people. Even today, many former secondary specialized school teachers are still proud of the special status of secondary specialized school education.

### 1.2. The Change in Social Functions Caused by the Reform of State-Owned Enterprises

State-owned enterprises are the main body operating technical training schools. However, they have fallen into an extremely difficult development situation and suffered substantial losses because of the rapid development of private enterprises. Based on this unfavorable situation, the Third Plenary Session of the 14th CPC Central Committee reformed the establishment of a modern enterprise system in accordance with the principles of "clearly-established ownership, well-defined power and responsibility, separation of enterprise from administration, and scientific management," with the purpose of making enterprises truly become subject to market forces. As the problems of state-owned enterprises became more and more severe, *Decision of the CPC Central Committee on Certain Major Issues Concerning the Reform and Development of State-Owned Enterprises* was approved on September 22, 1999. This document specifies that "according to the macroeconomic environment, the state's financial resources and changed circumstances, we should take feasible and effective measures to solve these problems in a planned way and by categories, so as to facilitate enterprises to increase capital and reduce debt as well as promote debt and asset restructuring. Governments at all levels should actively support and steadily carry forward the separation of the social functions of enterprise-operated schools."[3] "Separation of the social functions of enterprise-operated schools" is one of the most influential sentences on technical training schools. This is because technical training schools were classified as a social function of enterprises at that time. Now that it was a social function, it had to be separated. However, the problem of who would take over after separation was not handled properly, and it was no exaggeration for us to use the word "catastrophe" to describe the situation faced by technical training schools in some areas. Even today, only the technical training schools in a few provinces or regions such as Guangdong have been well preserved; the technical training school licenses in most provinces or regions have been revoked and merged, or come under the jurisdiction of education administration departments. The educational nature of technical training schools has been completely integrated with vocational middle schools. The disappearance of a large number of technical training schools will naturally lead to an acute decline in the enrollments of secondary vocational schools. From this perspective, it was not prudent to separate the social function of technical training schools from enterprises. However, if we cannot draw historical lessons at the level of group consciousness, then this historical tragedy may well repeat itself.

### 1.3. The Large-Scale Enrollment Expansion of Higher Education

On December 24, 1998, MOE issued *Education Revitalization Action Plan Facing 21st Century*, which proposes: "In order to enable more senior high school graduates to have access to higher education, the total number of junior and senior college students in 2000 will, under the premise of adopting new mechanisms and models, reach 6.6 million according to local needs, funding and possible changes in conditions. The incremental increase in the enrollment plan will be mainly used for the development of local higher vocational education; the scale of in-school postgraduates shall achieve a tangible improvement. The enrollment rate of higher education has increased from 9.1% (new standard) in 1997 to around 11% in 2000."[4]

Under the guidance of this policy, in 1999, "a total of 2,754,500 students were enrolled by junior and senior college education, an increase of 669,500, or 24.31% over the previous year," and "the gross enrollment rate of higher education reached 10.5%, increasing by 0.7% over the previous year"[5]; in 2000, "a total of 3.767 million undergraduates (senior college) and higher vocational (junior college) students were enrolled by higher education, an increase of 1.0131 million, or 36.78% over the previous year."[6] This growth rate was very astonishing. Therefore, 1999 is referred to as the year of enrollment expansion in higher education, marking the longest and largest enrollment expansion of China's higher education in history. In 2008, MOE said the enrollment expansion in 1999 was too sudden and required more control by gradually increasing the proportion of enrollments. However, in the context of the global financial crisis in 2009, enrollment expansion of postgraduate students began. The *Outline of the National Medium- and Long-Term Education Reform and Development Plan (2010–2020)* put forward the goal of "further improving the popularization of higher education and achieving a gross enrollment rate of 40%."[7] As the rapid enrollment expansion brought a decline in quality, MOE issued *Some Suggestions on the Overall Improvement of the Quality of Higher Education* in April 2012, which required "stabilizing enrollments and keeping the scale of undergraduate enrollments in state-run colleges and universities relatively stable"; it also came up with a number of measures that had a significant influence on subsequent educational practice. However, higher education did not stop its expansion pace. Only the objective changed. The document requested that "the incremental increase in the scale of higher education should be mainly used to develop higher vocational education, continuing education and postgraduate professional degree education and broaden non-government funded education and cooperation in school operations."[8] The enrollment expansion has continued until now. By 2015, a total of 7.3785 million junior and senior college students were enrolled in regular higher education, an increase of 164,500 over the previous year; the number of in-school students enrolled was 26.253 million, an increase of 776,000 over the previous year; the number of graduates was 6.8089 million, an increase of 215,200 over the previous year.[9] In the same year, it was announced that the gross enrollment rate of higher education in China reached 40%, five years ahead of the goal set forth by *Outline of the National Medium- and Long-Term Education Reform and Development Plan (2010–2020)*.

This is a controversial episode in history. In today's view, replacing quantity for quality has enabled more students to have access to higher education, and has had more positive effects on China's social development. It's generally acknowledged that enrollment expansion of higher education aims to alleviate college students' employment difficulties caused by economic recession. That's the reason why we continue to increase the enrollments of postgraduates when expanded college students encounter employment difficulties again. The introduction of this policy at that time did not exclude these consideration, because the policy of increasing enrollments in higher education was introduced during the period when laid-off workers were the most prominent problem in China. Nevertheless, it is still believed that this important policy was not introduced for this temporary purpose only. The policy makers judged at the time: "From present to the near future, the lack of internationally advanced and creative expertise has become one of the main factors that restrict China's capacity to innovate and compete."[10] This should be the primary starting point for the introduction of this policy.

Regardless of the purpose of the enrollment expansion of higher education, it had a lethal impact on the enrollments of secondary vocational education. For secondary specialized schools and technical training schools at that time, this is the equivalent of applying a hot flannel to the tip of an iceberg. Just think, how many junior high school graduates would choose to attend vocational schools when they suddenly had so many college entrance opportunities? Worse still, MOE also proposed the "employment-oriented" policy regarding vocational education at that time, which is still highly controversial. In 2002, the *Decision of the State Council on Vigorously Promoting the Reform and Development of Vocational Education* by MOE required "an increase in the proportion of secondary vocational school graduates entering higher education institutions, especially higher vocational schools."[11] In 2004, the "employment-oriented" policy was put forward. The word "employment-oriented" prominently appeared in *Some Opinions of MOE on Being Employment-Oriented and Deepening the Reform of Higher Vocational Education*. At the most extreme time, the enrollment rate of secondary vocational students was required to not exceed 5%. This policy aimed to reinforce the ability of vocational education to serve the industrial development, to improve students' skill levels, to adhere to the fundamental attributes of vocational education, and to prevent secondary vocational education from blindly pursuing enrollment rate targets. However, the control over students' opportunities for further study would inevitably interact with the above factors and aggravate the already tough situation of secondary vocational enrollment.

## 2. Major Countermeasures for the Sharp Decline in the Enrollments of Secondary Vocational Schools

Many countermeasures have been put forward to deal with the severe decline in the enrollments of secondary vocational schools. Without doubt, this downward trend was in the end temporarily contained by MOE with the policy of increasing enrolling 1 million people each year. However, we need to pay close attention to the reform measures that emerged under this stimulus. There were mainly three countermeasures proposed at that time: 1. Operate comprehensive secondary schools; 2. Transform from vocational school education to vocational training; 3. Operate five-year junior colleges.

### 2.1. Operate Comprehensive Secondary Schools

Vocational schools in Shanghai are active practitioners of comprehensive secondary schools, represented by the "Dual Enrollment, Dual Diploma" model of the Shanghai Changyang Middle School and the "Dual Channel" model of the East China Mode High School in Shanghai. The specific implementation process of the "Dual Enrollment, Dual Diploma" model[12] is students are required to learn all the compulsory courses and some professional basic courses for regular high schools in the first three years, of which 80% are cultural courses, 20% are technical specialized courses, and 3% in graduation; some students can take the college entrance examination when they graduate from grade 3; those students who do not take the college entrance examination or failed in the examination shall continue their fourth year of study. The basic implementation process of the "Dual Channel" model is school education is required to thoroughly reflect the two functions, namely, higher education preparation education and employment preparation education, and achieve bidirectional penetration of vocational education and general education in teaching content and approaches; students can obtain two diplomas or one diploma with several certificates from regular senior high school and vocational secondary school (or technical grade examination) after accomplishing the required courses, so as to cultivate "qualification + expertise"; in terms of class setting, it is divided into directional classes and non-directional classes, and students can have several opportunities for diversion in the senior high school stage; students in directional classes should complete the compulsory courses required by regular senior high schools in the first three years; they also need to study specialized courses and can take the college entrance examination; those students who fail in the examination can specialize in their professional subjects in the fourth year and the qualified students will be granted a technical secondary school diploma.

Comprehensive secondary schools were more popular at that time, because advocates strongly asserted that comprehensive secondary school is a kind of school that can allow students to pursue further studies and provide them guaranteed employment. This propaganda is, of course, extremely irrational. Students with low scores in the senior high school entrance examinations should also take into account both academic and vocational courses when studying in comprehensive secondary schools. How can they be equipped with the ability to pursue further studies and work? As a result, both pursuing further studies and employment are lacking in strength without doubt. However, driven by breaking through the school-operating dilemma, many schools were highly enthusiastic about operating comprehensive secondary schools. The subsequent practice showed that comprehensive secondary school is not adaptable to the environment of our country. After more than 10 years of school-operating practice, 28 comprehensive secondary schools in Shanghai automatically closed down at last because they failed to fill their classrooms.

In fact, the so-called comprehensive secondary schools experimented within our country were not real comprehensive secondary schools. Although these schools implemented both general education and vocational education, the vocational education here was grafted onto the general education. Vocational education is a "fallback" for those students who fail in the college entrance examination rather than a process on the basis of students' independent choice. It is college-oriented in essence. Secondary vocational education once again encountered the problem of decline in enrollments in the recent two years. In this context, comprehensive secondary schools were put forward again by some regions to solve this problem. Whether this strategy is feasible has plenty of models to draw upon.

## 2.2. Focus on Vocational Training

Another influential strategy is to transform vocational education from a school-based model to a vocational training-based model. That is, take postsecondary training as the main source of vocational skill acquisition in China. This idea was inspired by the British vocational education model. Professor Shi Weiping and I were the dominant power behind this strategy. We worked together and published the paper *Reflection and Exploration on the School-Operating Model of Urban Secondary Vocational Schools in China* in the 12th issue of *Educational*

*Research* in 2000, and *The Development Prospects of Urban Post-Secondary Training* in the 9th issue of *Chinese Vocational and Technical Education* in 2000, in which we systematically expounded this strategy and analyzed the following advantages of postsecondary training: 1. The primary task of urban secondary vocational schools is to orient to the tertiary industry, namely, the service industry; the training period of the service industry is usually short but requires higher levels of general cultural knowledge by students; and the implementation of postsecondary training is in accordance with the features of the urban industrial structure. 2. Postsecondary training is not only conducive to meeting the requirements for workers' basic cultural knowledge during the production process and job-transfer training, but also to meeting learners' requirement to improve their education level. 3. Postsecondary training is flexible enough to timely reflect the changes in the relationship between labor market supply and demand, achieve the best matching between labor force and occupation to the utmost extent, and enhance the efficiency of training. 4. Vocational schools no longer undertake or seldom undertake the teaching of culture courses; this can simplify the functions of vocational schools, help to carry out vocational and technical education and training, and improve the quality of vocational education. 5. Postsecondary training can contribute to solving the shortage of urban secondary vocational students at that time; implementing postsecondary training and incorporating a large number of youth into the scope of vocational and technical training can greatly enlarge the targeted participants and alleviate the conflict between students' supply and demand.[13]

These opinions, even in today's view, are still insightful. According to the realistic environment of the development of China's vocational education, it is impossible to transform the training model of multiple vocational schools from school education to vocational training (of course, there are also schools that have successfully realized this transformation, such as the Shanghai Real Estate School). This is because it is difficult to forecast the negative consequences of such reforms. If secondary vocational school education fails to settle down, the construction of vocational education system won't come into being today. Nevertheless, this strategy indeed reveals a major problem in vocational education models at that time. That is, too much emphasis is put on school vocational education, and vocational training is very weak. The core implication of this strategy is that we should develop vocational education within a broader vision. From this perspective, this strategy is far-sighted. Even today, our attention to vocational training system is far from enough; we still have a long way to go compared with the concept of "TVET" adopted by UNESCO. Dr. C.J. Zirkle from the Ohio State University took "see where you can find vocational education in the United States?" as the logical starting point for discussion when introducing the American vocational education system. This vision is much broader than ours.

### 2.3. Operate Five-Year Junior Colleges

This is a successful strategy established by Jiangsu province. Schools named after "xxx higher vocational and technical training school" can only be found in Jiangsu province. Jiangsu Union Technical Institute is the carrier for the implementation of this strategy. In June 2003, Jiangsu Union Technical Institute, approved by the People's Government of Jiangsu Province and registered by MOE in records for reference, was formally established in Jiangsu Province. It is an independently established regular junior college, which implements the school-operating model of "small brand institutes within a big institute." Under it, a number of higher vocational and technical training schools are set up as the branch institutes of the institute and several school points are also set up. The main functions of Jiangsu Union Technical Institute are: coordinate and assist higher vocational and technical training schools to formulate development plans; make overall plans and coordinate the annual enrollment plan for five-year higher vocational and technical training schools; organize higher vocational and technical training schools to carry out educational and teaching exchange, cooperation, and research; coordinate the major construction of higher vocational and technical training schools and the sharing of teaching resources between schools; take charge of enrollment management for students in five-year higher vocational and technical training schools; issuance of graduation certificates; etc. At present, the institute consists of 54 branch institutes such as the Nanjing Institute of Technology, 38 school points such the Jiangsu Drama School and 5 higher normal schools; set up 16 types and more than 130 five-year higher vocational majors; with nearly 200,000 students (Data source: Jiangsu Union Technical Institute Campus Network, February 2017).

The establishment of five-year junior colleges is an innovative model of operating vocational education in China and has played an important role in stabilizing the development of secondary vocational education in Jiangsu province.

## Part 2 Concern for the Weak Position of Skilled Talents in Employment

However, it is the internal factors that have a decisive influence on the development of things. All the above factors, such as the removal of job assignment policy in secondary technical training schools, the separation of the social functions of state-owned enterprises, and the enrollment expansion of higher education are just the external factors that led to the sharp slump in the enrollments of secondary vocational education. The internal factor lies in that the value of skilled workers has not been truly recognized by the society. In terms of wage levels, labor security, and chances for promotion, for example, skilled workers cannot compete with professionals at all. This is the most fundamental problem existing in the development of vocational education in China.

Guided by the policy of "letting some people get rich first," China's economy has developed rapidly from the 1980s to 1990s, and its achievements have drawn the attention of the world. However, only part of people got rich first during this period. To be precise, only a very small number of people became wealthy, mainly industrial operators. For most workers, although their living standard has also been greatly improved, the gap between the rich and the poor has been broadening rapidly. The protection of workers' rights and interests was far less than that in the planned economy era. China was in a critical period of transforming from a planned economy to a market-oriented economy during this period; a series of measures, systems, and platforms to protect worker's rights and interests in the planned economy era were destroyed; and the country mainly focused on supporting the development of enterprises. As a result, the government could not systematically research and solve the problem of protecting workers' rights and interests in market-oriented economic conditions; thus, the system of protecting workers' rights and interests was very imperfect and the status of workers was very humble; even highly skilled workers were not in a good condition. In this case, it was impossible for people to have a good impression on vocational education. After entering the 21st century, protecting workers' rights and interests and improving the wages of skilled workers have increasingly become the focus of social attention and the core of national policies. After more than 10 years of hard work, this situation has been greatly improved. However, this problem has not been completely solved. Skilled workers are still very humble in their social status, and it is still a critical factor that impedes the development of vocational education at present.

## 1. Manifestations of Skilled Talents' Disadvantaged Status in Employment

The following materials reflect workers' status from different aspects.

Look at a case first. Here is an undercover doctor's record in a factory.[14] The author had worked as a worker for 25 days in the factory, and offered an in-depth description of the workers' working and living conditions, the content of which was stunning. The case described in the report happened in 2015, so you can imagine the situation 15 years ago. Although this report is extracted from the internet, we can affirm it is basically true from the detailed description of its content. Furthermore, there are many similar reports that can corroborate each other.

### 1.1. Slender Income

For the social investigation, I worked as a worker for 25 days. I lived in Shangwei village, Zhangkengjing, Guanlan town, Longhua new zone, Shenzhen. Although it was called a "village," industrial production was its main function and the majority was labor-intensive manufacturing industry. Migrant workers gathered in such industrial parks. They had similar life and destiny. Both men and women had a face from which you could easily judge they were wage earners. During working hours, the pedestrians outside the parks were thinly scattered; after work, the roads would become a steady stream and bustling. Various kinds of household wastes could be seen everywhere. The stores mostly sold economical and practical goods. It was difficult to see various "high-end, magnificent, and classy" products belonging to the metropolis except in some hypermarkets. The police station's alarm reporting telephone could be seen every few tens of meters, which reminded everyone to take care of their personal and property security at any time.

The factory payment here worked out almost the same in the end. If a general worker did not often work overtime, he would earn about 2,000 yuan per month. If he overworked for a long time, for example, overworking 4 hours a day, his wage would be 3,000–4,000 yuan; it was generally impossible to exceed 4,000 yuan.

The basic wage was mostly about 1,800 yuan, which was established on the basis of the newly adjusted minimum wage standard in Shenzhen. Shenzhen started to implement the minimum wage of 1,808 yuan per month from February 1, 2014. It was the highest minimum wage in China at that time. The so-called minimum wage standard was the highest wage standard for workers in some private enterprises. Many small factories even failed to implement the minimum wage standard.

### 1.2. Inevitable Fines

February 20, 2014, was the fifth day for me in Shenzhen. I became a regular employee of Shenzhen Lecai Smartcard Technology Co., Ltd. Like many factories, Lecai was hiring a large number of people. There was almost no threshold to work as a general worker in such kind of small factory.

Before formal appointment, the company's front desk operator took a *New Employee Protocol* for me to sign. There were two kinds of words in the protocol that appeared frequently: one was mandatory, such as "must," "must obey," "must be confirmed by the supervisor or manager," etc.; the other was punitive, such as "punish," "deduct," "be dealt with as ..." and so on. Worker must wear work clothes and badges as required; otherwise, they will be punished by 10 yuan each time; whoever disturbs the order shall be punished according to related regulations; those who do not show up at work posts without reasons after clocking in will be dealt with as absenteeism ... All the terms in the protocol manifested the factory's barefaced strength and despotism. However, even confronted with such trenchant disciplines and regulations, workers could only choose to obey and had no ways to negotiate. These regulations of the factory were not a worthless piece of paper; various fine notices were often published on the bulletin board. These regulations were important management tools for the factory.

### 1.3. Closed Work

I was assigned to the punch press workshop. There were six or seven different types of machines in the punch press workshop. Only one worker operated one of the machines, and he became my master later. After a few days, I realized that each punch press workshop had only two workers in two shifts every day; each one was responsible for 12 hours of production.

Lecai is a factory that produces various kinds of cards, such as membership cards, advertising cards, etc. I was mainly responsible for producing membership cards during that period of time at the factory. A membership card contains 11 production processes: offset printing, coating, magnetic strip, positioning, compounding, punching, etc. The running punching machine is corresponding to "punching" process, which cuts a large card into 25 pieces of small cards. Every time a card is cut, it will make a sound like "deng." The powerful implosion would make the sound reverberate through the whole floor of workshops. I didn't feel it was ear-piercing when I heard this kind of noise at first, but I felt that it was some kind of torture for me after working in the workshop for a few hours.

The master had a precocious face, which did not match his 18-year-old age. Though diligent and practical, he was introverted and rarely had any workmates he could talk to in the factory. He was always watching a video while eating alone. It was not until later that I realized this position could confine workers' characters. The noise of the machine kept ringing in the 40-square-meter workshop. No one was here except the six or seven machines. The workshop was just like a small isolated island after its door was closed. It was perfectly normal for a person who has worked in this environment for a long time to become lukewarm and silent.

On the second day when I was in the factory, my master told me that a worker was injured in the punch press workshop some time ago. Later, my master also suffered an occupational injury. His palm was pressed by a hot thermoprinting machine. Fortunately, he was not severely injured. He did not become disabled, and only his two fingers and the back of the palm were stitched and bandaged. Workers have been operating the machine all day long, so occupational injury is not a small probability event. It is potentially an enormous threat to workers.

My daily action was to put a big piece of card on the punch machine and cut it into small pieces of cards. After continually working like this for an hour, my hands were still habitually moving and my mind gradually became numb. I felt that I was suffering from workshop phobia when I was looking at the unfeeling painted walls, the ground, and the cold machines that unshakably stood there every day.

### 1.3. Hard Life Circumstance

I lived in a free dormitory as other workers did. The door of the dormitory was very dilapidated and ramshackle, and even couldn't be locked. I put my wallet and mobile phone under the pillow when I went to sleep every night. Sometimes I would wake up at midnight and check if they were still there.

The dormitory can accommodate 8 people in total. In fact, the beds we slept on were very dangerous. The upper bunks had no railings; many screws on the bedstead were loose, and they were easy to fall apart with gravity. In order to make the bedsteads more solid, we put the heads and ends of the three bunk beds together so as to make them lean against each other firmly.

The dormitory would become very noisy after work. The sounds of bathing, laundry, and horseplay mixed together, which showed the excitement and ruggedness of the workers when free from the workshops.

It was not an exaggeration but a fact that four of the six people had no money for meals. I didn't dare to put much money in my wallet three days after I came to the factory. I usually put no more than 20 yuan. I was afraid of it being borrowed instead of being stolen or robbed. Just a few days after I came to the factory, three workers borrowed money from me, 10 yuan, or

20 yuan. They would not borrow much from me, 100 yuan at most, mainly for eating, buying daily necessities, cigarettes, etc. Later, I found that there were too many people who needed to borrow money or were likely to borrow money from me, and I couldn't deal with this as I only had a few hundred yuan. Therefore, when the third worker came to borrow money, I could only show him my empty wallet.

I took it for granted that the price of the place where workers gathered would be relatively low, but the actual reality is the opposite. The price here was not low, but higher than that of many cities and towns. My school was located in Liangxiang town, Fangshan district, Beijing. The bananas in the vegetable market were often sold at about 3 yuan per catty. However, bananas on any fruit stand here were sold at 4.5 yuan per catty. For the expenses outside the factory, workers spent much on fast food. Here, the snack priced at 10 yuan was the worst; better snack was 15 yuan, and the average was 12 yuan.

According to the introduction of some workers who had worked in Shenzhen for a long time, every time their wages rose, the price in the industrial parks would rise accordingly, such as the rent. What they really felt was that their wages did not rise but fall instead. They could get approximately 2,000 yuan per month many years ago; however, after the prices rose multiple times, their wage was only about 2,500 yuan.

Then, let's look at the analysis at the industry level. Take the iron and steel enterprise as an example. In the article *Research on the Wage Incentive Mechanism of Technical and Skilled Talents in Iron and Steel Enterprises*, Liu Li analyzes the reasons why technical and skilled workers are not highly enthusiastic about work and learning: First, their wage level is on the low side. Nowadays, most iron and steel enterprises implement the "structural wage system." Their wage structure is not unreasonable and only a small amount of "work" is linked with their work performance in their wages. As a result, the outstanding contributions created by the technical and skilled workers through their skills and experience could not be thoroughly reflected in their wages. Their wage level is not high and their wages do not match their contributions. Second, the improvement of techniques and skills is not thoroughly reflected in wages. Many iron and steel enterprises do not have a unit that is directly related to the improvement of employees' technical skills in the wage structure. Because of insufficient wage incentives, employees don't have enough motivation for conscious learning, and it's difficult to improve the enterprises' overall level of technical skills. Third, the promotion channel is narrow and the career development prospects are bleak. In the old state-owned enterprises, there is only the channel for the promotion of administrative posts, and only a small number of people can get career development through administrative posts. Because of the narrow promotion channel, technical and skilled talents in the enterprises can see no hope ahead and lose the motivation to work actively. Fourth, there is no effective performance evaluation mechanism to guarantee the internal fairness. Many enterprises do not have a true performance evaluation mechanism for all employees. Employees do not have quantitative assessment indicators and standards, and their work ability and work results cannot be evaluated fairly. This leads to the unequal distribution of bonuses and the little difference between the wage of technical and skilled workers with great contributions and that of ordinary employees.[15] These circumstances are commonplace.

Many enterprises even link the probationary wage proportion with academic qualifications and positions. The lower their academic qualifications and positions are, the lower wage proportion they will obtain, as shown in Tables 2.1 and 2.2. Obviously this is discrimination.

Table 2.1 The wage management system of an enterprise in Chongqing—the wage standard for initial job holders

| Serial Number | Academic Qualification | Wage Standard in the Probation Period (Proportion) | Notes |
|---|---|---|---|
| 1 | Graduates of junior secondary schools | 50% | Probation Period: 3–6 months |
| 2 | Graduates of senior high schools(including secondary technical schools) | 60% | Probation Period: 3–6 months |
| 3 | Graduates of secondary specialized schools | 70% | Probation Period: 3–6 months |
| 4 | Graduates of junior colleges | 80% | Probation Period: 3–6 months |
| 5 | Undergraduates | 90% | Probation Period: 3–6 months |
| 6 | Master graduates | 100% | Probation Period: 3–6 months |

From https://www.taodocs.com/p-107583993.html titled as the wage management system of a listed enterprise in Chongqing [EB/OL]. 2018-5-1.

Table 2.2 The wage management system of an enterprise in Chongqing—the wage standard for noninitial job holders and new employees during the probation period

| Serial Number | Employee Type | Working Experience | Salary Standard in the Probation Period (Proportion) | Notes |
|---|---|---|---|---|
| 1 | General professional and technical personnel, management personnel | Less than three years (including three years) | 90% | Probation Period: 3 months |
| 2 | | More than three years | 100% | Probation Period: 3 months |
| 3 | Technician, auxiliary worker, veteran worker | Less than four years (including four years) | 80% | Probation Period: 3 months |
| 4 | | More than four years | 100% | Probation Period: 3 months |
| 5 | Department manager and above | | 100% | Probation Period: 3 months |

From https://www.taodocs.com/p-107583993.html titled as the wage management system of a listed enterprise in Chongqing [EB/OL]. 2018-5-1.

In terms of the absolute number of wages, the wages of workers are usually distinctly lower than the wages of professional workers, as shown in Table 2.3.[16]

Table 2.3 Ningbo professional technical grade wage levels

| Serial Number | Professional Technical Grade | Average |
|---|---|---|
| 1 | Primary worker | 21,744 |
| 2 | Intermediate worker | 33,795 |
| 3 | High-level worker | 44,483 |
| 4 | Technician | 52,890 |
| 5 | Senior technician | 59,785 |
| 6 | Other staffs | 24,947 |
| 7 | Senior professional technician | 124,047 |
| 8 | Associate senior professional technician | 108,715 |
| 9 | Mid-level professional technician | 83,206 |
| 10 | Junior professional technician | 52,549 |
| 11 | Staff without technical positions | 30,926 |

Table 2.4 Career development channels for different types of posts

| Serial Number | Management | | Professional and Technical Post | | Production Operation | | Technician | |
|---|---|---|---|---|---|---|---|---|
| 1 | Senior | General manager | | | | | | |
| 2 | High-level | | | | | | | |
| 3 | General | | | | | | | |
| 4 | Senior | Vice-general manager | Professional and technical post at vice-general manager level | Senior | | | | |
| 5 | High-level | | | High-level | | | | |
| 6 | General | | | General | | | | |
| 7 | Senior | Department manager | Professional and technical post at manager level | Senior | | | | |
| 8 | High-level | | | High-level | | | | |
| 9 | General | | | General | | | | |
| 10 | High-level | Section supervisor | Professional and technical post at supervisor level | High-level | | | Technician post at supervisor level | High-level |
| 11 | General | | | General | | | | General |
| 12 | Probationary | | | Probationary | | | | Probationary |
| 13 | High-level | Office clerk | Professional and technical post at clerk level | High-level | Supervision group leader | High-level | Technician post at clerk level | High-level |
| 14 | General | | | General | | General | | General |
| 15 | | | | | Operator | | | |

More seriously, skilled workers usually are not only at the bottom of the enterprise in terms of post grades, but also have very limited promotion space, as shown in Table 2.4.

From https://www.taodocs.com/p-107583993.html titled as the wage management system of a listed enterprise in Chongqing [EB/OL]. 2018-5-1.

## 2. Reasons for the Weak Position of Skilled Workers in Employment

The weak position of skilled talents in employment can be attributed to both institutional and ideological reasons. The institutional reasons should be put first.

### 2.1. Institutional Reasons

In the planned economy era, workers were the masters of the country, and they had a high social status and were well-paid. In the market-oriented economy era, China's political system did not change, but a series of systems that guarantee workers' social status and economic treatment had been destroyed by market forces; a new institutional system had not been established; the state still focused on the development of enterprises: all these led to the weak position of skilled workers in employment. Some researchers made the following analysis: "Our country still follows the route of traditional planned economy system in terms of the management of skilled personnel. Since reform and opening-up, breakthroughs have been made, but some underlying problems still remain unresolved. For example, the distinct division of the dual identity of 'cadre-worker' and 'engineer-skilled worker' makes it difficult for workers to be promoted as a cadre. A skilled worker with knowledge and skills will always be a worker."[17] Other researchers also did similar analysis: "The traditional labor and personnel management system established during the planned economy period is a set of personnel management system 'which attaches less importance to occupation and more to grade.' The core of it is to strictly separate workers and cadres (including scientific and technological personnel) from the management system and manage them separately. Within the framework of this management system, cadres are usually regarded as professionals and workers are regarded as general workers; moreover, most of the highly skilled personnel (such as senior technical workers, technicians, etc.) are classified as workers. For example, technicians in enterprises are called the worker technicians, so as to distinguish them from the technicians and engineers in the technical cadre team. Therefore, it is difficult for them to be regarded as professionals. Although this management system is currently in the course of reform, it still exerts a tremendous and profound influence. It can be said that this is the institutional cause of the misalignment of highly skilled personnel."[18]

## 2.2. Ideological Reasons

The disadvantaged position of skilled talents in employment can also be attributed to the ideological reasons, namely, we fail to properly deal with the relationship between science and technology, thoroughly recognize the independent status of technology comparing with science and the value of technical knowledge.

Before the mid-19th century, science and technology could be said to be two fields that were almost completely separated with each other. After the mid-19th century, the relationship between science and technology has undergone fundamental changes, and scientific theories have begun to exert increasingly substantial influences on technological inventions. It is the development of organic chemistry that makes large-scale dyeing technology possible. Electric and magnetic research has laid scientific and theoretical foundations for electric power and electric lamps. Since then, the main source of technological invention has shifted from experience to science. Along with the rapid development of science, science is playing an increasingly important role in technological progress. Nowadays, we can almost say that technological inventions, especially high-tech inventions, will become impossible without the guidance of scientific theories.

In this context, people's views on the relationship between science and technology diverged. A comparatively popular view is that "although the difference of the effect of science on technology is a matter of degree, all technical activities are the continuation of science and technology must be the application of science; technology is even considered as applied science."[19] It makes sense to think of technology as the application of science. However, we must not take a step further on this view, and even regard technology as an appendage of science and completely deny the unique content and structure of technical knowledge itself. Unfortunately, we have taken this step consciously or unconsciously, and the step we have taken is not small. This step leads to the impoverishment of technological culture. It is the view of "only science, no technology" and the barren technological culture that are severely restricting the promotion of the social status of skilled workers.

The reasons for this misconception are both common and different in various countries. For China, the reasons possibly come from two aspects mainly: 1. Scientific theories are playing an increasingly important role in technological inventions. The great magic of scientific theory in technological inventions has hoodwinked people, and made people generally believe that technology is the application of science and an appendage of science; scientific theory can generate technology easily as long as it makes a major breakthrough. In many people's minds, "science and technology" has become "science without technology." This view is particularly prevailing in educational circles, no matter if it is conscious or unconscious. Although technological inventions are becoming increasingly dependent on scientific and theoretical breakthroughs in the contemporary era, science is just science and technology is just technology. They are still two independent domains. Technology is not a simple application of science. The process of transforming scientific theory into technology not only contains a great deal of exploitation and innovation and intuition and inspiration, but also involves a lot of social, political, economic, and practical knowledge. Furthermore, technological inventors are required to spare arduous efforts and even bear the risk of failure. 2. Technological culture is not thoroughly integrated with traditional Chinese culture. For China, both modern science and technology are exotic. Both of them originated from the West and were spread to China after the Opium War. They were the pearls of Western culture and collided with our traditional culture when spreading within our country. However, this collision process has undergone a sudden change. That is, scientific culture was successfully blended into traditional Chinese culture while technical culture failed to be blended into scientific culture by far. It is marked by the May Fourth Movement. The slogan of "science" and "democracy" was put forward during the May Fourth Movement, while "technology" was forgotten. Since the May Fourth Movement, China has scarcely made any effort to integrate technical culture with traditional Chinese culture. Therefore, we can say that technological culture has not been successfully integrated into China's mainstream culture at the ideological level since the May Fourth Movement. Currently, Chinese culture is still a kind of culture that is technologically barren. Even though we enjoy abundant and colorful material products brought to us by modern technology and culture every now and then, technological culture failed to be integrated with traditional Chinese culture. The failure is great concern to our cultural tradition that people attach more importance to theories and less to skills. However, in modern culture, culture without technology is not complete. This is because technology has made tremendous contributions to modern civilization.

# Part 3 Senior Skilled Workers and Technicians Are Also Professionals

We need to truly recognize the values of skilled workers and fully apply this into the labor employment of skilled people, so as to guarantee their due labor remuneration and rights and provide them the same respected status as other professional workers (such as scientists, doctors, and engineers). This is the premise for educators to be willing to choose vocational education consciously. A possible career development path that education may lead to is often more attractive to students than the innate benefits of education itself. This is an important feature of education in an era when vocational education is in parallel with general education. For example, when we talk about how Germany and Switzerland attach importance to vocational education, we will inevitably talk about how to improve the social status of skilled workers. Since reform and opening-up, the rises and falls of the development of vocational education in China are closely related with the changes of skilled workers' social status. At present, vocational education is stepping into a more and more steady track, and it is increasingly recognized and valued by all sectors of society. This is an important link for the modernization of vocational education. This change has much to do with the great transformation of the concept of status which is gradually realized through the efforts of all walks of life in vocational education circles in recent years. The actual recognition of skilled workers' values and guaranteeing them by systems in labor employment is the logical starting point for China to construct modern vocational education.

## 1. Policy Support for the Confirmation of Skilled Talents' Values

In 1985, *Decision of the CPC Central Committee on the Reform of the Education System* clearly took "improving the quality of the nation, bringing forth more talent and better talent" as the purpose of education reform, and proposed: "the construction of socialist modernization not only needs advanced scientific and technical experts, but also urgently needs millions of intermediate and junior technical personnel, managers, technicians and other urban and rural workers who have received good vocational and technical education. Without these technological workers, advanced science and technology and advanced equipment cannot become real social productive forces." However, this document, together with a series of important documents that followed, do not explicitly expound that "skilled workers are also professionals." Since then, throughout the 1990s, under the influence of the various factors mentioned above, our concept of professional has gradually been distorted.

The concept of professional that only attaches importance to qualifications and educational backgrounds has become the main obstacle that restricts the confirmation of skilled workers' value. Skilled workers fail to be included in the rank of "professional," and they are recognized by the society for a long time; thus, skilled workers do not have a high status in enterprises.

At the beginning of the 20th century, the successful reform of state-owned enterprises has enabled China's economy to gain the vigor to achieve a higher level of development. In 2003, China's GDP per capita exceeded 1,000 U.S. dollars, which is a historic achievement. On this basis, China began to try to find solutions to the strategic problems of economic development in the next period, and set forth the strategies for upgrading the industrial structure. That is, to transform from low value-added labor-intensive industries to high-value-added technology-intensive ones. At that time, enterprises were generally confronted with a shortage of highly skilled personnel in the process of industrial upgrading. In this context, China was increasingly apprehensive about the importance of cultivating skilled personnel, especially highly skilled personnel; in order to cultivate highly skilled workers, we must first disabuse the social concept of professionalism and incorporate skilled workers into the personnel management system of our country.

The first to initiate this process was the *Decision of the CPC Central Committee and the State Council on Further Enhancing the Development of Human Resources* (No.16 [2003] from the CPC Central Committee). The document requires "to establish a scientific talent concept" and points out: "Valued qualities exist among the people. Those who have certain knowledge or skills, can be engaged in creative work and make positive contributions to boosting the construction of socialist material civilization, political civilization and spiritual civilization, and building up the great cause of socialism with Chinese characteristics, will all be the assets required by the Party and the country. We must adhere to the principle of choosing personnel with both political integrity and professional competence, take morality, knowledge, capacity and performance as the main standard criteria for workers; we should choose talented people without sticking to one pattern, rather than just emphasize educational background, professional title, qualification and identity. We should encourage everyone to make contributions and become an asset." Furthermore, it also requires "to further improve the social status of highly skilled people and optimize the social environment for their growth."[20] The great significance of this document is, first of all, the breakthrough of traditional standards. As mentioned above, China has, for a long time, been identifying talented people according to the standard of "personnel with technical secondary academic qualification or above and junior titles or above," which was proposed in 1982. According to this standard, skilled workers are excluded from being classed as professionals.

Table 2.5 Main documents and significance of promoting the confirmation of the values of skilled personnel

| Documents | Key Contents | Meaning Analysis |
|---|---|---|
| *Decision of the State Council on Vigorously Developing Vocational Education* (No.35 [2005] from the State Council) | 1. Gradually improve the social status and economic income of the production and service front-line technical talents, especially the highly skilled talents, and implement special award policies and incentives for excellent skilled workers. | Improve the social status and economic income of skilled talents and implement award policies and incentives for excellent skilled workers |
| | 2. Extensively publicize the importance and function of vocational education, and propagandize the significant contributions of excellent skilled workers and high-quality workers in socialist modernization. | |
| *Opinions on Further Enhancing the Development of Highly Skilled Personnel* (No.15 [2006] from the General Office of the CPC Central Committee) | 1. Incorporate highly skilled workers into an important item of accelerating the strategy of reinvigorating China through human resource development, and underline, and underline how important and urgent it is to fully realize and deal with human resource work well.<br>2. Perfect the training system for highly skilled workers. | Examine the importance of dealing with human resource work well from the perspective of national strategy, effectively improve the social status and establish the values of highly skilled workers in terms of cultivation, examination and evaluation, commend incentives, enhancing social security, increasing funding investment and creating a positive atmosphere, and so on. |

| Documents | Key Contents | Meaning Analysis |
|---|---|---|
| | 3. Establish and perfect the examination and evaluation, competition selection and technical exchange mechanisms for highly skilled talents.<br>4. Establish a position management and commend incentive mechanism for highly skilled workers. | |
| | 5. Perfect the rational flow and social security mechanism for highly skilled talents.<br>6. Increase funding investment and do well in the basic work about highly skilled workers.<br>7. Create a good atmosphere that is beneficial to the growth of highly skilled workers. | |
| *Notice on Further Enhancing the Evaluation of Highly Skilled Personnel* (No.22 [2006] from the Ministry of Labor and Social Security<now MOHRSS>) | Make further breakthroughs in evaluating highly skilled workers in terms of age, qualification, identity and proportion restriction, concentrate on professional ability and work performance, and attach importance to the examination and evaluation of workers' professional ethics and knowledge; provide timely skill appraisal services for qualified highly skilled workers who meet the requirements of national professional standards. | Break through various kinds of boundaries, highlight capabilities and performances, and provide a more relaxed environment for the growth of highly skilled talent. |
| *Outline of the "11th Five-Year Plan" for the Construction of Highly Skilled Personnel Cultivation System* (No.10 [2007] from the Ministry of Labor and Social Security) | Enterprises should increase investment in the cultivation of production and service front-line skilled workers, especially highly skilled people; withdraw 1.5%–2.5% from the total wages of employees according to relevant regulations and take it as personnel education fund, in order to guarantee the cultivation of highly skilled workers as a priority. | Ensure enterprises' responsibility of cultivating highly skilled workers, and provide financial guarantees for the growth of highly skilled talent in enterprises. |

(*Continued*)

Table 2.5 Continued

| Documents | Key Contents | Meaning Analysis |
|---|---|---|
| *Opinions on Highly Skilled Personnel's Special Government Allowance Granted by the State Council* (N0.24 [2008] from MOHRSS) | The special government allowances granted by the State Council have been implemented since 1990., In the past, people who could enjoy the allowances were mainly selected among the professional skilled workers in enterprises and public institutions, and the high-level professionals who made great contributions in the fields of science, education, culture and health, and front-line industrial and agricultural production. From 2008, highly skilled workers could participate in selection. At present, various provinces and cities have also established government allowance systems for highly skilled workers. This is a great institutional breakthrough and is of great significance in changing people's concept of professional. | Clarify the amount, conditions, methods, and approvals, as well as the selection cycle, allowance standards and granting methods of selecting highly skilled workers who enjoy special government allowances |
| *National Program for Medium-and Long-Term Talent Development (2010–2020)* | The main measures for the construction of a highly skilled workforce: Improve the training system for highly skilled workers. Strengthen vocational training, construct a number of national demonstration training bases and public training bases for highly skilled personnel. Reform the school-operating mode of vocational education. Enhance the construction of the "Double-Quality Teachers" for vocational education. Implement the "Double Certificates" system, namely, academic certificates and professional certificates. Gradually implement the free secondary vocational education and subsistence allowance system for students. Implement the national invigorating plan for highly skilled talents. Promote diversified assessment for skilled workers. Formulate comprehensive approaches to promote the coordinated development of highly skilled workers and engineering technologists. Establish a mechanism to carry on the unique skills and techniques of highly skilled workers from generation to generation. Carry out various kinds of vocational skill competitions and post training activities. Perfect the national selection and commendation system for highly skilled workers, and further improve the income and social status of highly skilled workers. | While continuously stressing the improvement of the income and social status of highly skilled workers, it also proposes a series of approaches to perfect the training system for highly skilled workers. |

| Documents | Key Contents | Meaning Analysis |
|---|---|---|
| *Several Opinions on Deepening the Reform of the Income Distribution System* (No.6 [2013] approved and forwarded by the State Council) | 1. Improve the professional skills of workers. Perfect the professional training system for all workers, fully withdraw and rationally use the expenditures on educating and cultivating employees in enterprises, guarantee the minimum paid training time for employees. Perfect the mechanism for socialized vocational skills training, assessment, appraisal and certification, and standardize the fees for the certification of professional technical abilities. Improve the income and social status of skilled workers.<br>2. Perfect the mechanism in which technical elements participate in distribution. Establish and perfect the compensation system for scientific and technological innovation talent on the basis of their actual contributions, and encourage enterprises and public institutions to implement wage agreements and project wages for urgently-needed high-level and highly skilled workers. Strengthen intellectual property protection (IPR), complete the distribution policies which are beneficial to the transformation of scientific and technological achievements, exploit various distribution methods such as bringing scientific and technological achievements into business and the incentives for job dividend rights, and ensure the due shares of scientific and technological achievements in distribution. Perfect the special allowance system for high-level and highly skilled workers. | 1. Further guarantee the funding for the cultivation of skilled talent.<br>2. Put forward a series of specific measures to improve the income of skilled workers. |

(*Continued*)

Table 2.5 Continued

| Documents | Key Contents | Meaning Analysis |
|---|---|---|
| *Decision of the State Council on Accelerating the Development of Modern Vocational Education* (No.19 [2014] from the State Council) | People's governments at all levels shall create an environment for equal employment and eliminate all institutional barriers and employment discrimination that affect equal employment such urban and rural areas, industries, identities and gender; no Party and government offices, or enterprises and public institutions shall discriminate against graduates of vocational colleges. Deepen reforming the income distribution system and promote enterprises to improve the income level of skilled workers. Encourage enterprises to establish skilled duty allowance and special duty allowance system for highly skilled workers. | It is explicitly proposed to eliminate institutional barriers and employment discrimination, promote fair employment for skilled workers, and get to the basic facts of the problems. |
| *The 13th Five-Year Plan for Economic and Social Development of the People's Republic of China* | Implement the new apprenticeship system in enterprises. Improve the income of skilled workers, perfect the professional title appraisal system, and promote the connection of professional and technical titles and skill levels with the permission to settle down in large cities. | Further enable skilled workers to receive equivalent treatment institutionally. |

This document redefined the talent standard and proposed the principle of "four views of not concerning educational background, professional title, qualification and identity only" for higher appointment, which is a historical breakthrough in human resources.

The state has, on this basis, successively released a series of significant documents to boost the transformation of the concept of professionalism. Table 2.5 summarizes the main contents and significance of promoting the confirmation of the values of skilled personnel in these documents.

## Case 1: The Implementation of the Chief Technician System in Shandong Province[21]

On December 31, 2004, the General Office of the People's Government of Shandong Province printed and distributed the *Measures for the Administration of Chief Technicians in Shandong Province.* The *Measures* determine that 100 chief technicians will be selected in the whole province every year, with a four-year management duration. In terms of treatment incentives, the chief technician list will be incorporated into the high-level talent pool of Shandong province, and everyone will be granted 1,000 yuan as subsidies per month by the government during the management period; the province will organize some chief technicians to participate in activities such as political theory training, investigation of provincial and national conditions, consultation, and vocation; the enterprises and organizations where they work can implement annual salary system by referring to the enterprise operators, and the earnings which are transformed from their technological achievements shall be distributed to each individual according to a certain proportion; chief technicians of Shandong province shall be arranged to participate in the annual health inspections, which are organized at city level for high-level personnel; and the enterprises and organizations where they work shall arrange a 20-day paid vacation for them every year.

## Case 2: 114 Staff Are Hired as Worker Technicians and Offered High Salaries by Qianqiu Coal Mine[22]

Si Yingge, Publicity Department of Qianqiu Coal Mine, Yimei Group, Yima city (county-level), Henan province: In order to implement the strategy of invigorating the mine industry and creating a good atmosphere of respecting knowledge, talent, and advocacy skills, Qianqiu Coal Mine employs, according to its actual production requirements, 114 staff as worker technicians and senior worker technicians in the whole mine today and let them enjoy technical subsidies on the basis of open, just, and fair principles. They are recommended by grassroots units and pass systematic evaluation. All these aim to stimulate staff enthusiasm for learning technology. The employed worker technicians shall be hired for one year; the technicians and senior technicians shall be offered skilled duty allowance during the appointment period. The allowance standards for worker technicians and senior worker technicians are: 300 yuan per month for underground technicians; 200 yuan per month for technicians above ground; 1,000 yuan per month for underground senior worker technicians, and 600 yuan per month for senior worker technicians above ground. Dynamic management shall be implemented during the appointment period, along with sticking to the principle of combining daily assessment with regular assessment as well as qualitative assessment and quantitative assessment. When the appointment period expires, new assessment and employment will be carried out for technicians above ground, and the technical allowance will not be implemented for those who leave the posts of their original professions or are appointed as management personnel. The appointment of worker technicians is a major measure to promote the strategy of "enhancing the cultivation of talent and strengthening the group through improvement" for Qianqiu Coal Mine. This will surely have a positive and far-reaching influence on guiding and motivating many staff to fulfill their posts, foster their abilities diligently, achieve success in their posts, and upgrade their skills.

## Case 3: Issuance of the Enforcement Regulations of the Highly Skilled Talent Plan Issued by Taicang City (County-Level)

In order to accelerate the construction of highly skilled labor and create a good social environment for the growth of highly skilled workers, Taicang City Leading Talent Work Office and the Bureau of Human Resources and Social Security jointly formulated and issued the *Enforcement Regulations of the Highly Skilled Talent Plan in Taicang City* recently. The *Enforcement Regulations* point out that highly skilled workers are technical staff who work in front-line posts in production, transportation, and service; acquire proficiency in specialized knowledge and technology; have exquisite operation skills; and can solve operational problems of critical technologies and processes in work practice. The *Highly Skilled Talent Plan in Taicang City* is jointly organized and implemented by Taicang City Leading Talent Work Office and the Bureau of Human Resources and Social Security in Taicang. It plans to select and subsidize 20 outstanding highly skilled workers and 200 crucial highly skilled workers within 5 years. Among various enterprises in this city, front-line production highly skilled personnel (national professional qualification level 3 and above) can participate in the evaluation and selection of highly skilled workers in Taicang. The outstanding highly skilled and crucial workers can enjoy the following treatment during the identification period: the outstanding highly skilled workers can enjoy a government salary allowance for five years of 15,000 yuan per person each year; the crucial highly skilled workers can enjoy a government salary allowance for five years of 5,000 yuan per person each year. The outstanding highly skilled and crucial workers will be evaluated and selected once a year; they will be brought forth from the bottom to the top, up through level-by-level recommendation. The Bureau of Human Resources and Social Security in Taicang City is responsible for the tracking management and daily service for the highly skilled personnel in Taicang, and establishing archives for them and implementing examinations and evaluation.[23]

Some of the above policies have been fully implemented; some are still being implemented; and some are still unable to be implemented. Anyhow, the efforts at policy level have played a significant role in the confirmation of the value of skilled workers.

Under the guidance of national policies, many local governments and enterprises have introduced more specific measures to establish the due value of skilled personnel by improving their income and social status. Here are some cases.

## 2. Media Support for the Confirmation of Skilled Workers' Values

Extensive social attention has been paid to how to improve people's enthusiasm for skill practice and alleviate the shortage of skilled workers through increasing their income and improving their social status. During this process, the media played an important role in creating a good social atmosphere. In order to reflect the circumstances during this period more thoroughly, I excerpt some influential reports as follows:

In 2003, *People's Daily* published Lin Zhibo's article entitled *Selecting Talent without Sticking to One pattern*. He wrote in the article: "In order to change this situation, we must first establish correct talent evaluation standards. The correct talent evaluation standards should reflect the spirit of 'not sticking to one pattern.' The so-called pattern means the old standard. The establishment of a talent employment standard aims to guarantee the level of employing talented people and the impartiality of the hiring process. However, if we place too much emphasis on tangible factors such as educational background and qualification, and even only on educational background and qualification, then the old 'pattern' will become an obstacle for us to discover and make use of talented people and prevent talent from going unrecognized. The experiences from work tell us that the important way to overcome this is to have a 'pattern' but not sticking to the old 'pattern' and to establish a talent evaluation standard based on capacity and performance rather than educational background and qualifications. By doing so, we can establish a correct direction, reverse the tendency of pursuing education only and giving top priority only to seniority in the selection, and more extensively select talented people with excellent capacities and outstanding performance. In terms of comprehensive capability evaluation, special attention should be paid to people's innovative ability in practice. Innovation is the soul for the survival and development of a country and a nation, and it is also a critical factor of an individual's overall qualities. Take innovative ability as an important aspect of a person's abilities and conduct assessments and evaluation of it. This is actually deepened and extended ability-orientation and performance-orientation, and also the inevitable requirement for work to accomplish the ambitious goal of building a well-off society in an all-round way."[24]

On December 19, 2003, reporter Zhu Yu and Gu Ruizhen published an article entitled *Take Advantages of the East Wind to Set Sail Smoothly—Overview of National Work Capacity* on XINHUANET. This article directly criticized the problem of traditional standard talent identification and clearly requested that highly skilled workers are also professionals. According to the article: "For a long time, China always equated talent standards in accordance with 'personnel with technical secondary school degree or above and with junior professional title or above' which was proposed in 1982. As the reform and opening-up steps into a new stage, people have expressed doubts: Zhang Ruimin, the founder of the national industrial brand Haier, was only a senior high school graduate during 1966–1968; Wang Leyi, the innovator of greenhouse vegetable planting technology and leader of the plant industry revolution, was just an ordinary farmer who graduated from higher primary school. Are they professionals?" It proposed that "we should break through the previous concept of talent and establish a new one, which is the primary issue that must be solved first in judging work value … We must not only acknowledge scientists, engineers and technicians as professionals, but also acknowledge 'expert workers' such as highly skilled workers and technicians as professionals." The article also gave an example: "The fresh news 'Chief Worker' took place in the Urban Power Supply Company of Shanghai Municipal Electric Power Company. Recently, this company introduced the chief-post system, that is, to set up a 'chief-post' in a worker's post sequence so as to direct employees to learn technology and focus on developing their professional skills. The chief-post system sends a straightforward signal: people have more than one path to success and senior technical workers are scarce and unique talent!"[25]

On December 22, 2003, Xinhua News Agency *Beijing Times* organized authors to conduct an authoritative interpretation of the first national talent work conference. The authors gathered various views in *The Talent Work Conference Brings Four Major Changes*, in which there were mainly two items related to skilled workers: 1. The talent concept has made a historic breakthrough. The representative views are as follows: according to the World Bank budget analyst: "For a long time, Chinese people only focused on academic qualifications and professional titles; many people were engaged in false credentials and spent money on fake professional titles. With the development of society, many enterprises and organizations become more and more concentrated on people's practical abilities and work performance, which is a historical breakthrough in talent recognition concept." According to a researcher of the Center for National Studies in the Chinese Academy of Sciences: "The new elaboration about talent standards has broken through the traditional concept that 'The one who has studied to become a scholar stays on the highest rung of the social ladder', which will have a profound influence on the sociocultural development of China. At present, China's human resources market is artificially divided into labor market and talent market, which is a prominent manifestation of the old talent concept. In the eyes of some people, high-level technicians and experienced workers are not talented. Many places offer good treatment for management technical personnel, but neglect high-level technicians who also make great contributions. The scientific concept of talent will certainly enable more people's creativity to emerge and flow thoroughly." 2. High-skilled talent training will become a hot topic. Representative views include according to the Deputy Director of Man-Made Satellite Monitoring Station of Chinese Academy of Surveying & Mapping: "What we need most now is the people who can operate and repair the equipment. In the past few years, many people in this area left because of the arduous conditions; though the conditions become much better now, we still need that kind of professional talent most. I think that skilled workers will become increasingly valued after the talent conference, and the skills of talented people will also become more and more important."[26]

Luo Chuanyin published an article entitled *Perfect the Highly Skilled Talent Training System* in *China Personnel* and pointed out: "Investigations reveal that: enterprises don't have sufficient investment in training for staff; some enterprises are limited by scale and have difficulty cultivating staff by themselves; the employed works are old in age, low in education level and weak in individual learning, which impedes the cultivation and development of enterprises; some enterprises, after changing their operating mechanism, seek quick success and instant benefits, attach more importance to using the staff and less to cultivating them, or even provide no cultivation; the talent remuneration system is unreasonable: many enterprises do not have technical subsidies; the contrast between low income and high risk has made many young workers want to change their professional status and become a member of high-income low-risk managers and professional technicians."[27]

Yin Weimin published an article entitled *Promote the Spirit of World Skills Competition and Enhance the Construction of Skilled Personnel* in *Economic Daily* and stated: "1. Enhancing the construction of skilled workers is an important mission of the times … General Secretary Xi Jinping pointed out: 'Big industrial countries are all big countries with strong technicians, thus we must have a team made up of super skilled workers', 'As a manufacturing power, we should take talent as our foundation.' He required to 'vigorously build a team of highly skilled workers who can support the manufacturing industry and innovation in China.' These important statements improve the status of skilled workers to a new level and have a great significance and far-reaching influence on the construction of a skilled workforce. 2. Enhancing the construction of a skilled workforce is an important basis for China to transform from a big manufacturing country into a powerful manufacturing country. In recent years, China's economy has developed rapidly and the number of skilled workers has been growing steadily. By the end of 2014, there were 157 million skilled workers throughout China, of which 41.365 million were highly skilled professionals, an increase of 80% and 122%, respectively, compared to that in 2004 … Skilled workers in China only account for 20% of the employed; especially highly skilled professionals only account for 25% of skilled workers; the number of highly skilled professionals with 'high-grade, precise, advanced' skills is even less. However, in Western developed countries, especially in some powerful manufacturing countries, the number of highly skilled professionals account for more than 40% of the total number of skilled workers."[28]

## 3. The Contribution of Shanghai Vocational and Technical Education Forum to the Confirmation of Killed Workers' Value

In the process of confirming the value of skilled workers, an academic group has made a great contribution; many of its viewpoints have ultimately become state policy. This academic group is Shanghai Vocational and Technical Education Forum.

The predecessor of Shanghai Vocational and Technical Education Forum is a research group consisting of Yang Jintu, Meng Guangping, Cheng Yonglin, Yan Xueyi, Huang Kexiao, Lv Xinxiang, and Guo Yang in 1994. The main task of this group is to continuously discuss and explore the major issues about higher vocational and technical education. In 2000, the research group not only thoroughly thought about future research but also took the processing mechanism into consideration; it decided to establish Shanghai Vocational and Technical Education Forum on the basis of the research group. In December 2000, a conference was held at the Tianping Hotel-Shanghai, and the Shanghai Vocational and Technical Education Forum were officially established. The secretariat was set up in the Higher Technical Education Research Institute of the Shanghai Dianji University. On the basis of the original group members, some other members successively joined this Forum, including Xue Ximin, Wang Shizheng, Li Zongyao, Ma Shuchao, Xia Jianguo, Dong Dakui, Shi Weiping, Yang Ruofan, Xu Guoqing, and so on.

The main contribution of this organization to the confirmation of the skilled workers' value is that it demonstrates the independence of technology-based talent and skilled talent based on role-type classification theory of Purdue University and lays a theoretical foundation for confirming the value of skilled workers. This role-type structure theory divides personnel into four categories: 1. Academics, who are engaged in discovering and researching objective laws; 2. Engineers (designing, planning, and decision-making), who are engaged in designing, planning, and decision-making work that benefits the society directly; 3. Technology-based (technological, operating, and intermediate type) professionals, who are engaged in the work that directly benefits society in the front-line production or at the job site; 4. Skilled (skill-based, operative) workers, who work by relying on their operating skills in the front-line production or at the job site.[29]

According to this theory, researchers surveyed and investigated the job settings in enterprises and made the following basic judgments: "Currently China lacks the job series: technician—technologist—senior technologist; has no special definition of engineers who are engaged in on-site and technical work; technologists and senior technologists are incorporated into the workers and are isolated from technicians. As a result, it is easy for people to neglect the independent status of technology-based personnel. However, the extensive existence of technical roles is an objective fact; technical roles are a kind of job with distinctive characteristics ..."[30] They then put forward: "Social positions are not only hierarchical but also classified. Different hierarchies of positions are different in the depth of knowledge and ability, and different types of roles are different in their knowledge and ability structure. Therefore, the cultivation of different hierarchies and types of roles calls for different hierarchies and types of education; both workplace hierarchies and work roles require a reasonable structure, thus require a reasonable structure of education hierarchy and education type."[31]

Their views were collectively published in forms of papers, books, and academic conferences, which had an extensive and profound impact on the academic world and played an important part in confirming the value of technology-based and skilled personnel. Among them, the contributions of two researchers need to be particularly mentioned: Mr. Huang Kexiao and Mr. Yang Jintu.

As early as the early 1990s, Mr. Huang realized the importance of considering vocational education as a distinctive education type in Chinese academic system, and drew an education system diagram on the basis of the role-type theory. See Figure 2.2.[32] This diagram is not only conducive to confirming the type that vocational education belongs to, but also helpful to the clarification of the internal relationships within vocational education. It remains enlightening nowadays.

Figure 2.2 Classification diagram based on "science" and "technology"

| | |
|---|---|
| 总分类 | General Classification |
| 性质与内容 | Attribution and Content |
| 学校教育系列 | School Education Series |
| 学校 | School |
| 培养目标 | Training Target |
| 人才系列 | Talent Series |
| 基础教育 | Basic education |
| 社会、科学、技术、文化的基础知识技能 | Basic knowledge and skills about society, science, technology and culture |
| 基础教育 | Basic education |
| 普通中小学 | Regular primary and secondary school |
| 教育 | Education |
| 专门教育 | Specialized education |
| 科学教育 | Scientific education |
| 学术性(纯理论) | Academic(Pure theory) |
| 基础科学 | Basic science |
| 应用性(实用理论) | Applied (Pragmatic theory) |
| 技术科学 | Technical science |
| 应用科学 | Applied science |
| 高等(科学、技术)教育 | Higher (science, technology)education |
| 理科大学 | University of science |
| 各科大学(工、农、医、商、数等)技术科学大学 | University of various kinds of technical sciences(industry, agriculture, medicine, business, mathematics) |
| 工程学院 | College of engineering |
| 高等专科学校 | Junior college |
| 技术专科学校 | Technical college |
| 基础科学人员 | Basic science staff |
| 技术和应用科学人员 | Technology and applied science staff |
| 工程开发人员(工程理论工程设计人员以及生产开发人员) | Engineering developer (Engineering theory staff, engineering designer and production developer) |
| 科学人才 | Science talent |
| 技术教育 | Technical education |
| 技术性(专业技术) | Technical (Professional skill) |
| 技能性(操作技艺) | Skilled (Operating technology) |
| 设计 | Design |
| 工艺(过程) | Technology(Process) |
| 管理 | Management |

*(Continued)*

Figure 2.2 Continued

| | |
|---|---|
| 智能型 | Intelligent |
| 技能型 | Skill-oriented |
| 专业技术教育(职业技能教育) | Profession technical education (Vocational technical education) |
| 职业和技术教育 | Vocational and technical education |
| 各级各类人员职业培训进修学校或中心 | Vocational training continuation school or center for personal at all levels and of all types |
| 中等专业学校 | Secondary specialized school |
| 专业技术人员(中间转换人员) | Professionals |
| 职业学校 | Vocational school |
| 技工学校 | Technical training school |
| 生产操作人员 | Production operating staff |
| 工程技术人才 | Engineering technology personnel |

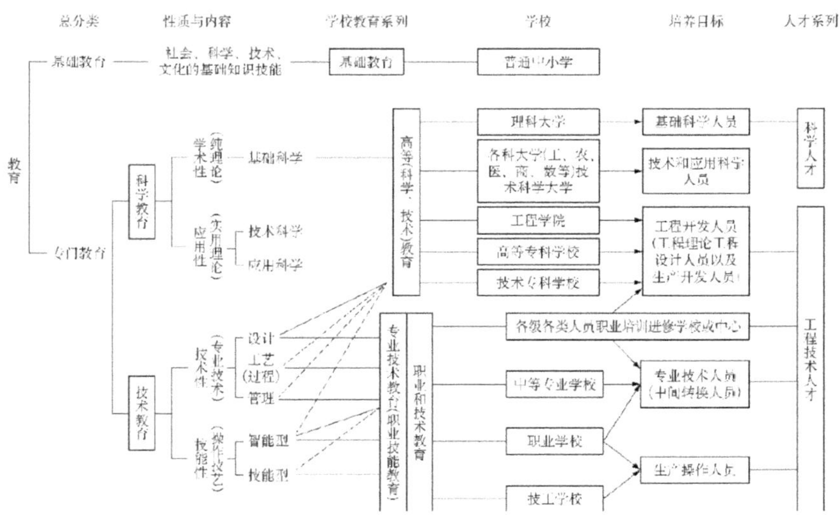


Mr. Yang is the leader of Shanghai Vocational and Technical Education Forum, and is known as the "Forum Host." He once served as the Director of the Department of Vocational and Adult Education in MOE. He explicitly advocates the reality of the existence of technology-based work-roles, the necessity of cultivating technology-based talent through the development of higher vocational education, and the independence of technical and skilled professionals; moreover, he also advocates the equality among workers and the great potential for everyone to become a professional. He astutely pointed out: "The ancient adage that 'Every profession produces its leading authority' is not only an advanced concept but also an objective reality that exists at all times and all over the world. Nowadays, the 'leading authority' refers to the outstanding person among all types of talents in all walks of life, who are usually referred to as elites. Furthermore, elites are also divided into categories, though the classifying methods are different."[33] He once served as the honorary President of SHSIPO since 2003, which enabled him to apply his vocational education concepts to school-operating practice. During his tenure, he put forward the school-operating idea that "believe that everyone is talented and help everyone to reach the height of that talent." This idea is similar to such statements: "Vocational education is a significant asset to guide young people to success," "Vocational education shall give everyone a chance to shine in his life," that were proposed by General Secretary Xi Jinping. The positive significance of this viewpoint lies in that we should not only thoroughly recognize the status of skilled professionals in the workforce, but also that everyone is possible to become an outstanding talent. This is a further deepening of the talent concept. Only when we believe that everyone is talented and can succeed can we make it possible to regard highly skilled people as professionals in reality.

## Notes

1 National Bureau of Statistics of China: National Statistics Bulletin on Education Career Development 1995, www.edu.cn/edu/tjsj/zhsj/jiao_yu_fa_zhan/200603/t20060323_11629.shtml
2 Vocational and Technical Education: 20 Years of Review and Witnessing, 1999, p. 23.
3 CPC Central Committee: Decision of the CPC Central Committee on Certain Major Issues Concerning the Reform and Development of State-Owned Enterprises, 1999.
4 MOE: Education Revitalization Action Plan Facing 21st Century, 1999.
5 MOE: National Statistics Bulletin on Education Career Development 1999, 2000.
6 MOE: National Statistics Bulletin on Education Career Development 2000, 2001.
7 Office of National Medium- and Long-Term Education Reform and Development Plan: Outline of the National Medium- and Long-Term Education Reform and Development Plan (2010–2020), 2010.
8 MOE: Some Suggestions on the Overall Improvement of the Quality of Higher Education, 2012.
9 MOE: National Statistics Bulletin on Education Career Development 2015, 2016.
10 MOE: Revitalization Action Plan Facing 21st Century, 1999.
11 MOE: Decision of the State Council on Vigorously Promoting the Reform and Development of Vocational Education, 2002.
12 Research Group "On Studying and Experimenting the Infiltrated 'Dual Enrollment, Dual Diploma' School-Operating Mode of Vocational School and Ordinary School in Secondary

Education" in Shanghai: Preliminary Exploration of the School-Operating Modes of Comprehensive Senior High Schools, Vocational & Technical Education Forum, No.5, 1999.
13 Shi Weiping, Xu Guoqing: Reflection and Exploration on the School-Operating Mode of Urban Secondary Vocational Schools in China, Education Research, No. 12, 2000.
14 Anonymous: An Undercover PhD - Terrified by the Assembly Lines in the Workshops for 25 Days, https://xueshu.baidu.com/
15 Liu Li: Research on the Wage Incentive Mechanism of Technical and Skilled Talents in Iron and Steel Enterprises, China Business • Theoretical Research, No. 16, 2013, pp. 43–44.
16 Chen Shida, He Peihua: On Job Hunting and Wages: The Latest Market Guidance Wage Levels in Zhejiang Province, Zhejiang University Press, 2009.
17 Song Fengjing: Skilled Talent Cultivation and Beijing's Economic Development, Hualing Press, 2005, p. 59.
18 Ding Dajian: The shortage of Highly Skilled Talents and the Misalignment of Their Value Evaluation, Private Education Research, No. 4, 2004, pp. 57–58.
19 Yang Peiting: The Theory of Science and Technology, Zhejiang Education Publishing House, 1985, pp. 97–98.
20 The CPC Central Committee and the State Council: Decision of the CPC Central Committee and the State Council on Further Enhancing the Development of Human Resources, 2003.
21 Yang Jintu: Major Changes in 30 Years: Overview of the Important Issues in Vocational Education in China in 1979–2008, Educational Science Publishing House, 2011, p. 246.
22 Si Yingge: 114 Staffs are Hired as Worker Technicians and Offered High Salaries by Qianqiu Coal Mine, Trade Union Information, No. 14, 2011, p. 38.
23 Issuance of the Enforcement Regulations of the Highly Skilled Talent Plan Issued by Taicang City (County-Level), Suzhou Human Resources and Social Security Network, www.tcrcsc.com/news_18617.html
24 Lin Zhibo: Select Talents without Sticking to One pattern, People's Daily, December 19, 2003.
25 Zhu Yu, Gu Ruizhen: Take Advantages of the East Wind to Set Sail Smoothly—Overview of National Talent Work, XINHUANET, December 19, 2003.
26 The Talent Work Conference Brings Four Major Changes, Beijing Times, December 22, 2003.
27 Luo Chuanyin: Perfect the Highly Skilled Talent Training System, China Personnel, October 25, 2010.
28 Yin Weimin: Promote the Spirit of World Skills Competition and Enhance the Construction of Skilled Talents, Economic Daily, December 16, 2015.
29 Chief editor Xue Ximin: Theory and Practice of Higher Vocational and Technical Education, Fudan University Press, 2000, pp. 17–18.
30 Secretariat of Shanghai Vocational and Technical Education Forum: Basic Understanding of Several Issues about Vocational and Technical Education - Studies on Shanghai Vocational and Technical Education Forum for the Past Decade, Higher Education Press, 2005, p. 65.
31 Secretariat of Shanghai Vocational and Technical Education Forum: Basic Understanding of Several Issues about Vocational and Technical Education - Studies on Shanghai Vocational and Technical Education Forum for the Past Decade, Higher Education Press, 2005, p. 56.
32 Liu Fonian: Review and Exploration—On Several Educational Theoretical Issues, East China Normal University Press, 1991, p. 353.
33 Yang Jintu: Talent Concept and Vocational Education, Vocational and Technical Education, No.36, 2008, pp. 66–69.

CHAPTER THREE

# Establishing the Strategic Position of Developing Vocational Education

The sharp decline in new student enrollments in secondary vocational education in China at the turn of the 20th and 21st centuries did not reflect the overall development of vocational education at that time. While vocational education was difficult to develop on the whole, higher vocational education had at the same time developed substantially. Eventually enrollments for secondary vocational education became stable and improved with everyone's efforts. It goes without saying that developing higher vocational education is of great importance, as it is a significant step forward in the establishment of China's vocational education system. This is the premise for the promotion of vocational education. Marked by the development of higher vocational education, China's vocational education is striding toward a new historical stage, which is intimately related to the critical shortage of highly skilled people brought about by industrial upgrading in China. In fact, the demand for establishing the value of skilled people is also connected to the shortage of highly skilled workers. The transformation from labor-intensive to technology-intensive industry not only requires a large number of engineers who are engaged in high-tech research and development, but also enormous technology-based and skilled experts who are proficient in advanced technology. Technological progress and economic development are the fundamental powers for the development of vocational education. Both are indispensable: economic development without technological progress only requires workers who have been trained for a short period of time; economic development without the application of technological progress only calls for people who can engage in high-tech research and development rather than those who can make use of high-technologies. This is proven by history again. The end result of the discussion is the establishment of the strategic position of vocational education in national policies, which marks the full prologue of the construction of modern vocational education. Whether it can adapt to the requirements of new economic and social forms for skilled personnel is a brand-new issue that vocational education confronts during this period.

## Part 1 Industrial Upgrading and Shortage of Highly Skilled Experts

Industrial upgrading is designed to increase the additional value of products through essential factors of product improvement, structure transformation, production efficiency, and product quality improvement and upgrading of industrial chains. In 2001, China officially joined the WTO, and the environment for economic performance has undergone tremendous changes, in which opportunities and challenges coexist. The Party and the State put forward a timely strategic target of economic development for industrial upgrading and China's economy began to move into a new round of high-speed growth. In this context, the severe shortage of highly skilled professionals became a hot topic for discussion among all relevant groups.

Figure 3.1 The practical training workshop in Jiangnan Shipyard Technical School (2003)

## 1. Focus on Improving the Industrial and Technical Levels

### 1.1. The Policy Path for Industrial Upgrading

In 2002, the 16th CPC National Congress was held. The 16th CPC National Congress Report proposed taking a new road to industrialization and vigorously implementing the strategy of rejuvenating China through science and education and of sustainable development with reference to economic construction and reform of the economic system. As the *Report* says: "Achieving industrialization still remains a formidable historical task in China's modernization process. Informationization is an inevitable option for China to accelerate industrialization and modernization. We shall adhere to driving informationization with industrialization and promoting informationization with industrialization and embark on a new industrialization road featuring high technology content, good economic returns, low resource consumption, minimal environmental pollution and full utilization of human resources." The concept of a "new industrialization road" marks a major change in the direction of China's industrial development. That is, to transform from labor-intensive and resource-intensive to knowledge-intensive and technology-intensive economic development. It is the result of a comprehensive judgment on the shortcomings in the previous economic development model and the direction of the world economy at that time and thereafter. This concept is the key concept that has played a guiding role in China's industrial development for more than a decade.

For example, the *Main Points for the Work of the State Council in 2006* (No. 12 [2006] from the State Council) requires: "Focus on improving the industrial and technical levels. Accelerate the development of advanced manufacturing industries, high-tech industries and modern service industries, and make great efforts to research and develop important technical equipment by relying on priority projects."[1]

*Decision of the State Council on Accelerating the Fostering and Development of Strategic Emerging Industries* (No. 32 [2010] from the State Council) points out: "Accelerating the fostering and development of strategic emerging industries is a significant measure to facilitate the upgrading of industrial structure and accelerate the transformation of the economic development model. Strategic emerging industries are mainly driven by innovation and can vigorously promote the development of surrounding industries; accelerating the fostering and development of strategic emerging industries contributes to quickening the transformation of the economic development model, helping to upgrade the industrial level, promote the upgrading of traditional industries and build a modern industrial system from a high starting point. It embodies the fundamental requirements for adjusting and optimizing the industrial structure."[2]

The State Council's *Industrial Transformation and Upgrading Plan (2011–2015)* (No. 47 [2011] from the State Council) proposed: "The '12th Five-Year' industrial transformation and upgrading requires taking the new industrialization road with Chinese characteristics and focusing on improving the capability of independent innovation in accordance with the essential requirements of constructing a modern industrial system, with scientific development as the theme, by centering on accelerating the transformation of the economic development model, and taking the reform and opening-up as the driving force; to promote the deep integration of informationization and industrialization, transform and upgrade traditional industries, foster and expand strategic emerging industries, accelerate the development of productive service industries, and comprehensively optimize technical structure, organizational structure, layout structure and industry structure; to develop industries based on and driven by innovation, intensive and high efficiency, eco-friendly, benefiting people's livelihood and endogenous growth, constantly heighten the core competitiveness and sustainable development capabilities of the industries, and lay a more solid foundation for building an industrial power and constructing a moderately prosperous society in an all-round way."[3]

*The '13th Five-Year' National Science and Technology Innovation Plan* (No. 43[2016] from the State Council) by the State Council proposed: "building a modern industrial technology system with international competitiveness, grasping the latest trends in the world's scientific and technological revolution and industrial transformation, with focus on the urgent requirements for improving China's industrial international competitiveness, intensifying the major technological development of key links in major fields, breaking through the technical bottlenecks in industrial transformation and fostering emerging industries, constructing an independently controllable technical system with reasonable structure, advanced management and open compatibility, and provide powerful support for China's industry to strive toward the high-end global value chain."[4]

## 1.2. The Realistic Situation of Industrial Upgrading

China's industrial upgrading is a continuous process. Before the concept of the new industrialization road was put forward, China's economic development was not just an increase in quantity. It also inevitably included an improvement in technological level at the same time. However, after the state clearly came up with this policy, the focus of economic development further fundamentally changed.

Figure 3.2 Intelligent machine manufacturing workshop

For example, *Wenhui Daily* published an article, *Shanghai's Economic Development over the Past Three Decades: A Giant Leap from Ten-Billion Level to Thousand-Billion Level*, in which data were used to analyze the tremendous changes in Shanghai's economy and society during the 30 years of reform and opening-up: 1. China's economic aggregate has achieved a big increase, and the comprehensive strength has been greatly enhanced. In 1978, Shanghai's GDP was only 27.281 billion yuan; it reached 1,128.885 billion yuan by 2007. On the basis of comparable prices, the average annual growth rate was 10.3% and the gross economic value expanded by 16 times. 2. The level of productivity continues to improve and the per capita GDP has reached a new stage. In 1978, the per capita GDP of Shanghai was less than US$1,500 if it is calculated by the permanent resident population and the current exchange rate; it jumped to US$2,000 in 1995, rose to US$3,000 in 1999, then over US$5,000 and reached US$8,728 in 2007, equivalent to the level of middle-income countries or regions in the world. 3. The rate of multipurpose utilization for energy has constantly increased. The energy consumption per 10,000 yuan of GDP in Shanghai dropped from 0.907 tons of standard coal in 2005 to 0.833 tons of standard coal in 2007, declining by 8.2%. 4. The economic structure has adjusted greatly and the structure of the three major industries has undergone major transformations. Since reform and opening-up, the structural proportion of Shanghai's three major industries was adjusted from 4:77.4:1.6 in 1978 to 0.8:46.6:52.6 in 2007. The proportion of the tertiary industry in GDP increased from 18.6% in 1978 to 52.6% in 2007, increasing by 34 percentage points. Secondary industry reached the stage of "adjusting while developing" from "developing while adjusting" and formed a new pattern of joint development of pillar industries, high-tech industries and urban industries. In 2007, industry realized an added value of 529.808 billion yuan, increasing by 15.2 times over 1978 if calculated at comparable prices, with an average annual growth of 10.1%. The six major industries, such as electronic information product manufacturing, automobile manufacturing, petrochemical engineering and fine chemical engineering, high-quality steel manufacturing, complete equipment manufacturing and bio-pharmaceutical manufacturing, achieved a total industrial output value of 1,450.294 billion yuan, accounting for 65.2% of the city's total GDP. The proportion increased by 10.7% compared with that in 2001. Among them, Shanghai's automobile production increased by 78 times compared with that in 1978; finished steel production increased by 5 times; steel ships for civil use increased by 11 times; and power generation assembly increased by 24.9 times.[5]

Under the guidance of the industrial upgrading policy, the speed for China to achieve the transformation of industrial form has quickened greatly; the technological level of enterprises has improved rapidly; some high-tech industries have stood out. The U.S. *Fortune* magazine released the list of the world's top 500 companies in 2017. 115 Chinese companies ranked on the list and the number of shortlisted companies is second only to U.S. What is especially praiseworthy is that three of the six shortlisted internet companies belong to China, playing an equal part with U.S. The three enterprises are Alibaba, Tencent, and JD.com. The reason why so many Chinese enterprises can enter the world's top 500 list is not a result of enterprise mergers as advocated by some Western scholars. The very important factor is the improvement of enterprises' technological levels, such as the high-speed rail industry. When looking back, we can indeed see the tremendous achievements in China's industrial upgrading over the past decade. Shanghai's large aircraft project will become an important engine for China's industrial upgrading in the next stage.

The National Bureau of Statistics analyzed the effects of industrial upgrading in *The Further Promotion of Supply-Side Structural Reform, the Speeding Up of Transformation and Upgrading—No. 10 of the Series of Economic and Social Development Achievements Since the 18th CPC National Congress*: from 2013 to 2016, the added value of high-tech industries increased by an average annual rate of 11.3%, and the growth rate was 3.8 percentage points higher than that of industrial enterprises above a designated size; the added value of equipment manufacturing industry grew at an average annual rate of 9.4%, and the growth rate was 1.9 percentage points higher than that of industrial enterprises above a designated size. In 2016, the added value of strategic emerging industries increased by 10.5% over the last year, 4.5 percentage points higher than the growth rate of industrial enterprises above a designated size. New products with high technology content and high added values are growing at a high speed. From 2013 to 2016, the output of sports utility vehicles (SUVs) increased by an average annual rate of 45.7%; the average annual growth rate of mobile communication base station equipment was 33.1%; 27.1% for photoelectronic devices, 22.1% for solar cells, and 19.1% for optical cable.[6]

Some researchers pointed out that China's industry has an obvious forward trend in the mid-to-high end. Knowledge-intensive and high value-added high-tech industries and equipment manufacturing industries in line with the transformation and upgrading direction have grown at a fast rate. In the first quarter of 2017, the added value of high-tech industries and equipment manufacturing industries increased by 13.4% and 12.0%, respectively, 6.6 and 5.2 percentage points higher than that of industrial enterprises above a designated size, respectively, accounting for 12.2% and 32.2% of the added value of industrial enterprises above a designated size.[7] The international community has fundamentally changed its impression of China's industrial technology and thoroughly appreciated China's advanced and powerful industrial technology in many fields.

Of course, industrial upgrading also brings another important issue, that is, humans are substituted by machines. This has been a very hot topic over the past two years. This situation seems to be particularly obvious in Dongguan city, Guangdong province. This is because Dongguan used to be a famous gathering place for labor-intensive enterprises. Someone once described the change in this way: "When walking into the factory of Dongguan DRN New Energy Technology Co., Ltd., you will find a very limited number of workers in the large workshop. Only 6 people work on the second generation production line that has been put into production, yet covering 28 processes such as filling, welding, detecting, and discharging. This automated production line created an output value of 460 million yuan for the enterprise last year, with a year-on-year growth of about 80%."[8] Humans substituted by machines is an inevitable result of industrial upgrading, and industrial upgrading itself is to substitute labor-intensive industries with technology-intensive industries. However, there is no need to excessively worry that the substituted people will have no work to do after industrial upgrading. This is because that industrial upgrading is not something recently new; it has come into being since technology was applied in enterprises. The people who were finally substituted have found new jobs, that is, to be engaged in high-tech jobs or transferred to the service industry. The people required by these jobs are highly skilled experts.

## 2. Highly Skilled Professionals Account for Only about 5% of Skilled Workers

While the industrial technology is upgrading at a rapid rate, the level of skilled people in China is not high enough to meet the needs of high-tech enterprises, which has become an increasingly obvious problem. The cultivation of highly skilled professionals has been a problem of wide concern for governments and society.

### 2.1. Shortage of Highly Skilled Experts

Researchers have attempted to use data to explain the low percentage of highly skilled workers at that time and the disparity with developed countries. However, there was no authoritative answer to the proportion of highly skilled workers in developed countries at that time. Some researchers said 20%, some said 30%, and some said 40%. Of course, these are all estimates. This is because the term used to describe highly skilled workers is inherently a unique concept in China and foreign countries have no corresponding statistical specifications. Therefore, it is extremely difficult to obtain precise data. Each country has different demands for highly skilled experts because of its different industrial models. For example, the manufacturing industries in Germany and Japan adopt the fine manufacturing route, so they have a very large demand for highly skilled experts; however, U.S. has a much lower demand for highly skilled workers because its manufacturing industry adopts the standardized manufacturing route. Accordingly, in view of present discussion of this issue, China should base its research on Germany and Japan because the goal of China's industrial development is to improve its standard of refined products. Although the data may not always be accurate, they can still play a role in explaining the shortage of highly skilled workers in China at that time. This issue is of concern to all sectors of society.

Shanghai is at the frontier of China's economic development; it has a favorable industrial base and its technology has always ranked among the country's leading level; it has a tradition of respecting skilled workers. According to Shanghai people, "shifu" (means master in English) is the way to address others respectfully. Therefore, Shanghai attaches special importance to the shortage of highly skilled people and has introduced some leading policies in terms of promoting the cultivation of highly skilled workers. At that time, the Shanghai Municipal Labor Bureau announced the following statistics and judgments on the status of skilled workers. That is, the total amount and structure of the professional skilled teams are still not compatible with the functional orientation of Shanghai as an international metropolis. The structure of skilled teams illustrates four of the following features: 1. In terms of hierarchical structure, the proportion of highly skilled expertise is small. The proportion of high-skilled professionals (including senior workers, technicians, and senior technicians) to the entire skilled team accounted for 5.39% in 1998 and 6.22% in 2002. Although the number has increased year by year, the proportion of highly skilled professionals is still relatively low and remains short-handed when compared to the proportion of about 30% in foreign developed countries. 2. In terms of age structure, the higher the skill level, the older the age structure will be. Taking the year 2002 as an example, the age distribution of intermediate and above average skilled workers in the city is: intermediate workers are dominated by young people aged 23–35 (31.06%) and 36–45 (43.69%); senior workers are mainly people aged 36–45 (48.28%) and 46–60 (30.33%); the category of technicians is dominated by middle-aged and elderly people aged 46–60 (45.90%) and 36–45 (44.26%), while senior technicians are mainly 46–60 years old (55.29%). The overall age structure of highly skilled talents is relatively large. 3. The overall educational standard is low in terms of academic structure. Taking the year 2002 as an example, the educational background structure of intermediate and above average skilled workers in the city is: junior high school and below accounts for 48.1%; secondary vocational and high school education accounts for 40.15%; junior college education is 7.17%; and undergraduate and above is 4.59%. 4. In terms of industry distribution, skilled workers are mainly in traditional industries and few skilled workers are in emerging industries. According to a sampling survey, skilled workers are mainly in traditional industries such as manufacturing, transportation, warehousing and mail business, electric power, fuel gas and water production and supply, and wholesale and retail industries, and they are still lagging behind in emerging industries such as the financial industry, information transmission, computer services, and software industries.[9]

At that time, some researchers calculated that China had about 70 million skilled workers in total, including over 2.8 million senior workers, technicians, and senior technicians, only accounting for about 4%, which is far smaller than the proportion of 20%–40% in developed countries. Some researchers have further pointed out that senior skilled workers, technicians, and senior technicians only accounted for 3.5% of the entire technical team in manufacturing and information industries in China; more than 1 million senior technicians were in demand; more than 2 million people needed training urgently.[10] This figure for Shanghai was 6.22% in 2002; the national data was slightly lower than this, but the gap is not very large. It can be said that these data reflected the overall situation of the highly skilled talent structure at that time. Such a shortage of skilled workers obviously cannot meet the requirements of industrial upgrading.

The severe shortage of highly skilled workers received high attention from the media, and major media have repeatedly reported this phenomenon. On April 7, 2005, *Xinmin Evening News (Daily)* published an article, *Seeking Technicians with an Annual Salary of RMB 500, 000*: a special recruitment for the highest salary for technicians in South China will be held at the China Hotel in Guangzhou. About 100 manufacturing and IT communication enterprises from places such as Shenzhen, Dongguan, as well as the world's top 500 enterprises, will come to Guangzhou to compete for skilled workers. Some deep-pocketed enterprises even generously offer an annual salary of 500,000 yuan and say that the salary can still be "negotiated" as long as they are urgently needed technical personnel. Some enterprises say that in Shenzhen three posts will "compete for" an intermediate technician and five posts will "compete for" a senior technician. Cases such as "hard to recruit a technician with a monthly salary of 6,000 yuan" and "unable to employ a senior technician with an annual salary of 160,000 yuan" frequently take place in the talent market. 50,000 yuan is the minimum annual salary the recruiting enterprises offer for the skilled workers. Many enterprises cannot recruit the talent they want at all. In 2005, the number of skilled workers in demand in Guangzhou was 1,534,800; at present, Guangzhou has about 1.208 million skilled workers, which is 326,800 less than the actual demand. Furthermore, there are only 39,800 senior technicians and technicians, and 171,700 senior workers, which is far less than the actual demand.[11] This report had great repercussions in society at that time, and the shortage of highly skilled professionals quickly became the focus of social concern.

However, in contrast to the severe shortage of highly skilled workers, a large number of college students could not find a job and quite a lot of college students had to work as low-skilled workers soon after higher education underwent a short-term substantial expansion. This phenomenon was reported by many media. On March 15, 2005, *Xinmin Evening News (Daily)* published an article, *Four out of Ten College Graduates Become Front-Line Technical Workers*, that said among the college graduates who were engaged in production skills posts, nearly four out of ten college graduates were junior college graduates or above, of which many were undergraduates. On March 20, 2005, the newspaper reported again that of more than 800 applicants, 368 are undergraduates and 3 are graduate students at a recruitment fair organized by Xiamen city.[12]

This phenomenon naturally initiates people's deep reflection on China's education system: now that so many college students are still working as workers and highly skilled professionals are very scarce in the labor market, why do we cultivate so many academic students? This had at least two effects on the development of vocational education during this period: 1. People became increasingly conscious of the importance of vocational education, which plays an important role in stabilizing the overall scale of vocational education. 2. People began to rethink the orientation of undergraduate education and to reconsider whether developing technology applied to undergraduate education. Based on this practical need, I cooperated with Professor Shi Weiping and published a paper, *A Study on the Significance and Strategy of Developing China's Undergraduate Technology* in *Research in Educational Development* (No. 12, 2003). Now, it has become an explicit requirement by MOE to transform local undergraduate courses into technology-applied undergraduate courses; some local undergraduate colleges that have a good understanding about the operation principles of higher education have been actively exploring the practicalities of switching paths.

### 2.2. The Concept of Highly Skilled Professionals

The increased focus on highly skilled professionals has triggered a discussion on what highly skill means. The main disagreement is does a highly skilled professional refer only to the skilled worker in the conventional sense, or to high-level technical talent who have intellectual abilities? Below are some representative viewpoints.

Lang Qunxiu researched the concept of highly skilled people from the historical evolution of the concept of highly skilled people, the types of highly skilled people, and the knowledge and ability features of highly skilled and talented people. Lang believes that highly skilled people are advanced applied experts who possess highly specialized knowledge and exquisite manipulative skills, and can use their hands and brain together and are among the front-line practitioners of production and service, including senior workers, technicians, and senior technicians. They can be divided into three categories: technical skill type, composite skill type, and knowledge skill type.[13] Liu Chunsheng started from the advanced, the superordinate concept of the highly skilled, and then analyzed the implications of what highly skilled people are from three aspects: relativity, generality, and complexity. First, in terms of relativity, there can be no absolute standards for the highly skilled; they are produced in relative comparisons. Second, in terms of generality, with the continuous advancement of society and the rapid development of advanced technology, skilled people not only rely on their skills to work, but also need to have necessary specialized theoretical knowledge and ability to resolve specific problems by relying their professional knowledge. More importantly, they also need to have the capacity to solve urgent issues on the spot. Third, in terms of complexity, they are the skilled front-line operators who should be able to solve difficult problems in production operations by using their knowledge and technological know-how and by updating their knowledge structure and technical structure constantly.[14] In brief, highly skilled and talented people in the modern sense are not only higher-level skilled workers, but also technicians, or at least technology involved.

He Yinglin and Song Xingchuan define the concept of the highly skilled in terms of its implications, extension, and growing trend. The implications are mainly related to three factors: knowledge, skill, and accomplishments, comparable to existing research criteria. However, from the perspective of extension, they believe that highly skilled experts belong to the elite of skilled workers; they account for a small proportion, and are roughly equivalent to the deputy senior and senior professional titles in professional and technical posts; only technicians and senior technicians can match highly skilled workers.[15]

Disagreements are certainly not very serious, and the differences in viewpoints are related to the working environment where the researchers are. Researchers in the labor system may advocate for an understanding of highly skilled experts in a narrow sense, and those in the education system will more likely include technical experts in the category of highly skilled workers, and think that they are the highly skilled people that are more needed by modern society. In consideration of the fact that technicians are difficult to strictly separate from skilled workers in practice, they are completely integrated in some industries, and the shortage of highly skilled experts is actually an overall problem for the front-line workers engaged in practical work at all levels. As a result, highly skilled talent here should still be understood in a generalized sense. As a matter of fact, along with the discussion on the shortage of highly skilled people, the discussion on the shortage of "gray collar" workers also occurs in Shanghai. Comparing "white collar" and "blue collar," "gray collar" workers are all people who possess both strong theoretical knowledge and operational ability and obviously cannot be defined in a narrow sense of what is a skilled person.

## 2.3. Policies to Promote the Development of Highly Skilled Experts

In relation to the shortage of highly skilled professionals, the CPC Central Committee and the State Council issued the *Decision of the CPC Central Committee and the State Council on Further Enhancing the Development of Human Resources* (No.16 [2003]) in December 2003. This document has included highly skilled workers into the category of high-level professionals for the first time and this policy has become one of major national employment strategies. The document pointed out: "Highly skilled and talented people among the working class is an indispensable force to facilitate technological innovation and achieve the commercialization of research findings. We should implement national highly skilled talent training projects and skills revitalization programs, and accelerate cultivating highly skilled talent through school education and training, enterprise on-the-job training, and independent self-study. We should perfect the vocational qualification certificate system for skilled workers, propel the reform of technician examination and evaluation system, integrate training, assessment, employment with salary, and gradually establish a mechanism for the development of highly skilled and talented people consisting of unified standards, autonomous declaration, social assessment and enterprise employment. We shall further improve the social status of highly skilled workers and optimize the social environment for their growth."[16]

In June 2006, the General Office of the CPC Central Committee and the General Office of the State Council issued *Opinions on Further Enhancing the Development of Highly Skilled Personnel*, requiring the work of enhancing highly skilled personnel as a major task to promote economic and social development and thoroughly apprehend how important and urgent it is to carry out highly skilled work. Moreover, it also explicitly put forward the guiding ideologies, aims, and tasks for highly skilled work, and emphasized how important and urgent it is to enhance the value of work for highly skilled people.

MOE had a quick response to the central government's policy, issued *Action Plan for Education Rejuvenation in 2003–2007*, and proposed implementation of the "vocational education and training innovation project": "a skilled workforce is important to propel technological innovation and achieve the transformation of scientific and technological achievements. We should enhance the construction of higher vocational and technical colleges and secondary vocational and technical schools, and extensively carry out job skills training. We should adapt to the requirements of taking a new road to industrialization … accelerate the training of a large number of skilled and practical personnel who are urgently needed by the software industry, especially all kinds of highly skilled experts at all levels."[17]

In order to implement the policy requirements for training a highly skilled workforce, the Ministry of Labor and Social Security officially launched the national high skill training project, which first initiated the cultivation of highly skilled workers in mechanical and electrical projects in 30 key cities and 11 industries (enterprise groups) throughout China. Six ministries and commissions including MOE also determined to implement "the training project for skilled people who are severely needed by the manufacturing industries in vocational colleges and modern service industries." They planned to select more than 500 vocational colleges as demonstration training bases for skilled trainees, and train more than 1 million urgently needed skilled people for selected major projects between 2003 and 2007. *The 13th Five-Year Plan for Economic and Social Development of the People's Republic of China* was released on March 17, 2016, and six major training projects were proposed. The "national revitalization plan for highly skilled personnel" is one of the six major projects, which requires the "construction of a number of skilled master studios, 1,200 training bases for highly skilled workers and the cultivation of 10 million highly skilled workers nationwide."[18]

Since then, "highly skilled professionals" has been the key word in related important documents by the Party and state, education and labor departments. For example, the State Council's *The "13th Five-Year" Plan for National Science and Technology Innovation* (No. 43 [2016] from the State Council) continuously proposes to "cultivate and bring up a number of world-class scientists, technology leaders, highly skilled talents and high-level innovation teams, enable young scientific and technological and talented people to stand out and expand innovative entrepreneur teams."[19]

## Part 2 Policy Path to the Formation of the Strategic Position of Vocational Education

If we carefully analyze the statements about the significance of the development of vocational education in the important national documents before and after 1998, we will find that there is a great difference between the two. This difference is so great that we can consider 1998 as the watershed for the development of vocational education in China since reform and opening-up. Since 1998, China's secondary vocational education has suffered the pain brought about by the sharp decline in enrollments. While suffering the pain, it also includes a newly formulated future for vocational education. That is, the establishment of modern vocational education.

The important difference is the use of the word "strategy." In the documents before 1998, no matter how important it was to develop vocational education, we rarely saw the development of vocational education expressed at the national strategic level. The *Decision of the CPC Central Committee on the Reform of the Education System* in 1985 just points out the economic and social construction is in severe need of millions of intermediate and junior technicians, management personnel, skilled workers, and other urban and rural workers who have received good vocational and technical education. Subsequent series of documents were basically carried out within this framework, though some slight differences existed in the way how these expressions were elaborated. The *Decision of the State Council on Vigorously Developing Vocational and Technical Education* in 1991 explicitly required that "the strategic position and role of vocational and technical education should be highly valued." Here the concept of "strategic position" was used for the first time. However, the decision failed to elaborate it on the implications involved.

Since 1998, a series of important background proposals, such as taking a new road to industrialization, the urgent need for industrial upgrading, the severe shortage of highly skilled personnel, the difficult development of vocational education, and the attitude of considering skilled workers as having equal status, all contributed to the creation of a new concept, that is, to put the development of vocational education at a national strategic position. This was not a trivial change.

Strategy was a military term referring to the tactics adopted by military generals to command the troops in battles. In modern society, the term "strategy" has an expanded meaning in the fields of politics and economy, and the meaning has evolved into a general and overall tactic, scheme, and countermeasure that can determine victory or defeat. Putting vocational education at a national strategic position, in other words, the state believes that the development of vocational education has an overall and long-term effect on the development of the whole country, and is a factor that can determine the success or failure of the country's future development. This is a brand new understanding about the significance of developing vocational education.

Logically speaking, the 15th the CPC National Congress put forward the strategy of rejuvenating China through science and education, and has elevated education to the height of national strategy. In order to implement the strategy of rejuvenating China through science and education, MOE promulgated *Action Plan for Education Rejuvenation for the 21st Century* in 1998. In this *Plan*, two parts are involved with vocational education. That is, the higher education part devotes some space to discussing the development of higher vocational education and specifically leaves a space to discuss the development of vocational education. In fact, vocational education occupies a relatively important position in the comprehensive documents released by MOE. However, as far as the vocational education interests are concerned, if there was no national document that directly addresses the strategic position of vocational education, they would always feel unconvinced of the importance of vocational education to social and economic development, and could not really attach much importance to it strategically. Frankly speaking, vocational educators always feel that they have stolen some glory from higher education and basic education, and they do not know how much glory is left after the glory is distributed to them. In people's minds, vocational education is a kind of low-status education, and the strategy of rejuvenating the country through science and education mostly reminds people of basic education and academic higher education.

This turning point has finally arrived. The *Decision of the State Council on Promoting the Reform and Development of Vocational Education* was an early document that explained the strategic status of vocational education in 2002. This document required a profound understanding of the important position of vocational education in socialist modernization and puts forward: "Promoting the reform and development of vocational education is a significant path to implementing the strategy of rejuvenating the country through science and education, promoting the sustainable development of the economy and society and enhancing international competitiveness; it is an inevitable requirement for adjusting economic structure, improving the quality of labor and accelerating the development of human resources; it is an important measure to broaden employment channels and promote employment and reemployment. In the new situation of China's entry into WTO and the rapid development of economic globalization, we should take serious measures to develop vocational education and achieve results."[20] Of course, vocational education here is still not placed at the strategic position of national development, and the importance of developing vocational education is just inferred from the perspective of implementing the strategy of rejuvenating the country through science and education.

In 2004, *Several Opinions on Further Enhancing Vocational Education* proposed that: "The current and future period is of important, strategic opportunities for the development of vocational education. Building a well-off society in an all-round way, taking a new road to industrialization, promoting urbanization, resolving the "Three Rural" issues (namely, agriculture, rural areas, and rural residents), improving industrial competitiveness and promoting employment and reemployment, all urgently require improving the qualities of labor and accelerating the cultivation of a skilled workforce. It is a strategic and urgent task to change the relatively backward situation of vocational education and fully embrace the basic role of vocational education in economic and social development."[21] These words completely clarify the great significance of developing vocational education in China. The statements of "basic role" and "strategic and urgent task" are significant, as they make clear the strategic significance of developing vocational education. This makes great sense to vocational education.

"Strategic significance" has become the basis for the development of vocational education in the important documents by the Party and the State ever since. Although some documents do not directly use the term "strategic," they basically set forth the significance of developing vocational education within this framework and require special attention be given to vocational education. For example, the paper *Decision of the State Council on the Vigorously Developing Vocational Education* in 2005 keeps this orientation: "Developing vocational education and accelerating the development of human resources is an important measure to implement the strategy of rejuvenating China through science and education and the strategy of reinvigorating China through human resource development, promote China's new road to industrialization, resolve the 'Three Rural' issues and promote employment and reemployment; it is an important path to comprehensively improving national qualities, transforming China's immense population pressure into an advantage, enhancing China's comprehensive national strength and building a harmonious society; it is an inevitable requirement for carrying out the Party's educational policies, complying with the laws of education and realizing the comprehensive, coordinated and sustainable development of education."[22]

In 2010, *Outline of the National Medium- and Long-Term Education Reform and Development Plan (2010–2020)* pointed out: "Developing vocational education is an important path to boosting economic development, promoting employment, improving people's livelihoods and resolving the "Three Rural" issues; it is the key link to relieve the labor supply and demand problem and it must be placed at a more prominent position. Vocational education should be geared to everyone and society, and attention should be attached to cultivating students' professional ethics, vocational skills, employment, and entrepreneurial abilities. By 2020, we shall build a modern vocational education system that meets the requirements of transformation of an economic development model and industrial restructuring, inculcates the concept of life-long education and the coordinated development of secondary and higher vocational education, satisfies people's requirements for receiving vocational education and the requirements of the economic society for high-quality, skilled personnel."[23]

The *Decision of the State Council on Accelerating the Development of Modern Vocational Education* in 2014 pointed out: "Accelerating the development of modern vocational education is a significant strategic deployment made by the Party Central Committee and the State Council. It is of great significance in further implementing the strategy of innovation-driven development, creating greater employment dividends and accelerating the changing pattern of structural adjustment and upgrading promotion."[24] At the national vocational education working conference this year, General Secretary Xi Jinping stressed: "Vocational education is an important component of the national education system and human resources development; it is a vital path for the majority of the young to open the door to success and to excel; it assumes the significant responsibilities of cultivating diversified talent, furthering technical skills and promoting employment and entrepreneurship. Therefore, we must pay great attention to it and accelerate its development."

In 2014, *Planning for the Establishment of a Modern Vocational Education System (2014–2020)* pointed out: "With the advance of new industrialization and the development of science and technology, the modern vocational education system has increasingly become an important support for national competitiveness. Especially since the international financial crisis, U.S., Europe, Japan, Russia, India and other countries and regions have taken the improvement of modern vocational education system as a strategic choice to strengthen national competitiveness, and the development of the substantial economy in particular, with efforts to build a consolidated sustainable workforce and technology competitive advantages in a new round of international competition."

Placing the development of vocational education at the height of national strategy is not only a reasonable judgment on the status of vocational education, but also signifies the entry of the development of vocational education into a new stage in China. This brand new stage can be summarized with one term, that is, the construction of modern vocational education. The term "modern vocational education" was officially put forward in *Decision of the State Council on Accelerating the Development of Modern Vocational Education* in 2014. However, from the perspective of development practices, the construction of modern vocational education should be pushed forward to 1998. After this critical period, we will see that a series of core concepts about modern vocational education, such as a modern vocational education system, industry-academy cooperation, curriculum construction, and double-quality faculty development, have come to the fore one after another and become the main focal point for the development of vocational education during this period. A large number of master and doctor's authorization stations concerning vocational and technical education emerged throughout the country during this period, which greatly improved the academic level of vocational education and provided a rich theoretical foundation for the scientific development of vocational education. In 2002, 2004, and 2005, the national vocational education working conference was held three times within a short period of four years. However, the convention is that this conference is held every five years. This also indirectly demonstrated that vocational education was in a critical period of development at the time. Confronted with an extremely tough development situation, will vocational education continue to decline, or break through mountains of difficulties and usher in a new situation? This question has already had a reply today. With efforts from all relevant parties, we have successfully embarked on the latter path. The successful leap from the developmental path has laid a solid foundation for vocational education to finally become an education type in its own right.

## Part 3 Theoretical Explanation of the Functions of Vocational Education

Theoretical papers expounding the importance of developing vocational education are of great significance for the research of vocational education from multiple perspectives. For example, in terms of economic development, vocational education is considered to be the educational factor that is most related to economic development and plays a fundamental role in supporting economic development. This is because tens of thousands of high-quality and technically skilled people need to be cultivated through vocational education. In terms of social equity, vocational education is believed to have enabled a large number of disadvantaged families to acquire the skills that are required to increase their income. Therefore, it is beneficial to promote social equity. In terms of individual development, vocational education is considered to be the education path that is more suitable for some students. For those who fail to enter the academic education system, vocational education provides them with another more suitable education and enables them the opportunity for career development. In order to further enhance people's understanding on the importance of developing vocational education, I shall list some theoretical views of famous German and U.S. scholars below:

## 1. Interpretation of the Functions of Vocational Education by German Scholars

"The experience gained through work-based learning opens the door to people's future work"[25] thoroughly reflects the basic belief that most European countries have in developing vocational education. They believe that experience and learning skills are of genuine and practical value for individual employment and future development. They also believe that skills are essential to support economic development. Germany, for example, considers vocational education as the secret weapon of economic development. Therefore, vocational education has always been a very important component of its education system and also in most European countries.

The BMBF (Bundesministerium für Bildung und Forschung: German Federal Ministry of Education and Research) has fully acknowledged the significance of developing vocational education and has pointed out early on that "vocational education and further study, as well as high qualification standards, are the preconditions for a country's development, especially its innovation capacity."[26] Sondermann, the head of BMBF Vocational Education Department, proposed at the conference of BIBB (Bundesinstitut für Berufsbildung: German Federal Institute of Vocational Education) in 2011 that the "German vocational education system imparts high-quality professional capabilities and qualifications. Compared with other countries, youth accounts for a high proportion of the population entering the labor market and having a low unemployment rate, which is the greatest importance that vocational education has for the employment system in Germany." Ms. Scheffler was the head of Vocational Education Department and State Minister of Culture who was responsible for school affairs at this joint conference. She pointed out that "vocational education (including dual-system vocational education and full-time school vocational education as well as further education) is an important pillar to guarantee specialized labor supply."[27] Its up-to-date vocational education development report, which clearly points out once again that: the "dual-system vocational education is an important pillar for innovation, economic competitiveness and social cohesion in Germany. The quality of vocational education, the concept of a comprehensive vocational system, the favorable transition from professional training to work, and the low youth unemployment rate within the EU, are the decisive actors for German vocational education to succeed and obtain recognition internationally."[28]

DIHK (Deutscher Industrie- und Handelskammertag; German Chambers of Industry and Commerce) also discovered in a survey that the "German dual-system vocational education is not only a successful model but also the pillar of the German national economy. Enterprise can guarantee their sustainable development by means of apprentice training, which is the foundation of competitiveness of enterprises. The precise connection of labor market demand means that the youth unemployment rate in Germany remains at a low level among European countries. The dual-system vocational education provides youth with multiple development opportunities, favorable employment and wage income prospects, and lower unemployment rates than college graduates."[29]

A study by Bertelsmann Fund mentioned that: "At present, there are 5.7 million unemployed young people under the age of 25 in EU. The unemployment rate of the youth in this age group is over 50% in Greece and Spain. Countries like this tend to pay close attention to dual-system vocational education when seeking for ways to better transition from school to profession. The theoretical examination of vocational schools is connected with the practical experiences of enterprises, which ensures that enterprises have professional and technical workers who are closely related to practical needs. Moreover, it is also the secret to the successful transition from school to the job market."[30]

In addition, many other German scholars have also acknowledged the positive role of vocational education in the whole society in various kinds of published reports. For example, the renowned German scholar Professor Rauner has repeatedly elaborated on the importance of developing vocational education. He wrote an article in 2008 analyzing the six reasons for modernized dual-system vocational education to be integrated into the vocational education system: first, seen from the perspective of developing learning theories, situation-based learning is the most effective form for the development of professional capacity; second, dual-system vocational education has been proved to be an educational form to enhance corporate innovative and competitive capacities; third, vocational education promotes the identity acknowledgment of vocational education, and thus plays a decisive role in integrating teenagers' professional enthusiasm with the society; fourth, the well operating dual-system vocational education can reduce the difficulty in entering the employment system from vocational education; fifth, corporate training funds in dual-system vocational education can be raised; sixth, the high quantity of training and the high quality dual-system of vocational education can guard against poverty.[31] The *Handbook of Technical and Vocational Education and Training Research* edited by Professor Rauner has been translated into multiple languages including Chinese. The preface to the English version says: "Vocational education is of crucial importance to the development of the global economy; it has cultivated a large number of intermediate-level technical workers for the employment system …" In 2014, the Chinese version was published. In the introduction collaboratively written by Professors Rauner and Maclean it is emphasized again that "vocational education has always been considered to be the critical factor to enhance corporate competitiveness and in maintaining the national economic development level."[32]

In terms of individual development, Gepperth pointed out in his speech at the International Vocational Education Conference held in Hangzhou that "Vocational education not only targets professional qualifications, but also helps young people become imaginative, able to undertake responsibilities and act independently from a humanistic perspective."[33] Professor Schmidt also believed that "those young people who have successfully entered and completed the dual-system vocational education can achieve high quality training standards that are acknowledged by the labor market and usually engage in professional jobs smoothly. It is a channel for young people to integrate into the society."[34]

Academics, Walden, Beicht, and Herget explained the significance of developing vocational education from the corporate perspective in that the "Double-system vocational training can bring diverse and direct economic benefits to enterprises. For example, qualified employees with special knowledge and skills are the important source of corporate competitiveness. This can make employees better acknowledge and improve their perception of their affiliation with the enterprise. Qualified employees can respond flexibly to unexpected circumstances in the market and accelerate the implementation of corporate investment and innovation."[35]

## 2. Interpretation of the Functions of Vocational Education by U.S. Scholars

In the U.S. education system, vocational education is not as important as most European countries. However, the functions of vocational education in economic, social, and individual development are highly acknowledged in U.S. society. In the history of the U.S. education over the past century, the important position of vocational education has never wavered, and all reforms were implemented on the basis of how to better develop vocational education and how to develop more appropriate vocational education. Miller has systematically catalogued the development of the U.S. vocational education, and believed that the viewpoints of the following scholars play an important role in supporting the development of the U.S. vocational education.[36] European countries consider employment and economic development as the basic starting point of the development of vocational education. Unlike European countries, while attaching full attention to the importance of the economic and social functions of vocational education, the U.S. pays more attention to the importance of vocational education to individual career development and considers it as a fundamental component of quality-oriented education. Therefore, the U.S. implements vocational education for all in the secondary education stage.

### 2.1. The Prosser Principles (1940)

Many principles relating to U.S. vocational education come from Charles Prosser in the 1940s. Prosser and Quigley jointly proposed the following principles of vocational education, often referred to as the Prosser principles. Prosser mainly explains the significance of vocational education from the perspective of how to improve the efficiency of social operations, and his main principles are: 1. Each profession has a minimum production capacity requirement for each individual, and each individual must have this capacity to guarantee employment. If vocational education fails to provide individuals with this capacity, then it will be ineffective for both individuals and the society. 2. Vocational education must recognize that individuals must be trained so as to meet the requirements of the labor market, even as modern professions have more ways to improve efficiency and appeal to better working conditions. 3. If the training provided by vocational education can meet the requirements of the group and benefit from it, the social services provided by vocational education will be more effective. 4. When vocational education methods can better adapt to learners and take into consideration the characteristics of the group served, vocational education will become more socially beneficial.

### 2.2. Keller Principles (1948)—"primacy of the person"

Keller uses "primacy of the person" as the subtitle of his work *Principles of Vocational Education*. He mainly explains the significance of vocational education in terms of individual development. He thinks that vocational education is not simply the preparation for life, but life itself. His principles include: 1. Vocational education indicates a comprehensive, efficient, and happy life; 2. Vocational education assumes that life has a range of purposes, and it becomes apparent in meaningful professions; 3. Vocational education provides services for diversified individuals; 4. Vocational education undertakes a democratic mission; 5. Vocational education attaches importance to the development of students.

### 2.3. Barlow Principles (1967)

The U.S. vocational education system developed in a gradual and stable process. In the early 1900s, the industrialization process required a better trained workforce, and vocational education was considered as the best way to prepare for work. The NSPIE (National Society for the Promotion of Industrial Education) provides extensive information exchange for various groups and promotes the formation of a series of principles, such as the Barlow principles. The main points of the principles are: 1. Vocational education is a national issue for discussion. It involves business, industry, agriculture, labor, education, and public affairs, and all these contribute to economic development. They are still the hot issues discussed by the U.S. Congress today. 2. Vocational education can contribute to national defense and improve social welfare—vocational education can provide individuals and families with the means of improving economic welfare; provide capable workers for the nation and support certain war efforts by use of their skills. This principle has been gradually expanded nowadays. 3. Career preparation for young people and adults is a public liability—vocational education can help individuals to develop meaningful and productive work as well as necessary life skills, knowledge, and attitudes in a democratic society. The basic principle of a democratic society is that individuals should have the opportunity to thoroughly develop their potential.

### 2.4. Miller Principles (1985)

Miller summarized a series of principles based on the fundamental principles of vocational education and contemporary principles. These principles are closely connected to practices and are used to guide vocational education programs and policy development from every angle. Miller's vocational education principles are the most comprehensive, and mainly incorporate three parts: people, curriculum, and method. Related discussions of the significance of vocational education are: 1. Vocational education is beneficial to eliminate gender discrimination and stereotypes; 2. Vocational education can serve individuals with special requirements; 3. Vocational education is a constituent part of the public education system; 4. Federal legislation on vocational education is a response to the strategic requirements of the country.

### 2.5. John Thomson Principles (1973)

The key points of John Thompson's principles include: 1. Vocational education can foster market-oriented individuals and make them production tools by developing his or her capacities to demonstrate skills; 2. Vocational education is a means of acquiring the basic capabilities required by fair competition in the labor market; 3. Vocational education is economic education because it orients toward the requirements of the labor market and can make contributions to the economic strength of a country; 4. Vocational education is production education that serves the economic system and is socially effective.

## 3. How to Make Vocational Education Better Accepted by Learners

Chinese scholars have also comprehensively clarified the significance of developing vocational education. Mr. Huang Yanpei earlier summarized three major principles for developing vocational education: preparation for individual livelihood, preparation for individual service to the society, and preparation for improving national and international productivity. If we combine these principles with the reality today and carefully study the three sentences, we will become more conscious of their profound significance and their broad and long-term vision.

The important documents mentioned above have fully explained and promoted the significance of developing vocational education, thoroughly integrated specific problems of economic development in contemporary society, and thus are more policy-targeted.

However, academic theories are just one aspect of developing vocational education; whether it can be ultimately developed depends on how well learners accept vocational education. Systematic approaches need to be adopted to make vocational education better accepted by learners. For example, improvement of working conditions proposed at the end of this book is a distinctly important factor. However, reasonably explaining the significance of developing vocational education is also a strategy that we need to take into consideration.

As for the reason I put forward this question, I wonder whether my colleagues, who are immersed in developing vocational education and think their efforts are of great value to their students and the society, have ever thought about it: when we lift up our voice for the equivalent scale of vocational education with general education, how will non-vocational educators and parents look upon our assessment? Instead of appreciating us, some voices think we are almost committing a crime. They despise and condemn this opinion and argue that introducing so many students to vocational education makes general education no longer accessible to them and can destroy many students' academic careers. What they really want to express is: what right do you have to expect so many students to accept this kind of despised vocational education? According to this logic, the more we develop vocational education, the more harmful it will be to the society; it is these people who are devoted to developing vocational education that make general education no longer accessible to so many students.

We can completely contradict this viewpoint in the same way, but this won't facilitate the settlement of this issue. Which view is right is not what I will discuss here, but the reason why such big differences arise and how to resolve them. Because of different standpoints, knowledge background and life experiences, it may be impossible to completely resolve the difference. However, will the discourse environment for the development of vocational education become more favorable if we can look at some problems out of the scope of vocational education and adopt some viewpoints that can be understood and accepted by different social groups?

When looking back at the developmental history of vocational education over the past few decades, we seem to indeed enclose ourselves within vocational education and increasingly detach the discourse from the discussion of the whole educational system. For example, in terms of the significance of developing vocational education, China has a negative attitude about vocational education and the strength of vocational education itself is relatively weak. As a result, vocational education colleagues naturally gather within vocational education circles to establish a system of discourse, in order to strive for status and acknowledgment for themselves: God rewards those who work hard. Fortunately, the central leaders have accepted some basic ideas about the development of vocational education that have been formed in recent years; former central leaders all have emphasized the need to establish the strategic position of the development of vocational education and explicitly stated it in State Council documents.

However, the effect may not be so perfect if we do not broaden our scope and look at this issue from the perspective of others, such as parents and students, and adopt some policies that are not well accepted by parents and students in practice. For example, "vocational education should be roughly equivalent in scale to general education" is a policy statement of this kind. This policy is considered as an important principle for establishing the strategic position of vocational education in practice and was affirmed by *Decision of the CPC Central Committee on the Reform of the Education System* in 1985. It is an important achievement of vocational education development since reform and opening-up. It has played a crucial role in the formation of vocational education system nowadays and satisfied the demands for a skilled workforce in industry during the economic boom cycle.

Nowadays, however, it is necessary to reflect on whether this policy is reasonable under current and future social conditions.

Regarding this policy, parents may think: if only there was no vocational education, our children would go to regular senior secondary school; if you develop vocational education how can you develop it on roughly same scale with regular education? Do you want to mislead more students? Of course, this is not the jumping-off point of the policy. However, their understanding is also reasonable from this perspective. When vocational education is of poor quality and unable to bring students favorable career development opportunities, it will be against the "people-oriented" principle to force some people to accept vocational education. This certainly doesn't mean to abolish the policy that vocational education should be roughly of equivalent scale to regular education. After all, the establishment of a clear enrollment ratio of vocational education to that of regular education is extremely important for the healthy development of the entire education system in China. However, under the current development circumstances, we should not guarantee the development of vocational education only by means of restricting the new student enrollment, but also study and train hard to enable vocational education to become a complete system vertically and communicate smoothly with regular education horizontally. Furthermore, we should create quality vocation education so as to attract students. In other words, we should demonstrate the strategic position of vocational education to the society through the associated implications of economic and social development. This is the core spirit of "making vocational education more attractive" proposed by MOE and the basic fulcrum for the development of vocational education in China since the 21st century. Supported by this concept, vocational education has made great steps toward modernization, achieved substantial progress, and made great achievements in various fields for the past two decades.

## Notes

1 State Council: Main Points for the Work of the State Council in 2006, 2006.
2 State Council: Decision of the State Council on Accelerating the Fostering and Development of Strategic Emerging Industries, 2010.
3 The State Council: Industrial Transformation and Upgrading Plan (2011–2015), 2011.
4 The State Council: The '13th Five-Year' National Science and Technology Innovation Plan, 2015.
5 Zhang Xiaoming: Shanghai's Economic Development over the Past 3 Decades: A Giant Leap from Ten-Billion Level to Thousand-Billion Level, Wenhui Daily, December 30, 2008.
6 National Bureau of Statistics: The Further Promotion of Supply-Side Structural Reform, the Speeding Up of Transformation and Upgrading—No. 10 of the Series of Economic and Social

Development Achievements Since the 18th CPC National Congress, http://www.stats.gov.cn/tjsj/sjjd/201707/t20170714_1513096.html.

7 Guo Tongxin: The Constant Promotion of Transformation and Upgrading, the Unceasing Enhancement of Development Momentum, People's Daily, April 27, 2017.

8 JinYanming, Ye Yongyin: The Quiet Transformation of Talent Structure after "Human Substituted by Machines" in Dongguan, https://www.mmsonline.com.cn.

9 Shanghai Municipal Labor and Social Security Bureau (now Shanghai Municipal Human Resources and Social Security Bureau): Relevant Circumstances about Enhancing Vocational Training and Accelerating the Establishment of a Professional Skilled Talent Team in Shanghai, 2003.

10 Ouyang Yuliang, Gao Zhimin, Wang Liangjian: An Overview of Research on Highly Skilled Talents, Vocational and Technical Education, No. 34, 2006, pp. 16–19.

11 Yan Li: Seek for a Technician with an Annual Salary of RMB 500,000, Xinmin Evening News (Daily), April 7, 2005.

12 Reporter: Four out of Ten College Graduates Become Front-Line Technical Workers, Xinmin Evening News (Daily), March 15, 2005.

13 Lang Qunxiu: Analysis on the Connotation of Highly Skilled Talent, Vocational and Technical Education, No. 22, 2006, pp. 18–20.

14 Liu Chunsheng, Ma Zhenhua: Definition of Highly Skilled Talent, Communication of Vocational Education No. 3, 2006, pp. 16–18.

15 He Yinglin, Song Xingchuan: Research on the Concept of Highly Skilled Talent, Vocational & Technical Education Forum, No. 1, 2006, pp. 18–20.

16 The CPC Central Committee and the State Council: Decision of the CPC Central Committee and the State Council on Further Enhancing the Development of Human Resources, 2003.

17 Ministry of Education: Action Plan for Education Rejuvenation in 2003–2007, 2004.

18 The 13th Five-Year Plan for Economic and Social Development of the People's Republic of China, 2016.

19 The State Council: The "13th Five-Year" Plan for National Science and Technology Innovation, 2016.

20 The State Council: Decision of the State Council on Vigorously Promoting the Reform and Development of Vocational Education, 2002.

21 Seven departments including MOE: Several Opinions on Further Enhancing Vocational Education, 2004.

22 State Council: Decision of the State Council on Vigorously Developing Vocational Education, 2005.

23 Office of National Medium-and Long-Term Education Reform and Development Plan: Outline of the National Medium-and Long-Term Education Reform and Development Plan (2010–2020), 2010.

24 State Council: Decision of the State Council on Accelerating the Development of Modern Vocational Education, 2014.

25 Sun Yuzhi: Modern Apprenticeship in Europe, China Labor and Social Security Publishing House, 2016, pp. 12–13.

26 BMB+F. Duale Berufausbildung an der Schwelle zum nächsten Jahrtausend. Herausforderungen bewältigen voneinander lernen. Bericht der Konferenz zur Duale Berufsausbildung in Dänemark, Deutschland, Liechtenstein, Luxemburg, Nieserlande, Österreich, Schweiz. Bonn. 1999. 2.

27 Thomas Sonderman/Beate Scheffler, Berufsbildung 2020-Konsequenzen für die Weiterentwicklung des Berufskonzepts. Berufsbildung in Wissenschaft und Praxis. 4/2012.
28 Bundensminiterium für Bildung und Forschung. Berufsbildungsbericht 2017. Bundesministerium für Bildung und Forschung (BMBF). Bonn 2017: 10.
29 DIHK. Ausbildung 2015. Ergebinisse eine DIHK Online Unternehmensbefragung. Berlin 2015: 7.
30 Dr. Jörg Dräger/Clemens Wieland. Vorwort [R]//Dieter Euler. Das duale System in Deutschland-Vorbild für einen Transfer ins Ausland? Eine Studie im Auftrag der Bertelsmann Stiftung [R]. Gütersloh: Bertelsmann Stiftung, 2013: 4–5.
31 Felix Rauner. Innovative Berufsbildung-von einem Versorgungs-zu einem Innovationsprojekt. In: Dorothea Piening/Felix Rauner. Innovative Berufsbildung-Auf die Attraktivität für Jugendliche und Unternehmen Kommt es an! Lit Verlag Berlin 2008. 25–31.
32 Felix Rauner, Rupert Maclean: Handbook of Technical and Vocational Education and Training Research (Volume 1), Beijing Normal University Press, 2014.
33 Rainer Gepperth. Grußworte und Referate vor dem Plenum. Symposium zur beruflichen Bildung 1994 Hangzhou. 12.
34 Christian Schmidt. Übergänge und Übergangssystem vor dem Hintergrund einer nachhaltigen Entwicklung des Berufsbildungssystem. In: Andreas Fischer/Dietmar Frommberger. Vielfalt an Übergängen in der beruflichen Bildung-Zwölf Ansichten. Schneider Verlag, 2013: 74.
35 Günter Walden, Ursula Beicht, Hermann Herget. Warum Betriebe (nicht) ausbilden, BWP 2002(02).
36 J.S. Scott, M. Sarkees-Wircenski. Overview of career and technical education [M]. The U.S.: American Technical Publishers. 2008(418).

CHAPTER FOUR

# Constructing a Modern Vocational Education System with Chinese Characteristics

The first link for constructing modern vocational education is to establish a modern vocational education system and the core is to establish a vocational education system consisting of secondary vocational education, higher vocational education, and technological applicable undergraduate education. In the report of the 19th CPC National Congress, there were only 21 words (in Chinese) that are directly related to vocational education: "perfect vocational education and the training system, deepen industry-education integration and school-enterprise cooperation." It can be seen that within the scope of the highest policies, people attached most importance to two aspects: first: system construction; second, school-enterprise cooperation. A modern vocational education system is the physical foundation for the construction of modern vocational education. All the elements of modern vocational education, such as school-enterprise cooperation, specialty, curriculum, and faculty, must be constructed on it. Only by constructing such a system can vocational education transform from grading to classification. When Chinese vocational education contains secondary vocational education only, students can only change the nature of education and enter regular education if they want to continue their studies. With the development of higher vocational education, higher vocational students can only choose to enter academic undergraduate schools due to the lack of corresponding undergraduate education. How can such vocational education become a distinctive and valued type of education? It is nothing but an appendage of regular education. When vocational education at different academic levels develops, we still need to establish a cohesive relationship within them so that they can form a modern vocational education system. In the first chapter, I described in detail the development history of secondary vocational education since reform and opening-up. So in this chapter, I will discuss the continuing development of modern vocational education system based on that foundation.

## Part 1 Actively Developing Higher Vocational Education through Multiple Approaches

Higher vocational education achieved quantitative development at the end of the 20th century. It has made a breakthrough in upgrading vocational education from secondary level to a higher level, and pushed Chinese vocational education a big step further in terms of system construction.

### 1. Exploration of higher vocational education

Higher vocational education as discussed here refers to traditional specialist vocational education. With the development of technological applicable undergraduate education, the references to the term "higher vocational education" began to differ in different literature and some have incorporated technological applicable undergraduate education in it. Higher vocational education has existed as a school-operating form as early as in the Qing Dynasty. Mr. Yang Jintu believes that "China's higher vocational and technical education, in terms of the basic service orientation and qualities it cultivates, should start in the 'higher industrial school for agriculture, industry and commerce' which was founded in the late Qing Dynasty. During the period 1898–1909, a total of 17 higher industrial schools were established with the approval of the Education Division of the Qing Government. In 1909, there were still 13 schools and 1,690 students."[1] Junior colleges established between the founding of new China and reform and opening-up are generally considered to belong to higher vocational education in terms of its school-operating form, although it was a kind of compressed undergraduate education in practice. By the end of the 20th century, higher vocational schools were ultimately integrated with higher professional schools, and they were collectively referred to as "higher vocational and professional schools," addressing the form of two closely connected concepts. This was because higher professional education did not want to be included into higher vocational education.

Figure 4.1 Gate of Yellow River Hydraulic Engineering College

From the early days of reform and opening-up to 1998, higher education had been expanding its enrollment over the 20 years. Although Chinese vocational education gave priority to the development of secondary vocational education during this period, we have never stopped our pursuit in exploring higher vocational education. In the 1980s, we mainly developed higher vocational education in the form of establishing vocational universities. On August 27, 1980, Jinling Vocational University was established, which is the first "vocational" university in China. On April 28, 1983, the State Council approved and forwarded the *Report on Accelerating the Development of Higher Education* issued by MOE and SDPC: "While expanding the scale of higher education, we should, according to the requirements of four modernizations (modernization of agriculture, industry, national defence and science & technology) in our country, adjust and reform the internal structure of higher education and increase the proportion of specialist and short-term specialties," "actively advocate large cities, medium-sized cities with robust economic growth and large enterprises to develop junior colleges and short-term vocational universities."[2] In 1985, *Decision of the CPC Central Committee on the Reform of the Education System* clearly proposed: "While developing vocational and technical education, we should focus on secondary vocational and technical education, facilitate the leading role of secondary specialized schools and actively develop higher vocational and technical colleges and universities … gradually establish an industry-supported, well-structured vocational and technical education system, which incorporates vocational education from primary to senior level and is able to communicate with regular education."[3] This document proposed, in the long term, to proactively develop higher vocational education and propel it to the level of higher education, so as to build a vocational education system. In 1985, the former National Education Commission deployed three regular secondary technical training schools and started experimenting with "five-year technical specialties" in these schools, namely, the Xi'an Aeronautical Engineering School, the Earthquake School of China Earthquake Administration, and the Shanghai Motor Manufacturing School. Although people realized the significance of developing higher vocational education during that period, these types of schools were either called vocational universities, or continued to be called technical colleges. These schools have never been officially named "vocational and technical colleges" (or "professional colleges" in some places), which shows that people still had lingering doubts about the development of higher vocational education.

## 2. The Formal Birth of Higher Vocational Education

The 1990s was a crucial period for the development of higher vocational education. This is because a large number of schools that were officially named "vocational and technical colleges" came into being in higher vocational education during this period. They were established as a new form of vocational education and higher education in China's education system, and higher vocational education has become a decisive field for education research in China.

In fact, higher vocational education was highly valued by Chinese vocational education until the release of *Decision of the State Council on Vigorously Developing Vocational and Technical Education* in 1991. There was just this understatement: "try to do a good job in establishing a number of higher vocational schools which can train highly skilled senior operating personnel."[4] From this we can see development focus still lies on secondary vocational education. Moreover, "higher vocational schools which can cultivate skilled senior operating personnel" mentioned here are not the higher vocational colleges we have now. On April 28, 1994, Shenzhen Higher Vocational and Technical College was established. It is the first higher education institution that is named a "vocational and technical college" in China, and is a milestone in the history of China's higher vocational education. In 1994, the national education work conference, which was convened by the Party Central Committee and the State Council, systematically put forward the task of developing higher vocational education, and again made the development of higher vocational education the focus of the educational circles and society. This conference was an important turning point in the development of higher vocational education in China, and the development of higher vocational education in

China has been substantially promoted ever since.[5] *Opinions of the State Council on the Implementation of "Outline of China's Education Reform and Development"* was issued in July 1994 and clearly proposed to "actively develop diversified vocational education and training after senior high school, and actively develop higher vocational education through such methods as reforming the existing junior colleges, vocational universities and adult colleges, and organizing flexible and diverse higher vocational classes."[6]

Figure 4.2 Gate of Shenzhen Polytechnic

*Vocational Education Law of the People's Republic of China,* which was issued in 1996, stipulates: vocational school education is divided into vocational school education at primary, secondary, and higher level, which authorizes the legal status of higher vocational education. *Higher Education Law of the People's Republic of China* released in 1998 also explicitly endows the legal status of higher vocational education in higher education: higher education institutions refer to universities, independent colleges, and junior colleges, including higher vocational schools and higher adult education schools.

However, higher vocational education has achieved realistic large-scale development due to the push by mass higher education. 1999 is a year of enrollment expansion for higher education, so it is also the starting year for the large-scale development of higher vocational education in China. On December 24, 1998, MOE promulgated the *Action Plan for Education Rejuvenation for the 21st Century,* which proposed that "actively developing higher vocational education is an urgent demand to improve the quality of national science, technology and culture, postpone employment and develop national economy." "In terms of diploma-oriented higher vocational education, we can reform, reorganize and restructure the existing junior colleges, vocational universities and independent adult colleges and select some qualified secondary technical training schools to operate higher vocational colleges (referred to as 'three reforms and one supplement'). Besides, we can also establish higher vocational and technical colleges in some undergraduate colleges and universities without constructing new schools in general." "We should gradually delegate responsibilities and powers of enrollment planning, entrance examinations and diploma issuance of higher vocational education to provincial people's governments and schools through pilot programs, and then provincial people's governments shall coordinate local existing higher vocational education resources under the national macro-direction."[7]

In 1999, MOE released *Opinions of the Trial Implementation on Developing Higher Vocational and Technical Education According to New Management Models and Operational Mechanisms* (No. 2 [1999] from MOE), proposing five paths to developing higher vocational education: First, short-term vocational colleges, vocational and technical colleges, and private colleges with higher education qualifications. In principle, the preceding schools are responsible for this trial task. Second, regular junior colleges. Third, higher vocational education institutions (secondary colleges) established in undergraduate colleges and universities. Fourth, as a transitional measure, a very small number of key national secondary vocational schools is reorganized, which are approved by MOE to develop both higher vocational education schools and secondary vocational education schools (develop higher vocational education in key specialties only). Fifth, adult colleges whose school-operating conditions meet the eligibility criteria stipulated by the state. However, it is necessary to adjust the training scale of adult off-job education according to schooling-operating conditions.[8] Although we have designed so many development paths, in practice higher vocational colleges that upgrade from secondary vocational schools have become the main force of higher vocational education in China, and nearly 80% of national demonstration vocational schools have upgraded from secondary vocational schools.

In 1999, the *Decision of the CPC Central Committee and the State Council on Deepening Education Reform and Comprehensively Promoting Quality Education* proposed: "Proactively develop higher education through diversified forms. By 2010, the higher education enrollment rate of the peer population in China should increase from the current nine percent to about fifteen percent." "Higher vocational education is an important component of higher education. It is necessary to vigorously develop higher vocational education and train a large specialized workforce, who can master the necessary theoretical knowledge and attain strong practical ability that are severely needed by first-line production, construction, management, service industries and rural areas. The existing vocational colleges, independent adult colleges and some junior colleges should be gradually transformed into vocational and technical colleges (or vocational colleges) through reforming, reorganizing and restructuring. And by encouraging undergraduate colleges and universities to independently develop or cooperate with companies to develop vocational and technical colleges (or vocational colleges). People's governments of provinces, autonomous regions, and direct-controlled municipalities may develop comprehensive and community-based vocational and technical colleges (or vocational colleges) according to the overall planning of local educational resources."[9] It's clear that this document has taken a big step forward in the development ideas of higher vocational education: 1. Unify various higher vocational education institutions into vocational and technical colleges (or vocational colleges), which are extremely beneficial and necessary to change the scattered pattern of higher vocational education and make it become a valuable and legitimate type of education; 2. Allow local governments to develop new vocational and technical colleges, which changes the policy of "without constructing new schools in general" in *Action Plan for Education Revitalization in the 21st Century*. This policy has greatly inspired local governments' enthusiasm to develop higher vocational education. As a result, higher vocational education has flourished and various university towns have appeared. Of course, every coin has two sides. Delegating power to local governments has stimulated the development of higher vocational education. However, this power has been decentralized to provinces and cities at each level, and even to districts and counties. As a result, higher vocational colleges held by districts and counties came into being. Some districts and counties failed to evaluate their financial resources adequately, which led to the problems of insufficient financial resources and low school-operating standards in the process of developing higher vocational education.

By expanding school-operating approaches and decentralizing school-operating powers, China's higher vocational education has achieved rapid progress. The specific development is shown in Tables 4.1, 4.2, 4.3, and Figures 4.3 and 4.4. The data in Table 4.2 and 4.3 are organized according to the data in Table 4.1. As can be seen from these tables and images, there were only 442 higher vocational schools throughout China in 2000, and the number reached 1,047 in 2004, more than doubled in just four years; in 2000, the new student enrollment of higher vocational schools was only 487,000, and it reached 2.374 million by 2004, nearly five times than that of 2000; in 2003, the new student enrollment in higher vocational schools exceeded that of other higher education institutions, occupying half the number in higher education.

Table 4.1 Development status of national higher vocational schools in the period 1978–2015[38]

| School Type Year | Number of Schools | | Number of Full-Time Teachers (10,000 people) | | Number of New Student Enrollment (10,000 people) | | Number of Students at School (10,000 people) | | Number of Graduates (10,000 people) | |
|---|---|---|---|---|---|---|---|---|---|---|
| | Regular Higher Education Schools | Higher Vocational (Technical) Schools | Regular Higher Education Schools | Higher Vocational (Technical) Schools | Regular Higher Education Schools | Higher Vocational (Technical) Schools | Regular Higher Education Schools | Higher Vocational (Technical) Schools | Regular Higher Education Schools | Higher Vocational (Technical) Schools |
| 1978 | 598 | … | 20.6 | … | 40.2 | … | 85.6 | … | 16.5 | … |
| 1980 | 675 | … | 24.7 | … | 28.1 | … | 114.4 | … | 14.7 | … |
| 1985 | 1,016 | … | 34.4 | … | 61.9 | … | 170.3 | … | 31.6 | … |
| 1990 | 1,075 | … | 39.5 | … | 60.9 | … | 206.3 | … | 61.4 | … |
| 1995 | 1,054 | … | 40.1 | … | 92.6 | … | 290.6 | … | 80.5 | … |
| 2000 | 1,041 | 442 | 46.3 | 8.7 | 220.6 | 48.7 | 556.1 | 100.9 | 95.0 | 17.9 |
| 2001 | 1,225 | 628 | 53.2 | 12.4 | 268.3 | 66.6 | 719.1 | 146.8 | 103.6 | 19.3 |
| 2002 | 1,396 | 767 | 61.8 | 15.6 | 320.5 | 89.1 | 903.4 | 193.4 | 133.7 | 27.7 |
| 2003 | 1,552 | 908 | 72.5 | 19.7 | 382.2 | 199.6 | 1,108.6 | 479.4 | 187.7 | 94.8 |
| 2004 | 1,731 | 1,047 | 85.8 | 23.8 | 447.3 | 237.4 | 1,333.5 | 595.7 | 239.1 | 119.5 |
| 2005 | 1,792 | 1,091 | 96.6 | 26.8 | 504.5 | 268.1 | 1,561.8 | 713.0 | 306.8 | 160.2 |
| 2006 | 1,867 | 1,147 | 107.6 | 31.6 | 546.1 | 293.0 | 1,738.8 | 795.5 | 377.5 | 204.8 |
| 2007 | 1,908 | 1,168 | 116.8 | 35.5 | 565.9 | 283.8 | 1,884. 9 | 860.6 | 447.8 | 248.2 |
| 2008 | 2,263 | 1,184 | 123.8 | 37.7 | 607.7 | 310.6 | 2,021.0 | 916.8 | 512.0 | 286.3 |
| 2009 | 2,305 | 1,215 | 129.5 | 39.5 | 639.5 | 313.4 | 2,144.7 | 964.8 | 531.1 | 285.6 |
| 2010 | 2,358 | 1,246 | 134.3 | 40.4 | 661.8 | 310.5 | 2,231.8 | 966.2 | 575.4 | 316.4 |
| 2011 | 2,409 | 1,280 | 139.3 | 41.3 | 681.5 | 324.9 | 2,308.5 | 958.9 | 608.2 | 328.5 |
| 2012 | 2,442 | 1,297 | 144.0 | 41.3 | 688.8 | 314.8 | 2,391.3 | 964.2 | 624.7 | 320.9 |
| 2013 | 2,491 | 1,321 | 149.7 | 43.7 | 699.8 | 318.4 | 2,468.1 | 973.6 | 638.7 | 318.7 |
| 2014 | 2,529 | 1,327 | 153.5 | 43.8 | 721.4 | 338.0 | 2,547.7 | 1,006.6 | 659.4 | 318.0 |
| 2015 | 2,560 | 1,341 | 157.3 | 45.5 | 737.8 | 348.4 | 2,625.3 | 1,048.6 | 680.9 | 322.3 |

Note: 1. "…" indicates that the statistic is missing; 2. In order to compare, the figure lists some data about the development of regular higher education institutes.

Table 4.2 The proportion of the number of higher vocational school students to the total enrolled number of regular higher education (%)

| Year | Regular Higher Education Schools | Undergraduate Universities | Higher Vocational (Technical) Schools Higher Vocational Schools |
|---|---|---|---|
| 1978 | 100.0 | 100.0 | … |
| 1980 | 100.0 | 100.0 | … |
| 1985 | 100.0 | 100.0 | … |
| 1990 | 100.0 | 100.0 | … |
| 1995 | 100.0 | 100.0 | … |
| 2000 | 100.0 | 81.9 | 18.1 |
| 2001 | 100.0 | 79.6 | 20.4 |
| 2002 | 100.0 | 78.6 | 21.4 |
| 2003 | 100.0 | 56.8 | 43.2 |
| 2004 | 100.0 | 55.3 | 44.7 |
| 2005 | 100.0 | 54.3 | 45.7 |
| 2006 | 100.0 | 54.3 | 45.7 |
| 2007 | 100.0 | 54.3 | 45.7 |
| 2008 | 100.0 | 54.6 | 45.4 |
| 2009 | 100.0 | 55.0 | 45.0 |
| 2010 | 100.0 | 56.7 | 43.3 |
| 2011 | 100.0 | 58.5 | 41.5 |
| 2012 | 100.0 | 597 | 40.3 |
| 2013 | 100.0 | 60.6 | 39.4 |
| 2014 | 100.0 | 60.5 | 39.5 |
| 2015 | 100.0 | 60.1 | 39.9 |

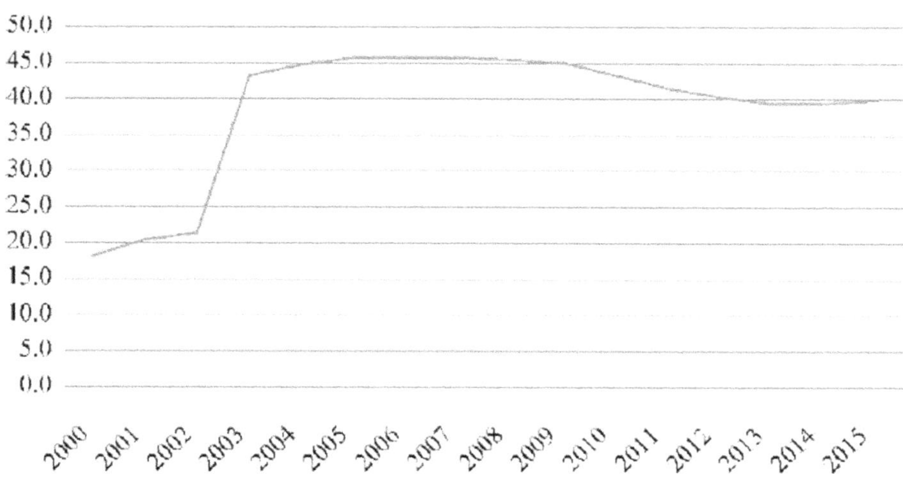


Figure 4.3 The annual trend in the proportion of higher vocational school students to the total enrolled number of regular higher education (2000–2015)

The ratio of students enrolled in higher vocational schools (%)

Table 4.3 The proportion of new student enrollments in higher vocational education to the total enrolled number of regular higher vocational education (%)

| Year | Regular Higher Education School | Undergraduate University | Higher Vocational (Technical) School |
|---|---|---|---|
| 1978 | 100.0 | 100.0 | … |
| 1980 | 100.0 | 100.0 | … |
| 1985 | 100.0 | 100.0 | … |
| 1990 | 100.0 | 100.0 | … |
| 1995 | 100.0 | 100.0 | … |
| 2000 | 100.0 | 77.9 | 22.1 |
| 2001 | 100.0 | 75.2 | 24.8 |
| 2002 | 100.0 | 72.2 | 27.8 |
| 2003 | 100.0 | 47.8 | 52.2 |
| 2004 | 100.0 | 46.9 | 53.1 |
| 2005 | 100.0 | 46.9 | 53.1 |
| 2006 | 100.0 | 46.3 | 53.7 |
| 2007 | 100.0 | 49.8 | 50.2 |
| 2008 | 100.0 | 48.9 | 51.1 |
| 2009 | 100.0 | 51.0 | 49.0 |
| 2010 | 100.0 | 53.1 | 46.9 |
| 2011 | 100.0 | 52.3 | 47.7 |
| 2012 | 100.0 | 54.3 | 45.7 |
| 2013 | 100.0 | 54.5 | 45.5 |
| 2014 | 100.0 | 53.1 | 46.9 |
| 2015 | 100.0 | 52.8 | 47.2 |

Higher vocational education has reached a scale that has fundamentally changed the school-operating pattern of Chinese vocational education and higher education.

## 3. Curriculum and Associated Development of Higher Vocational Education

After achieving rapid progress in higher vocational education, a more important issue begins to confront the people, that is, the development of curriculum, teaching standards, and operating policy of higher vocational education. It involves two key issues: 1. what kind of students should be admitted and trained, namely, the orientation of higher vocational training; 2. how to educate and train students, namely, the quality and path of higher vocational training. The newly developed higher vocational education has rapidly shifted from expansion to operating policy development.

The proportion of new student enrollment in vocational educational schools (%)

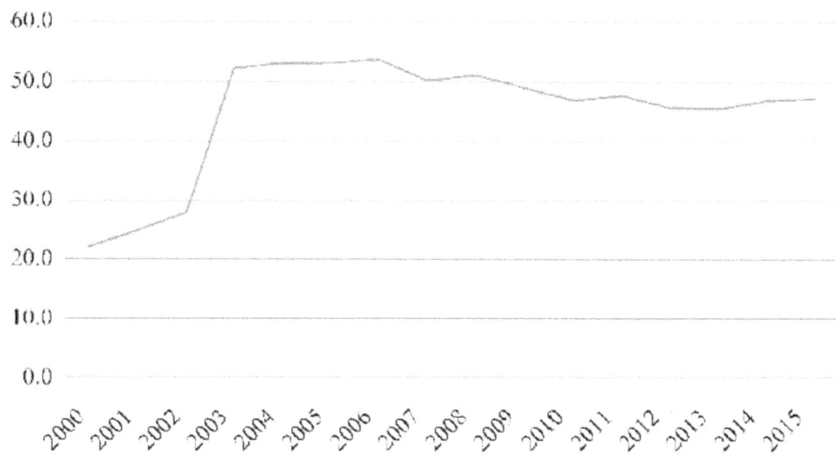


Figure 4.4 The changing trend in the proportion of new student enrollment of higher vocational schools to the total enrolled numbers in regular higher education

## 3.1. Orientation of Higher Vocational Student Training

Before higher vocational education can develop on a large scale, the basic task of education in China is to train technical workers and technicians in secondary vocational education, namely technical training schools and secondary specialized schools, respectively; vocational high schools train both technical workers and technicians at the same time; universities train academic students. Higher professional education is required to target at training application-oriented students; however, people's understanding has been unclear in terms of the boundary between application-oriented students and academic students and the clear distinction between training methods. Moreover, schools always aspire to orient students to a higher level. This actually makes higher vocational education a compressed form of undergraduate education. Generally speaking, this kind of educational structure is distinctive. With so many higher vocational institutions established now, what is the training objective? In the preceding 20 years of higher school education experiments, people basically held the view that higher vocational school targets training technical students. The students it trains should neither be positioned at the level of skilled workers nor at the level of engineering and academic professionals, but at the level of technical competency between skilled workers and engineering professionals, that is, at the level of ability targeted by secondary specialized schools. However, the training objective is higher than that of secondary specialized schools. This view is advocated by the members of Shanghai Vocational and Technical Education Forum, with Mr. Yang Jintu as the core advocate.

*Opinions of MOE on Reinforcing the Cultivation of Higher Vocational and Technical Talents* (No. 2 [2000] from the Department of Higher Education, MOE) puts forward: "Training models of higher vocational education are basically characterized by focusing on the training of high-tech professionals; to design students' knowledge, ability, quality structures and training programs with the purpose of adapting them to social requirements and taking technical application ability as the main line; students should be characterized as having appropriate basic theoretical knowledge, strong technical application ability, wide knowledge and high standards, etc."[10] This document takes "practical high-tech professionals" as the goal of training in higher vocational education, which was widely recognized by all walks of life. However in 2004, *Opinions on Being Employment-Oriented and Deepening the Reform of Higher Vocational Education (No. 1 [2004] from the Department of Higher Education, MOE)* proposed that: "Higher vocational education should take service as the purpose and employment as the orientation, and follow the path of integrating industry, production and research. Higher vocational colleges should take the initiative to adapt to the requirements for economic and social development, determine the goals of school operation based on employment, identify the position of schools in the development of regional economies and industry, strengthen the reform of the training model, and persist in attracting 'down-to-earth, retainable, practical' highly skilled students with strong practical abilities and good professional ethics and oriented toward first-line production, construction, management and the service industry"[11] The proposal of the training objective of "highly skilled students" led to two major viewpoints: whether vocational education should be based on technical knowledge or skill ability. This immediately caused great controversy in higher vocational education circles, which continues today.

Most people are naturally against the concept of being highly skilled, and they advocate restoring the training position of "practical high-tech professionals." The document drafters at that time adopted the concept of "highly skilled" only to highlight the school-operating position of "taking service as the purpose and employment as the orientation" in higher vocational education and emphasized that higher vocational education should focus on cultivating students' skills.

(Employment orientation was quite controversial at that time. Many people proposed that the further education function of vocational education should not be denied.) They perhaps even did not realize the specific meaning of the concept of skilled workers and the fundamental difference with technical professionals in the order of expertise. However, according to classification theory, there is an important difference between skilled work and technical work in terms of knowledge and ability. Moreover, secondary vocational schools basically target training skilled students (the boundaries of the three types of secondary vocational schools are becoming increasingly vague). So, people are extremely concerned that it will be difficult to distinguish the training objectives of higher vocational education and secondary vocational education after setting training "highly skilled students" as the objective of higher vocational education. If people fail to distinguish, scholars worry about whether the higher education attribute of higher vocational education can be accurately reflected. People in charge of operating higher vocational schools are worried about whether they will be included among secondary vocational schools. There is indeed a "high" in being "highly skilled." However, as many people have seen, "high" skill cannot equate with "high" academic level, because "high" skill can be achieved through repetition training. They found evidence from the education classification system of UNESCO and think that we must upgrade intellectual complexity if we want to develop advanced-level higher vocational education.

The concept of being "highly skilled" did have some adverse effects on the direction of developing higher education at that time. Some higher vocational colleges have blindly strengthened the training of students' operational skills without fully comprehending the spirit of the documents. They largely removed or reduced theoretical courses and lowered the theoretical teaching of higher vocational education to a level that did not meet the basic requirements of higher education, thus severely affecting the embodiment of the advanced-level higher vocational education. In order to change this situation and upgrade higher vocational education to higher education, MOE put forward the concept of "high-end skills" again. For example, *Notice on Supporting Higher Vocational Schools to Improve the Ability of Developing Professional Service Industries* (No. 11 [2011] from the Department of Vocational and Adult Education, MOE) in 2011 has the following statement: "Strengthening specialty construction of higher vocational colleges and training high-end skilled and specialized workers is an important way to develop modern industries."[12] Here, the word "high-end" is adopted instead of "highly," with the hope that higher vocational education would train a higher-level skilled and specialized workforce. However, no matter how "high-end" they are, they still belong to a class of skilled workers and there is no substantial change in the hierarchical level. As a result, a chorus of criticism was provoked. The root cause lies in the failure to resolve the problem of what kind of workers should be cultivated by higher vocational education.

This problem has continued until now. Taking technical professionals as the training objective of higher education, the technical undergraduate education to be discussed below finally appeared. The training objective proposed in 2002 has never reappeared in higher vocational education. This is extremely unfavourable for the development of higher vocational education. With the development of technological undergraduate education, higher vocational education will confront a greater squeeze within the school-operating space. Given the policy guidance that no upgrade is allowed, the next issue that needs to be studied seriously is how then to develop higher vocational education. However, even if it is clearly stated that higher vocational education should target at training technical students, it doesn't mean the problem of the orientation of higher vocational school operation is solved. This is because there are no satisfactory answers to the problem of "what on earth does technical competency mean," and technicians have a very vague status in the employment structure of our country. We can see this from the development of technological undergraduate education.

Of course, it is not appropriate to set skilled workers as the training objective of higher vocational education; however, it is also not necessarily suitable for technical experts: 1. Is it certain that skilled students need not be cultivated for high vocational training? Some high-level skilled people also need to master comparatively complex theoretical knowledge, and need to be cultivated by higher vocational education, such as master-level mechanical workers; 2. Does higher vocational education only cultivate technicians? In fact, higher vocational education also incorporates a large number of design specialties, such as arts and crafts design, costume design, etc. Besides, it contains many management specialties. The higher vocational specialty directory also includes the specialty of teacher training. As a school-operating form, higher vocational education has such a complicated and comprehensive student training structure that we can only describe its overall orientation. However, it is difficult to classify it into a certain type of work status. It is more practical to list the types of skilled workers that higher vocational education may cultivate than to get bogged down in endless conceptual debates. At the level of curriculum development, this problem is generally solved through specifying the specific occupation relevant to each higher vocational specialty.

### 3.2. Quality and Path of Higher Vocational Training

While solving the problem of the training objective of higher vocational students, higher vocational circles have been haunted by another problem. That is, the quality and path of higher vocational training. "Quality" is a highly flexible concept, and what is meant needs to be specifically defined in practice. For example, reaching the basic school-operating level can be said to be a quality requirement, but the pursuit of excellence can also be said to be a quality requirement. For the newly established higher vocational education, quality refers to the basic school-operating level, especially the basic level of higher education, and improvement on this basis. Since many higher vocational colleges are upgraded from secondary vocational schools, how to make these schools genuinely achieve higher education levels is a matter of concern. Path refers to the student training model, curriculum model, and teaching model that reflect the features of higher vocational education. Higher vocational education belongs to vocational education from the sense of education type, and belongs to higher education from the sense of academic structure level. As a new education form, how to carry out student education? Due to the lack of practical school operation experiences and insufficient experience of other countries, the higher education circle is not very familiar with this issue. In order to solve this problem, MOE has implemented a number of actions that have achieved significant results.

In 2000, MOE released the *Standards Setting for Higher Vocational Schools (Provisional)* (No. 41[2000] from MOE), which aims to standardize the basic school operating conditions for higher vocational colleges. The regulations include: 1. When a higher vocational school is to be established, it must be equipped with a full-time headmaster (dean) and a vice headmaster (dean) who have high political qualities, management abilities, and noble characters; are familiar with higher education; and have worked in deputy senior or above professional and technical posts in higher education institutions. At the same time, it should also be equipped with full-time moral education workers, who have worked in deputy senior professional and technical posts or above, and departmental and specialty leaders, who have working experience in higher education; 2. When a higher vocational school is to be established, it must be equipped with a teaching faculty consisting of full-time and part-time teachers, and the number of it should be consistent with specialty setting and the number of students at the school; 3. When a higher vocational school is to be established, there must be land and school buildings in line with specialty types and scale of the school; 4. It must be equipped with necessary internship training places, teaching apparatus and equipment, books and reference materials in line with the specialty setting; 5. The curriculum setting must highlight the features of higher vocational schools; 6. The number of specialties that shall enroll students for the first time should be around 5 after the school is established; 7. The funds required for various works such as the basic construction investment and normal teaching of higher vocational schools must come from stable and reliable sources and be tangibly guaranteed.[13] This document specifies the requirements from seven aspects. For new higher vocational schools, this document makes detailed regulations on the number of students at the school and the school-operating conditions the schools should reach within four years. This document is of fundamental importance to higher vocational schools that have just developed on a large scale.

Demonstrative higher vocational education is an important measure for the country to upgrade higher vocational education. The concept of "demonstrative higher vocational education" first appeared in *Action Plan for Education Revitalization for the 21st Century* in 1998: "select 30 existing schools to build demonstration vocational and technical colleges."[14] *Decision of the State Council on the Vigorously Developing Vocational Education* (No. 35 [2005] from the State Council) increased 30–100, known as the "211 Project" in higher vocational education. In 2006, MOE issued the *Opinions of MOE and MOF on Implementing the Construction Plan of National Demonstration Higher Vocational Colleges and Accelerating the Reform and Development of Higher Vocational Education* (No. 14 [2006] from the Department of Higher Education, MOE), which aims to implement the construction task of 100 demonstration higher vocational colleges: "Support the construction of 100 high-level demonstration colleges; enable more than 600,000 students to directly benefit from the schools; provide various social training for more than 2 million people; focus on constructing 500 featured specialty groups with wide coverage of industries, good school operating conditions, close integration of industry and education and high quality student training; cultivate and introduce competent 'Double-Quality Teacher' specialty leaders and teachers, employ technicians and skilled craftsmen in the enterprise industry and employ top quality full-time and part-time teachers; set up 4,000 high-quality professional core courses and 1,500 kinds of special teaching materials and teaching courseware, each specialty to promote the upgrading of more than 3 specialty-related courses in the region and industry and significantly improve teaching qualities; develop and promote teaching resources sharing in key industries supported by the state so as to provide quality services for students' independent learning; build a public service platform using modern information and provide technical support for high-quality teaching resource sharing; promote counterpart support between demonstration institutions and economically underdeveloped regions and facilitate the exchange between secondary and higher vocational colleges in the region, and improve the overall quality of higher vocational education."[15] Then MOE issued *Opinions of MOE and MOF on Implementing the Construction Plan of National Demonstration Higher Vocational Colleges and*

*Accelerating the Reform and Development of Higher Vocational Education* (No. 14 [2006] from the Department of Higher Education, MOE), with the purpose of the specific deployment of this work. In *Several Opinions on Comprehensively Improving the Teaching Quality of Higher Vocational Education* (No. 16 [2006] from the Department of Higher Education, MOE), MOE continued to strengthen the construction tasks of 100 demonstration institutions: "The state will implement a construction plan of demonstration higher vocational colleges, with a focus on supporting the construction of 100 demonstration institutions, closely integrating higher vocational colleges with economic and social development across the country, strengthening school operations, improving the teaching quality in an all-round way and promoting the sustainable and healthy development of higher vocational education."[16] It also put forward clear and explicit construction ideas such as a student training model, curriculum model, industry-university co-operation, training base, teachers, and especially proposed that "higher vocational colleges should strengthen their quality consciousness, enhance the construction of the quality management system in particular, focus on process monitoring, attract employers to participate in the evaluation of teaching quality, and gradually improve the teaching quality assurance system with schools as the core, education administrative departments as the guide, and with social participation."[17]

In 2006, the construction of 100 national demonstration higher vocational colleges was officially launched. From the above construction guidelines, the construction focused on the school operating elements such as curriculum, teacher, and student training models; hardware construction, which accounted for a small proportion, although this project has prompted local governments to invest in higher vocational hardware. In 2010, MOE and MOF decided to continue to promote the "National Construction Plan for Demonstration Higher Vocational Colleges," to increase the number of key national construction institutions and add about 100 key higher vocational colleges. Inspired by the construction of national demonstration higher vocational colleges, many provinces and cities have launched construction plans for local demonstration vocational colleges. The construction work has greatly contributed to local governments' investment in higher vocational colleges and improved the image of higher vocational colleges as highly valued among the people. This has not only greatly improved the hardware facilities in a large number of higher vocational colleges, but also substantially upgraded the administrative and teaching level of the colleges and enhanced the social image of higher vocational education. It also played a major role in the process where higher vocational education has eventually become a valued and distinctive type of higher education.

In 2011, MOE issued the *Notice on Supporting Higher Vocational Schools to Improve the Ability of Developing Professional Service Industries* (No. 11 [2011] from the Department of Vocational and Adult Education, MOE) (the management authority of higher vocational education was assigned to the Department of Vocational and Adult Education at the end of 2010), which further improved the level of higher vocational education on the basis of constructing demonstration higher vocational universities and colleges. This document firstly comprehensively appraised the overall situation of higher vocational colleges in China at that time: "The level of specialty construction cannot well adapt to the requirements of promoting vocational education reform and innovation, building a modern vocational education system and serving the economic and social development and modernization construction, which is obviously reflected in the inflexible management systems and operational mechanisms and insufficient school-operating vitality; specialty settings are disjointed with industrial development, course content is disjointed with the application of industrial technology, teaching means and methods have no clear aims; the quantity, quality and structure of the teaching staff cannot meet the requirements for training high-end skilled professionals, the construction and management system of double-quality teachers has not yet been established; graduates' practical ability and professional attitude cannot fully meet work requirements, schools' practical training conditions and workplace environments need to be improved urgently and training of students professional spirit needs to be strengthened urgently."[18] The specific measure is to focus on supporting the construction of a number of key industries that closely match the requirements of industrial development, deeply integrate schools with enterprises, enjoy high social recognition, and good employment.

In 2015, MOE issued the *Action Plan for Innovation and Development of Higher Vocational Education (2015–2018)* (No. 9 [2015] from the Department of Vocational and Adult Education, MOE), which aims to further upgrade higher vocational education. After 20 years of development, China's school operating level of higher vocational education has greatly improved and our vocational education structure has fundamentally changed. However, it's clear that higher vocational education still needs to be further improved, especially faculty development. At the same time, higher vocational colleges are also suffering huge operating pressures brought about by the expansion of undergraduate education promotion and the transfer of a number of undergraduate colleges toward the direction of technical schools. Under these pressures, whether higher vocational education consciously moves forward or unconsciously shrinks backward will determine the future of higher vocational education.

## Part 2 Directing Some Local Undergraduate Institutions to Transform into Technical Institutions

As early as 1965, the U.S. educator H. A. Foechek predicted: "At some point in the future, there may be at least four basic types of bachelor's degree programs at the undergraduate level: science, engineering science, engineering, and engineering technology."[19] To upgrade vocational education to the level of undergraduate education is not only a requirement for a high-tech workforce within industry but also a requirement of building a modern vocational education system for vocational school students to further enhance their academic qualifications within the vocational education system. The discussion on the necessities and strategies of developing application-oriented undergraduate education in China began in the early 21st century. In 2003, Professor Shi Weiping and I jointly published a paper entitled *On the Significance and Tactics of Developing University Technology Education in Contemporary China* in *Research in Educational Development*. This was also the core issue of Shanghai Vocational & Technical Education Forum at that time. Researchers mainly demonstrated the necessity of developing technical undergraduate education from the perspective of perfecting the technical training system starting from the question of how to implement school orientation after some technical colleges were upgraded to undergraduate institutions. After 2010, developing technological undergraduate education began to become a national policy.

Figure 4.5 Shanghai Institute of Technology

## 1. The Policy Path to the Development of Technical Undergraduate Education

The policy of developing technical undergraduate education at the national level is proposed within the background of many undergraduate institutions blindly pursuing research-based positioning, emphasizing basic theory teaching without sufficient training of students' practical abilities, thus creating a great dilemma for undergraduate graduate employment; at the same time, the industry was severely deficient in high-tech workers.

In view of this problem, *Outline of the National Medium-and Long-Term Education Reform and Development Plan (2010–2020)* puts forward the following ideas for higher education reform: "Adapt to the requirements of national and regional economic and social development, establish a dynamic adjustment mechanism, and continuously optimize the structure of higher education ... Focus on expanding the scale of application-oriented, competent and skilled workers."[20] Strengthening the cultivation of application-oriented students in higher education is formally put forward as a major issue for restructuring higher education in this document, which had a far-reaching influence on Chinese education. In 2011, MOE issued *Instructions of MOE on Promoting the Coordinated Development between Secondary and Higher Vocational Education* (No. 9 [2011] from the Department of Vocational and Adult Education, MOE), which required "improving the system of high-end skilled trainees through application-oriented undergraduate education." In 2014, MOE released *Instructions of MOE on Further Promoting Educational Reform and Cooperative Development in Yangtze River Delta* (No. 7 [2014] from MOE), which clearly proposed: "According to the requirements of regional economic and social development, especially industrial transformation and upgrading, guide some local undergraduate universities to transform into application-oriented applied-technology universities and allocate more resources to application-oriented applied-technology universities in line with the changes in the annual enrollment plan, expenditure allocation per student and major construction projects."[21] This document is of great significance to the development of applied-technology undergraduate education. It is precisely under the policy of "guiding some local undergraduate universities to transform into applied-technology universities" that technical undergraduate education has achieved substantial progress. Lu Xin, Vice Minister of MOE, played a critical role in formulating this policy. She strongly advocated for transforming 600 local undergraduate universities into applied-technology undergraduate universities.

Since then, the development of applied-technology undergraduate education has become an important part of vocational education reform and development policies. The main documents focus on elaborating it and some documents provide extensive detail. For example, the *Decision of the State Council on Accelerating the Development of Modern Vocational Education* (No. 19 [2014] from the State Council) requires: "Guide the transformation and development of regular undergraduate institutions. Guide a group of regular undergraduate institutions to transform into applied-technology institutions by means of pilot and demonstration projects to focus on developing undergraduate vocational education. When an independent college is transformed into an independent university, we should encourage it to orient toward an applied-technology university. Establish a classification system for colleges and universities, implement systematic management, and accelerate the establishment of classification settings, assessment, guidance, and appropriation systems. Policies and measures such as enrollment and investment should remain as priorities for our policy agenda for applied-technology institutions."[22]

*Planning for Modern Vocational Education System Construction (2014–2020)* also requires that: "We should develop applied-technology institutions and cultivate undergraduate professional students on the basis of operating the existing specialist vocational (junior) colleges well. Applied-technology institutions are an important part of the higher education system and has equal status with other regular undergraduate institutions." "Guide a number of undergraduate colleges and universities to transform and develop. Support undergraduate institutions to comprehensively transform into applied-technology institutions which orient toward service industries and local economic and social development. Encourage independent colleges to transform into independent applied-technology institutions. Encourage undergraduate institutions and demonstration higher vocational schools to train high-level application-oriented technical students through collaborative teaching and joint training."[23]

In 2015, MOE released a special document *Instructions on Guiding Some Local Regular Undergraduate Universities to Transform into Application-Oriented Universities* (No. 7 [2015] from MOE), which instructs some pilot local undergraduate universities to transform in the direction of cultivating application-oriented, technical and skilled trainees through 22 measures and in four aspects. These policies are more concrete.

*Opinions of MOE on the Work of Setting Up Colleges and Universities in the "Thirteenth Five-Year Plan" Period* (No. 3[2017] from MOE) divides China's higher education into three types: research-based type, application-oriented type, and vocational skill-oriented type. This clarifies the independent status of applied-technology undergraduate education in higher education. "Research-based institutions mainly focus on cultivating innovation-oriented students in academic research and carry out theoretical research and innovation. They are qualified for conferring academic degrees including bachelor, master and doctor, and postgraduate education accounts for a large proportion. Application-oriented institutions are mainly engaged in cultivating application-oriented students at undergraduate level or above who can serve the economic sector, and also in research on social development and technology applications. Vocational and technical institutions are mainly engaged in cultivating specialist technical students for working at the front-line of production, management and service, and actively carry out or participate in the reform and innovation of technical services and skills application."[24]

In *The "Thirteenth Five-Year" Plan for China's Educational Development (No.4 [2017] from the State Council)*, the State Council continued to put forward the requirements for adjusting the structure of higher education: "Give priority to developing technological application-oriented universities and small-scale specialist colleges. Accelerate establishing a number of high-level application-oriented colleges and universities and higher vocational schools which can serve local economic and social development. Incorporate qualified technical colleges into the college and university sequence according to the regulations applicable to colleges and universities."[25]

## 2. Local Practice of Developing Applied-Technology Undergraduate Education

Under the guidance of a series of policies released by MOE, local governments have actively launched the transformation of local undergraduate colleges and universities. The specific implementation plan is formulated by each province and city; pilot first and then popularize; the transforming object is limited to 600 local undergraduate colleges and universities, accounting for about 50% of the total undergraduate institutions. The colleges and universities directly under central ministries and agencies are out of the limited scope of these policies.

Cingta Query summarized relevant data and found that by November 19, 2015, 13 provinces (cities) had successively issued plans and 181 colleges and universities had been determined to completely transform into applied-technology colleges and universities or just to include some specialties. The specific situations included: 1. The plan issued by Zhejiang province was the most rigorous. A total of 41 regular undergraduate colleges and universities actively applied for applied-technology transformation, accounting for about 80% of the total number of colleges and universities in the whole province; 2. The plan issued by Guangxi Zhuang Autonomous Region was also very strong, where

19 colleges and universities were determined to be included in the selection scope of an undergraduate college transformation pilot; 3. In Hubei province, 18 undergraduate colleges were approved to completely transform into technology colleges and universities, accounting for about 30% of the total number of undergraduate colleges and universities in the whole province. Besides, some specialties in 5 universities were approved for pilot transformation; 4. In Henan province, 15 colleges and universities were identified to participate in two pilots; 5 undergraduate schools were identified as pilot schools the first time, and another 10 pilot schools were identified on the basis of voluntary applications in September 2014; 5. Jiangxi province identified 10 undergraduate colleges (2 provincial undergraduate colleges, 3 local undergraduate colleges, 3 private undergraduate colleges, and 2 independent colleges) as the first batch of pilot schools for transformation; 6. Hebei province identified a total of 10 pilot universities, and set up special subsidy funds to support the transformation and development of pilot schools. 7. In Jilin province, 9 local undergraduate colleges were transformed into applied-technology modern universities. In addition, some secondary colleges and specialty clusters of 24 undergraduate universities were chosen for pilot transformation; 8. In Gansu province, 6 undergraduate colleges and 2 independent colleges, namely, Lanzhou Jiaotong University, Bowen College of Technology and Engineering, LUT, were listed as the first batch of pilot schools for transformation; at the same time, other provincial undergraduate colleges and universities were encouraged to carry out pilot transformation work in secondary colleges or specialties (groups) according to their actual development needs; 9. Liaoning province issued the *Opinions on Implementing the Transformation of Undergraduate Colleges and Universities into Application-Oriented Type*, which proposed that by 2017, except for the colleges and universities under ministries and commissions, the proportion of specialties in training application-oriented students shall reach 70% in the whole province and the annual application-oriented students trained shall be about 120,000. In 2015, about 10 colleges and universities (including private colleges and universities) and 100 specialties were selected to carry out school transformation and specialty transformation in advance; 10. In Chongqing, a total of 6 colleges and universities participated in the pilot of transforming them into applied-technology universities; 11. Sichuan province identified a total of 3 colleges and universities to carry out reform pilots; 12. Hunan province identified 2 universities to launch pilot projects; 13. Shanghai did not make a list of the schools that could completely transform into universities but identified the first batch of undergraduate applied-technology pilot specialties in Shanghai municipal colleges and universities, with 26 specialties from 16 universities selected.[26]

## 3. Several Problems in Transforming Local Undergraduate Institutions into Applied-Technology Institutions

The development of applied-technology undergraduate education is undoubtedly of great significance to perfecting the vocational education system and providing more career development paths for vocational school students. For example, the Shanghai Municipal Education Commission stipulated that the specialties included in the transformation list could only recruit secondary vocational graduates. This policy has played an important role in enhancing the attractiveness of secondary vocational schools. Objectively speaking, the policy released by MOE on transforming local undergraduate colleges and universities into applied-technology schools gets down to the fundamental problem of higher education in China, and is important in promoting diversified higher education and making student training better adapt to social demand. This policy created significant repercussions in education circles after it came out. Many people thought carefully before declaring their approval of this policy.

### 3.1. School Transformation or Specialty Transformation

It was undoubtedly correct to guide some undergraduate colleges and universities to transform into applied-technology ones. However, this policy is confronted with a primary problem, namely, whether to reorient these colleges and universities toward applied-technology schools as a whole, or only introduce some suitable specialties and then gradually make these schools more applied-technology oriented? These are two completely different ways of thinking. From the above examples of implementing this policy in various provinces and cities, we can see that Shanghai has adopted a distinctive strategy. Shanghai actively implemented the policy of MOE, but it only implemented this policy at the specialty level, rather than reposition entire schools as applied-technology schools. This strategy actually seems reasonable, as it not only makes this policy easier to accept by most colleges and universities, but also greatly reduces the resistance that this policy faces in the implementation process. Furthermore, it can implement the transformation requirements into specialties and achieve genuine transformation.

From the perspective of reducing policy implementation resistance, most undergraduate colleges and universities that were required to transform were actually unwilling to do so. According to the summary of Cingta Query, transformation plans of 13 provinces and cities are listed, and a total of 181 colleges and universities participated in the pilot. However, it certainly will not be so easy to implement these plans in practice. Even for the 181 colleges and universities, some of them are not completely happy to voluntarily transform. Teachers in these schools are strongly resistant to transformation.

The reason why these schools are unwilling to transform is inevitably related to the understanding of the leaders and teachers in these schools. In fact, there is no lack of applied-technology research and corresponding teacher training in the discipline construction and training in undergraduate colleges and universities. Some research is highly practical and produced mature marketable products. However, this research and teaching exists in research-oriented universities that have not been transformed. If research-oriented universities do not conduct application-oriented research, we can't explain why they attract such large-scale horizontal scientific research funds. In research-oriented universities, we can see agricultural experts do research in the field all the year round; sociologists do research on street corners all the year round; educators do research in the classroom all the year round, and engineering experts do research in the laboratory and on construction sites all the year round. Their actions are consciously directed toward practical outcomes. Genuine experts are certain to attach great importance to application-oriented research. Applications will never be reduced, and will increase the academic level of research. If local undergraduate colleges and universities think that being engaged in practical research indicates a decline in school level, it is because they do not really understand the true essence of research and student cultivation.

This presents a contradiction, that is, colleges and universities that are not required to become application-oriented are conscientiously doing application-oriented research while those which are clearly required to transform into application-oriented schools are unwilling to transform. Why? Is it completely because the leaders and teachers in local colleges and universities are insufficiently aware of this policy? Not exactly. The transformation policy should be fully implemented from the perspective of local colleges and universities. Local colleges and universities generally have a concern that they will be placed beneath research-oriented universities by social values and related policies after being labeled as "application-oriented" schools. This is because application-oriented school means something completely different for research-oriented universities and local undergraduate colleges. For research-oriented schools, "application" may possibly mean having to swallow their pride and be willing to look deep into practice. However, it indicates move to a lower level and the impossibility of reaching academic heights for local undergraduate colleges. This is ingrained thinking in society. If these concerns are not excluded from local undergraduate colleges at implementation level, there will be great resistance to policy implementation.

Furthermore, requiring the entire college to transform is still subject to the influence of administrative thinking, and is inconsistent with the actual situation and operation rules of discipline setting in colleges. In general, academic and application-oriented disciplines coexist in a university. If all disciplines of a university are required to become application-oriented, then some basic disciplines will fail to transform. If they are forced to transform, this will severely damage the development of the disciplines. If all disciplines are transformed, then the overall applied model will make the school lose its academic status and reputation, and deprive application of an academic foundation, which will cause serious damage to the development of the disciplines in the school. The discipline system of a university is also an ecological environment. We should not interfere with it too much, or the ecological balance will be destroyed.

Therefore, from the perspective of implementing transformation, it is not only feasible but also beneficial to the healthy development of colleges and universities if we can transform it on the basis of specialties and even part courses of specialties.

### 3.2. Applied Technology or Technological Applicability

Regarding the transform direction, many concepts are mentioned, even if they are not completely unified in the documents. Common terms include "application-oriented," "applied technology," "technology-applied," "technological applicable," etc. Many concepts are used without a refined distinction, indicating that people do not have a clear understanding of the essence of transformation. Vague concepts will naturally affect the practical process. We can only say that the first 181 pilot colleges and universities have accomplished project application; they are still in the initial stage of transformation in practice; some even have not begun to do substantial work. One of the important reasons is that people generally do not have a clear understanding of the essential content and path of transformation.

Of these concepts, "applied" is first and foremost inappropriate. This is because the application of basic theory is not a separate link, but a process of a long sequence of events. For example, engineering science is also included into the scope of application, because it has begun to apply basic theories. If we understand the specific content of transformation in this way, then it will obviously have no too much practical significance. The "application" discussed here should be the application of technology, namely, the application of methods and actions. Then this will touch on the second concept, "applied technology," the most frequently used concept. However, whether this concept is appropriate or not needs to be discussed. This is because "applied technology" can be understood as "research on applied technology," or as "applying technology into work." They are two completely different levels of positioning. If it is the former, it positions a specialty at a quite high level, as research on applied technology is not easier than research on basic theory. The application attribute of preceding research-oriented universities are mainly means to be engaged in the research and development of applied technology. A university has no problem to be completely positioned in the research and application of technology, but this requirement is obviously too high for local colleges and universities. Therefore, the concept of "technology application" will be more accurate if the transformation is mainly for local colleges and universities. "Technology application" means to apply technology, and it can be just the reform within the teaching scope.

When the term "technology application" is chosen, we will be confronted with the question: whether it is "technology-applied" or "technological applicable." This is because the two terms are much different in connotation. The former is to classify schools or specialties into a certain type, whereas the latter more accurately reflects certain attributes of the school. The concept of "technological applicable" should be more appropriate. Regardless of the development of the school or specialty type, thinking should be cautiously used. In terms of implementation strategy, we should not easily classify a school or specialty into a certain type; instead, we can try to improve some of its attributes. In fact, the word "application" is easier to be understood in a general sense. However, it will be very difficult if we want to manipulate it. For example, to clearly distinguish whether research is basic research or application-oriented research and whether the student training is academic or applied. Any research and education has its academic and applied attributes, but merely as a difference of degree. In this case, it is not suitable to classify a specialty as a certain type.

There is also a concept that is used occasionally, that is, vocational undergraduate. This concept is not recommended to be used. As mentioned above, the concept of "higher vocational education" has led to a dispute over technology and skill in terms of school operating orientation for higher vocational schools. There is absolutely no need to continue this dispute at undergraduate level. There is no doubt that undergraduate schools should be positioned as "technology." Now the question is, what on earth does technology refer to? Since our country has no complete ranking of technical roles, we can't have a deep understanding about its knowledge and ability structure. In the education classification system promulgated by UNESCO, there is indeed a category of "technological applicable undergraduate education," which belongs to 5A-2.[27] According to career structure theory, it targets training of not only traditional technicians but also field engineers. This is a compound target of training. Within the engineering field, the concept "field engineers" becomes increasingly complex, as engineers are further divided into such types as engineering scientists, engineering planners, and construction engineering. For technological applicable undergraduate education, it targets the training of practical engineers. We have such titles as "field engineer" and "product engineer" in our daily expressions.

### 3.3. Is It Easier for Local Undergraduate Institutions to Transform?

We have taken several factors into consideration when determining local undergraduate institutions as the object of transformation. One consideration is whether more local undergraduate institutions should transform, and if so, whether it is easier for them todo so. If the transformation is positioned as "applied-technology application," then local undergraduate institutions should indeed transform. However, whether it is easier for them to transform is not necessarily the case.

First, in terms of teachers' practical capacities, current local colleges, and universities are no more advantaged than research-oriented universities. In order to successfully achieve this transformation, local undergraduate colleges and universities must carry out in-depth training of teachers' practical capacities. The critical issue here is not whether local colleges and universities can provide adequate training opportunities, but whether teachers are willing to train conscientiously. Second, we may assume that local colleges and universities will integrate with local industries more closely; thus, it will be conducive to realizing transformation. In fact, however, whether local colleges and universities are closely integrated with local industries has nothing to do with spatial distance. Many of the current examples of cooperation are transnational. Whether schools can establish a close partnership with enterprises depends on the schools' reputation and technological R&D strength. In this regard, research-oriented universities have great advantages.

Third, local undergraduate colleges and universities do not have the advantage that research-oriented universities have in terms of an open and flexible system as well as teachers' conscientious spirit. The operation mechanisms of all "application"-oriented universities are remarkably open and flexible. In terms of external cooperation, the so-called openness indicates breaking through the scope of the discipline field itself and establishing complex cooperative relations within various social domains in which the disciplinary knowledge is applied, including cooperation in attracting the right students and research projects. As for the so-called flexibility, it means establishing diversified management standards and requirements so that the management system can better adapt to factors such as project management, teacher recruitment, and requirements for teacher promotion. Developing technology-oriented undergraduate education requires not only the input of relevant school-operating elements, but also the establishment of an open and flexible operation mechanism. In this respect, local undergraduate colleges and universities are not as advantaged as research-oriented universities.

Local undergraduate colleges and universities should transform toward the direction of technological application. However, they lack basic conditions in many aspects in the transforming process. This is the dilemma faced by the current development of technological applicable undergraduate education.

## Part 3 Facilitating the Coordinated Development and Interconnection of Secondary and Higher Vocational Schools

Building a perfect vocational education system has always been the core goal pursued by China's vocational education. With the maturing of higher vocational education and the development of technology-oriented undergraduate education, China's vocational education has gradually improved at an academic structural level, and the vocational education system has finally built a solid identity.

### 1. Policy Path to the Construction of a Modern Vocational Education System

Although the concept a "modern vocational education system" was proposed in the paper, *Decision of the State Council on Vigorously Promoting the Reform and Development of Vocational Education* in 2002, the goal of building a "vocational education system" was put forward in the *Decision of the CPC Central Committee on the Reform of the Education System* in 1985: "Gradually establish an industry-supported, well-structured vocational and technical education system which incorporates vocational education from primary to senior level and is able to communicate with regular education."[28] This goal has run through almost all important documents since reform and opening-up. For example, in 1991, the *Decision of the State Council on Vigorously Developing Vocational and Technical Education* proposed: "Initially establish a basic framework of vocational and technical education system with Chinese characteristics which incorporates vocational education from primary to senior level, is industry-supported, well-structured, diversified and able to communicate and coordinate with other education."[29] The *Vocational Education Law of the People's Republic of China* in 1996 required: "Implement education diversity at different stages with a focus on post-secondary education, establish and improve vocational school education and vocational training simultaneously, and set up a vocational education system in which it can coordinate communication and development with other educational institutions."[30]

With the improvement of vocational education in the academic system, the task of accelerating the construction of the vocational education system is becoming more and more urgent at the national level. After higher vocational education developed on a large scale, secondary vocational education and higher vocational education have been respectively managed by the Department of Vocational and Adult Education and the Department of Higher Education for a long time. This leads to a serious disconnect between the two. For example, the specialty catalogues of the two are difficult to dock with each other, which greatly hinder secondary vocational students' further study in the vocational education system. After recognizing this problem, MOE clearly proposed the "continuous specialty" of higher vocational education in the 2010 edition of the secondary vocational specialty catalogue. However, this does not address the underlying cause at all.

In 2005, *Decision of the State Council on Vigorously Developing Vocational Education* proposed: "Further establish and improve a modern well-structured, diversified, flexible and open, self-developed vocational education system with Chinese characteristics which can adapt to the socialist market economic system, meet people's requirements for lifelong learning, closely integrate with market demand and labor employment, allow school-enterprise cooperation and work-integrated learning."[31] This document puts the word "modern" in front of the original concept of a "vocational education system," and puts forward the concept of a "modern vocational education system."

In 2010, *Outline of the National Medium-and Long-Term Education Reform and Development Plan (2010–2020)* continued to use the term, "modern vocational education system," and proposed: "By 2020, a modern vocational education system, which can adapt to the requirements for the transformation of an economic development model and the adjustment of industrial structure, reflect the concept of lifelong education, and allow the coordinated development of secondary vocational education and higher vocational education, will have been established, in order to satisfy people's requirements for receiving vocational education, and meet the economic and social need for high-quality workers and a skilled workforce."[32]

From relevant expressions in the above documents, we can see that the vocational education system mainly refers to a system composed of all kinds of vocational schools at all levels and internally connected. For example, the second part of a "vocational education system" in the *Vocational Education Law of the People's Republic of China* elaborates all kinds of entities that implement vocational education at all levels. Therefore, the concept of a "modern vocational education system" can be understood as follows: secondary vocational education and higher vocational education connect with each other and coordinate development to constitute a system, and can adapt to the industrial structure. This is not substantially different from the definition of a "vocational education system" in previous documents. The word "modern" mainly reflects a more ideal academic system within a different industrial, social, and educational environment.

In 2014, the *Decision of the State Council on Accelerating the Development of Modern Vocational Education* (No. 19 [2014] from the State Council) continued to follow the earlier understanding of the concept of a "modern vocational education system." It proposed "systematic training and a diversified workforce" as the principle for the construction of modern vocational education, and required it to "facilitate the close connection between secondary vocational education and higher vocational education, to fully implement the important role of higher vocational education in optimizing the structure of higher education."[33] In the section on "accelerating the construction of a modern vocational education system," this document addresses five major issues: consolidate and improve the level of secondary vocational education, innovate and develop higher vocational education, guide the transformation and development of regular undergraduate colleges and universities, perfect diversified channels for the growth of vocational education students, and actively develop various forms of continuing education. This document elaborates on the specific content of the five issues. Only according to this document can we think that a modern vocational education system is considered as an element of modern vocational education. That is to say, it is mainly understood as the improvement of the implementing agencies at all levels of vocational education, the construction of an internal connection system, then on this basis the construction of a communication bridge with regular education, as well as the construction of a connection system that adapts to changes in the industrial structure.

However, the concept of "modern vocational education system" began to change in *Planning for Modern Vocational Education System Construction (2014–2020)* in 2014. The title of the document relates to the construction of a modern vocational education system. When explaining the goals for constructing a modern vocational education system, it follows the meaning of a modern vocational education system in previous documents: "In 2015, the framework of a modern vocational education system will have been established … levels of training will be more optimal; specialty structure will better adapt to market demand; secondary vocational education will be comprehensively connected with higher vocational education; industry-education integration and a school-enterprise cooperation system will be established; a modern vocational college system will be formed; the ability of vocational education to serve national development strategies will be further enhanced and vocational education will be more attractive." "By 2020, a modern vocational education system with Chinese characteristics will be basically established … the level and structure of the vocational education system will be more scientific, college layout and specialty settings will adapt to the needs of the economic sector."[34] This description about the extension of a modern vocational education system is basically the same as described in previous documents. The core remains: all kinds of implementing agencies of vocational education at all levels, the internal connection system, and the basic operating characteristics of this system. However, when stating the specifics of construction, this document encompasses all aspects of vocational education, which leads to a conceptual difference: does a modern vocational education system only refer to the school system or the entire vocational education system?

In terms of the modernization of the entire vocational education system, the vocational education circle has always used another phrase, namely "modern vocational education" instead of the phrase "modern vocational education system." As mentioned above, it is only used to refer to the modernized vocational education school system and its connections. It is particularly important to maintain conceptual stability for the development of theory and practice. People possibly intended to include more content while drafting this document. However, such expression led to confusion between the terms "modern vocational education" and "a modern vocational education system."

## 2. Local Practice in Constructing a Modern Vocational Education System

Under the guidance of national policies, local education administrative departments have actively promoted the construction of a modern vocational education system, which mainly focuses on establishing connections among secondary vocational education, higher vocational education, and technology-oriented undergraduate education. This is because in practice it is the most prominent problem. We can also consider it as the main implication of the word "modern" in a modern vocational education system. The work has been further carried out in Jiangsu province, Beijing, and Shanghai, but especially in Jiangsu province.

### 2.1. Practice in Jiangsu Province

Jiangsu province has established a modern vocational education system mainly in the following four forms:

1. "3+2" or "3+3" staged training in secondary vocational schools and higher vocational schools. That is to say, students shall spend 3 years on secondary vocational education, and 2 or 3 years on higher vocational education.

During the 5- or 6-year period of study, the counterpart pilot secondary vocational schools and higher vocational schools shall formulate a comprehensive, coordinated, interconnected teaching system to fit with students' theoretical knowledge courses and skills training course requirements at secondary and higher vocational level and systematically educate senior skilled students. Students of this project can enter higher vocational education through voluntary enrollment.

2. "3 + 4" staged training in secondary vocational schools and regular undergraduate colleges. That is to say, students shall spend 3 years in secondary vocational education and 4 years in regular undergraduate education. During the 7-year period of study, the counterpart pilot secondary vocational schools and undergraduate colleges shall formulate a coordinated, comprehensive, and interconnected teaching system to fit with students' theoretical knowledge courses and skills training course requirements, and systematically cultivate high-end technical professionals at undergraduate level. Students of this project can enter undergraduate education through the counterpart qualifying recruitment standards. For the "3+4" model, the test content focuses on professional skills and an academic level of secondary vocational education subjects. The standards are jointly formulated by undergraduate colleges and secondary vocational schools and submitted to Jiangsu Provincial Education Examination Authority for validation.
3. Staged training in higher vocational schools and regular undergraduate colleges. That is to say, students shall spend 3 years in higher vocational education (5 years in five-year higher vocational education); after passing a qualification exam, students shall spend 2 years in regular undergraduate education. During the period of study, the counterpart pilot higher vocational schools and undergraduate colleges shall formulate a coordinated, comprehensive, and interconnected teaching system to fit with students' theoretical knowledge courses and skills training courses, and systematically cultivate high-end technical students at undergraduate level. Undergraduate enrollment of this project can include a "specialized subject to undergraduate course" channel, and a "specialized subject to undergraduate course" selection method is jointly formulated by undergraduate colleges and higher vocational schools and then submitted to Jiangsu Provincial Education Examination Authority for validation.
4. Joint training by higher vocational education and regular undergraduate education. Higher vocational schools cooperate with regular undergraduate colleges and universities to jointly recruit students through an

undergraduate college enrollment plan for "second tier universities" and cultivate four-year undergraduate high-end technical professionals. During the study period, the counterpart pilot higher vocational schools and undergraduate colleges and universities shall formulate a coordinated, comprehensive, interconnected and teaching system to fit with students' theoretical knowledge courses and skills training courses according to the standards of cultivating undergraduate applied students and the requirements for high-end technicians, in order to make sure that students in higher vocational schools and undergraduate colleges and universities study in flexible and diverse ways, as well as to cultivate undergraduate applied technicians with high-level technical skills.

### 2.2. Practice in Beijing

Beijing's modern vocational education system is characterized by the construction of a hierarchical education system. According to their understanding, hierarchical vocational education is an expandable vocational education staged hierarchy, which is established with postsecondary education diversion as the origin and the 5-level structure as the main body, to adapt to the complicated requirements for the social division of labor and the characteristics of workforce hierarchical structures, by comprehensively referring to the established student evaluation standards for skill and technology, school education systems, vocational qualification systems, and the general features of social organizations and enterprise management structures, transnational enterprise training systems and experience of international vocational education systems (see Figure 4.6).[35] On this basis, it is necessary to further establish a progressive relationship and inter-linking mechanisms for different standards and functions at different levels within the hierarchical vocational education system, establish open mechanisms and operational rules for the requirements of the economic sector and people's learning, and form a series of systems and norms to instruct vocational educational institutions to carry out education activities and guide educators to receive vocational education.

The explanations of each level of vocational education are as follows:

1. Vocational education level 1 and level 2 belong to "basic vocational education," with the purpose of training junior and intermediate workers with certain skill levels. Vocational education level 1 is mainly related to the vocational preparation education after the stage of compulsory education. It aims to assist the incoming labor force to meet the entry criteria of basic vocational qualifications, and cultivate junior workers with necessary professional qualities and basic skills so that they can work in non-technical posts or simple skill-oriented posts. Vocational education level 2

is equivalent to secondary vocational education under the current system. It mainly trains intermediate workers with certain professional qualities and skill levels for front-line production and service, who can work in general skill-oriented posts.

2. Vocational education level 3 and level 4 belong to "enhanced vocational education," with the purpose of cultivating practical and applied high-quality skilled workers. Vocational education level 3 belongs to vocational preparation education after senior high school. It aims to cultivate skilled workers with good professional qualities and certain management abilities, who can work in moderately complex skill-oriented posts and assistant management posts. Vocational education level 4 is equivalent to higher vocational education under the current system. It trains highly skilled people with good professional qualities for front-line production, construction, management, and service, who can work in comparatively complicated skill-oriented and management posts.

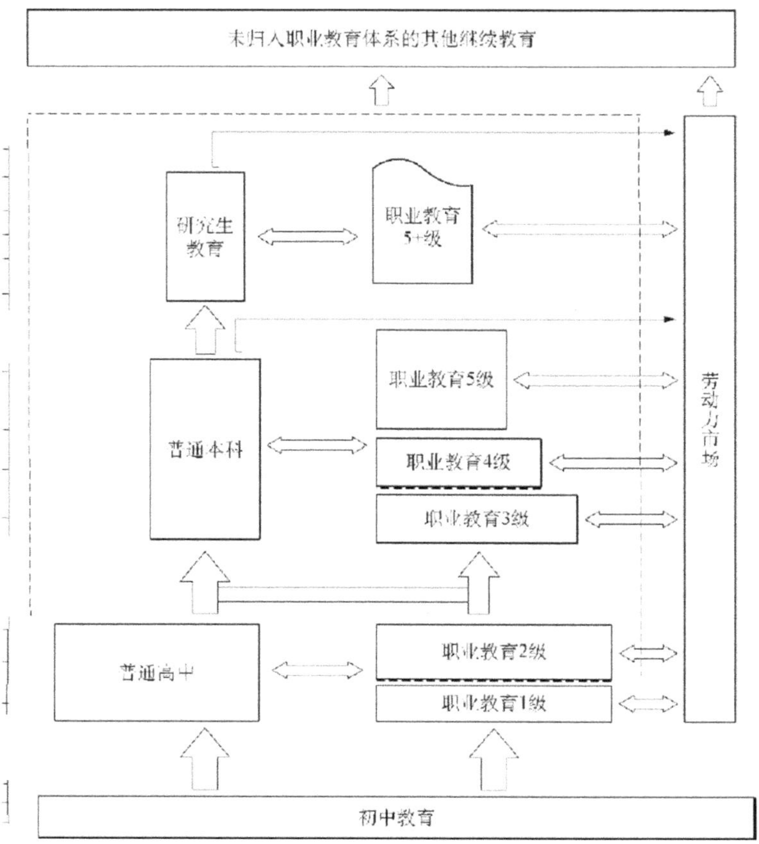

| | |
|---|---|
| 未归入职业教育体系的其他继续教育 | Other kinds of continuing education that are not included in the vocational education system |
| 研究生教育 | Postgraduate education |
| 普通本科 | Regular undergraduate |
| 普通高中 | Regular senior high school |
| 初中教育 | Junior middle school education |
| 职业教育5+级 | Vocational education level 5+ |
| 职业教育5级 | Vocational education level 5 |
| 职业教育4级 | Vocational education level 4 |
| 职业教育3级 | Vocational education level 3 |
| 职业教育2级 | Vocational education level 2 |
| 职业教育1级 | Vocational education level 1 |
| 劳动力市场 | Labor market |

Figure 4.6 The concept of a staged hierarchy of Beijing vocational education

3. Vocational education level 5 and level "5+" belong to "expandable vocational education." Vocational education level 5 mainly cultivates applied technological professionals with high professional qualities, cultural qualities, competencies, and abilities, who can work in complex technology-oriented and important management posts. Vocational education level "5+ " cultivates top-line graduates who have a professional spirit, a pioneering sense, leadership, innovative capacity, the ability to solve major production tasks, and key technical problems of major engineering projects, and can engage in design R&D, engineering technology, and senior management posts. Among these levels, level "5+" is open-ended. Some specialties may, with the development of science and technology, reach above level "5+," or more possibly, level 6, level 7, or higher.

They believe that this hierarchical design has formed a vocational education system with bottom-up training objectives, progressive training standards, smooth cohesion between education content and requirements, an open and flexible admission system and forms, rigorous and scientific quality assurance and assessment.

## 2.3. Practice in Shanghai

Shanghai puts forward in the *Planning on the Construction of Modern Vocational Education System in Shanghai (2014–2030)* that various forms should be adopted on the basis of strengthening higher vocational education and actively developing and applying undergraduate education, so as to broaden the cohesive channels between secondary vocational education and junior college education, between junior college education and undergraduate education, and establish a smooth career development path (see Figure 4.7). A total of 9 cohesive paths are designed:

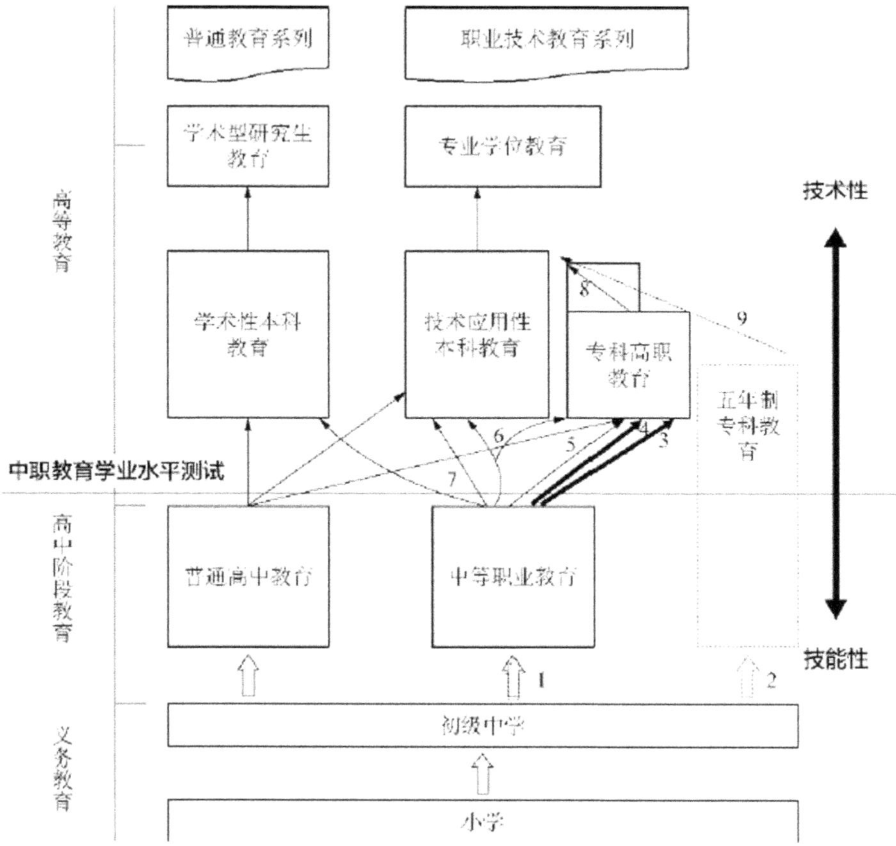


| | |
|---|---|
| 高等教育 | Higher education |
| 普通教育系列 | Regular education series |
| 学术型研究生教育 | Academic postgraduate education |

| | |
|---|---|
| 学术性本科教育 | Academic undergraduate education |
| 职业技术教育系列 | Vocational and technical education series |
| 专业学位教育 | Professional degree education |
| 技术应用性本科教育 | Technological applicable undergraduate education |
| 专科高职教育 | Specialist higher vocational education |
| 五年制专科教育 | Five-year specialist education |
| 中职教育学业水平测试 | Secondary vocational academic proficiency test |
| 高中阶段教育 | Senior high school education |
| 义务教育 | Compulsory education |
| 普通高中教育 | Regular senior high school education |
| 中等职业教育 | Secondary vocational education |
| 初级中学 | Junior middle school |
| 小学 | Primary school |
| 技术性 | Technology-oriented |
| 技能性 | Skill-oriented |

Figure 4.7 The concept for school cohesive paths based on a modern vocational education system in Shanghai

Note: The dashed line shows the school types or paths that do not exist in Shanghai. The orientation of the educational nature of professional degrees still remains controversial, so this diagram shall not discuss its cohesion for the time being. Vocational education series upgrades with the academic levels; the skill component of student cultivation gradually weakens and the technique component gradually increases.

Path 1: Enter secondary vocational education through the senior high school entrance examination. This path is an existing and mature academic path from compulsory education to senior high school education. It is necessary to further reform the internal specialty establishment and perfect the specialty layout so that the specialty structure can better match the industrial labor demands.

Path 2: Enter a five-year specialist education through the senior high school entrance examination (however, Shanghai had not established a five-year junior college up to the deadline of this book).

Path 3: Interconnected training in secondary vocational education and higher vocational education. It has become the main path for secondary vocational school students to enter higher education.

Path 4: Enter specialist higher vocational education through independent enrollment. This path requires further improvement of the independent school entrance examination system, and highlights professional examinations and skill examinations in accordance with major categories of professional examinations.

Path 5: Enter specialist higher vocational education or applied technological undergraduate education through the counterpart college entrance examination. It is the main path for secondary vocational school students in Shanghai to enter higher education. However, it is necessary to further improve the counterpart college entrance examination system and make it accord with material selection of vocational education and consistency in cultivating students.

Path 6: Enter higher education through the common college entrance examination. This path requires further perfection of the college entrance examination system and makes it accord with material selection of vocational education and consistency in cultivating students.

Path 7: Interconnected training in secondary vocational education—applied undergraduate education ("3+4").

Path 8: Cohesive training in specialist education—applied undergraduate education (specialist origin "3+2").

Path 9: Cohesive training in five-year specialist education—applied undergraduate education (five-year specialist origin "5+2"). It aims to incorporate the advantages of the scheme for a continuous course of five years in curriculum integration and further connect to the continuous training of undergraduate education. However, the premise is to establish five-year specialist education.

## 3. A Design to Achieve the Construction of a Modern Vocational Education System in China

As mentioned above, in current practice, the key to constructing a modern vocational education system is to establish an internally cohesive system for vocational education. From the solutions to this problem at home and abroad, there are two paths: 1. Cohesion at entity level. That is, to establish a cohesive relationship between specific secondary and higher vocational schools and technological applicable undergraduate universities. Secondary and higher vocational schools and technological applicable undergraduate universities, which have the desire to establish a cohesive relationship, are required to sign an agreement first. Then, education administrative departments will organize experts to conduct project appraisals. Schools whose projects pass the appraisal process will obtain an enrollment plan and then implement integrated training for students. Students of this kind of project can enter higher education schools without participating in the unified college entrance examination. This model has been adopted by the U.S. National Education Technology Plan (NETP). Such institutions as community colleges, local vocational and technical training schools, comprehensive secondary (high) schools, four-year colleges or universities, various apprentice organizations and private educational institutions are required by the federal government to participate and sign an agreement on the implementation of "NETP."[36] The practice as described earlier in Jiangsu and Shanghai also belongs to this model, which plays a dominant role in constructing an internally consistent system of vocational education in China. 2. Cohesion at criteria level. That is, to link up the professional teaching standards of secondary vocational education, higher vocational education, and technological applicable undergraduate education, so as to enable students to obtain a smooth path to further study within vocational education. This model is adopted by Britain and Australia. The practice in Beijing is striving for this. Compared with consistency at institutional level, consistency at criteria level transcends specific educational institutions, and realizes the overall cohesion of the vocational education curriculum system. It not only achieves the goal of consistency and cohesion, but also provides students with enormous choices. Therefore, it is the ultimate goal that the construction of a modern vocational education system should pursue.

We can't say the consistency of system construction at the sponsoring entity level is wrong. This is because, achieving consistency between secondary and higher vocational education (including consistency within applied technology undergraduate education) is not as simple as achieving this between senior high school education and university education. Senior high school education and university education are two completely different types of education, and there is no conflict or contradiction between them. However, secondary vocational education and higher vocational education belong to two levels of education of the same nature. Many internal complicated and paradoxical problems need to be resolved. If we do not achieve consistency between secondary vocational education and higher vocational education at sponsoring entity level, then the cohesion between them is likely to fail. From the enrollment perspective, for example, even if clear corresponding relations and ideal professional teaching standards at all levels are established between the specialty catalogues of various levels of vocational education, the counterpart specialties and standards could still fail to be fully integrated into the training of technical skills because of students' excessive freedom in specialty selection while pursuing their educational goals. Another example: while a cohesive relationship will be finally implemented within student training, cohesion at this level can only be achieved with the support of the cohesion of teachers. Only by establishing the cohesive relationship on the basis of the cooperation of the sponsoring entities can this cohesive relationship be constructed.

However, it is not nearly enough only to conceptualize the consistency required to achieve cohesion between secondary vocational education and higher vocational education at the sponsoring entity level. This is because the cohesion between secondary vocational education and high vocational education at this level is only a partial cohesion, and it is impossible to form a consistent system. The ultimate goal of establishing a modern vocational education system in China is to set up a professional teaching standard system based on the cohesion between secondary and higher vocational education. *Instructions of MOE on Promoting the Coordinated Development between Secondary and Higher Vocational Education* (No. 9 [2011] from the Department of Vocational and Adult Education, MOE) realized the importance of this issue and proposed to "gradually prepare professional teaching standards that are consistent between secondary and higher vocational education."[37] However, this is a scientific and professional job. At present, the construction difficulty in this field in China mainly lies in the organization and implementation in the development process rather than the mastery of development techniques.

## Notes

1 Yang Jintu: Review of the Development History of Chinese Higher Vocational Education in the 20th Century, Vocational & Technical Education Forum, No. 13, 2017.
2 State Council: Report on Accelerating the Development of Higher Education, 1983.
3 CPC Central Committee: Decision of the CPC Central Committee on the Reform of the Education System, 1985.
4 State Council: Decision of the State Council on Vigorously Developing Vocational and Technical Education, 1991.
5 Yang Jintu: Review of the Development History of Chinese Higher Vocational Education in the 20th Century, Vocational & Technical Education Forum, No. 13, 2017.
6 State Council: Opinions of the State Council on the Implementation of "Outline of China's Education Reform and Development", 1994.
7 MOE: Action Plan for Education Rejuvenation for the 21st Century, 1998.
8 MOE: Opinions of the Trial Implementation on Developing Higher Vocational and Technical Education According to New Management Modes and Operational Mechanisms, 1999.
9 State Council: Decision of the CPC Central Committee and the State Council on Deepening Education Reform and Comprehensively Promoting Quality Education, 1999.
10 MOE: Opinions of MOE on Reinforcing the Cultivation of Higher Vocational and Technical Talents, 2002.
11 MOE: Opinions on Being Employment-Oriented and Deepening the Reform of Higher Vocational Education, 2004.
12 MOE: Notice on Supporting Higher Vocational Schools to Improve the Ability of Developing Professional Service Industries, 2011.

13 MOE: Standards Setting for Higher Vocational Schools (Provisional), 2000.
14 MOE: Action Plan for Education Rejuvenation for the 21st Century 1998.
15 MOE, MOF: Opinions on Implementing the Construction Plan of National Demonstrative Higher Vocational Colleges and Accelerating the Reform and Development of Higher Vocational Education, 2006.
16 MOE: Several Opinions on Comprehensively Improving the Teaching Quality of Higher Vocational Education, 2006.
17 MOE: Several Opinions on Comprehensively Improving the Teaching Quality of Higher Vocational Education, 2006.
18 MOE: Notice on Supporting Higher Vocational Schools to Improve the Ability of Developing Professional Service Industries, 2011.
19 Yan Xueyi: On Vocational and Technical Education, Shanghai Scientific and Technological Literature Press, 1999.
20 Office of National Medium-and Long-Term Education Reform and Development Plan: Outline of the National Medium-and Long-Term Education Reform and Development Plan (2010–2020), 2010.
21 MOE: Instructions of MOE on Further Promoting Educational Reform and Cooperative Development in Yangtze River Delta, 2014.
22 State Council: Decision of the State Council on Accelerating the Development of Modern Vocational Education, 2014.
23 Six departments including MOE: Planning for Modern Vocational Education System Construction (2014–2020), 2014.
24 MOE: Opinions of MOE on the Work of Setting Up Colleges and Universities during the "Thirteenth Five-Year Plan" Period, 2017.
25 State Council: The "Thirteenth Five-Year" Plan for China's Educational Development, 2017.
26 Cingta Query: The 181 Universities are a Step Ahead of Other Universities in Transforming Themselves into Application-Oriented Universities, http://www.360doc.com/content/16/0311/14/7592490_541311539.shtml.
27 Pan Manyuan: My View on the Orientation of Application-Oriented Undergraduate Colleges and Universities, Research in Education Development, No. 21, 2007.
28 CPC Central Committee: Decision of the Central Committee of the CPC on the Reform of the Education System, 1985.
29 State Council: Decision of the State Council on Vigorously Developing Vocational and Technical Education, 1991.
30 The Nineteenth Session of the Eighth National People's Congress: Vocational Education Law of the People's Republic of China, 1996.
31 State Council: Decision of the State Council on Vigorously Promoting the Reform and Development of Vocational Education, 2002.
32 Office of National Medium-and Long-Term Education Reform and Development Plan: Outline of the National Medium-and Long-Term Education Reform and Development Plan (2010–2020), 2010.
33 State Council: Decision of the State Council on Accelerating the Development of Modern Vocational Education, 2014.
34 MOE: Planning for Modern Vocational Education System Construction (2014–2020), 2014.

35 Li Yuhong: Research on the Classification System of Vocational Education—On the Construction of Classification Standards for Marketing Vocational Education, China Fortune Press, 2012.
36 Stewart, B.R. & Bristow, D.H. (1997) Tech prep programs: the role and essential elements, in Journal of vocational and technical education, Volume 13, Number 2.
37 MOE: Instructions of MOE on Promoting the Coordinated Development between Secondary and Higher Vocational Education, 2011.
38 National Bureau of Statistics: China Statistical Yearbook (2016), http://www.stats.gov.cn/tjsj/ndsj/2016/indexch.htm.

CHAPTER FIVE

# Developing Vocational Education Based on the Needs of Industry and Enterprises

It is an important mission for modern vocational education to promote school-enterprise cooperation as the basis for the successful construction of school-operating entities. Cooperation with the business sector in workforce training is a basic rule for the operation of vocational education at all times all over the world. The differences between vocational education patterns in various countries are largely reflected in the proportion of responsibilities that schools and enterprises assume. For example, Japanese enterprises assume the primary responsibility for vocational education, and many enterprises have established excellent vocational training systems; German enterprises cooperate with vocational schools in student training, and exert their influence in workforce training under the world-renowned "dual system"; U.S. schools assume the primary responsibility for vocational education, and enterprises have participated in training vocational students through various programs. However, regardless of the patterns, "enterprise's involvement" is the foundation for developing vocational education well. Without enterprise involvement, vocational education will have difficulty in making progress with curriculum development, teacher training, and the implementation of modern apprenticeship schemes. Before reform and opening-up, China implemented a planned economy. Under this economic model, it was easy to solve the problem of enterprises' involvement in student training in vocational education. At that time, the two main implementation institutions of vocational education, secondary technical training schools and vocational schools, were either operated by economic departments or by enterprises; vocational education entrenched itself deeply in industry and enterprise. After reform and opening-up, however, the connection between enterprise and vocational school gradually disintegrated as a result of the market economy. In order to rebuild this connection, all school-operating levels of vocational education have made extremely strenuous efforts.

Figure 5.1 Hangzhou Vocational & Technical College signing the cooperation agreement with the Fair Friend Enterprise Group

## Part 1 The Policy Path to Promoting School-Enterprise Cooperation

Through an analysis of relevant documents, we find there are three main intertwined concepts on this topic: industry-education integration, school-enterprise cooperation, and a combination of work-study (there are also many similar concepts, such as industry-academy cooperation). The three concepts are actually three levels of the same thing: industry-education integration as a concept at the system level, that is, the integration of industry systems and education systems; school-enterprise cooperation as a concept at the entity level, that is, the cooperation between vocational schools and enterprises; work-study combination as a concept at the learning and teaching level, that is, the combining of work and study. As a frequently used concept, "school-enterprise cooperation" can be divided into a broad sense and a narrow sense. The broad sense of school-enterprise cooperation includes industry-education integration, school-enterprise cooperation (in a narrow sense), and combining work-study, whereas the narrow sense of school-enterprise cooperation only refers to school-enterprise cooperation at the entity level. Sometimes we also see such concepts as industry-university-research (referring to scientific research institutions) cooperation and industry-university-government cooperation, which can be considered as an extended concept of school-enterprise cooperation (some may be redundant). Vocational education operation is confronted with the prominent problem of establishing a cooperative relationship between schools and enterprises. We can divide the development of China's school-enterprise cooperation policies since reform and opening-up into three stages:

## 1. School-Enterprise Cooperation at the Subconscious Stage

We should pay attention to establishing connections with the industrial sector while operating vocational education. From the intellectual history of vocational education, this connection can be said to have come into being since the birth of modern vocational education in China. The earliest vocational schools in China were established by the advocates of the Westernization Movement. Mr. Huang Yanpei, a pioneer of vocational education during the period of the Republic of China, was perfectly conscious of this problem. He wrote: "Positively speaking, those who operate vocational schools must simultaneously communicate and be in contact with all educational and professional circles; those who advocate vocational education also need to devote some effort to participate in the progress of the whole society."[1]

However, in the first 20 years after reform and opening-up, "school-enterprise cooperation" did not feature prominently in important documents of the state and MOE and was usually skated over in one sentence. These documents were conscious of school-enterprise cooperation, but this consciousness was still at a relatively vague level, much less of a thorough design of the implementation strategies of school-enterprise cooperation. Therefore, it is called "the subconscious stage." There may be two reasons for this: 1. People mainly attached importance to how to restore and develop vocational schools at that time, and had not enough time to think about the deep-seated problems of the implications for the construction of vocational education. 2. Industry and enterprise were highly enthusiastic about participating in vocational education at that time, and assumed considerable responsibilities in fact. For example, secondary technical training schools were operated by economic sectors, and technical training schools were operated by enterprises. So, the problem of school-enterprise cooperation was not very prominent. The hidden reason behind this was that China's economy was still highly planned by the end of the 1990s.

This can be seen from careful analysis of the documents that are of great significance to the development of vocational education since reform and opening-up. The *Decision of the CPC Central Committee on the Reform of the Education System* in 1985 did not specifically address the issue of school-enterprise cooperation, and just mentioned that "secondary vocational and technical education must be closely integrated with the requirements of economic and social development." At the same time, it was emphasized that we should fully activate the enthusiasm of enterprises, public institutions, and operating departments to develop vocational education. The two statements are not the same concept as school-enterprise cooperation we discuss here. The former talks about the need for vocational education to serve economic and social development functionally, while the latter talks about how to expand the operating forces of vocational education.

There was just an understatement in the *Decision of the State Council on Vigorously Developing Vocational and Technical Education* in 1991: "All kinds of vocational and technical training schools and training centers should actively develop school-operating industries and manage production practice bases well according to their teaching needs and conditions. Industry-education integration and combining work-study should be advocated."[2] The two important concepts of "industry-education integration" and "combining work-study" appeared here. However, they were not raised as important issues and the implications were not elaborated either.

In the *Outline of China's Education Reform and Development* (No. 3 [1993] from the CPC Central Committee) in 1993, we can only find a relevant statement: "We should, under the guidance of the government, advocate joint school operations, take the road of industry-education integration, make more use of loans to develop school-operating industries, enhance schools' self-development capacities, and gradually achieve a factory (farm)-for-school scheme."[3] The purpose of "industry-education integration" here is not to reform the student training model, but to solve the problem of insufficient funds for vocational education through the factory (farm)-for-school scheme, and enhance the self-development capacities of vocational schools. Under the direction of this document, establishing school-operating enterprises and "breaking down walls for opening shops" were very prevalent in vocational schools in the 1990s. These economic behavior in vocational schools did enhance economic strength at the very beginning. However, this kind of behavior subsequently diverted school educational resources away and was not related to schools' student training on the one hand, while some economic corruption problems also appeared on the other hand. As a result, these behaviors were gradually alleviated and terminated due to the difficulties in finding funds for operating schools.

*Vocational Education Law of the People's Republic of China* in 1996 put forward this issue from the perspective of vocational schools: "While implementing vocational education, vocational schools and vocational training institutions should integrate industry with education, serve regional economic construction, keep close contact with enterprises and cultivate practical and proficient workers."[4] The starting point is simply to improve the industrial service functions of vocational education without basing them on the establishment of school-enterprise cooperation while an understanding of its implications is quite superficial.

The *Action Plan for Education Revitalization for the 21st Century* in 1998 devotes a great deal of time to the development of vocational education and adult education, but it only mechanically mentions that: "Vocational education and adult education should take the road of industry-education integration."[5]

## 2. School-Enterprise Cooperation at the Conscious Stage

In the 21st century, the status of school-enterprise cooperation in important documents has changed markedly. It is reflected in: 1. increasingly prominent status; 2. increasing length; 3. more and more detailed and in-depth expositions on the content. All these reflect the fact that school-enterprise cooperation has become the core of vocational education in our country. The possible reasons are: 1. With more and more attention to the underlying structure of vocational education, people are increasingly conscious of the great significance of school-enterprise cooperation to successfully operating vocational education. 2. At the end of the 20th century, secondary vocational education suffered a sharp decline in enrollments. Confronted with this dilemma, people proposed two ways to explore the way out: one was to highlight the regular education component in vocational education, such as operating comprehensive secondary (high) schools; the other was to truly develop a distinctive vocational education, such as the proposal of an "employment-oriented" goal. Although people widely debated the "employment-oriented" policy, we finally chose the latter in practice. People have profoundly understood that the fundamental way for developing vocational education lies in developing a distinctive vocational education. School-enterprise cooperation is the most distinguishing feature of vocational education. 3. As the reform of economic system deepens, economic sectors and enterprises have drastically withdrawn from vocational education and thus the reestablishment of the school-enterprise cooperation relationship has become a problem that vocational education must make great efforts to solve. People explicitly realized the importance of school-enterprise cooperation in this period and began to focus on specific issues as to how to push the cooperation further. Therefore, this period is called the conscious state. Research literature on school-enterprise cooperation substantially increased during this period.

The *Decision of the State Council on Vigorously Promoting Vocational Education Reform and Development* (No. 16 [2002] from the State Council) in 2002 is the first document that gives high priority to school-enterprise cooperation. The title of the second section of the document is: "Promote the reform of the management system and the school-operating system, facilitate vocational education to be closely integrated with economic construction and social development." Although there is no explicit adoption of school-enterprise cooperation or other similar concepts, that is what the sentence "facilitate vocational education to be closely integrated with economic construction and social development" intends to express. Moreover, this sentence positioned the reform at the level of management systems and school-operating systems. However, in terms of specific content, it is a pity that this section mainly elaborates the reform of the school-operating system, focuses on establishing and gradually improving the hierarchical, localized, government-coordinated, socially engaged vocational education management system under the leadership of the State Council, without enough explanation about how to facilitate vocational education close integration with economic construction and social development. In the section of "Deepen educational and teaching reform; adapt to social and corporate needs," the document clearly proposes the task of establishing a school-enterprise cooperation mechanism: "Strengthen the relations between vocational schools and employers such as enterprises and industries, and establish a mechanism which can closely integrate vocational schools with the labor market."[6] But it goes only so far, without more profound content. Therefore, this stage can only be called "the conscious stage."

In 2004, MOE released the *Action Plan for Education Rejuvenation in 2003–2007*. The section on vocational education is entitled "Take employment as the orientation and work hard to transform the school-operating pattern of vocational education," which systematically sets forth the specific mission of constructing school-enterprise cooperation: "Aim at employment promotion, further transform the guiding ideology of higher vocational and technical colleges and secondary vocational and technical training schools, implement diverse, flexible and open student training patterns, integrate education and teaching with production practice, social services and technology promotion, strengthen the training of practical teaching and employability. Enhance the collaboration with industries, enterprises, units of scientific research and technology promotion, propel 'customized training' and 'modular training' models; explore ability-oriented teaching models for the requirements of job groups; be market-oriented, consistently develop new specialties, reform curriculum provisions, adjust teaching content; strengthen professional ethics education; vigorously enhance the cultivation of 'double-quality' teachers, and encourage professionals, managers and personnel with special skills in enterprises and public institutions to serve as full-time and part-time teachers."[7] The content structure of this text is actually not rigorous enough; however, its significance lies in the statement that school-enterprise cooperation has evolved from a prominent position in the document to a stage of deepening its specific content, and produced many new concepts at that time, such as customized training models and "double-quality" teachers.

In order to implement this plan, seven departments including MOE issued *Several Opinions of Seven Departments including MOE on Further Enhancing Vocational Education* in 2004, in which the concept of "school-enterprise cooperation" was officially proposed for the first time: "Vocational colleges must persist in service-guided and employment-oriented principles, be society-oriented and market-oriented when operating schools, propel industry-education integration and reinforce school-enterprise cooperation."[8] But the expression goes only so far.

## 3. School-Enterprise Cooperation at the Systematic Design Stage

After brief deliberation, while continuing to retain its prominent status, school-enterprise cooperation begins to appear in a number of important documents and its content is distinctly more embodied and systematized. This shows that our country has begun to systematically design and carry forward school-enterprise cooperation, and it has become the core content of the national policies on vocational education.

The *Decision of the State Council on Vigorously Developing Vocational Education* (No. 35 [2005] from the State Council) in 2005 is the first document that systematically elaborates school-enterprise cooperation. In this document, there are three sections that are most closely linked to school-enterprise cooperation: 1. Adhere to employment orientation and deepen the reform of vocational education: "Work hard to carry forward the training model of combining work-study and school-enterprise cooperation. Closely connect with enterprises, reinforce students' productive fieldwork and social practice and reform the traditional student training model which centers on schools and classrooms. Secondary vocational school students must go to the employing units such as enterprises for work experience in the last year. Higher vocational college students shall spend no less on half a year on practical training. Establish a system for enterprises to receive vocational college students for internships ..." 2. Actively facilitate institutional reform and innovation and improve the development vitality of vocational education. Specifically, "promote joint school operation by public vocational schools and enterprises and form a school-operating entity which is an integration of school and enterprise with school ahead and factory (farm) behind. Promote the integration and reconfiguration of public vocational school resources, and take the road of scaled, collectivized and chain-oriented school operations." 3. Develop vocational education on the basis of industrial enterprises and propel the close integration of vocational colleges and enterprises. To be specific, "competent authorities of industries and industry associations should, under the guidance of national education guidelines and policies, carry out prediction of labor demand within the industry, formulate education and training programs, organize and guide vocational education and training in the industry; participate in the formulation of vocational qualification standards, vocational skills appraisal and certificate issuance for the unique types of work in the industry; participate in formulating professional qualification standards, professional skills appraisal and certificate issuance for specific types of positions in the industry; involve in formulating competence baselines for training institutions and qualification criterion for practitioners; take part in national education and teaching evaluation and related management over vocational colleges and universities."[9]

Here, we select three statements that are directly related to school-enterprise cooperation. Besides, some other contents are more or less related to school-enterprise cooperation, such as faculty development. This document has 6,677 words in total (in Chinese). In such an extremely important document, school-enterprise cooperation is endowed with such a prominent status and length, which shows how profound the understanding was and how much people were concerned with its significance at that time. This document also forms the basic principles of school-enterprise cooperation construction: 1. At the country level, it facilitates competent authorities of industries and industry associations to participate in vocational education and embodies the content of industry-education integration; 2. At the level of school-operating systems, it allows enterprises to participate in operating vocational colleges in various forms; 3. At the teaching model level, it mainly fosters the cultivation of students' practical abilities.

This policy framework has been extended in subsequent work plans and important documents by MOE. *Main Points for the Work of the State Council in 2006* requires: "Vigorously promote combining work-study practices and school-enterprise cooperation, establish and improve the work experience system for students, and carry out pilot work-study programs."[10] *Main Points for the Work of the State Council in 2007* requires: "Work hard to promote the concepts and systems of school-enterprise cooperation, combining work-study and work-study programs."[11]

*Main Points for the Work of the State Council in 2008* requires vigorously developing vocational education and focusing on quality improvement: "Deepen the reform of vocational education and teaching. Vigorously carry forward school-enterprise co-operation and work-study programs, improve and gradually implement the system of one-year work experience in secondary vocational education and half-year work experience in higher vocational education and endeavor to improve the system of work-study programs. Extensively carry out customized training."[12] *Main Points for the Work of the State Council in 2009* continues to require: "Vigorously promote school-enterprise cooperation and combining work-study and actively promote work-study programs, learning and working alternation, and work experience."[13] These statements are basically consistent and the policies are stable.

*Outline of the National Medium-and Long-Term Education Reform and Development Plan (2010–2020)* follows on from the above statement: "Adhere to the service-guided and employment-oriented principle, promote education and teaching reform. Implement the student training model of combining work-study, school-enterprise cooperation and work experience." At the same time, it is particularly important to strengthen the guiding role of the industries institutionalized school-enterprise cooperation, and construct a stable mechanism for enterprises to participate in vocational education: "Arouse the enthusiasm of industrial enterprises. Establish and improve the school-operating mechanisms which is led by government, guided by the industry and participated in by enterprises, formulate laws and regulations to promote school-enterprise co-operation, and drive institutionalized school-enterprise cooperation."[14] Then in 2011, MOE issued *Opinions of MOE on Emphasizing the Guiding Role of Industries and Promoting the Reform and Development of Vocational Education* (No. 6 [2011] from the Department of Vocational and Adult Education, MOE), and proposed: "Encourage industry and enterprise to fully participate in all levels of education and teaching," "Promote the school-operating pattern of industry-education integration and school-enterprise cooperation, achieve the connection of professions with industry, enterprise and work role," "To emphasize the role of the teaching-guidance committees of industrial vocational education," and "Simplify the instruction system and working mechanisms of the vocational school education and teaching industry. Vocational schools should establish institutions for school-operating consultation, specialty setting assessment and teaching guidance in which industry and enterprise participate."[15] Under the guidance of these documents, vocational education teaching-guidance committees of various industries have been established.

Since then, almost all the important documents have continued the above expressions, without much innovation in content. So, I will not list them all here.

# Part 2 Overview of the Practice of School-Enterprise Cooperation

Under the guidance of national policies, vocational colleges have carried out extensive exploration and practice in school-enterprise cooperation. The following is an analysis of the progress of school-enterprise cooperation from two levels: the overall progress and case practice. The analysis is difficult to thoroughly cover the overall situation of school-enterprise cooperation. This is because such practices carried in China's vocational education are too varied in their content.

## 1. Analysis of the Overall Progress of School-Enterprise Cooperation

Prior to analysis, it is necessary to establish that the practice of school-enterprise cooperation was not started until relevant policies are promulgated, and practices and policies are interactional. The practice of operating vocational colleges must be carried out under the guidance of national policies without doubt. We can see almost all vocational colleges focused on school-enterprise cooperation after 2005; they adopted multiple approaches to make use of resources as much as possible, and implemented diversified practice patterns of school-enterprise cooperation. However, before the official release of the documents, some local practices rapidly developed. This is because, before extensive practice, there are many pilot projects which often preceded universal policies intended for vocational colleges. For example, in terms of school-enterprise cooperation, some places started to introduce the German "dual system" model as early as the 1980s. In 1983, China cooperated with Germany to establish the architecture vocational education center in Nanjing, then established the Second Automobile Vocational Education Center in Second Automobile Works Co. in China (now Dongfeng Motor Corporation), and then collaboratively built the Shanghai Electronic School.[16]

The following survey reports reflect the general conditions of school-enterprise cooperation.

1. In 2009, the China Association of Staff and Workers Education and Vocational Training published *School-Enterprise Cooperation Has Become a Normal Teaching Model in Technical Training Schools—Research Report on the Cultivation of Chinese Technical Students* in *Vocational and Technical Education.*[17] In the survey, 200 questionnaires were released and 150 were collected; the respondents were 42 technician colleges, 96 senior technician schools, and 12 regular technical schools. The research conclusions,

which are worthy of comment, include: ① Currently, the overwhelming majority of technical schools and vocational schools have widely realized that only by cooperating with enterprises can they foster talented students that truly meet the requirements of enterprises and social production; most schools have adopted school-enterprise cooperation as a normal model of school teaching and realistically implemented it in daily teaching; a considerable number of enterprises have accepted the teaching model of school-enterprise cooperation. ② The schools and enterprises that carry out school-enterprise cooperation have basic guarantees in funding, and enterprises have basically accepted that school-enterprise cooperation students will come to take internships. ③ Manufacturing is the most common specialty carried out by school-enterprise cooperation. ④ The main problems faced by current school-enterprise cooperation are: first, the enthusiasm of enterprises to participate in school-enterprise cooperation; second, the system construction of relevant national policies. These two issues are actually closely related to each other.

2. Wang Wenjin published the *Survey Report on School-Enterprise Cooperation in Enterprises* in *Chinese Vocational and Technical Education* in 2009.[18] The survey scope of the report covers six places, Beijing, Tianjin, Jiangsu, Guangdong, Shandong, and Wenzhou and the number of enterprises surveyed was 135. The research conclusions, which are worthy of comment, include: ① Most enterprises well understand all the national documents concerning school-enterprise cooperation; ② Enterprises participate in school-enterprise cooperation mainly in the form of providing various practice opportunities; ③ Most cooperation is a superficial cooperative relationship; no long-term and stable cooperative relationships have been established yet; most enterprises believe that the current school-enterprise cooperation lacks a long-term mechanism; ④ Enterprises are widely concerned that interns lack security guarantees; ⑤ What enterprises hope to obtain from school-enterprise cooperation is a qualified reserve of human resources.
3. Bi Jieli and Wang Lin published *Survey and Analysis Report on Skilled Student Training through School-Enterprise Cooperation* in *China Training* in 2010.[19] This report covers more than a dozen provinces and cities including Beijing, Tianjin, Hebei, Shandong, Heilongjiang, Guangdong, Shanxi, Gansu, and Anhui and 100 enterprises are surveyed in this report. The research conclusions, which are worthy of mention, include: ① The proportion of small-scale enterprises, which carry out school-enterprise cooperation, is lower than that of large-scale enterprises. Large enterprise

leaders have a better understanding of the significance of school-enterprise cooperation than small enterprise leaders; ② The manufacturing industry has the largest number of enterprises participating in school-enterprise cooperation; ③Human resources department managers have a deeper understanding of school-enterprise cooperation than enterprise leaders, and the understanding of large enterprises is better than that of small enterprises.

4. Pan Haisheng, Wang Shibin, and Long Deyi published an investigation report, *Analysis of the Status and Influencing Factors of School-Enterprise Cooperation for China's Higher Vocational Education* in *Research in Higher Education of Engineering* in 2013.[20] This investigation surveyed 117 enterprises and 87 higher vocational colleges. The enterprise samples mainly came from nine east and central regions where manufacturing industries were relatively developed, covering eight industries, including manufacturing, railway transportation, modern service, photovoltaic , shipping, chemical, electronic and information industries, and the aircraft industry. Samples of higher vocational colleges came from 11 different provinces. The research conclusions, which are worthy of mention, include: ① From the new employees recruited by the sample enterprises each year, students from vocational colleges that have cooperation with enterprises are not advantaged; ② More than 90% of the specialties in the sample higher vocational colleges adopt the school-operating pattern of school-enterprise cooperation; ③ Vocational colleges have limited channels and ways to cooperate with enterprises. Active contact of higher vocational colleges accounts for the major proportion; ④ Practical training is the main form of school-enterprise cooperation at present; ⑤ Enterprises are more likely to use students as production employees, and pay less attention to skills training; ⑥ In terms of student internships, enterprises provide very little supporting funds; ⑦ Both schools and enterprises believe that school-enterprise cooperation is the critical factor to improve the quality of vocational education and enhance the competitiveness of enterprises; both sides believe that school-enterprise cooperation should not be limited to superficial forms of cooperation such as practical training, but also should strengthen their cooperation in other areas such as training, technology research and development, and establishment of alliance organizations.

5. The National Education Inspection Team summarized the development of school-enterprise cooperation in *The National Education Inspection Report: Focus on Secondary Vocational Education (Abstract)* (No. 3 [2011] from the National Education Inspection Team): ① Put forth efforts to improve policies and regulations and enhance institutional improvement. In

2008, Zhejiang province issued *Regulations of Ningbo City on the Promotion of Vocational Education School-Enterprise Cooperation*, and Ningbo became the first city which had special legislation for vocational education school-enterprise cooperation in China. In 2010, such places as Shandong, Shaanxi, Gansu, and Guangxi listed the formulation of *Regulations on the Promotion of Vocational Education School-Enterprise Cooperation* as their work objective. ② Operate schools in various forms, to enhance new school-enterprise co-operation progress. Each region has intensified communication and cooperation between secondary vocational schools and industries & enterprises through such forms as "customized" training, school-enterprise resource sharing, collaborative development of specialized courses, co-construction of training bases, and joint vocational skills competitions. ③ Facilitate work-study schemes, and the reform of the student training model has achieved initial success.

According to the sampling survey, nearly 70% of teachers and 80% of students believe that work experience positions are completely consistent or basically consistent with the job groups of their specialties; about 60% of students say that the enterprises pay the internship subsidy in full monthly during the work experience period and the enterprises also appointed special internship instructors to solve difficult problems during internship so as to improve their practical skills. The main problem is that industry and enterprise still have not fully participated in educational teaching management, specialty setup, and curriculum establishment of secondary vocational schools; schools and enterprises lack institutional guarantees for their rights and responsibilities; long-term mechanisms for school-enterprise cooperative school operation have not been established yet.[21] Generally, we can summarize the progress of school-enterprise cooperation as follows:

### 1.1. Significant Progress Has Been Made in China's School-Enterprise Cooperation

1. School-enterprise cooperation has been established as the basic school-operating characteristic of vocational education

In the past decade, school-enterprise cooperation has been highlighted in vocational education documents by almost all education administrative departments; almost all vocational colleges have been involved in promoting school-enterprise cooperation when introducing their overall school-operating plans. This is true not only in developed regions, but also in less developed regions. Some regions have confronted many real problems in promoting school-enterprise cooperation, such as the backward development of local industries and the difficulty in finding enterprises to cooperate. However, the "advocacy" for school-enterprise cooperation was widespread nonetheless. Nearly half of the scientific research projects and published papers were related to school-enterprise cooperation each year. All these phenomena show that we have firmly established the important position of school-enterprise cooperation in vocational education.

2. School-enterprise cooperation has been tangibly promoted in vocational colleges

While vocational colleges have widely realized the importance of school-enterprise cooperation, school-enterprise cooperation has also been substantially promoted in vocational education: ① Most vocational colleges have partner enterprises; some vocational colleges that are outstanding in school-enterprise cooperation have established firm partnerships with renowned enterprises in the relevant industry; ② School-enterprise cooperation has been very extensive in content, such as providing internship positions for vocational college students, selecting excellent enterprise staff to participate in curriculum development of vocational colleges and to serve as part-time principal lecturers in certain courses, participating in teaching quality assessment of vocational colleges, and providing teaching attachments for vocational schools. This progress can be reflected in a number of ways. For example, one of the intentions of school-based curriculum development in vocational colleges is to implement important enterprise research and convene relevant enterprise experts to analyze work tasks and professional abilities. It's a link that well illustrates the level of school-enterprise cooperation in a vocational college. This is because vocational colleges will have difficulty finding qualified corporate experts without the support of extensive school-enterprise cooperation. Such activities, even if rarely carried out, find it difficult to reach a high professional level. However, we find that vocational colleges are usually able to find qualified enterprise experts in both developed and less-developed regions. Of course, as revealed in the above survey, in terms of school-enterprise cooperation, the cooperation at curriculum development level is far less extensive and thoroughgoing than that in work practice. Nevertheless, it has made progress on the whole and has been comprehensively carried out in some regions and schools. The reason why enterprises fail to extensively and deeply participate in vocational school curriculum establishment lies in that vocational colleges haven't mastered the skills that enable enterprises to better participate in curriculum development, rather than that enterprises are not willing to do so.

It should be specially noted that although the German "dual system" has not been widely popularized in China, some pilot projects have been carried out very well, almost approaching the prototype of Germany, such as the cooperation between Taicang Secondary Vocational School and Taicang German Enterprises Technician Training Center. This cooperation began in 2001. In 2004, Taicang Secondary Vocational School jointly established the Schaeffler Training Center with Schaeffler Co. Ltd. These centers specialize in such vocational training as grinding apparatus, mechanical engineering, mechanical & electrical engineering, electronic engineering, numerical control, clothing, and vehicle repair. The dual-system student training model, which was jointly carried out by Pujiang Secondary Technical School of Sichuan Province and Chengdu Bosheng Precision Machinery Co. Ltd. in mechanical manufacturing, is also quite successful.

3. School-enterprise cooperation has achieved a diversified structure

While school-enterprise cooperation has widely achieved substantial progress, each vocational college has shown its special prowess and created various school-enterprise cooperation models, thus forming a diversified structure of school-enterprise cooperation. In terms of cooperative partners, some vocational colleges choose the single cooperation model, that is, a specialty only establishes deep cooperation with a very influential enterprise; some vocational colleges choose the multiple cooperation model, namely, they establish cooperative relationships with all those enterprises that can promote specialty establishment (such as Ningbo Polytechnic). In terms of cooperation depth, some vocational colleges only establish contractual cooperation; some directly bring enterprises into schools and establish a "factory-in-school" program; some are even deeply integrated with enterprises and form a community (such as Hangzhou Vocational & Technical College). In terms of cooperation content, some vocational colleges mainly position school-enterprise cooperation as a specialty development consultation strategy; some closely integrate the teaching process with enterprises' production processes and create an order-tracking model of teaching (such as Shanghai Business and Information School in the Qingpu district); some particularly implement school-enterprise cooperation through technical services (such as Wenzhou Vocational & Technical College). Which cooperation model is adopted depends on the school-operating requirements of vocational colleges and the characteristics of local enterprises.

4. Progress in system construction of school-enterprise cooperation

In order to better facilitate the implementation of school-enterprise cooperation, MOE has discussed and drafted school-enterprise cooperation regulations.

Prior to this, many provinces and cities issued local school-enterprise cooperation regulations. For example, Ningbo implemented *Regulations of Ningbo City on the Promotion of Vocational Education School-Enterprise Cooperation* in 2009; Henan province promulgated *Methods of Henan Province on the Promotion of Vocational Education School-Enterprise Cooperation (Trial)* in 2012; in the same year, Hangzhou Municipal People's Government also released *Several Opinions of Hangzhou Municipal People's Government on Promoting School-Enterprise Cooperation in Secondary Vocational Education.* These regulations not only provided ideas and guarantees for the promotion of school-enterprise cooperation, but also regulated the problems that may arise in school-enterprise cooperation and define the measures to resolve them. As a result, they significantly advanced school-enterprise cooperation.

### 1.2. School-Enterprise Cooperation Still Confronts Many Fundamental Problems in China

While achieving the above progress, school-enterprise cooperation also confronts many problems in development. These problems mean that China's school-enterprise cooperation is only a kind of school-operating activity, rather than a constituent part of China's vocational education system.

1. The basis for a national system of school-enterprise cooperation has not yet been established

The first problem that China's school-enterprise cooperation faces is that it has not yet been established as a national system. At the state level, industry-academy cooperation is mainly promoted in the form of policy documents, and this promotion is primarily realized through public advocacy and financial support. However, in order to deepen school-enterprise cooperation and make it a basic feature of vocational education like developed countries, we need to solve some major problems in the development of school-enterprise cooperation, such as the basic requirements for the content and form of school-enterprise cooperation, the obligations of enterprises in school-enterprise cooperation, etc. Furthermore, it should be noted that school-enterprise cooperation may bring about the problem of unclear property rights between schools and enterprises. Such a situation has already occurred in some vocational schools, and it is urgent to establish relevant systems to solve this problem.

2. Enterprises' school-enterprise cooperation consciousness has not yet been fully activated

There haven't been any substantial changes in schools' enthusiasm and enterprises' concern for school-enterprise cooperation. Most enterprises accept school-enterprise cooperation in order to obtain excellent mechanics, or due to a personal relationship with vocational school leaders, or because they are driven by certain economic benefits. Very few enterprises participate in school-enterprise cooperation for the purpose of better cultivating technical and skilled students and establishing a student guarantee foundation for industrial development. Enterprises participate in school-enterprise cooperation for interest or human relations, let alone reaching the level of social responsibilities. This shows China's school-enterprise cooperation lacks a solid social foundation. This situation is dangerous because it is often difficult to maintain school-enterprise cooperation for long without a social foundation. We can stimulate enterprises' motivation to participate in school-enterprise cooperation through both the system and the media. We have been complaining that enterprises have less consciousness in participating in school-enterprise cooperation. However, has there been any school-enterprise cooperation propaganda specifically targeted at enterprises? Is there any platform for enterprises to talk about school-enterprise cooperation at state level at present?

It seems not in my memory. Even nongovernmental organizations such as the Chinese Society of Vocational and Technical have failed to motivate entrepreneurs to participate in the system plans. We have been calling on ourselves to implement school-enterprise cooperation, while these people already know the significance of school-enterprise cooperation.

3. The role of school-enterprise cooperation in student training needs to be refined

At present, although the content of school-enterprise cooperation has been deepened in general, it is still at the developmental stage. There is still much room for the improvement in the quality of student training in vocational schools. The biggest role of school-enterprise cooperation in student training should be reflected in transforming workplace capability requirements into curriculum standards, genuinely developing teaching materials based on work knowledge and establishing a teaching resources database based on such materials as practice work-books, work orders, and cases. Only when we make substantive breakthroughs at these levels and make vocational education classroom teaching truly based on the actual work to be done can vocational education become real vocational education. However, no substantial progress has been achieved in the reform of vocational education in these areas. Therefore, it can be judged that the form of school-enterprise cooperation in vocational education still outweighs the content in general and we still need to continue to deepen the role of school-enterprise cooperation in student training. However, this is the most difficult link in school-enterprise cooperation, which requires methodological support.

4. Prominent interscholastic imbalance in school-enterprise cooperation

Evident interscholastic differences still exist in school-enterprise cooperation. School-enterprise cooperation in some vocational colleges has grown to a considerable scale; the models are also unique; it plays an increasingly important role in student training. For example, studios, which are established by many vocational colleges, basically can run well on the basis of school-enterprise cooperation. However, school-enterprise cooperation in some vocational colleges is still at the initial stage. This difference is reflected not only in the vocational colleges with different school-operating levels in the same region, but also in the vocational colleges in different regions as well as in different kinds of vocational colleges in the same region. Generally speaking, school-enterprise cooperation with vocational colleges in developed areas is much more mature than that of vocational colleges in less-developed areas; school-enterprise cooperation with secondary technical schools and vocational schools is much more mature than that of vocational high schools; school-enterprise cooperation with vocational high schools is much more mature than that of secondary vocational schools.

5. Negative factors affecting school-enterprise cooperation still exist

It should be noted that while striving to facilitate school-enterprise cooperation, we will also encounter many factors that can make school-enterprise cooperation more negative and can quickly ruin people's tremendous earlier efforts in a flash. In the late 1990s, during state-owned-enterprises reform, enterprises were required to divest nonproductive functions, in order to allow enterprises to focus on profitable production and services and get state-owned enterprises out of trouble as soon as possible. However, this policy also had extremely remarkable side effects on school-enterprise cooperation. At present, some negative factors that affect school-enterprise cooperation also arise. For example, the vocational colleges that belonged to industries are classified under the corresponding jurisdiction of the Education Department. The introduction of a reform measure certainly produces its own problems to be solved. While solving the targeted problems, however, we also need to systematically think about the new problems it may bring, especially the effect on other areas. Now that school-enterprise cooperation is so important for vocational education, we need to attach special importance to this dimension in the policy-making process.

## 2. Case Study of School-Enterprise Cooperation

The above is an analysis on the overall progress of school-enterprise cooperation in China. Next, we will further analyze several cases, so that we can have a deeper understanding about the actual situation of school-enterprise cooperation progress and consider more concrete experiences. All provinces, cities, and vocational colleges have made great efforts to promote school-enterprise cooperation and have achieved good results and experiences. On October 29–31, 2002, MOE convened a national experience and information exchange conference on industry-university-research cooperation in higher vocational and technical education in Yongzhou city, Hunan province; many excellent cases were exchanged during the conference; *Chinese Vocational and Technical Education* also introduced a series of school-enterprise cooperation cases with outstanding achievements in 2012 and 2013. Here I will make an analysis on the practice of school-enterprise cooperation in two regions (Shanghai and Hangzhou) and a vocational college (Hangzhou Vocational & Technical College). The reason why they are selected for analysis is that they all have something especially worthy of learning.

### 2.1. The Practice of School-Enterprise Cooperation in Shanghai

Shanghai's vocational education, especially secondary vocational education, has been ahead of other regions of the country since the founding of the new China. This is related to the fact that Shanghai has led the country with its economic level. Developed industries and service industries will inevitably require the support of a large number of high-level skilled workers. "Old masters" in Shanghai are a group that people are very impressed with and have respect for. Their excellent skills support the development level of Shanghai's industries and services. After entering the 21st century, Shanghai successfully accomplished industrial restructuring; it mainly focuses on advanced manufacturing industries and takes the lead in developing high and innovative technology in manufacturing industries. For example, Shanghai Baosteel is the most advanced in steel smelting technology in China; the large aircraft project is also based in Shanghai. The economic scale of services has overtaken other industries in Shanghai, accounting for more than 70% of the total GDP. Moreover, the service industries occupy a high proportion in modern service industries, such as finance and shipping. Correspondingly, the specialty structure of vocational schools has also been successively transformed along with the transformation of the industrial structure. The development practice of Shanghai's vocational education shows that the development of advanced manufacturing industries and modern service industries will further push up the requirements of industrial development for highly skilled workers, other than obsolescent skilled workers.

The favorable industrial foundation provides fertile soil for the development of vocational education in Shanghai, including the promotion of school-enterprise cooperation. As a result, it is characterized by school-enterprise cooperation by technical experts. That is, school-enterprise cooperation in Shanghai's vocational education is characterized by mainly being implemented at technical expert level. For example, technical experts are hired to participate in and instruct a variety of vocational educational professional activities, such as project appraisal, curriculum reform, skills identification, teacher cultivation, etc. In Shanghai, it has become the norm for technical experts to participate in various vocational educational professional activities. A large number of high-level and experienced technical experts are active in various vocational educational professional activities in Shanghai. Some technical experts establish contacts with vocational schools through corporate recommendation at the very beginning, while others directly establish contacts with vocational schools through other means. No matter which way the contact is established, ultimately school-enterprise cooperation is carried out at the individual level. In other words, Shanghai's school-enterprise cooperation is carried out by independence of the cooperation with enterprises from the cooperation with technical experts. This is the biggest characteristic, and also a point worth learning.

The biggest features of this kind of school-enterprise cooperation are: 1. Schools obtain much "tangible benefit." School-enterprise cooperation is carried out at the technical expert level, and this makes the content of school-enterprise cooperation surpass the limitations of only providing practice opportunities for students, and enables it to probe deeply into various professional collaborative activities. This form of cooperation really contributes to facilitating teachers' understandings of the actual work situations, improving teachers' skill levels and deepening curriculum establishment. 2. This "tangible benefit" is relatively easy to obtain. Cooperation at technical expert level can bypass enterprises, and be achieved by directly employing technical experts to participate in various professional activities. This enables school-enterprise cooperation to avoid many institutional barriers and achieve rapid promotion.

The formation of this school-enterprise cooperation model is first and foremost related to the favorable industrial foundations existing in Shanghai that can provide a number of technical experts with high skills and high sense of social responsibility for this kind of school-enterprise cooperation model. This is the prerequisite for the formation of the school-enterprise cooperation model to be based on technical experts. Furthermore, the formation of the school-enterprise cooperation model in Shanghai is also related to another two factors: 1. The maturity level of vocational education in Shanghai. There is no doubt that Shanghai's vocational education also attaches great importance to fundamental system construction. The same is true in the field of school-enterprise cooperation. Comparatively speaking, Shanghai's vocational education has devoted more effort to curriculum establishment and teaching reform. Such extra emphasis on work focus is related to the fact that Shanghai's vocational education has established a comparatively stable institutional system due to long-term historical development. Moreover, Shanghai's secondary vocational schools have basically not been upgraded to higher vocational schools, which also objectively enables Shanghai's vocational education system to maintain stability. This kind of vocational education development model focusing on related underlying structural foundations enables Shanghai's vocational education to implement more school-enterprise cooperation activities at the technical expert level. 2. The long-standing commercial culture in Shanghai. Shanghai is a commercial city in the Yangtze River Delta. The long-standing commercial culture has made school-operators of vocational education more pragmatic. They would rather devote more effort to substantial professional cooperation than just be content with some superficial contract signing and arrangements.

### 2.2. Practice of School-Enterprise Cooperation in Hangzhou

Hangzhou is also an economically developed city in the Yangtze River Delta. It has the same long-standing commercial culture as Shanghai. This culture also creates the pragmatic spirit embodied in all kinds of vocational education development work in Hangzhou. However, the technological foundation of Hangzhou's industry lags far behind Shanghai, which makes the focus of its school-enterprise cooperation different from that of Shanghai. Besides, Hangzhou's vocational education is significantly different from Shanghai's vocational education, that is, most of its high-quality secondary vocational schools have upgraded to higher vocational schools by taking advantage of the great development of higher vocational education. This makes much of its infrastructure for vocational education likely to start anew. This is true not only for higher vocational schools, but also for secondary vocational schools. Consequently, while promoting school-enterprise cooperation, Hangzhou has devoted considerable effort to system construction, including establishing vocational education groups, constructing various channels of cooperation, and integrating common cooperative content such as various elements of corporate culture into campus culture. Hangzhou's school-enterprise cooperation is characterized by its fund guarantee.

In 2012, Hangzhou Municipal People's Government released *Several Opinions of Hangzhou Municipal People's Government on Promoting School-Enterprise Cooperation in Secondary Vocational Education*, which requires it to implement special funds and guarantee school-enterprise cooperation: "1. Implement internship funds for students. Secondary vocational schools shall bring students' internship liability insurance premiums into schools' appropriation budgets. Secondary vocational school students shall receive an internship living allowance of no less than 50% of the minimum wage standard per month during the internship period in the enterprise. Financial departments at the same level shall, according to the actual number of students who are ultimately accepted by enterprises for internship and whose accumulated internship time is over one month, grant each person 200 yuan per month as reward, and gradually increase the reward according to the minimum wage standard, with the purpose of improving interns' working conditions. Part of the funds shall be assumed by finance and be included in the annual budget of public secondary vocational schools. Private secondary vocational schools shall be subsidized at the same level of finance according to this standard, and then schools shall uniformly pay the subsidies to enterprises. 2. Implement enterprise funding. Those enterprises whose costs (including material consumption, energy consumption, and service charges for teachers and administrative staff) are increased due to the admission of interns from secondary vocational schools shall enjoy appropriate tax preferences and financial subsidies. 3. Implement subsidies for external part-time teachers. The funds required for public secondary vocational schools shall be assumed to be financed at the same level and included in schools' annual budget; the funds required for private secondary vocational schools shall be included in school-operating costs. 4. Continue to strengthen financial support. Give support to constructing a number of municipal secondary vocational school demonstrative training bases, high-grade municipal vocational education off-campus training bases, and municipal school-enterprise cooperation staff education demonstration training bases, which rely on secondary vocational schools, integrate resources of industry and enterprise, and aim to serve local industrial transformation and upgrading and employee training. Municipal education bureaus and finance bureaus will, according to the actual situations of local base construction, collaboratively formulate relevant methods for 'substituting subsidies with rewards.'"[22]

The above text is a detailed excerpt on the section of school-enterprise cooperation funding from the document in Hangzhou, in order to enable readers to have a more nuanced understanding about the specifications of its funding support.

The reason why I present Hangzhou's financial arrangement as a case is to remind readers that it is necessary to provide adequate financial support for the school-enterprise cooperation model, which is mainly promoted by schools. Governmental purchase of enterprise services may be a strategy to solve the problem of school-enterprise cooperation in China.

### 2.3. The Practice of School-Enterprise Cooperation in Hangzhou Vocational and Technical College

In terms of school-enterprise cooperation at the vocational school level, Hangzhou Vocational & Technical College is a case worthy of analysis. The school-enterprise cooperation began to be heavily promoted at the end of 2008. However, it only took several years to make significant advances to enable school-enterprise cooperation to play a substantial role in the reform of the college personnel training model. This is highly original in Zhejiang province and even within all vocational colleges nationwide. The rapid advancement of school-enterprise cooperation in this college may be attributed to the favorable geographical advantages (Hangzhou) and the resources owned by the leaders of this college. However, the fundamental factor lies in its strategy of promoting school-enterprise cooperation. The reason why I analyze it as a case is that this case allows us to see the effects brought by positive attitudes and pragmatic strategies when most vocational schools are pessimistic about the promotion of school-enterprise cooperation.

The school-enterprise cooperation strategies of the Hangzhou Vocational & Technical College can be reduced to two points: 1. School-enterprise integration mechanisms; 2. Establishment of substantive cooperation projects.

The school-enterprise integration mechanisms, usually called the school-enterprise community, is a kind of secondary school-enterprise co-management mechanism, which is collaboratively established by the colleges and enterprises at the secondary college level, and carried out under the leadership of the council. For example, the management of Fair Friend Institute of Electromech is jointly composed of the Electromech Institute and the Fair Friend Enterprise Group; the enterprise leader directly serves as the vice-president of the Institute, department heads and teaching and research office leaders; at the same time, Fair Friend Institute of Electromech is listed as an entity as the training base for staff in the Fair Friend Enterprise Group and is operated as its subordinate enterprise, which has become an important part of the enterprise' development strategies. This kind of council is jointly established by schools and enterprises and has a single subject; colleges have transferred important administration authorities to enterprises, so that school-enterprise cooperation has changed from the "cooperation" of "two sides" into "one community" of "one side." As a result, enterprises are enthusiastically motivated to participate in vocational education. Enterprises are not as enthusiastic about cooperating with vocational colleges, which is a bottleneck in promoting school-enterprise cooperation. However, the case of Hangzhou Vocational &Technical College tells us that enterprises do not lack enthusiasm to cooperate most of the time; they just need to find the interest to support their participation in cooperation; moreover, we should thoroughly take into consideration the reasonable interest requirements of the enterprises in cooperation. Enterprises are market entities. Only when their interests are fully considered can school-enterprise cooperation be promoted.

It will be difficult to further school-enterprise cooperation if we are only confined to the construction of school-enterprise co-management mechanisms without support of specific quality cooperation content. As a market entity, enterprises are often more down-to-earth; they are not willing to waste energy on meaningless cooperation. Only substantial cooperation can fundamentally motivate enterprises' enthusiasm to participate in school-enterprise cooperation and substantively promote school-enterprise cooperation. This is the second important lesson we can get from the case of the Hangzhou Vocational &Technical College. After establishing a school-enterprise community with the corresponding enterprise, each secondary college immediately confirms and implements a series of substantial cooperation projects. For example, enterprises select excellent technical experts and engineering technicians, and let them become deeply involved in specialty setup, curriculum development, and even new product research & development. The teachers and students of the knitting major in Highfashion Womenswear Institute even manage to research and design 70% of the new clothing, which are launched by the enterprise every year. It was developed by the teachers and students of the profession. It is precisely because of the link of cooperation projects that we can continue to implement and deepen school-enterprise cooperation.

## Part 3 How to Facilitate School-Enterprise Cooperation under Market Economy Conditions

In retrospect, the development course of school-enterprise cooperation in vocational education in China since reform and opening-up, we can see that China has gradually deepened its understanding of the significance and content of school-enterprise cooperation with the development of vocational education practice; practice work has been advancing as a whole, and many excellent cases have occurred; but progress is below expectation. Considering the stage school-enterprise cooperation is in at present, we need to deeply examine some issues.

## 1. Paths to the Construction of School-Enterprise Cooperation Systems under Market Economy Conditions

The problems that people can directly experience with school-enterprise cooperation are: 1. Systematic construction is difficult to advance. Even if most vocational colleges in some regions have established good school-enterprise cooperation networks, such cooperation fails to be systematic and is easily disturbed by external factors and then collapse quickly. Of course, this kind of school-enterprise cooperation is not what we expect. 2. Enterprises are generally very passive about school-enterprise cooperation. We can only find school-enterprise cooperation cases achieving substantive results in such places where the conditions are very favorable and the cooperation is actively promoted by vocational colleges. Confronted with setbacks, people may have two extreme emotions: one is disappointment, that is, thinking it's impossible to realize school-enterprise cooperation under the social conditions in China; the other is impatience, namely, being eager to take a series of powerful measures at once, including imposing tax on enterprises, and obliging enterprises to participate in school-enterprise cooperation through legal and administrative means. Both impulsive reactions contribute little to the resolution of problems.

Faced with these problems, we should take notice of a common phenomenon: very few countries have really perfect school-enterprise cooperation systems, even in developed countries. Take the "dual system" as an example. Only a few Northern European countries such as Germany and Switzerland are doing well in it. Even in Germany, the numbers of enterprises that genuinely participate in school-enterprise cooperation only account about 20% of the total number; moreover, German enterprises' motivation to participate in school-enterprise cooperation tends to fluctuate with the external economic environment. For example, in the 1990s, with the intensified economic competition, enterprises were more inclined to pursue economic interests; labor-capital relationships in German enterprises became tense at one time; and enterprises become less motivated to participate in school-enterprise cooperation. Another example is Japan. With the continuous business economic recession since the 21st century, the lifetime employment system has suffered setbacks, which even threatens the existence of the training system within the enterprise. If we consult experts from these countries on how to establish a school-enterprise cooperation system, they often reply in one sentence: it will be a long time, maybe 200 years. This reply is actually worthy of our deep thought. It's a fact that school-enterprise cooperation is particularly difficult to carry forward in our country. However, the primary reason is not that we are not hardworking, but that we take this problem so lightly that we fail to be thoroughly conscious of its complexity; as a result, we are so impatient that we set construction goals that are contrary to the current conditions.

The reasons why China's school-enterprise cooperation system is complicated are that: 1. Enterprises are economic entities rather than education entities; their main mission is to provide material products and services to the society; and they are not supposed to undertake the task of public education. Governments have no right to force enterprises to participate in school-enterprise cooperation. As a market entity, an enterprise can operate freely as long as it does nothing illegal. If we expect enterprises to undertake the task of public education, we must provide guidance from outside. It is useless to blindly review how school-enterprise cooperation was deepened in the planned economy era. This is because the attributes of enterprises have completely changed in the market economy era. 2. School-enterprise cooperation system is a kind of social system. The essential difference between a social system and an artificial object lies in that: the latter can be built completely according to the will of people and the products can be made to highly match the original designs; while the former is achieved through the process of human interaction, which means that it is a highly uncertain dynamic process. We can propose a construction plan for a social system. However, it will be difficult for us to be certain about the final result; it can even develop toward the opposite direction. We cannot mechanically apply the laws of the natural world when planning social development. 3. The development history of enterprises in modern sense is very short. Strictly speaking, it can only be counted from the time of reform and opening-up. Over more than 30 years of development, we already have a number of very large and even internationally competitive enterprises, and the total number of enterprises has also grown rapidly. However, it is too demanding for us to require Chinese enterprises to establish Western enterprises' culture and spirit within such a short period of time.

It should be especially noted that school-enterprise cooperation after reform and opening-up is an issue about establishing school-enterprise cooperation relationships in the market economy era. Since we are in the market economy era, we must think about this issue by putting it in the market economy institutional environment, rather than think about it in the previous way we did in the planned economy era. Unfortunately, we precisely deviated at this point. Rethinking the statements about school-enterprise cooperation in the past few years, we can find almost all statements put forward requirements for enterprises from the perspective of education; some requirements are completely unrealistic sometimes, without considering enterprises as independent market entities, or analyzing what the existing enterprises can do in fact. All these lead to our failure in making comparatively realistic planning for the goals and paths for constructing a school-enterprise cooperation system in China.

Under market economy conditions, enterprises independently operate according to laws and market rules and set the pursuit of profit as the primary target. Other targets are attached to this. This is the essential purpose of an enterprise under market economy conditions. Under these circumstances, there are only four ways to let enterprises undertake goals beyond their essential purposes: enterprises voluntarily do so; purchase their services from outside; restrict their behavior by laws; and partially transfer interests to enterprise as peer exchange. Among the four strategies, the third strategy can only exist in the coordinated market economy model, such as in Germany and Japan. The success of the German "dual system" is most relevant due to its economic model. However, in the current economic operational situation in China, much freedom has been given to enterprises in order to stimulate their vitality. In such an economic model, the third strategy is unlikely to work. Therefore, we can only establish school-enterprise cooperation relationships through other three strategies in China. Unfortunately, our thinking is based precisely on the third strategy at present. This is the primary reason why China's school-enterprise cooperation is trapped in a dilemma. Therefore, the construction of a school-enterprise cooperation system in China should first determine the current forms and strategies for cooperation according to the current economic model, and then gradually advance the school-enterprise cooperation model together with the transformation of the economic model, so as to gradually approach the German model. It is a long process for the economic model to transform because it depends on the mutual balancing of various factors. As a result, we should have a long-term plan for the transformation of the school-enterprise cooperation model.

## 2. Basic Strategies for the Construction of School-Enterprise Cooperation System under Market Economy Conditions

According to the above analysis on the background and path ahead, we need to have a good mastery of the following four basic strategies for the construction of China's school-enterprise cooperation system:

### 2.1. Set Reasonable Development Goals

When formulating the future development goals of China's school-enterprise cooperation, we will be confronted with a key problem: will we set the German model or the U.S. model as our reference point?

As mentioned above, Germany's school-enterprise cooperation takes enterprise as the main driver; that is, enterprise is the main undertaker of vocational education tasks, and the role of the government is to cooperate with enterprises in the implementation of vocational education, such as providing apprentices with cultural knowledge and professional theoretical knowledge through vocational schools. The most prominent advantage of this model lies in that it enables enterprises to truly participate in training a technical and skilled workforce. However, the operation of this model must be guaranteed by a social mechanism, which can coordinate enterprises' behaviors to undertake vocational education tasks. Germany's economic operating model is called a coordinated market economy by academic circles, and such a mechanism exists in this economic model. Germany has played a prominent role in the European debt crisis, and new liberalism has suffered a series of setbacks in the U.S. and in Britain recently. All these make the international community increasingly interested in Germany's economic operating model.

The school-enterprise cooperation in the U.S. takes the government as the main body; that is, government is the main undertaker of vocational education tasks, and an enterprise is completely a market entity and operates freely according to the laws of the market. Enterprises' undertaking of vocational education needs to be realized through governmental purchase of services. In this model, enterprises' participation in vocational education is in an extremely unstable state. This is because enterprises will stop purchasing when they don't have any funds to purchase. In this model, even if the enterprises are participating in school-enterprise cooperation, their participation is confined. This is because education is not their main job, and they won't consciously cultivate their capacities in this respect. Although this model has many deficiencies, we have no choice but to adopt this model in a high-level free market economy.

Judging from the characteristics of current economic operations in China, we can only consult the U.S. model more in terms of the school-enterprise cooperation model. However, we can also learn from the strengths of the German model as much as possible, such as enhancing the stability of school-enterprise cooperation. As for future development, we should judge from the result of the economic transition model.

## 2.2. Enhance Financial Support

In current market economy conditions in China, the construction of school-enterprise cooperation system mainly relies on purchasing school-enterprise cooperation services from enterprises, or equally exchanging and sharing resources with enterprises. This can be proven by all the excellent school-enterprise cooperation cases presented above. This kind of school-enterprise cooperation requires a large amount of financial support. Furthermore, as a part of school-enterprise cooperation, schools also need much capital expenditure, such as the recruitment of technical experts, the purchase of students' work-related injury insurance. The experiences of Western countries show that financial support is an important guarantee for the successful implementation of school-enterprise cooperation under free-market economy conditions. For example, the school-enterprise cooperation in the U.S. came into being spontaneously; it did not develop rapidly in the first few decades; after the 1960s, school-enterprise cooperation developed rapidly due to a large amount of funding. In the 1990s, some laws were enacted to attract enterprises to participate in vocational education, and encourage the continuous development of various existing models of school-enterprise cooperation, thus facilitating the rapid development of school-enterprise cooperation in the U.S.

### 2.3. Developing Well-Established Industry Associations

From the development perspective, China is a country focusing on manufacturing industries, and it needs a more stable and well-embedded school-enterprise cooperation relations to support the cultivation of highly skilled experts required by industrial upgrading. However, this school-enterprise cooperation model must be constructed based on the premise of transforming the economic model; the transformation of the economic model depends on the aims of different interest groups in the market economy. However, government is not completely passive in this process. On the contrary, it can adopt appropriate strategies to actively guide the transformation of the economic model. One of the important strategies is to instruct well-established industry associations to coordinate enterprises' economic and educational behaviors in virtue of industry associations. That is, to develop the intermediate forces of modern social governance systems.

There are many industry associations in China at present, but we can't equate our industry associations with Western industry associations. Generally speaking, the existing industry associations are still not powerful enough and cannot effectively play a coordinating role in industries; some industry associations have even become a tool for a few interest groups to become industrial monopolists; some are engaged in their own economic interests and do not really play a coordinating role in industries. Therefore, it is a very complicated process for industry associations to develop and become well-established, and government needs to actively regulate and instruct their business development.

### 2.4. Promoting School-Enterprise Cooperation Legislation

So far, China has not yet issued any special laws for school-enterprise cooperation, but the promotion of school-enterprise cooperation urgently calls for the release of such laws: 1. School-enterprise cooperation is a very sophisticated relationship. Student cultivation through school-enterprise cooperation is a model with many potential risks. Many complicated problems need to be resolved according to laws, such as clear property rights, occupational injury compensation and workplace restrictions, etc. 2. Enterprises' behaviors need legal restrictions so that school-enterprise cooperation can become systematized. It is a strategy to coordinate corporate behavior by developing industry associations, but they are nongovernmental organizations after all. They can just influence enterprises' behavior and have no legal effect. Systematic school-enterprise cooperation needs to put restrictions on enterprises' market behavior, so that it can devote some effort to undertake social responsibilities in the pursuit of profits. This transformation in enterprises' behavioral patterns depends on legal means. The issue we need to carefully consider in legislation is to what extent shall corporate behaviors be constrained. This needs to be determined according to China's dominant economic policies and how acceptable to enterprises they actually are. Therefore, it is a process of gradually becoming clear.

## Notes

1 Edited by China Vocational Education Association: Collected Works of Huang Yanpei on Education, Shanghai Educational Publishing House, 1985, p. 155.
2 State Council: Decision of the State Council on Vigorously Developing Vocation and Technical Education, 1991.
3 CPC Central Committee, State Council: Outline of China's Education Reform and Development, 1993.
4 The Nineteenth Session of the Eighth National People's Congress: Vocational Education Law of the People's Republic of China, 1996.
5 MOE: Action Plan for Education Revitalization for the 21st Century, 1998.
6 State Council, Decision of the State Council on Vigorously Promoting Vocational Education Reform and Development, 2002.
7 MOE: Action Plan for Education Rejuvenation in 2003–2007, 2004.
8 Seven departments including MOE: Several Opinions of Seven Departments including MOE on Further Enhancing Vocational Education, 2002.
9 State Council: Decision of the State Council on Vigorously Developing Vocational Education, 2015.
10 MOE: Main Points for the Work of the State Council in 2006, 2006.
11 MOE: Main Points for the Work of the State Council in 2007, 2007.
12 MOE: Main Points for the Work of the State Council in 2008, 2008.
13 MOE: Main Points for the Work of the State Council in 2009, 2009.

14 Office of National Medium-and Long-Term Education Reform and Development Plan: Outline of the National Medium-and Long-Term Education Reform and Development Plan (2010–2020), 2010.
15 MOE: Opinions of MOE on emphasizing the Guiding Role of the Industries and Promoting Reform and Development of Vocational Education, 2011.
16 Vocational and Technical Education: 20 Years of Review and Witnessing, 1999, p. 111.
17 China Association of Staff and Workers Education and Vocational Training: School-Enterprise Cooperation has Become a Normal Teaching Model in Technical Training Schools - Research Report on the Cultivation of Chinese Technical Students, Vocational and Technical Education, No. 30, 2009.
18 Wang Wenjin: Survey Report on School-Enterprise Cooperation in Enterprises, Chinese Vocational and Technical Education, No. 2, 2009.
19 Bi Jieli, Wang Lin: Survey and Analysis Report on Skilled Training through School-Enterprise Cooperation (I), China Training, No.6, 2010.
20 Pan Haisheng, Wang Shibin, Long Deyi: Analysis on the Status and Influencing Factors of School-Enterprise Cooperation for China's Higher Vocational Education, Research in Higher Education of Engineering, No. 3, 2013.
21 The National Education Inspection Team: The National Education Inspection Report: Focus on Secondary Vocational Education (Abstract), 2011.
22 Hangzhou Municipal People's Government: Several Opinions of Hangzhou Municipal People's Government on Promoting School-Enterprise Cooperation in Secondary Vocational Education, 2012.

CHAPTER SIX

# Vocational Education Should Actively Serve Economic Development

Being market-oriented and serving industry are not only the basic strategies for developing vocational education but also the basic functions of vocational education. Serving the industry is the purpose, while being market-oriented is the method. Serving the industry does not indicate that we can completely ignore human's requirements for development. All kinds of education confront the dilemma of balancing the requirements for social development and individual development. The special feature of vocational education is that only when it preferentially meets the requirements for social development can it better satisfy the requirements for individual development. In terms of vocational specialty, only when it can facilitate a promising career can it be appealing to students and thus be "socially just." During the development of vocational education over the past four decades, we can see that with upgrading industrial structure, the previously popular specialties are no longer popular and now previously unpopular specialties become very popular. For vocational schools with different specialty orientations, they also have undergone rises and falls in upgrading their industrial structures. Over the past four decades since reform and opening-up, China has made remarkable economic achievements. These achievements are certainly not only an increase in GDP, but also accompanied by upgrading industrial structure. Vocational education has always actively studied the changing trend of upgrading industrial structure during this process, and made timely adjustments to its specialty structure. As a result, its specialty structure has always basically matched the industrial structure to better serve industry development. This is also an important part of the construction of modern vocational education.

Figure 6.1 The busy modern port

# Part 1 Promoting the Optimization and Upgrading of the Industrial Structure

## 1. Policy Paths to Upgrading Industrial Structure

Upgrading Industrial Structure refers to the process or trend of industrial structure to transform from a low level to a higher level.[1] It is a process of upgrading the industrial structure to a new level through adjustment of the industrial structure according to the evolution of industrial structure. The directions of upgrading industrial structure include: 1. Upgrading from an economic structure dominated by light textile industries to one dominated by heavy chemical industries; 2. Upgrading from an economic structure focusing on raw materials to one focusing on processing and assembling; 3. Upgrading from low value-added labor-intensive industries to high value-added technology-intensive industries. Furthermore, the focus of the whole national economy upgraded from primary industry to secondary industry, and then to the tertiary industry.[2] The primary reason for the upgrading of industrial structure is technical progress and changes in comparative advantages. Countries with low technological levels, abundant labor resources, and natural resources may remain at a low level in the industrial structure.

As technology advances and the economy develops, it is possible to upgrade the industrial structure if proper conditions exist and if we can adjust the industrial structure in a timely manner.

Both international experience and China's practice show that the optimization and upgrading of industrial structure are highly correlated with sustainable economic growth. Since the developing economy took off, long-term rapid growth was realized on the basis of a rapid transformation of the economic structure. It can be said that the process of industrialization is not only a process of continuous increase in economic aggregate, but also a process of economic structural adjustment and upgrading. Through empirical research on the development experience of dozens of countries after the World War II, scholars such as Hollis B. Chenery concluded that "development means successful change of economic structure," which is accepted by most scholars at home and abroad.[3] The process of structural transformation and upgrading is accompanied by rapid economic growth, which generally has the following characteristics: 1. In terms of economic aggregate, the proportion of the output value and employment of primary industry continues to decline, and secondary and tertiary industries successively become the dominant growth industries; 2. Some high growth industries have burgeoned one after another and promoted continuous high-speed economic growth; 3. The proportion of fund-intensive, technology-intensive and high value-added industries has been rising constantly and pushed the entire economy toward a resource-saving, technology-intensive, and knowledge-intensive direction.

China's upgrading of industrial structure is consciously carried out under the guidance and support of national policies. At different industrial development stages, China's government formulates the basic directions for industrial restructuring according to the actual conditions of industrial development and the growing trends of international industries. The overall directions are: 1. To enhance the basic industries; 2. To develop high and new technology industries, upgrade manufacturing industry; 3. To increase the proportion of service industry.

As early as 1989, *Decision of the State Council on the Main Points of the Current Industrial Policies* (No. 29 [1989] from the State Council) made the following judgments according to the basic conditions of China's industrial structure at that time: "At present, the total domestic demand is greater than the total domestic supply and serious problems still exist in the industrial structure. This is mainly due to the following reasons: the excessive production capacity of the processing industries, lack of production capacity of basic industries such as agriculture, energy sources, raw materials and transportation; the excessive production capacity of general processing industries, lack of advanced processing capacity; low-level industrial structure of export products, large export volume of domestic short-term products, and the contradiction with domestic market supply. These problems not only affect the rational utilization and allocation of resources in China, but also impede the stable development of the economy and the improvement of macro-economic benefits." To define these problems, the document put forward: "In the current and future period, the basic direction and task of formulating industrial policies and adjusting industrial structure is to concentrate efforts on developing basic industries such as agriculture, energy, transportation and raw materials, enhance industries that can increase effective supply, strengthen future economic development potential; at the same time, control the development of general processing industries so that they can harmoniously develop with basic industries."[4]

However, the profound changes of the industrial structure, especially the rapid development of high and new technology industry and service industry, occurred after the 21st century. This is because the development of the two requires substantial economic foundations and conditions. After entry into the 21st century, industrial restructuring became the kernel of China's industrial development policies. Some key documents are selected below for analysis.

*Interim Provisions on Promoting the Industrial Structure Adjustment* (No. 40 [2005] from the State Council), which was issued by the State Council in 2005, is a critical document for China to implement industrial restructuring policies. This document defines the targets of China's industrial restructuring: promote the optimization and upgrading of industrial structure, facilitate the healthy and coordinated development of the primary, secondary and tertiary industries, gradually establish an industrial structure, which is based on agriculture, guided by high and new technology industry, supported by basic industry and manufacturing industry, and allows the all-around development of service industry, adhere to development in a resources-efficient, clean, and safe manner so as to achieve sustainable development. The direction and key points of industrial restructuring include: 1. Consolidate and enhance the fundamental roles of agriculture in the economy, expedite the transformation from traditional agriculture to modern agriculture; 2. Strengthen infrastructure construction such as energy sources, transportation, hydraulic engineering and information, and reinforce protection for economic and social development; 3. Focus on developing advanced manufacturing industries by revitalizing the equipment manufacturing industry and strengthen its role as the foundation of economic development; 4. Accelerate the development of high and new technology industry and further enhance its leading role in economic growth; 5. Increase the proportion of service industry, optimize its structure and facilitate its all-around and rapid development; 6. Vigorously develop a recycling economy, build a resource-saving and environment-friendly society, and coordinate economic growth with population resources and the environment; 7. Optimize industrial organization structure and adjust regional industrial distribution; 8. Implement an open and mutually-beneficial strategy, open wider to the outside world and facilitate the upgrading of domestic industrial structures.[5]

A series of subsequent important documents continued and deepened the orientation of "industrial restructuring": 1. *Main Points for the Work of the State Council in 2006* (No. 12 [2006] from the State Council) requires: "Expedite the pace of developing advanced manufacturing industry, high and new technology industry and modern service industry, work hard to research and develop major technical equipment on the basis of key projects."[6] 2. *Several Opinions of the State Council on Accelerating the Development of the Service Industry* (No. 7 [2007] from the State Council) released in 2017 requires: "Vigorously develop production-oriented service industries, facilitate the organic integration and interactive development of modern manufacturing and service industry; vigorously develop the service industry for people's well-being, actively expand the scope of new style services and continuously foster new growth points for the service industry."[7] 3. *Main Points for the Work of the State Council in 2007* (No. 8 [2007] from the State Council) requires: "Put forth effort to optimize the industrial structure. Encourage and support the service industry to speed up its development pace, especially modern services such as logistics, finance, information, consulting, tourism and community service, actively develop the rural service industry … accelerate the development of high and new technology industry, revitalize the equipment manufacturing industry and widely apply advanced technologies to transforming and upgrading traditional industries."[8] 4. *Decision of the State Council on Accelerating the Fostering and Development of Strategic Emerging Industries* (No. 32 [2010] from the State Council) requires: "Accelerating the fostering and development of strategic emerging industries is a major measure to promote the upgrading of industrial structure and accelerate the transformation of economic development model."[9] 5. In *Industrial Transformation and Upgrading Plan (2011–2015)* (No. 47 [2011] from the State Council), the State Council proposed: "The industrial structure is further optimized. The scale of strategic emerging industries has expanded significantly and added-value has accounted for about 15% of the industrial added-value; the development level of relevant production-oriented service industries has improved significantly. The scaled economic industries have significantly become more concentrated and a number of internationally competitive enterprise groups have been fostered."[10] *The '12th Five-Year' Plan for the National Development of Strategic Emerging Industries* (No. 28 [2012] from State Council) issued by the State Council in 2012 proposes: "By 2020, we will endeavor to make strategic emerging industries an important motive force for national economic and social development, make the added-value account for 15% of GDP, make some industries and key technologies world-advanced, make energy conservation and environmental protection, new-generation information technology, biology and high-end equipment manufacturing industries the pillar industries of the national economy, and new energy, new material and new energy automobile industries the leading industries of the national economy."[11] 7. *Guiding Opinions of the State Council of the People's Republic of China, on Accelerating Development of Productive Service and Promoting Industrial Structure Adjustment and Upgrading* (No. 26 [2014] from the State Council) released in 2014 requires: "We should be guided by the needs of industrial transformation and upgrading, further accelerate the development of productive service industries, instruct enterprises to further break out of the 'large and all inclusive' 'small and comprehensive' structure, separate and outsource non-core businesses, extend to the high-end value chain, and gradually promote China's industry to transform from a manufacturing-oriented to a service-oriented type."[12]

## 2. The Current Situation of Upgrading Industrial Structure

Under the dynamic guidance of the policies, China's industrial structure has undergone fundamental changes.

### 2.1. Structural Transformation of the Three Major Industries

Figure 6.1 shows the structure data of the output values of China's three industrial sectors from 1978 to 2015 and Figure 6.2 shows the number of employees in the three industrial sectors in China from 1978–2015 (according to the data of the National Bureau of Statistics). Figures 6.2, 6.3, and 6.4 are drawn according to relevant data and show us the changing trends more directly. From these data, we can see: 1. Before 1984, the ratio of the output value of the three industrial sectors in GDP presented a "secondary-primary-tertiary" structure; in 1985, the added value of tertiary industry surpassed that of primary industry for the first time, and presented a "secondary-tertiary-primary" structure; in 2012, the added value of tertiary industry exceeded that of secondary industry for the first time, and formed a high-quality "tertiary-secondary-primary" industrial structure. 2. The transformation and upgrading of the industrial structure brought about changes in the number of employees in the three industry sectors: before 1993, the number of employees in the three industrial sectors showed a "primary-secondary-tertiary" structure; in 1994, the number of employees in tertiary industry exceeded that of secondary industry for the first time, and presented a "primary-tertiary-secondary" structure; in 2011, the number of employees in tertiary industry surpassed that of primary industry for the first time, and tertiary industry became the industry sector with the largest number of employees among the three main industrial sectors; after 2002, the number of employees in primary industry began to decline sharply; in 2014, the number of employees in the secondary industry exceeded that of primary industry for the first time, showing a "tertiary-secondary-primary" structure. This change accords with the Petty-Clark Theorem. That is, with the increase in national income per capita, the labor force shall shift from primary industry to secondary industry, and then to tertiary industry. In terms of the distribution of the labor force in the three industrial sectors, the numbers of the labor force reduced in primary industry and increased in secondary and tertiary industries.

Table 6.1 The output value structure of China's three industrial sectors between 1978 and 2015[33]

| Time | GDP | Added Value of Primary Industry | Added Value of Secondary Industry | Added Value of Tertiary Industry |
|---|---|---|---|---|
| (Year) | (100 Million RMB) | (100 Million RMB) | (100 Million RMB)) | (100 Million RMB) |
| 1978 | 3 678.7 | 1 018.5 | 1 755.2 | 905.1 |
| 1979 | 4 100.5 | 1 259 | 1 925.4 | 916.1 |
| 1980 | 4 587.6 | 1 359.5 | 2 204.7 | 1 023.4 |
| 1981 | 4 935.8 | 1 545.7 | 2 269.1 | 1 121.1 |
| 1982 | 5 373.4 | 1 761.7 | 2 397.7 | 1 214 |
| 1983 | 6 020.9 | 1 960.9 | 2 663 | 1 397 |
| 1984 | 7 278.5 | 2 295.6 | 3 124.8 | 1 858.1 |
| 1985 | 9 098.9 | 2 541.7 | 3 886.5 | 2 670.7 |
| 1986 | 10 376.2 | 2 764.1 | 4 515.2 | 3 096.9 |
| 1987 | 12 174.6 | 3 204.5 | 5 274 | 3 696.2 |
| 1988 | 15 180.4 | 3 831.2 | 6 607.4 | 4 741.8 |
| 1989 | 17 179.7 | 4 228.2 | 7 300.9 | 5 650.6 |
| 1990 | 18 872.9 | 5 017.2 | 7 744.3 | 6 111.4 |
| 1991 | 22 005.6 | 5 288.8 | 9 129.8 | 7 587 |
| 1992 | 27 194.5 | 5 800.3 | 11 725.3 | 9 668.9 |
| 1993 | 35 673.2 | 6 887.6 | 16 473.1 | 12 312.6 |
| 1994 | 48 637.5 | 9 471.8 | 22 453.1 | 16 712.5 |
| 1995 | 61 339.9 | 12 020.5 | 28 677.5 | 20 641.9 |
| 1996 | 71 813.6 | 13 878.3 | 33 828.1 | 24 107.2 |
| 1997 | 79 715 | 14 265.2 | 37 546 | 27 903.8 |
| 1998 | 85 195.5 | 14 618.7 | 39 018.5 | 31 558.3 |
| 1999 | 90 564.4 | 14 549 | 41 080.9 | 34 934.5 |

(*Continued*)

Table 6.1 Continued

| Time | GDP | Added Value of Primary Industry | Added Value of Secondary Industry | Added Value of Tertiary Industry |
|---|---|---|---|---|
| 2000 | 100 280.1 | 14 717.4 | 45 664.8 | 39 897.9 |
| 2001 | 110 863.1 | 15 502.5 | 49 660.7 | 45 700 |
| 2002 | 121 717.4 | 16 190.2 | 54 105.5 | 51 421.7 |
| 2003 | 137 422 | 16 970.2 | 62 697.4 | 57 754.4 |
| 2004 | 161 840.2 | 20 904.3 | 74 286.9 | 66 648.9 |
| 2005 | 187 318.9 | 21 806.7 | 88 084.4 | 77 427.8 |
| 2006 | 219 438.5 | 23 317 | 104 361.8 | 91 759.7 |
| 2007 | 270 232.3 | 27 788 | 126 633.6 | 115 810.7 |
| 2008 | 319 515.5 | 32 753.2 | 149 956.6 | 136 805.8 |
| 2009 | 349 081.4 | 34 161.8 | 160 171.7 | 154 747.9 |
| 2010 | 413 030.3 | 39 362.6 | 191 629.8 | 182 038 |
| 2011 | 489 300.6 | 46 163.1 | 227 038.8 | 216 098.6 |
| 2012 | 540 367.4 | 50 902.3 | 244 643.3 | 244 821.9 |
| 2013 | 595 244.4 | 55 329.1 | 261 956.1 | 277 959.3 |
| 2014 | 643 974 | 58 343.5 | 277 571.8 | 308 058.6 |
| 2015 | 689 052.1 | 60 362.1 | 282 040.3 | 346 149.7 |

(Data source: it's drawn according to the data in Table 6.1)

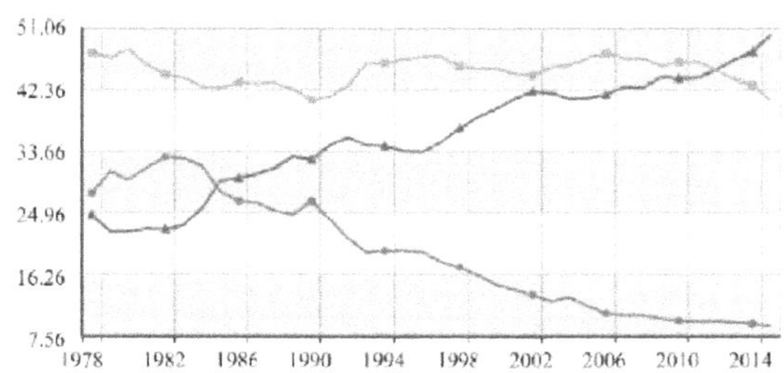


Three industrial structures - The added value of the first industry (%)

Three industrial structures - The added value of the secondary industry (%)

Three industrial structures - The added value of the third industry (%)

Figure 6.2 Variation trajectory chart of the output value structure of China's three industrial sectors between 1978 and 2015

Table 6.2 The numbers of employees in China's three industrial sectors between 1978 and 2015[34]

| Time | Number of Employees | Number of Employees in Primary Industry | Number of Employees in Secondary Industry | Number of Employees in Tertiary Industry |
|---|---|---|---|---|
| (Year) | (Ten Thousand) | (Ten Thousand) | (Ten Thousand) | (Ten Thousand) |
| 1978 | 40 152 | 28 318 | 6 945 | 4 890 |
| 1979 | 41 024 | 28 634 | 7 214 | 5 177 |
| 1980 | 42 361 | 29 122 | 7 707 | 5 532 |
| 1981 | 43 725 | 29 777 | 8 003 | 5 945 |
| 1982 | 45 295 | 30 859 | 8 346 | 6 090 |
| 1983 | 46 436 | 31 151 | 8 679 | 6 606 |
| 1984 | 48 197 | 30 868 | 9 590 | 7 739 |
| 1985 | 49 873 | 31 130 | 10 384 | 8 359 |
| 1986 | 51 282 | 31 254 | 11 216 | 8 811 |
| 1987 | 52 783 | 31 663 | 11 726 | 9 395 |
| 1988 | 54 334 | 32 249 | 12 152 | 9 933 |
| 1989 | 55 329 | 33 225 | 11 976 | 10 129 |
| 1990 | 64 749 | 38 914. 1 | 13 856. 3 | 11 978. 6 |
| 1991 | 65 491 | 39 098. 1 | 14 015. 1 | 12377. 8 |
| 1992 | 66 152 | 38 698. 9 | 14 355 | 13 098. 1 |
| 1993 | 66 808 | 37 679. 7 | 14 965 | 14 163. 3 |
| 1994 | 67 455 | 36 628. 1 | 15 312. 3 | 15 514. 7 |
| 1995 | 68 065 | 35 529. 9 | 15 655 | 16 880. 1 |
| 1996 | 68 950 | 34 819. 8 | 16 203. 3 | 17 927 |
| 1997 | 69 820 | 34 840. 2 | 16 547. 3 | 18 432. 5 |
| 1998 | 70 637 | 35 177. 2 | 16 599. 7 | 18 860. 1 |
| 1999 | 71 394 | 35 768. 4 | 16 420. 6 | 19 205 |
| 2000 | 72 085 | 36 042. 5 | 16 219. 1 | 19 823. 4 |
| 2001 | 72 797 | 36 398. 5 | 16 233. 7 | 20 164. 8 |
| 2002 | 73 280 | 36 640 | 15 681. 9 | 20 958. 1 |
| 2003 | 73 736 | 36 204. 4 | 15 927 | 21 604. 6 |
| 2004 | 74 264 | 34 829. 8 | 16 709. 4 | 22 724. 8 |
| 2005 | 74 647 | 33 441. 9 | 17766 | 23 439. 2 |
| 2006 | 74 978 | 31 940. 6 | 18 894. 5 | 24 142. 9 |
| 2007 | 75 321 | 30731 | 20 186 | 24 404 |
| 2008 | 75 564 | 29 923. 3 | 20 553. 4 | 25 087. 2 |
| 2009 | 75 828 | 28 890. 5 | 21 080. 2 | 25 857. 3 |
| 2010 | 76 105 | 27 930. 5 | 21 842. 1 | 26 332. 3 |

*(Continued)*

Table 6.2 Continued

| Time | Number of Employees | Number of Employees in Primary Industry | Number of Employees in Secondary Industry | Number of Employees in Tertiary Industry |
|---|---|---|---|---|
| 2011 | 76 420 | 26 594. 2 | 22 543. 9 | 27 281. 9 |
| 2012 | 76 704 | 25 773 | 23 241 | 27 690 |
| 2013 | 76 977 | 24 171 | 23 170 | 29 636 |
| 2014 | 77 253 | 22 790 | 23 099 | 31 364 |
| 2015 | 77 451 | 21 919 | 22 693 | 32 839 |

(Data source: according to the data in Table 6.2)

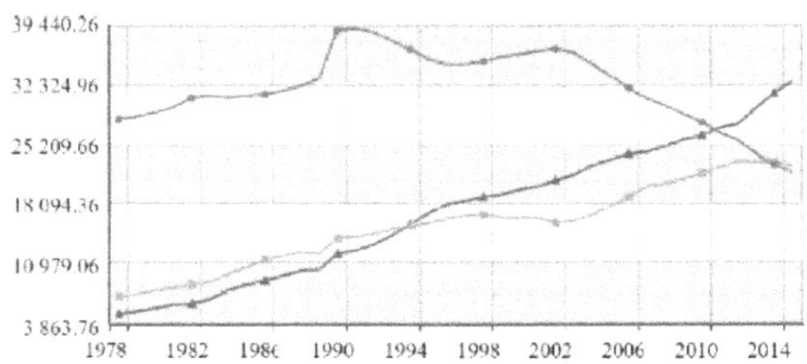


Number of employees in primary industry (ten thousand)    Number of employees in secondary industry (ten thousand)    Number of employees in tertiary industry (ten thousand)

Figure 6.3 Broken line graph of the number of employees in China's three industrial sectors between 1978 and 2015

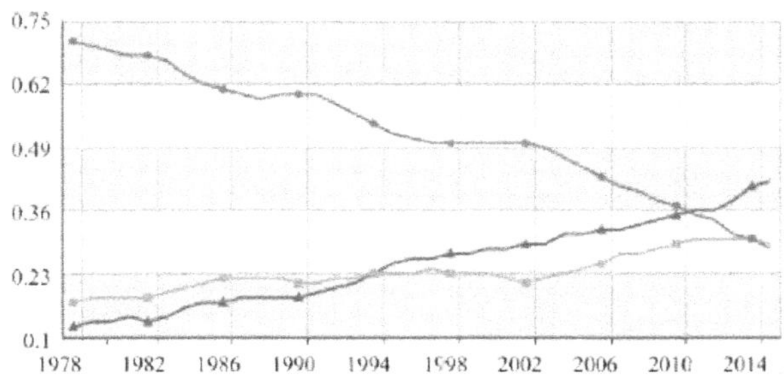


The proportion of the number of employees in primary industry

The proportion of the number of employees in secondary industry

The proportion of the number of employees in tertiary industry

Figure 6.4 Graph of the proportion of the number of employees in China's three industrial sectors between 1978 and 2015

(Data source: it's drawn according to the data in Table 6-2)

### 2.2. The Development of High and New Technology Industries

With the rise of GDP since reform and opening-up, China's high and new technology industries have also developed rapidly and promoted the widespread upgrading of the industrial structure. High-growth industries, which play an important role in economic development, also varied in structure during different historical periods: 1. From the late 1970s to the first half of the 1980s, the high-growth industries that promoted economic growth were mainly traditional industries such as light industry, textile industry, machinery industry, and building materials industry; 2. In the mid-and-late 1980s, a new generation of household electrical appliances such as color TVs, refrigerators, washing machines, and air conditioners became the new high-growth industries; 3. After a brief adjustment in the late 1980s, since 1992 China's economy entered a new round of rapid growth. During this period, the high-growth industries were mainly infrastructure and basic industries such as roads, ports, electric power, communication equipment manufacturing, and extractive industries; 4. Since the beginning of the 21st century, industries such as information, automobile, real estate, iron, and steel have developed rapidly, and once again facilitated rapid economic growth. In addition, the proportion of high-tech and value-added industries keeps growing. For example, the growth rate of the information industry, a new high-growth industry, was over 20% for eight consecutive years since 1997. According to the National Bureau of Statistics, the added-value of high and new technology industries, which focused on information industry, reached 661.4 billion RMB in 2004, up 23.1% over 2003; the added-value of high and new industries accounted for 5% of GDP for the first time, signaling that high and new technology industry has become one of the pillars of the national economy in China.[13]

By the early 21st century, China had basically become a large manufacturing country. According to the statistics of the World Bank, the proportion of added-value of China's manufacturing industry to that of the world has grown from 2.7% in 1990 to 17.6% in 2010, successively surpassing such large manufacturing countries as Britain, France, Italy, Germany, and Japan.[14] Over the period from 1980 to 2010, the export volume of manufacturing industry rapidly increased from less than 10 billion U.S. dollars to 1,476.9 billion U.S. dollars, jumping ahead of Japan, the U.S., and Germany successively and China became the world's largest exporter in manufacturing industry. According to the statistics of UNIDO, among ISIC's 22 major categories, China's manufacturing industry had seven major categories that ranked the first in the world, and 15 major categories that were among the top three in the world.[15] In spite of the significant increase in the total industrial output value, the whole society also attached great importance to the problem about how to further upgrade high-tech products and increase the added-value.

At that time, heated discussions were held among all sectors of the society about the fact that China needed to export 800 million shirts to afford an airbus. This showed that China had to export a large number of low value-added commodities for foreign high-tech and high value-added products. How to transform from a large manufacturing country to a manufacturing powerhouse became the core direction of China's industrial development at this stage.

High-speed railway was the first industry to take solid steps in this direction. Over the past decade, China's high-speed rail industry has developed rapidly and become an important engine for industrial upgrading. The earliest passenger-dedicated high-speed railway line in China was the Qinhuangdao-Shenyang high-speed railway line, which came into service in October 12, 2003, with a projected speed of 200 kilometers per hour. It reserved the ability to speed up to 250 kilometers per hour. The total length is 404 kilometers, and the total investment was about 15 billion RMB. The Qinhuangdao-Shenyang high-speed railway is of great importance in the developmental history of China's railway and laid a solid technical foundation for the development of China's high-speed railway. In 2014, the opening of China's new railway lines reached an all-time record: the length of railroad lines in service exceeded 112,000 kilometers and the length of high-speed railway lines surpassed 16,000 kilometers, firmly ranking the system the first in the world. It is believed that Shanghai's large aircraft manufacturing project and artificial intelligence will become an important engine for China's next phase of industrial development. It's hoped that the history that "China needed to export 800 million shirts to afford an airbus" can be ended with the large aircraft project.

In regard to the overall situation of upgrading industrial structure in China, General Secretary Xi Jinping drew the following conclusion at the 2014 APEC Summit: Since reform and opening-up, China's economy has been developing at top speed. Although there have always been doubts about the irrational economic structure, the characteristics of the economic structure are generally compatible with the specific stage of development in our country. For the past few years, with the transition stage of the economic development in China, optimization of economic structures has begun to show an evident characteristic style: first, the proportion of the added-value of the service industry exceeds that of secondary industry; second, the growth rate of high and new technology industry and equipment manufacturing industry is higher than the average industrial growth rate; third, consumption contributes more to economic growth than investment. From here, China's economic development begins to become "higher in quality and better in structure."[16]

# Part 2 Promoting Specialty Structures That Connect to Industrial Demand

Upgrading industrial structure will necessarily bring about changes in workforce demand structure. Vocational education has always attached great importance to the connection between student education and training structure and labor demand structure. Important documents all emphasize that student education and training of vocational education should meet industrial requirements and guide the adjustment of student education and training structures of vocational colleges mainly by adjusting specialty catalogues and releasing labor demand data. China's secondary vocational education has developed much earlier than higher vocational education, and both of them have been under the jurisdiction of different departments for more than 10 years after higher vocational education developed on a large scale. So next, I will sort out the policy paths to specialty structural adjustment of secondary vocational education and higher vocational education.

## 1. Policy Paths to Specialty Structural Adjustment of Secondary Vocational Education

It has always been that the basic school-operating guidelines for China's vocational education are designed to serve the requirements of economic development. The main documents relevant to vocational education highlighted the function of vocational education to service economic development. As early as 1985, *Decision of the CPC Central Committee on the Reform of the Education System* proposed: "Secondary vocational and technical education must be closely integrated with the requirements of economic and social development."[17] In 1986, *Vocational Education Law of the People's Republic of China* clearly stipulated: "Vocational schools and vocational training institutions should implement industry-education integration in order to serve regional economic construction and closely integrate with enterprises in order to educate and train practical and skilled workers."[18] In 2010, *Outline of the National Medium-and Long-Term Education Reform and Development Plan (2010–2020)* proposed: "Vocational education should be incorporated into the planning for economic, social and industrial development, so as to promote the scale and specialty structure of vocational education to adapt to the needs of economic and social development."[19] The State Council issued *Decision on Accelerating the Development of Modern Vocational Education* in 2014 and put forward: "Promote speciality structure to integrate with industrial requirements, adjust and improve the regional distribution of vocational schools, set up specialties scientifically and rationally and improve the mechanisms for the dynamic adjustment of specialties according to industrial development."[20] *The '13th Five-Year' Plan for China's Educational Development* (No. 4 [2017] from the State Council) detailed a plan for school layout on how to better execute this function: "Adjust and improve the layout of vocational schools according to urbanized and industrial structures and optimize the structure of vocational education system according to the requirements of industrial development for technical and skilled labor. Encourage industrially developed regions to make plans for secondary vocational schools in the counties. Set up new higher vocational schools mainly in small and medium cities and industrial cluster districts. Establish a number of secondary vocational schools in poverty-stricken regions where the population is concentrated and industrial development is needed and focus on supporting poor secondary schools to establish secondary vocational schools that accord with the requirements of local economic and social development. Facilitate the scientific orientation of regional vocational schools according to the positioning of each main functional area, so that each vocational school can concentrate its efforts on developing characteristic advantageous specialties (clusters) required for local economic and social development. Spare no efforts to build a number of high-level vocational schools that can serve key industrial fields such as modern industrial development and anti-poverty development, form a technical skills educating and training pattern supported by key vocational schools in key national industries, and that serve the adjustment and optimization of industry structure."[21] As a matter of fact, among vocational education development policies in China, so much emphasis was put on the economic developmental function of vocational education that many scholars advocated the human developmental function of vocational education while emphasizing its economic developmental function. This exactly accords with Comrade Xi Jinping's statement that vocational education should "give everyone a chance to shine in life."

In order to better implement vocational education's economic developmental function and better match the student education and training structure with the demand structure, we necessarily need to develop a specialty catalogue that thoroughly reflects the labor demands of enterprises. In the integrated design of vocational education talent training systems, MOE and the Ministry of Labor have always attached great importance to formulating and amending the specialty catalogue.

### 1.1. Revision and Improvement of Professional Catalogues before 1998

After the development in the 1980s, the scale of secondary vocational education has gradually recovered, and national policies have attached importance to how to better match student education and training structures with the demand structure. On October 17, 1991, the State Council stated in *Decision on Vigorously Developing Vocational and Technical Education*: "We should rationally plan the layout and specialty setup of vocational and technical training schools so as to meet the actual requirements of the society."[22] In order to implement this guiding principle, the State Education Commission (now MOE) issued the *Notice on Amending the Specialty Catalogue for Regular Secondary Specialized Schools* on January 27, 1992, which requested regular secondary specialized schools to thoroughly revise their specialty catalogue. At the end of 1992, the revision of the specialty catalogue for regular secondary specialized schools was completely accomplished. On January 12, 1993, the National Deliberative Assembly on specialty catalogues for regular secondary specialized schools was convened in Jinan city, Shandong province. On March 23, 1993, the State Education Commission published the *Notice of the State Education Commission on Promulgating "The Specialty Catalogue for Regular Secondary Specialized Schools"* (hereinafter referred to as the *Notice*), and decided that *The Specialty Catalogue for Regular Secondary Specialized Schools* would be released and implemented. From the academic year of 1994–1995, all the regular secondary specialized schools in China must enroll students according to the new specialties listed in *The Specialty Catalogue for Regular Secondary Specialized Schools*. *The Specialty Catalogue for Regular Secondary Specialized Schools* in 1993 was the last version, which set up a specialty catalogue for secondary vocational schools according to subjects. This specialty catalogue was divided into nine subjects: engineering, agriculture, forestry, medicine and health, finance and economics, management, politics and law, art, and sports. Each subject has its subsubjects. For example, engineering is divided into geology and metallurgy. Each category has its sub-specialties, with 518 specialties in total. The *Notice* particularly emphasizes: "While implementing *The Specialty Catalogue for Regular Secondary Specialized Schools*, we should not just change the specialty names, adjust and merge the specialties. What is more important is to educate and train qualified secondary professionals for China's economic construction and social development in the new era."[23]

In 1995, the General Office of the Ministry of Labour (now MOHRESS) issued the first edition of *The Specialty Catalogue of Technical Training Schools*, which included 169 specialties. It aimed to adapt to the requirements of economic construction and technological advances, as well as strictly standardizing teaching management in technical training schools. This specialty catalogue was formulated according to *The Profession Catalogue of the People's Republic of China* and the actual production practice of enterprises. This profession catalogue highlighted that its formulation should accord with the needs of economic construction and the production practices of enterprises. In the 1990s, secondary specialized schools had a different school-operating orientation from technical training schools, so the two specialty catalogues complemented each other.

### 1.2. Formulation of the 2000 Edition of Specialty Catalogue

In 1998, the General Office of MOE released the *Notice of the General Office of MOE on Formulating the Specialty Catalogue for Vocational Senior High Schools* (No. 2 [1998] from the Department of Vocational Education). The specialty catalogue for vocational senior high schools was originally intended to standardize specialty setup. Vocational senior high schools had not developed for a long time; different places applied different principles in specialty setup; a nationally standardized specialty catalogue had not been formulated yet: all these led to the non-standard and unreasonably diverse specialty setups in vocational senior high schools and unscientific divisions and names of some specialties. For example, some specialties were the same in name but far different in content; some were the same in content but different in name; specialty setup covered undefined occupational scopes, or the range of occupations covered varied so greatly that it was difficult to be geared to the labor market. The *Notice of the General Office of MOE on Formulating the Specialty Catalogue for Vocational Senior High Schools* emphasized that this specialty catalogue was formulated specially for the purpose of enabling vocational senior high schools to better adapt to the requirements of the socialist market economy and social progress. The *Notice* embodies this purpose in the formulation principles of the specialty catalogue: 1. The specialty catalogue should adapt to the occupational classification and occupational grade standards formulated by the state and at the same time reflect the characteristics and rules of vocational senior high school education. Professional specialties shall be classified and arranged mainly according to industrial structure, management structure, scientific, and technological structure. Each specialty should have its basic professional competence requirements for production, service, technology and management, and a curriculum system that highlights application and practicality. 2. The specialty catalogue should be formulated on the basis of adapting to the current economic and technological development level in China and look ahead to the needs of professionals. 3. We should pay attention to learning and referencing the advanced experience at home and abroad, and attach great importance to the demands for competent labor in the occupations and positions that have burgeoned with economic and social development in recent years.

*The Specialty Catalogue for Secondary Vocational Schools* (hereinafter referred to as *The Catalogue*) was finally released in 2000. Chen Guang, who was the Director of the Textbook Division, was responsible for the revision. He believed that the starting point for the revision of the 2000 edition of the specialty catalogue was as follows: 1. Adapt to the industrial restructuring policy proposed by the state to "vigorously enhance primary industry, adjust and improve secondary industry, and actively develop tertiary industry," and optimize the specialty setup and layout of secondary vocational schools; 2. Occupation patterns have changed, with old occupations disappearing and new occupations burgeoning; 3. With the development of science and technology, the basic knowledge and skills required by vocational groups are increasingly assimilating, and this makes some specialties similar in content; 4. The market economic system has been established and improved, forcing vocational education specialties to be market-oriented and broadening the original narrow caliber of specialties; 5. Adapt to the construction and further improvement of the vocational education system, connect to higher vocational development and integrate with the lifelong education system; at the same time, upgrade the goal of segmenting workers and cadres into educating and training a high-quality labor force and secondary specialized professionals; 6. Unify the diverse pattern to create a uniform specialty catalogue for vocational senior high schools and adult secondary technical training schools. Therefore, the release of a systematic catalogue for senior high schools will meet the demands of the times.[24]

The 2000 edition of the specialty catalogue no longer sets up specialties according to subjects, but industries. Specialties are divided into such 13 categories: agriculture and forestry, resource and environment, energy, civil and hydraulic engineering, processing and manufacturing, communication and transportation, information technology, medicine and health, trade and tourism, finance and economics, culture, art and sports, social public services and other categories; specialties are set up under each major category. For example, planting, agronomy, and horticulture are set up under agriculture and forestry. All the categories can be divided into 270 specialties. Each specialty includes different specialized directions. For example, the planting specialty is divided into crops, fruits & vegetables, ornamental plants, plant protection, seeds, tobacco, tea, forage and feed crops, turf production and maintenance, etc. All the specialties can be divided into 470 specialized areas.[25]

### 1.3. Formulation of the 2010 Edition of the Specialty Catalogue

In 2010, MOE published a new specialty catalogue for secondary vocational schools. *Notice of MOE on Printing and Distributing "The Specialty Catalogue for Secondary Vocational Schools (Revised in 2010)"* (No. 4 [2010] from the Department of Vocational and Adult Education, MOE) explains the main purpose of amending the specialty catalogue: "Facilitate the reform and innovation of secondary vocational education, better support industrial construction, serve economic and social development, promote specialty setup of secondary vocational education to better match the needs of occupations, and instruct secondary vocational schools to set up specialties in a scientific and rational manner."[26] It also stipulates implementing dynamic management of the Catalogue, amending the Catalogue every three years, timely release and supplementing the Catalogue according to changes in labor demands in economic and social development and the circumstances of specialty construction in various places. Compared with the original Catalogue, the revised new Catalogue has made large adjustments in the content, specialty names, professional (skill) descriptions, corresponding occupations, vocational qualification certificate designs, continuing learning specialty descriptions, etc. The number of specialty categories has increased from 13 to 19; the number of specialties has increased from 270 to 321; the professional (skill) descriptions (namely, the original "specialization descriptions") has increased from 470 to 927; describing 1185 occupations, 720 vocational qualification certificates and 554 continuing learning specialties.[27] Judging from the specific adjustment of the specialty setup, *The Specialty Catalogue of Secondary Vocational Schools (Revised in 2010)* has well reflected the changes in occupations in the three major industrial sectors.

In order to adapt to the changes of primary industry, the Catalogue has set up many specialties that reflect the requirements of modern agriculture for a professional and technical workforce, such as agricultural production technology, modern agronomic technology, sightseeing agriculture management, modern forestry technology, pet protection, and management and aquaculture. In order to adapt to the changes of secondary industry, the Catalogue has set up many specialties that embody the requirements of high and new technology industries for a professional and technical workforce, such as ecological environmental protection, solar energy and biogas technology applications, intelligent building equipment installation and operation, fine chemical engineering, urban trail transit vehicle operation and maintenance, computer graphic design, computer animation and game production, biotechnological pharmacy, drug and food inspection, and website artistic design. In order to adapt to the changes in tertiary industry, the Catalogue has set up many specialties that reflect the needs of modern service industries for a professional and technical workforce, such as urban rail transit operation management, customer information services, rehabilitation technology, beauty and body care, hairdressing and image design, leisure services, monopoly businesses, logistics services and management, Western cuisine cooking, leisure sports services and management, community legal services, housekeeping services and management, elderly services, and management.

## 2. Policy Paths to the Structural Adjustment of Higher Vocational Education Specialties

### 2.1. Formulation of the 2004 Edition of the Specialty Catalogue

In 2004, MOE issued *The Instructive Specialty Catalogue for Higher Vocational and Technical Education in Regular Colleges and Universities (Trial)* (No. 3 [2004] from MOE to all colleges and universities). The catalogue is divided into 19 categories: farming, forestry, husbandry and fishing, communication and transportation, biochemistry and medicine, resource development and mapping, material and energy, civil engineering, water conservancy, manufacturing, electronic information, environmental protection, meteorology and security, light textile and food, finance and economics, medicine and health, tourism, public services, cultural education, arts and design and media, public security, and law, with 78 sub-categories and 532 specialties. In no time, MOE issued *Administrative Measures for Specialty Setup of Higher Vocational and Technical Education in Regular Colleges and Universities (Trial)* (No. 4 [2004] from MOE to all colleges and universities), which required colleges and universities to "start from their own school-operating conditions such as the teachers and practical training of higher vocational and technical education and pay special attention to adjusting and setting up specialties in accordance with the transformation principles of economic development and occupations under market-oriented economy conditions"[28]

### 2.2. Formulation of the 2015 Edition of the Specialty Catalogue

In 2013, MOE published *Notice of MOE on the Amending "The Specialty Catalogue for Higher Vocational Schools"* (No. 6 [2013] letter from the Department of Vocational and Adult Education, MOE), and began to amend the 2004 edition of the specialty catalogue. The revision work took 2 years. In 2015, MOE released *Notice of MOE on Printing and Distributing the "Administrative Measures for Specialty Setup of Higher Vocational Education (Specialist)" and "The Specialty Catalogue for Higher Vocational Education (Specialist) in Regular Colleges and Universities (2015)"* (hereinafter referred to as the *Notice*) (No. 10 [2015] from the Department of Vocational and Adult Education, MOE) and officially announced the 2015 edition of the specialty catalogue for higher vocational education. The *Notice* clarified the principles of amending the specialty catalogue: "actively adapting and serving development; inheritance and innovation, flexible setup; scientific norms, embodying features; connection promotion, system construction."[29] It addition, it required dynamic management of the specialty catalogue, amending it every five years and supplementing it once a year.

The revision of *The Specialty Catalogue for Higher Vocational Schools* made references to *Industrial Classification for National Economic Activities(2011), Regulation on the Classification of Three Industries(2012)*, *Occupational Classification System of People's Republic of China (2015 Edition), The Specialty Catalogue of Secondary Vocational Schools(Revised in 2010)* and *The Undergraduate Specialty Catalogue for Regular Colleges and Universities(2012)*, etc. It specified classification according to industries and professions, taking into account discipline classification for the specialty division and adjustment and connecting major specialty categories to corresponding industries, specialty categories to corresponding occupations and, in principle, specialties to corresponding occupation groups or technological fields. Compared with the previous catalogue, the revised catalogue made major adjustments in its system structure. It has set up such four distinct areas "describing specialty direction," "main corresponding occupation categories," "connected secondary vocational specialties," and "continued undergraduate specialties." The major categories maintained the original 19 unchanged, and adjustments were made to ranking and division; the number of specialty categories increased from the original 78–99; the number of specialties reduced from the original 1170–748; illustrating 746 specialty directions, 291 main corresponding occupation categories, 306 connected secondary vocational specialties and 343 continuing undergraduate specialties. Primary industry mainly involves the major categories of farming, forestry, husbandry, and fishing and sets up 51 specialties; secondary industry involves 8 major categories such as resource environment and security, energy, power and materials, and sets up 295 specialties; tertiary industry involves 11 major specialty categories such as communications and transportation, electronic information, and sets up 401 specialties. The ratio of the number of specialties related to the three industry sectors is 6.8:39.4:53.8, which is more aligned with the industrial restructuring requirements of China.

In order to adapt to the changes of primary industry, the Catalogue has set up many specialties that reflect the requirements of modern agriculture for a professional and technical workforce, such as agriculture and equipment, modern agricultural technology, leisure agriculture, ecological agricultural technology and horticultural techniques, green food production and inspection. In order to adapt to the changes of secondary industry, the Catalogue set up many specialties that reflect the requirements of high and new technology industries for a professional and technical workforce, such as new energy automobile technology, high-speed railway engineering technology, CRH maintenance technology, intelligent traffic technology applications, contamination restoration and ecological engineering technology, cleaner production and emission reduction technology, photovoltaic technology and applications, solar optothermal techniques and applications, photovoltaic material preparation technology, new building material technology, building intelligent engineering technology, automatic production equipment and applications, photoelectric manufacturing and application technology, new energy equipment technology, industrial robot technology, UAV application technology, and intelligent product development. In order to adapt to the changes in tertiary industry, the Catalogue has set up a number of specialties that reflect the requirements of modern service industries for professional and technical workforce, such as high-speed rail passenger transport services, environmental assessment and counseling, safety health and environmental protection, rehabilitation engineering technology, service outsourcing, chain operation management, exhibition planning and management, leisure sports, elderly services, and management.

## Part 3 Practice of Adapting Specialty Restructuring to Industrial Restructuring

There is no doubt that the education and training restructuring will be finally carried out in specialty setup and enrollments in vocational schools. Due to the special emphasis of MOE on vocational education's function to serve the service industry, and guided by the revision of the specialty catalogue and the release of labor demand data, local education administrative departments and vocational schools have always attached great importance to timely adjustment of specialty setup and enrollments according to industrial development changes. This makes the education and training structure of vocational education increasingly adaptable to the demand structure for an industrial workforce, and has gradually become basically compatible. Next, I will take Shanghai and Jiangsu as examples.

### 1. Local Practice: Make Education and Training Structures More Compatible with Labour Demand

First, let's look at the education and training of higher vocational students in Shanghai. In 2012, there were 32 independent higher vocational schools and 148,000 students in higher vocational and technical training schools in Shanghai. In terms of specialty structure, 32 independent schools set up 766 specialties in Shanghai in 2012; the average number of specialties for each school was 24.7 and the average number of students for each specialty was 150. 766 specialties covered 18 main specialties in higher vocational and technical education.[30] Industry distribution: there were 13 specialties for primary industry, accounting for 2% of the total number of specialties; 134 for secondary industry, accounting for 17% of the total number; 619 for tertiary industry, accounting for 81% of the total number (see Figure 6.5). It can be seen from the data that Shanghai's higher vocational specialties are mainly oriented to tertiary industry, which was basically coincident with Shanghai's industrial structure.

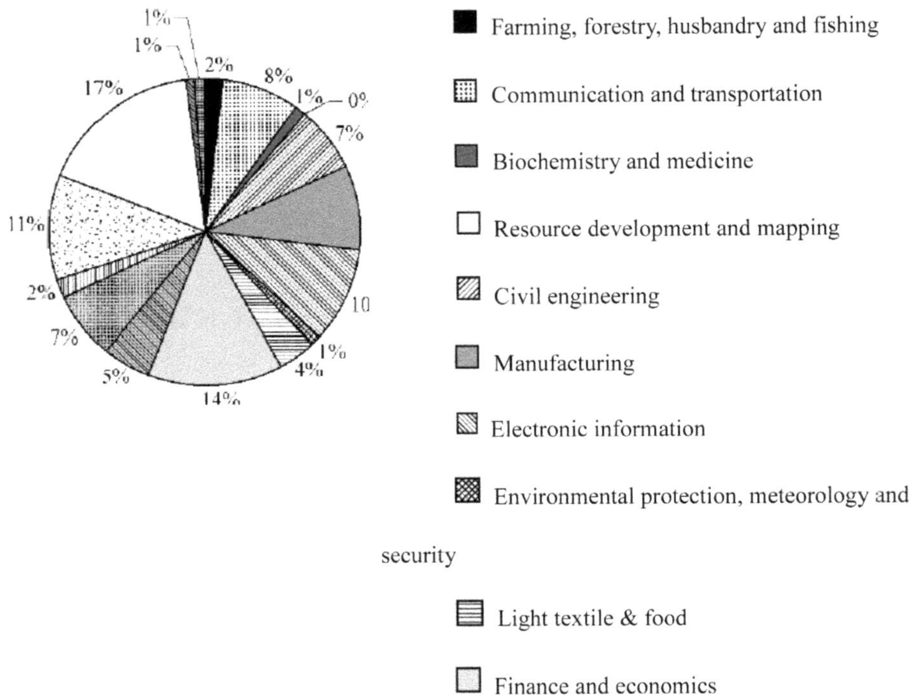


Figure 6.5 Distribution of the main specialties of the independent higher vocational schools in Shanghai in 2012

(Data source: Department of Higher Education, Shanghai Municipal Commission of Education)

Among the service specialties in higher vocational schools in Shanghai, the category of arts and design and media includes the largest number of specialties. Compared with other categories, the numbers in this category of specialties has remained the highest from 2008 to 2012, and shows an increasing trend. The proportion of the number of the specialties per year was 20.3%, 18.7%, 19.8%, 21.3%, and 25.5%. The other categories with large numbers of specialties include the main categories of electronic information, finance and economics, and cultural education. However, the category of finance and economics has not changed significantly over the past 5 years. Except for that, the categories of electronic information and cultural education have presented a declining trend in the 5 years. In particular the category of electronic information has markedly declined.[31] The specific data are shown in Tables 6.3 and 6.4.

Table 6.3 Distribution of the main specialties of 30 higher vocational schools in Shanghai

| Main Categories of Specialties | Number of Specialties | | | | | Proportion to the Total Number of Specialties (%) | | | | | Number of Schools Which Set Up the Specialties | | | | | Proportion to the Total Number of Schools (%) | | | | |
|---|---|---|---|---|---|---|---|---|---|---|---|---|---|---|---|---|---|---|---|---|
| | 2008 | 2009 | 2010 | 2011 | 2012 | 2008 | 2009 | 2010 | 2011 | 2012 | 2008 | 2009 | 2010 | 2011 | 2012 | 2008 | 2009 | 2010 | 2011 | 2012 |
| Electronic information | 86 | 86 | 97 | 85 | 62 | 16.3 | 15.6 | 15.4 | 12.3 | 10.4 | 24 | 24 | 24 | 22 | 17 | 80 | 80 | 80 | 73.3 | 56.7 |
| Medicine and health | 18 | 22 | 36 | 54 | 41 | 3.4 | 4.0 | 5.7 | 7.8 | 6.8 | 7 | 8 | 10 | 11 | 10 | 23.3 | 26.7 | 33.3 | 36.7 | 33.3 |
| Finance & economics | 82 | 93 | 92 | 105 | 98 | 15.6 | 16.9 | 14.6 | 15.2 | 16.4 | 23 | 22 | 23 | 20 | 19 | 76.7 | 73.3 | 76.7 | 66.7 | 63.3 |
| Tourism | 41 | 35 | 50 | 53 | 51 | 7.8 | 6.4 | 7.9 | 7.7 | 8.5 | 21 | 21 | 23 | 20 | 20 | 70 | 70 | 76.7 | 66.7 | 66.7 |
| Cultural education | 80 | 90 | 92 | 108 | 79 | 15.2 | 16.3 | 14.6 | 15.7 | 13.2 | 21 | 22 | 24 | 21 | 19 | 70 | 73.3 | 80 | 70 | 63.3 |
| Public services | 12 | 14 | 18 | 18 | 12 | 2.3 | 2.5 | 2.9 | 2.6 | 2.0 | 8 | 8 | 8 | 7 | 6 | 26.7 | 26.7 | 26.7 | 23.3 | 20 |
| Arts & design & media | 107 | 103 | 125 | 147 | 153 | 20.3 | 18.7 | 19.8 | 21.3 | 25.5 | 22 | 22 | 23 | 21 | 20 | 73.3 | 73.3 | 76.7 | 70 | 66.7 |
| Communication and transportation | 18 | 24 | 15 | 13 | 8 | 3.4 | 4.4 | 2.4 | 1.9 | 1.3 | 11 | 10 | 9 | 8 | 5 | 36.7 | 33.3 | 30 | 27 | 17 |
| Light textile & food | 24 | 16 | 30 | 26 | 24 | 4.6 | 2.9 | 4.8 | 3.8 | 4.0 | 10 | 10 | 11 | 10 | 9 | 33.3 | 33.3 | 37 | 33.3 | 30 |
| Public security | 2 | 5 | 5 | 13 | 8 | 0.4 | 0.9 | 0.8 | 1.9 | 1.3 | 1 | 1 | 1 | 2 | 1 | 3.3 | 3.3 | 3.3 | 6.7 | 3.3 |
| Law | 4 | 2 | 2 | 2 | 2 | 0.8 | 0.4 | 0.3 | 0.3 | 0.3 | 3 | 3 | 3 | 4 | 3 | 10 | 10 | 10 | 13.3 | 10 |
| Civil engineering | 23 | 27 | 29 | 23 | 24 | 4.4 | 4.9 | 4.6 | 3.3 | 4.0 | 10 | 11 | 13 | 11 | 10 | 33 | 33.3 | 43.3 | 33.3 | 33 |
| Manufacturing | 24 | 26 | 24 | 28 | 28 | 4.6 | 4.7 | 3.8 | 4.1 | 4.7 | 15 | 15 | 15 | 15 | 14 | 20 | 20 | 20 | 20 | 46.7 |
| Farming, forestry, husbandry and fishing | 5 | 8 | 16 | 15 | 9 | 1.0 | 1.5 | 2.5 | 2.2 | 1.5 | 4 | 4 | 5 | 4 | 4 | 13.3 | 13.3 | 16.7 | 13.3 | 13.3 |
| Total number of specialties | 526 | 551 | 631 | 690 | 599 | | | | | | Total number of schools | | | | | 30 | | | | |

(Data source: Department of Higher Education, Shanghai Municipal Commission of Education)

Table 6.4 Distribution of enrollments in the main specialties in 30 higher vocational schools in Shanghai

| Main Categories of Specialties | Number of Enrollments | | | | Proportion to the Total Enrollments of the Specialties (%) | | | |
|---|---|---|---|---|---|---|---|---|
| | 2009 | 2010 | 2011 | 2012 | 2009 | 2010 | 2011 | 2012 |
| Electronic information | 4 126 | 3 626 | 4 187 | 3 902 | 11.5 | 10.7 | 11.2 | 10.6 |
| Medicine and health | 2 079 | 300 | 2 845 | 2 582 | 5.8 | 0.9 | 7.6 | 7.0 |
| Finance & economics | 7 234 | 7 484 | 6 696 | 7 843 | 20.2 | 22.0 | 17.8 | 21.3 |
| Tourism | 3 383 | 3 275 | 3 375 | 2 981 | 9.4 | 9.6 | 9.0 | 8.1 |
| Cultural education | 5 589 | 5 787 | 5 656 | 5 354 | 15.6 | 17.0 | 15.1 | 14.6 |
| Public services | 1 037 | 681 | 708 | 767 | 2.9 | 2.0 | 1.9 | 2.1 |
| Arts & design & media | 5 628 | 5 778 | 5 807 | 6 447 | 15.7 | 17.0 | 15.5 | 17.5 |
| Communication and transportation | 1 888 | 2 044 | 1 906 | 1 898 | 5.3 | 6.0 | 5.1 | 5.2 |
| Light textile & food | 1 549 | 1 409 | 2 361 | 1 567 | 4.3 | 4.2 | 6.3 | 4.3 |
| Public security | 1 000 | 1 120 | 1 492 | 686 | 2.8 | 3.3 | 4.0 | 1.9 |
| Law | 162 | 163 | 136 | 155 | 0. 5 | 0. 5 | 0.4 | 0.4 |
| Civil engineering | 1 011 | 1 225 | 1 219 | 1 251 | 2.8 | 3.6 | 3.2 | 3.4 |
| Manufacturing | 811 | 686 | 649 | 790 | 2.3 | 2.0 | 1.7 | 2.1 |
| Farming, forestry, husbandry and fishing | 399 | 364 | 502 | 522 | 1.1 | 1. 1 | 1.3 | 1.4 |

(Data source: Department of Higher Education, Shanghai Municipal Commission of Education)

In terms of the enrollments of various specialties, the categories of finance and economics, arts and design and media, design, and cultural education are not only widely established in higher vocational schools; however, they have the largest number of enrollments. These categories are popular for admission to higher vocational schools in Shanghai. Compared with the specialty distribution in previous years, however, there is no significant difference in the enrollment numbers among these main categories. Between 2008 and 2012, the category of finance and economics was the one with the largest number of enrollments in higher vocational schools in Shanghai, whose average enrollments have accounted for 20.3% of the total number for the past 5 years. It was followed by the category of arts and design and media, whose number of enrollments accounted for 16.4% of the total. As for the categories of electronic information and cultural education, the number of their enrollments accounted for about 10% of the total. The proportion of the enrollment number of other categories has been generally less than 10% of the total enrollments.

As a province with a developed economy and vocational education, Jiangsu province has always attached great importance to how the specialty structure of vocational education is adaptable to the industrial structure. Experts have organized two rounds of large-scale scientific research on this issue since 2009. The second round of research drew the following conclusions: 1. The graduation numbers have adapted well to industry occupation requirements. The relative gap between the demand and supply of vocational graduates has been alleviated year by year. However, the gap between the absolute demand and absolute supply still remains prominent. A greater variety of skilled labor is needed for high and new technology industries, strategic emerging industries and particular advanced industries; 2. In terms of training structure, the specialty setup has basically covered all categories of industrial development in Jiangsu province; the proportion of specialty enrollments has been basically consistent with that of employee demands in the three industrial sectors; 3. The specialty structure of secondary vocational education has been consistent with the structure of leading industries and emerging industries to some degree. However, they are not highly adaptable to each other; few specialties which are highly technological and high in school-operating cost have been established; specialty setup lags behind or some specialties have not been established for long.[32]

## 2. How to Rationally Understand the Degree of Coincidence in Training Structures with Demand Structure

Making the training structure more adaptable to the demand structure of vocational education is an intrinsic requirement for both the industrial cycle and the vocational education cycle. Only by improving the degree of coincidence can demand of the industrial complex for a professional and technical workforce be satisfied, and vocational school graduates obtain jobs corresponding to their capacities. The problem now is how to rationally understand how compatible they are with each other. This involves studying the methodology as it relates to this issue.

There is a trend when examining this issue. That is, people are more often looking for a quantified and accurate conclusion and hope to use very precise data to reflect the degree of coincidence to provide early warnings and advice. This kind of data is certainly a valuable source for guidance of specialty setup and new student enrollments in vocational schools. The problem is whether the findings of this kind of study are reasonable? Is this kind of data available? Is it reliable if it is obtained? Many studies use the "job vacancies-to-seekers ratio" of the labor market as the indicator to reflect the degree of coincidence between supply and demand. This indicator is of some reference value when judging the degree of coincidence between the two, but it may not make any sense in many cases. This is because enterprises have various sources of qualified employees, and not all enterprises recruit them through the formal labor market. This will seriously affect the accuracy of both demand and supply data. For example, vocational school graduates are usually recommended for employment by the graduate schools directly and few are employed through the labor market. In order to accurately calculate the degree of coincidence, we need to solve the three problems: 1. The acquisition of the demand data; 2. The acquisition of the supply data; 3. The calculation of the degree of coincidence between supply and demand according to the indicator. However, in reality the three problems are all confronted with tough technical difficulties.

In terms of the first problem, is it possible to obtain accurate enterprise labor demand data? Although we can often see various labor demand data released at home and abroad, and even the prediction data on future labor demand, whether these data are accurate and reliable still need to be scrutinized: 1. It is difficult to directly obtain big data on enterprise labor demands. It's easy to obtain the labor demand data of an enterprise, but comparatively difficult to obtain the labor demand data of a region. The larger the research scope is, the more enterprises there will be, the more complicated the differences and changes among enterprises will be, and the more difficult it will be to obtain accurate big data on labor demand. Unless people can develop a platform, which can be used to measure enterprise labor demand, and all enterprises advise in a timely manner the required labor data of various types into the platform. 2. If we fail to obtain direct data, we will often use GDP to estimate the quantity of the labor demanded. However, does the growth of industrial GDP necessarily indicate an increase in labor demand? As a matter of fact, GDP growth and labor demand need to take enterprise technology, occupation data, and corporate human resource policies as the intermediate variables, however growth in GDP does not necessarily lead to an increase in labor demand. For example, if automation technology is introduced, the quantity of labor required may still decline; if an enterprise reduces job setups, it will also lead to a decline in labor demand; in terms of corporate human resources policies, for example, overtime work will reduce the demand for labor. Therefore, it is extremely inaccurate to draw direct inferences from the changes in labor demand through changes in GDP. 3. In order to calculate labor demand data accurately, we can seek for parameters that are highly correlated with changes in the quantity of labor needed. But this has always been a difficult technical problem. Useful parameters can be found in some industries, such as the medical industry: the number of nurses needed can be calculated according to the numbers of the patients treated in the hospital; in the automobile maintenance industry, we can calculate the number of maintenance workers that are needed in the future according to the average number of automobiles a worker can repair; but for most industries, it is difficult to find such parameters. 4. Some studies also hoped to calculate the demand of different levels of skilled labor for industrial development. It is a data which is more difficult to be calculated. This is because, for most jobs, enterprises have difficulty in judging which level of skill is required. In most cases, all levels of skill are fine. However, the higher the degree it is, the more accurate it will be.

For the second problem, it is easy to calculate statistics for supply data from the current year's graduates and it can even reach a relatively accurate level. The reason why I say so is that in addition to choosing jobs relevant to specialties, many vocational school graduates choose to continue their studies; some choose to change careers, and the number of the students who choose to change careers accounts for a considerable proportion. Therefore, it will be more difficult and even impossible to obtain complete supply data. This is because a large amount of substituted employment exists in the labor market, including: 1. Changing careers, which is particularly common in the service industry; 2. Short-term skills training. Enterprises carry out short-term training for unskilled workers in order to meet urgent requirements; 3. Lowering the academic levels. For example, undergraduates working as workers; 4. Employing specialist and retired personnel; 5. Trans-regional labor recruitment, such as the large-scale recruitment of workers from the inland to the coastal areas, etc. These phenomena show that vocational school is just a channel to provide labor for enterprises.

In terms of the third problem, does accurate calculation of the degree of coincidence exist? Even if we can obtain the above data accurately, the two sets of data don't need to be highly coincident. This is because people's abilities are adaptable. Individuals are not confined to a single and precisely defined job, but possess the employment transfer ability from a certain job. Moreover, this adaptability will expand with the enhancement of corporate training. While studying the degree of coincidence between the supply and demand of vocational education graduates, we should never underestimate the corrective role that enterprises play in human resources development. Furthermore, we should also see that different schools have different training orientations even in the same specialty. For some broadly orientated specialties, such as mechatronics, the differences vary considerably. This phenomenon will naturally affect the judgment of the degree of coincidence and also affect the statistics on the quantity of labor supply. Specialty caliber is the basic statistical unit. The smaller it is, the slighter the data error will be.

If we think it is possible with any certainty and practical guidance to calculate how labor supply can meet the demand in different industries under the premise of thoroughly taking various influencing variables into consideration, then it will be almost a meaningless job to integrate the coincidence data of various industries and find out the overall level of how labor supply is docked with labor demand. This is because the coincidence data of different industries are not comparable and they cannot be mathematically calculated. For example, in some industries, employees do not change their occupations frequently, and a slight mismatch between supply and demand will affect practice significantly, such as specialist doctors; while in some other industries, employees change their occupations frequently, and even a large mismatch between supply and demand won't affect practice too much, such as business executives.

The above is a methodological discussion on the calculation of the degree of coincidence between labor training structure and the demand structure. The results indicate that: 1. It's necessary to attach importance to the degree of coincidence. It is a crucial concept that instructs vocational schools to establish specialties and determine the enrollments. However, in terms of the research capability at present, we can only carry out macroscopic research on the descriptive analysis of labor demand, and thereby guide the specialty setup of vocational schools. For example, the service industry is the largest industry in the industrial structure in Shanghai, and it is a labor-intensive industry. If we make an analysis on the overall size, industrial form, and potential labor demand of the service industry in Shanghai, then the analysis results can be used to instruct the specialty setup of vocational schools. If most vocational schools mainly focus on engineering specialties, then we need to adjust the specialty structure. The pursuit of accurate calculation of degree of coincidence at the macro level is difficult to achieve at present. 2. We can carry out some quantitative research at the micro level, such as research according to different occupations; on preschool teachers for example; research according to different regions, on a certain vocational school. The smaller the range of our attention is, the more accurate results we will obtain and the better it can guide practice. For research at this level, both the changes in the employment of vocational school graduates over the past years and the changes in enterprises' attitude toward recruitment, are important signals for changes in regional labor demand. 3. While studying this issue, we should not overly pursue accurate calculation results, or deny the role of qualitative analysis in research. Instead, we should make a profound analysis of cases, or an in-depth description and analysis on the actual manifestation and occurrence mechanism of the issue. This is often more valuable than most macro data. Furthermore, the internal organizations and changing processes of society are very sophisticated and we should more often obtain the data range influenced by certain variables instead of accurate data.

## Notes

1 Wang Tongsan: Quantitative Economics in the 21st Century (Volume 3), Social Sciences Academic Press (China), 2003, p. 125.
2 Yin Ming: Handbook of Socialist Market Economy, Hehai University Press, 1993, p. 67.
3 Jiang Xiaojuan: The Improvement and Upgrade of Industrial Structure: New Tasks in the New Stage, Finance & Trade Economics, No. 4, 2005.
4 State Council: Decision of the State Council on the Main Points of the Current Industrial Policies, 1989.
5 State Council: Interim Provisions on Promoting the Industrial Structure Adjustment, 2005.
6 State Council: Main Points for the Work of the State Council in 2006, 2006.
7 State Council: Several Opinions of the State Council on Accelerating the Development of the Service Industry, 2007.
8 State Council: Main Points for the Work of the State Council in 2007, 2007.
9 State Council: Decision of the State Council on Accelerating the Fostering and Development of Strategic Emerging Industries, 2010.
10 State Council: Industrial Transformation and Upgrading Plan (2011–2015), 2011.
11 State Council: The '12th Five-Year' Plan for the National Development of Strategic Emerging Industries, 2012.
12 State Council: Guiding Opinions of the State Council of the People's Republic of China, on Accelerating Development of Productive Service and Promoting Industrial Structure Adjustment and Upgrade, 2014.
13 Jiang Xiaojuan: The Improvement and Upgrading of Industrial Structure: New Tasks in the New Stage, Finance & Trade Economics, No. 4, 2005.
14 Large Country Economic Transformation Research Group: From a Big Country of Human Resources to a Manufacturing Powerhouse, Economic Science Press, 2012.
15 Same as the above footnote.
16 Wang Yun, Zeng Zheng: Continuous Optimization and Upgrade of Industrial Structure is an Important Trait of the New Normal, Gmw.cn, http://news.xinhuanet.com/fortune/2016-01/05/c_128597450.htm

17 State Council: Decision of the CPC Central Committee on the Reform of the Education System, 1985.
18 The Eighth National People's Congress: Vocational Education Law of the People's Republic of China, 1996.
19 State Council: Outline of the National Medium-and Long-Term Education Reform and Development Plan (2010–2020), 2010.
20 State Council: Decision on Accelerating the Development ofModern Vocational Education, 2014.
21 State Council: The '13th Five-Year' Plan for China's Educational Development, 2017.
22 State Council: Decision on Vigorously Developing Vocational and Technical Education, 1991.
23 State Education Commission (now MOE): Notice of the State Education Commission on Promulgating "The Specialty Catalogue for Regular Secondary Specialized Schools," 1993.
24 Da Hai: Interview with Chen Guang, Director of the Textbook Division, and the Department of Vocational and Adult Education, MOE, on the Formulation and Management of the Specialty Catalogue of Secondary Vocational Schools: New Circumstances, New Principles and New Features, Vocational and Technical Education, No. 30, 2001.
25 Deng Zemin: The Specialty Catalogue for Secondary Vocational Schools, Chinese Vocational and Technical Education, No. 16, 2010.
26 MOE: Notice of MOE on Printing and Distributing "The Specialty Catalogue of Secondary Vocational Schools (Revised in 2010)," 2010.
27 MOE: The Specialty Catalogue of Secondary Vocational Schools (Revised in 2010), 2010.
28 MOE: The Instructive Specialty Catalogue for Higher Vocational and Technical Education in Regular Colleges and Universities (Trial), 2004.
29 MOE: Notice of MOE on Printing and Distributing the "Administrative Measures for Specialty Setup of Higher Vocational Education (Specialist)" and "The Specialty Catalogue of Higher Vocational Education (Specialist) in Regular Colleges and Universities (2015)," 2015.
30 Shanghai education portal website: edu.sh.gov.cn.
31 Data source: http://www.edu.sh.gov.cn/sjfb/201309/261592.html
32 Yin Weimin, Wang Fang, Liu Keyong: Early Warning Report on the Goodness of Fit of the Specialty Structure of Vocational Schools with the Industrial Structure in Jiangsu Province (2016), Jiangsu Phoenix Education Publishing, Ltd, 2017.
33 National Bureau of Statistics: National Data, http://data.stats.gov.cn/easyquery.htm?cn=C01.
34 National Bureau of Statistics: National Data, http://data.stats.gov.cn/easyquery.htm?cn=C01

CHAPTER SEVEN

# Establishing a Competency-Based Curriculum and Teaching Model

Curriculum and teaching are the core of education. Vocational education must firmly grasp and reflect its own characteristics to establish itself as a distinct type of education. Furthermore, they are also the key ingredients to ensure the quality of vocational education. Therefore, since reform and opening-up, we have embarked on a course of curriculum construction while taking the first steps toward the basic construction of vocational education, such as perfecting the school system and facilitating industry-education cooperation; furthermore, people's increasing consciousness of the importance of relevant curriculum and teaching construction has pushed the activity level of curriculum and teaching construction gradually from the edge to the core, and from local to nationwide. Curriculum construction aims to improve curriculum quality, and it must be accompanied by teaching standards while improving curriculum quality. However, there is an important difference in constructing the path between this field and other fields. That is, in the construction of most vocational education fields, including teacher training to be discussed later. It's basically carried out under the guidance of policies, while vocational curriculum and teaching norms are established under the guidance of both academic research and policies, and sometimes the role of academic researchers must precede policy guidance. Therefore, we should tackle curriculum construction and teaching norms of vocational education in China since reform and opening-up along two main lines: deepening the process of theoretical research and the evolution process of policy making.

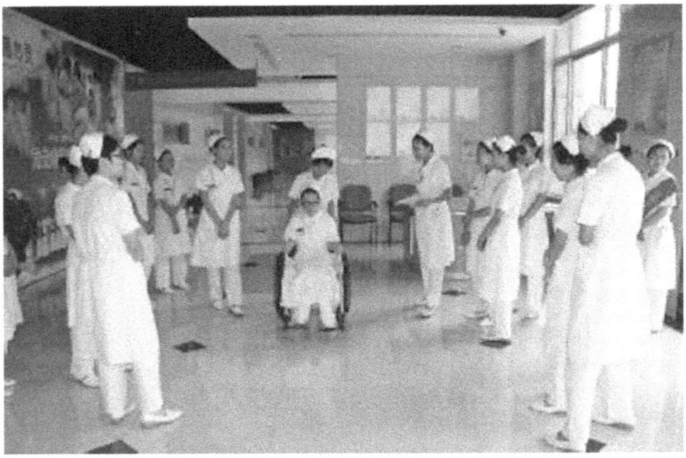

Figure 7.1 Nursing students role-playing

## Part 1 Vocational Curriculum Construction at the Conceptual Stage

Over the past four decades since reform and opening-up, the course of vocational curriculum construction should take the transition from the 20th and the 21st centuries as the turning point. The characteristics of vocational curriculum construction in the 1980s and 1990s can be summarized by the term "conceptual." The conceptual stage means that people's understanding of a problem is only a perception at the superficial level, and they propose solving strategies of a problem based on their subjective thinking of the problem. People often prefer to use the term "empirical" to describe problem-solving strategies at the initial stage, but this term is not appropriate here as the collection of accurate data is premature. This is because experience is often based on in-depth practice, and the construction theories of vocational curriculum which are proposed at this stage are not based on long-term and in-depth curriculum practice. It's prominently characterized by people's subjective perception. The use of the term "conceptual" can have continuity with the scientific stage of vocational curriculum construction after the 21st century. This is because the use of the term "scientific" here does not mean the form of knowledge which is defined by experimental testing in natural science, but the process of deepening theoretical research to approach the essence of curriculum problems and corresponding solutions. As keenly perceived by the author of *20 Years of Review and Witnessing*: "We haven't had a genuine curriculum theory of our own, because vocational education practice has not developed to the level where we can advance our own curriculum theory ... Faced with the rising storm of the knowledge economy at the turn of the century, we can really feel a wishful sense of urgency and anxiety."[1] In addition, some phrases that were used in the past are not used here, such as "curriculum development," "curriculum reform," but "curriculum construction" instead. This is because "curriculum construction" covers a wider range, and all behaviors that increase curriculum acquisition such as "developing curriculum," "purchasing curriculum," "introducing curriculum," and "reforming curriculum" can all be incorporated into the concept of "curriculum construction."

Strictly speaking, China did not take any concerted action on curriculum construction in the 1980s. This is because China's first curriculum theory, namely *Modern Curriculum Theory* by Zhong Qiquan, was published in 1989. As the birthplace of curriculum theory in China, the Department of Education of East China Normal University did not offer any curriculum theory for undergraduate courses at that time; only some postgraduates were inclined to pay attention to curriculum theory. The study of curriculum theory began to prevail in China's pedagogy after the mid-1990s. One of the major reasons is that at the beginning of the founding of new China, our pedagogical discipline system borrowed from the former Soviet system, while the former Soviet Union education had no curriculum theory but teaching theory only. As a result, although curriculum theory has developed in the U.S. and other countries for more than half a century and reached a fairly high academic level over that time, educational circles in China knew very little about its specific content. Vocational curriculum theory was developed under the influence of the general education curriculum theory, so it appeared later in China. In 1993, Mr. Huang Kexiao published an article, *On the Curriculum Reform of Vocational and Technical Education* in *Vocational & Technical Education Forum*, which was on the early research literature on vocational curriculum construction in China. As a pioneer in curriculum research of vocational education in China, Mr. Huang has also been recognized by vocational education circles. After that, there were several sporadic monographs on vocational curriculum from different angles such as *CBE Theory and Practice* compiled by the China CBE expert study group in 1993 and *A Teaching Model of Modern Vocational and Technical Education* edited and published by Liu Denggao in 2000. The two works mainly introduced internationally well-received curriculum models such as MES and CBE. In 1995, Shang Yuanming edited and published *Research on Curriculum Systems of Vocational Secondary Schools,* made an in-depth investigation and analysis of the curriculum problems of vocational secondary schools at that time, and attempted to propose solutions. In 2001, Mr. Huang published a monograph, *Introduction to Vocational and Technical Education Curriculum*, which is the first systematic monograph on vocational curriculum construction in China. The academic contribution of these achievements lies in that it has initiated the research on vocational curriculum in China. However, in terms of its content, it still centers on Western curriculum models and the conceptual description of vocational curriculum problems in China.

Although China did not take any sustained or in-depth action on vocational curriculum construction in the 1980s, early national policies were concerned with such issues as the importance of vocational curriculum construction and the determination of the main direction of curriculum construction. For example, *Decision of the CPC Central Committee on the Reform of the Education System* in 1985 points out: "Quite a lot of the curriculum is outdated in content, rigid in teaching methods, underdeveloped in practice, too narrow in specialty settings, and separated from the needs of economic and social development to varying degrees, and lags behind the development of contemporary science and culture."[2] In addition, vocational curriculum construction is often mentioned in other important documents, but has limited relevance to these areas. For example, the *Decision of the State Council on Vigorously Developing Vocational and Technical Education* (No. 55 [1991] from the State Council) proposes: "We should reform the teaching content and teaching methods, highlight practical teaching, and enhance vocational skills training; pay attention to enhancing adaptability, practicality and flexibility in teaching arrangements; vocational and technical training schools should not only attach importance to moral and intellectual education but also strengthen aesthetic education, sports and health education, so as to improve education quality in an all-around way."[3]

In the 1980s, China did not deeply reform the vocational curriculum, and mainly standardized the curriculum. MOE promulgated *Several Plans for the Two-Year Teaching Arrangements of Engineering Specialties in Secondary Specialized Schools* in 1979 and required that: "Secondary specialized schools should base its curriculum content on reality, carefully select content with appropriate depth and breadth and avoid being too much and deep in content." However, it also emphasized: "Secondary specialized schools should pay attention to strengthening basic theory teaching."[4] In 1979, MOE proposed in *Regulations Concerning the Work of Full-Time Secondary Specialized Schools* that: "Students should receive education at the senior high school level and learn specialized knowledge based on this." "Secondary specialized schools should enhance the teaching of basic theories and basic knowledge, and overcome the erroneous viewpoint of looking down upon theories and book learning."[5] These requirements were put forward in response to the problem due to the neglect of knowledge learning during the Cultural Revolution. Here it proposed the requirement that the academic knowledge level of secondary specialized schools should be equivalent to senior high school level, which has become the bottom line for the reform of the basic academic curriculum in secondary vocational schools, in spite of the existence of different opinions and realistically beyond reach. In 1986, the State Education Commission put *Opinions on Formulating Teaching Plans for (Three-Year) Vocational Senior High Schools* (No. 008 [86] from the Department of Vocational Education, MOE) into trial use, which was officially promulgated in 1990 after several years of trial and revision. This document makes detailed and explicit provisions on vocational education training objectives, curriculum setup and teaching hours, and it mainly contributes to the standardized curriculum of vocational senior high schools. For example, the document defines the training objective of vocational senior high schools as: "The task of vocational high schools is to train intermediate skilled workers, farmers at intermediate technical level, middle-level administrators, technicians and other employees." The curriculum is divided into three categories: the political and cultural strand, the specialized strand, and the internship strand. It also stipulates that the proportion of political and cultural course content, specialized course and internship course content is generally 3:3:4 for the industrial, agricultural, and medical category, 4:3:3 for liberal arts category, and 2.5:2.5:5 for some specialties and professions that require strong skills. The specific proportions can be reasonably flexible according to different specialties, professions and training objectives. At the same time, it even specifies the requirements for the number of teaching weeks and class hours: "During the three years, students should be in school for 150 weeks in total, including 105–111 weeks for teaching, 12 weeks for exam review, 24–27 weeks for winter and summer vacations, and 3–6 weeks for optional things. In terms of teaching time, there should be 60–70 weeks for theoretical teaching of the industrial, agricultural, and medical category, 70–80 weeks for the liberal arts category, 50–60 weeks for the specialties and professions that require strong skills, and the rest are allocated as weeks for internship."

"The number of theoretical teaching hours should be 28–32 class hours per week; the number of the total hours of the industrial, agricultural and medical category should be 1,800–2,100 class hours; the total number of the liberal arts category should be 2,100–2,400 class hours; the total number of specialties and professions that require strong skills should be 1,500–1,800 class hours; the total number of production practice time should be 36–48 class hours per week."[6] Such detailed regulations are not only necessary but also important for newly-established vocational senior high schools. It differs from the previous two documents in that it highlights the requirements for practical teaching. Special attention was paid to vocational education textbooks during this period. In 1993, the former State Education Commission released *Opinions on the Planning for Vocational and Technical Education Textbooks* (No. 13 [1993] from the Department of Vocational Education, MOE), and put forward national and provincial planning principles and proposed that the focus of textbook planning was quality improvement. However, no related content to textbook construction models and ideas was included except for management regulations.

The 1990s was an important stage for the initiation of curriculum reform of vocational education in China. The curriculum construction during this period mainly focused on the introduction of CBE that was a prevailing model in many developed countries in the 1980s. Curriculum reform struggled through some pilots and controversies of the CBE curriculum model. Under the direction of MOE, the Canada-China College Linkage Program (CCCLP) started to be established with the support of Canadian International Development Assistance (CIDA) from 1989. In October 1991, this program held the first "DACUM" workshop in Chengdu, China, and officially introduced CBE education ideas and curriculum models to China. This has triggered a nationwide upsurge of CBE curriculum research and practice in the 1990s. See Table 7.1.

Table 7.1 Significant events in introducing and promoting CBE in China[23]

| Time | Location | Theme |
|---|---|---|
| March 4–8, 1991 | Xiamen | Seminar on Canada-China College Linkage |
| November 4–9, 1991 | Chengdu | Symposium on Curriculum Development (DACUM) |
| November 17–25, 1992 | Beijing | Symposium on the Introduction of CBE |
| May 10–15, 1993 | Nanjing | Seminar on Chinese Project Coordinators |
| December 8–11, 1993 | Changzhou | Seminar on Adult and Continuing Education |
| January 9–20, 1995 | Shijiazhuang | Advanced Training Courses on CBE and DACUM |
| October 14–26, 1995 | Beijing | Shooting CBE TV documentaries in China |
| October 31—November 3, 1995 | Beijing | International Symposium on Environment and Education |
| April 16–18, 1996 | Nanjing | International Symposium on Vocational Education Mode and Curriculum Development |

The core idea of the CBE curriculum model is to organize courses based on occupational capacity modules. This is completely different from the three-stage curriculum model, which had been implemented in vocational education in China for some time before then. The three-stage curriculum divided the curriculum into three categories: a basic cultural course, a basic specialized courses and a specialized course, and the specialized course included a specialized theory course and a specialized practice course. The curriculum was carried out in the order from basic cultural course to basic specialized course and then specialized courses. This kind of curriculum model borrows from the curriculum model of specialized education in universities. The fundamental philosophy is to let students accumulate systematic specialized theoretical knowledge first, and then help students to form practical abilities by comprehensively applying their specialized theoretical knowledge. After nearly 30 years of efforts in curriculum reform, the three-stage curriculum model still remains the dominant curriculum model of vocational education in China up until now, which shows the difficulties in reforming the curriculum model.

Figure 7.2 Analysis on work tasks and occupational capabilities

The advantage of the three-stage curriculum model is that students can acquire relatively systematic and solid specialized theoretical knowledge. For the specialties requiring high theoretical knowledge, such as mechanical manufacturing, this curriculum model has certain advantages. However, it has the following serious defects in practice in training skilled people: First, the starting point of curriculum design is to master theoretical knowledge rather than the abilities required for professions. This makes it easy to disconnect from the needs of professions. However, the important purpose of restoring secondary vocational education in the 1980s was to cultivate skilled workers needed for economic construction, and serving economic construction was the basic direction for developing vocational education at that time. The three-stage curriculum model could not make sure that this requirement for curriculum development technology would be realized. Although it also emphasized this mission, it could only manifest as words. Second, it's easy to lead to too much theoretical knowledge and weaken the cultivation of practical capacities. This is because the three-stage curriculum model considers theoretical study as the basis of practical ability training, and reflects the requirements for theoretical knowledge in the form of a basic specialized course and a specialized theoretical course. Although all important documents have pointed out that vocational curriculum should concentrate on cultivating practical abilities, the characteristics of this curriculum model itself easily lead to the core position of theoretical knowledge in curriculum. Third, it is easy to teach theory disconnected from practice. In such a curriculum model, theory and practice are different courses. Although we emphasize that theory should serve practice, we did not provide any clear curriculum development technology for the linkage between theory and practice. As a result, this will inevitably mutually disconnect theory from practice. At that time, it was called the "dichotomy" between theory and practice. CBE curriculum was introduced to overcome these problems in the curriculum. Moreover, the three major problems can be well solved by organizing courses with the competence model of professions as the focus.

The introduction of the CBE curriculum model refreshed vocational education operations at that time, and it was actively piloted. Although the CBE model was widely publicized at that time, the first training events were held in Chengdu, Shanghai, and Jiangsu, the places where the pilots were intensively carried out. Shanghai Municipal Commission of Education focused on the major project "Research and Experiment on Vocational Curriculum Reform and Textbook Construction" which was sponsored by National Education Sciences Planning in China: the 9th Five Year Plan (1995~1999), initiated the "10181" project in 1996. In other words, China planned to spend 5 years accomplishing the reform and compilation of demonstration textbooks in 10 public courses and completing compilation of textbooks in 18 typical specialties and professions, and spend 10 years or so establishing a secondary vocational curriculum and textbook system which reflected the characteristics of China, in Shanghai through continuous experiments, summaries, and research. The project was based on the principles set out in the CBE curriculum model.

Although this attempt at curriculum reform has not fundamentally reversed the curriculum model at the practical level, it has indeed carried out curriculum development by strict use of capability analysis. Curriculum developers have followed the requirements of CBE curriculum development, hired corporate technical experts to develop capability modules so as to form some DACUM diagrams.

The pilots of the CBE curriculum model have also provided an important opportunity for vocational teachers to understand the special rules of vocational curriculum design and laid a good conceptual foundation for the all-around promotion of competency-based curriculum reform in the 21st century. The primary reason why the curriculum model failed to be fundamentally reversed was that it was unaware of how to convert capability analysis modules into curriculum. This was also the core issue in vocational curriculum construction at that time. Mr. Meng Guangping, the former Director of the Department of Vocational and Technical Education of MOE, once told me that China sent a delegation to Canada, with the purpose of understanding how the conversion process was realized at the time. The core task was to figure out this process, but no result was achieved. It now appears that the reasons why we failed to convert capability analysis outcomes into curriculum are that on the one hand, capability analysis had its own defects at that time, that is, it could not distinguish the task analysis from capability analysis; on the other hand, our consciousness did not completely accept the idea of organizing courses according to competency modules directly. When all we can imagine is a three-stage curriculum, we certainly can't achieve conversion. The conversion problem drew much attention at the time. For example, Mr. Jiang Naiping, an important researcher of vocational curriculum, excitedly pointed out that my research has exploited a direction for the conversion of task analysis outcomes into curriculum after seeing my research findings on distinguishing the logical paths to task analysis in an article.

Practitioners are generally curious about the CBE curriculum model and actively bring it up in discussions, but pioneers of vocational curriculum research have been studying how to avoid the CBE curriculum model. What they are most concerned about is: the CBE curriculum model will weaken students' theoretical knowledge learning, restrict the scope of their capability training, and go against students' adaptation to the job market and future development. Therefore, they advocate this curriculum model can only be applied to vocational training, and cannot be completely applied to school vocational education. Mr. Meng Guangping once talked to me about one matter: he spent a night trying to persuade an important researcher on vocational curriculum to accept the CBE curriculum model, but failed. That's where their divergence of opinion lies. Later, in order to make researchers accept the CBE curriculum model, Mr. Meng adopted an indirect approach. In other words, he proposed to distinguish the competency-based curriculum from the competency analysis method used in developing competency-based curriculum; he thought that people just do not accept the analysis method rather than the curriculum model, because they are certain that vocational curriculum should develop students' abilities. Actually, I can feel Mr. Meng's heart here. However, the CBE curriculum model has its particular implications, and it is quite different from the general curriculum philosophy that advocates cultivation of students' abilities. If we distinguish this curriculum model from its development technique, we won't really master this curriculum model well.

The researchers are unanimous in their concerns about the CBE curriculum model, but have completely different settlement strategies. For example, Mr. Huang Kexiao proposed the strategy of the "model of multi-element integrated education." He advocated that we should not just implement one curriculum model in a professional curriculum system; instead, we should learn widely from the strengths of multiple curriculum models, and construct a curriculum system supported by the best of various curriculum models. He particularly proposed to build technical subject curriculum. He once attempted to explain the underpinnings of a technical subject curriculum, but seemingly not very successfully. The solution strategy proposed by Mr. Jiang was a "broad basis, flexible module" curriculum model. Obviously, this kind of curriculum model does not completely deny the CBE curriculum model, as the "flexible module" refers to the competency-based curriculum. He added "broad basis" on this foundation to try to offset the problems in the CBE curriculum model. Other researchers have proposed the concept of a "personality-oriented" curriculum model, in order to highlight the importance of "students" in curriculum design.

The starting point for researchers to raise these concerns is to build a more reasonable vocational curriculum system. Some viewpoints are of great significance to the study of vocational curriculum. For example, the "model of multi-element integrated education" proposed by Mr. Huang must be used in practice, the pluralistic talent training objectives and the diversified knowledge types of vocational education determine that vocational curriculum models must be diversified, but no country only adopts the CBE curriculum in its school vocational curriculum. His concept of technical subject curriculum is worthy of in-depth study by curriculum researchers and is of great significance for the construction of a higher vocational curriculum and a technology applicable undergraduate curriculum. Their concerns are important in that they provide a protective screen to prevent a vocational curriculum slide from "emphasizing theory, underestimating practice" to "emphasizing practice, underestimating theory." This situation did occur in the reform of vocational curriculum in the early 21st century and some vocational schools completely became partial to skills training under the guidance of "useful and sufficient" theoretical knowledge. Of course, some concerns are a result of a lack of in-depth understanding of the CBE curriculum model. For example, the curriculum model explicitly defines occupational capability as the sum of knowledge, skill and attitude, thus the "personality-oriented" concept has no academic or theoretical basis for its existence. Since knowledge is included in ability, the concerns of Mr. Huang and Mr. Jiang seem to be too one-sided.

The more important problem lies in that these concerns are just responses to a number of factors, and do not go deeply into the theoretical basis of the CBE curriculum model. Therefore, the academic value produced by the theoretical research of vocational curriculum during this period is relatively limited, and correspondingly it plays a limited role in facilitating vocational curriculum construction. In fact, the above concerns can be completely solved by deepening the design of CBE curriculum development techniques. After deepening the design, this curriculum model can even be applied to higher vocational education and even technology applicable undergraduate education. This is because the CBE curriculum model originates from professional education. That is, from teacher education in the U.S. in the 1960s. We must adhere to taking the CBE curriculum model as the dominant model of vocational curriculum construction, otherwise vocational curriculum will never extricate itself from the three fundamental problems existing in the three-stage curriculum.

The above is just an analysis on specialized course construction, and its main content was still "standard" during this period. In other words, it means to supervise and urge vocational schools to set up the basic cultural courses that should be established, meet the requirements of basic cultural courses for the categories and number of class hours stipulated in *Opinions on Formulating Teaching Plans for (Three-Year) Vocational Senior High Schools* in 1990, and the basic cultural courses should be "equivalent to the level of regular senior high schools." At the same time, however, a considerable number of schools partially focused on basic cultural courses, and inappropriately increased basic cultural courses, with the so-called purpose of fostering students' "development potential." As a result, this led to the failure to properly realize the training objectives of vocational education. Since the issue of basic cultural courses was not very serious and relevant research had not been carried out in depth at the time, people hadn't begun to be concerned about reform of basic cultural courses.

## Part 2 Vocational Curriculum Construction in the Scientific Stage

The period from the early 21st century to now is very important for the reform of the vocational curriculum in China. If China's vocational curriculum construction was mainly characterized by the standardization of curriculum and the introduction of small-scale pilots of the Western curriculum models in the 1990s, then this period should be mainly characterized by the comprehensive development of curriculum reform and the in-depth transformation of the curriculum model. Moreover, not all course construction activities were carried out under the guidance of policies during this period; many were implemented by vocational schools spontaneously and even directly by teachers. Vocational school administrators and teachers gave unprecedented attention to curriculum construction and it became the core of the development of vocational education in China during this period. The reasons can be summarized in the following three ways. First, after developing for more than 20 years since reform and opening-up, China's vocational education has reached the basic level in terms of the construction of school-operating entities and people have become more and more conscious of the significance of curriculum construction and all that it implies. Moreover, curriculum construction has been generally considered as the core and key of the essential prerequisites of curriculum construction. Second, higher education expansion has brought about a sharp decline in the quality of secondary vocational students. If we don't implement curriculum reform and continue to carry out the "three-stage" curriculum, we will have difficulty in carrying on classroom teaching. For example, the reason why the influence of the "broad basis, flexible module" curriculum model suddenly suffered a sharp decline during this period was that people widely realized that "broad basis" was already an unattainable goal. Third, the rapidly developing higher vocational schools are confronted with strong curriculum construction requirements to create their own characteristics and levels. Fourth, the substantial progress in the level of curriculum research has greatly broadened people's understanding of the new model of vocational curriculum construction and inspired people's interest in curriculum development.

## 1. Progress in Vocational Curriculum Research

Vocational curriculum construction is chiefly characterized by the remarkable improvement in the level of research during this period. The number of people specializing in vocational curriculum research has increased compared with that in the 1990s, but the improvement during this period is more reflected in the enriched research findings and quality improvement. It is generally believed by vocational education circles that the most important researchers on curriculum during this period are Professor. Jiang Dayuan from the Central Institute for Vocational and Technical Education of MOE, Professor Zhao Zhiqun from Beijing Normal University, and me, known as the "troika" of vocational curriculum research. The academic paths of Professor Jiang and Professor Zhao are mainly to do with the study and introduction of the German curriculum model, and to localize it in some aspects. For example, Professor Jiang emphasizes that his systematic courses of the working process do not indiscriminately imitate the German model, but are independently explored to some degree. As for my academic path, I mainly base my research on the thorough absorption of the research findings of foreign vocational education courses, absorb myself in Chinese practice, confront the problems China faces, and explore vocational curriculum theories and models with Chinese characteristics.

As for the research findings of Professor Jiang and Professor Zhao, readers can thoroughly master them through their work and papers, and I won't go into it further here. One point to address here is the great improvement of their theoretical research level compared with that of the past. For example, Professor Jiang published a monograph, *Research on the Mainstream Teaching Thoughts of Vocational Education in Contemporary Germany*, and Professor Zhao Zhiqun published a monograph, *New Learning Concepts of the Technical and Vocational Education and Training*. Both are highly academic works. Here I will only summarize my research findings.

My research on vocational curriculum is mainly carried out along two paths, namely, how to understand curriculum and how to develop curriculum. The former is the study of curriculum theories of vocational education and the latter is research on the development techniques of vocational curriculum construction. Up to now, my main achievements in this field are as follows: 1. *Research on Practice-Oriented Vocational Curriculum*. This monograph was my first work in the field of vocational education. It mainly systematically explains the meaning of "practice" in vocational curriculum. Traditional vocational curriculum also attaches importance to practice, as highlighted in the documents analyzed above. However, the problem we confront is why we can't actually implement the practice we have always emphasized so much? This issue constitutes the starting point of my research in this work. The basic conclusions are: although traditional vocational curriculum theory attaches great importance to practice, its supporting philosophy is "practice is the application of theory"; we won't truly pay attention to practice in curriculum when we only consider practice as a result of theoretical application. In terms of knowledge theory, theory is equal with practice, and we should put this as the main logical thread for vocational curriculum construction and let theory serve practice. These are the basic ideas of a practice-oriented vocational curriculum and they are fundamentally significant for the construction of vocational curriculum that meets the requirements of the relevant laws. 2. *Vocational Curriculum Theory*. This book aims to construct a basic theoretical system for a vocational curriculum, which involves the most basic problems of vocational curriculum construction. The core is to construct, by use of the structuralist approach, three basic categories of vocational curriculum theory: discipline theory and occupational theory, general theory and specialty theory, basic theory and practical theory. Through sorting out the three basic categories, this book clarifies the essence of the complicated problems in vocational curriculum and various representative viewpoints. 3. *Project-Based Curriculum of Vocational Education: Principles and Development.* This monograph aims to elaborate the basic concepts and development techniques of a project-based curriculum of vocational education. Project-based curriculum is a kind of vocational curriculum model that I advocate. A project-based curriculum in vocational education differs from the one in regular education and higher education, especially in development techniques. The biggest feature is how to reflect the "occupational" requirements in project-based curriculum. 4. *Vocational Curriculum, Teaching and Teachers.* The purpose of this monograph is to deepen the research on key theoretical issues in vocational curriculum construction, teaching, and teacher training. The courses and teaching problems involve areas such as the psychology, knowledge theory, and methodological foundations of vocational curriculum reform, the reform of the vocational curriculum and teaching organization models, the construction of vocational curriculum connection systems and vocational teaching materials, and the development of vocational curriculum resources.

The above research findings obviously have drastically exceeded the research achievements in the 1990s in terms of the theoretic depth and refined degree of development techniques and played an extremely important role in facilitating the construction of vocational curriculum in China. As a result, this period is called the scientific stage of vocational curriculum construction.

Although we have produced abundant research findings, we are still regretful we are weak in theoretical research on the basic cultural curriculum. Due to the decline in the quality of student sources, most vocational schools are confronted with the difficulty in carrying on with the original basic cultural curriculum. Faced with this dilemma, people have put forward many reform suggestions. Some people advocate that the basic cultural curriculum should serve the specialized curriculum, and some advocate that it should reflect a competence-based curriculum concept and cultivate students' competence. These reform ideas were very popular at the beginning, but they all encountered problems when they were implemented. For example, when the first concept was implemented, we found that not all basic cultural curriculum courses could serve a specialized curriculum, such as many aspects of mathematic knowledge; for some basic cultural curriculum courses, if we put too much emphasis on serving the specialized curriculum, we will disintegrate the targets of the curriculum itself, such as Chinese. Another example is the second viewpoint. Too much emphasis on the cultivation of basic cultural curriculum abilities will make some basic cultural curriculum become skilled and lose its nature as a "cultural" curriculum, such as reforming Chinese into speech and eloquence, and practical writing. Because of the lack of systematic reform ideas, some vocational schools have begun to think of a basic cultural curriculum as being useless and blindly cut it down. This will prevent us from achieving the training objectives. I have specially arranged a chapter to discuss basic cultural curriculum reform in *Vocational Curriculum Theory*, but I'm confined to a conceptual description of the problems and fragmentary thoughts on solving strategies, and failed to form a systematic theory on basic cultural curriculum construction.

## 2. Diversified Implementation of Vocational Curriculum Construction

Theoretical enlightenment, administrative promotion, and vocational schools' identity have taken a full swing in vocational curriculum construction during this period. Various levels and types of curriculum construction projects have brought about the extensive implementation of vocational curriculum construction activities, and greatly propelled the construction process of vocational curriculum construction in China. In 2008, MOE promulgated *Opinions of MOE on Further Deepening the Teaching Innovation of Secondary Vocational Education* (No. 8 [2008] from the Department of Vocational and Adult Education, MOE), and established the overall direction for vocational curriculum construction during this period: "Deepen curriculum reform and strive to form an employment-oriented curriculum system. Facilitate secondary vocational schools transforming from discipline-based to competency-based teaching, target developing students' occupational capabilities, adjust the curriculum structure, rationally determine the proportion of the class hours of various courses and standardize teaching.[7]"

However, it was not easy to sort out the curriculum construction projects during this period. This is because they were not carried out in an orderly way according to the procedures of curriculum construction, but implemented at various levels in various forms within projects at the same time. Table 7.2 makes an attempt to sort out these projects. In terms of the level, the projects were carried out at the national, local and school levels; in terms of the content, they can be divided into three categories: basic curriculum norms, special construction projects and comprehensive construction projects; as for special construction projects, they can be divided into three categories: the construction of specialized curriculum, the construction of basic cultural curriculum, and the construction of implementation conditions.

Table 7.2 Construction projects of various types of vocational curriculum

| Content Level | Basic Curriculum Norms | Special Construction Project | | | Comprehensive Construction Project |
|---|---|---|---|---|---|
| | | Construction ofSpecialized Curriculum | Construction of Basic Cultural Curriculum | Construction of Implementation Conditions | |
| The state | Curriculum setting norms | Development of specialized teaching standards and curriculum standards<br>Teaching materials development<br>Curriculum resources development | Curriculum standards development<br>Teaching materials development | Training bases construction | High-quality curriculum<br>Demonstrative schools' construction |
| Local places | | Development of specialized teaching standards and curric-ulum standards<br>Teaching materials development | Curriculum standards development<br>Teaching materials development | Training bases construction | High-quality curriculum<br>Demonstrative schools' construction<br>Brand specialty construction |
| Schools | | Development of specialized teaching standards and curriculum standards<br>Teaching materials development | | Training bases construction | High-quality curriculum construction |

## 2.1. Basic Curriculum Norms

Since entering the 21st century, MOE has proceeded with the construction of basic curriculum norms. The core is to standardize the basic curriculum settings for vocational schools, and other aspects such as the use of teaching materials. It aims to establish a policy framework for the formulation of student training projects in vocational schools. It is completely implemented at the national level; local governments and vocational schools do not have this authority, but only to implement the general guidelines of MOE on curriculum settings.

In 2001, MOE released *Opinions on Curriculum Settings and Teaching Arrangements for Moral Education in Secondary Vocational Schools*, and stipulated that "the moral education courses of secondary vocational schools are divided into compulsory courses and elective courses. The compulsory courses include four courses such as occupational ethics and occupational guidance, basic knowledge of philosophy, basic knowledge of economics and politics, and basic knowledge of law.

Elective courses shall be set up according to actual conditions and shall be organized and implemented by local schools after being submitted to the Department of Vocational and Adult Education of MOE for examination and approval."[8]

Table 7.3 Teaching arrangements for moral education compulsory courses

| Grade | Semester | Course | Class Hours |
|---|---|---|---|
| Grade one | The first semester | Occupational ethics and occupational guidance | 32–36 |
| | The second semester | Basic knowledge of law | 32–36 |
| Grade two | The third semester | Basic knowledge of economics and politics | 32–36 |
| | The fourth semester | Basic knowledge of economics and politics | 32–36 |
| Grade three | The fifth semester | Basic knowledge of philosophy | 48–54 |

In 2008, MOE promulgated *Several Opinions of MOE on Further Deepening the Teaching Innovation of Secondary Vocational Education* (No. 8 [2008] from the Department of Vocational and Adult Education, MOE), and required: "Increase the proportion of professional skill courses; the class hours of professional skill courses (including work experience) generally accounts for two-thirds of the total class hours; set up professional courses by adopting the specialized course structure of foundation platforms and specialized direction according to the competency requirements of corresponding occupations (groups)." It also stipulates the use of teaching materials: "Fully utilize the role of the National Secondary Vocational Education Textbook Examination and Approval Committee, establish and improve the classroom access system for textbooks. Textbooks for compulsory courses such as moral education and basic cultural courses shall be uniformly planned and organized by the state, and textbooks for professional skill courses shall be planned by the state and local regions together. Textbooks for the basic courses of some main specialties and the core courses of key specialties shall be prepared uniformly by the state. Actively develop training courses and practical operation instruction textbooks."[9] The basic spirit of this document is to strengthen the teaching of specialized courses, which is aligned with the "employment-oriented" school-operating philosophy established at that time.

In 2009, MOE released *Principles and Opinions on Formulating Teaching Plans for Secondary Vocational Schools* (No. 2 [2009] from the Department of Vocational and Adult Education, MOE). This document is important for basically standardizing the whole student training process in secondary vocational education. In this document, important content on curriculum construction included: "The curriculum is divided into two categories: basic public courses and professional skills courses. The basic public courses include moral education, cultural courses, sports and health courses, art courses and other elective public courses. Professional skills courses 'adopts the course structure of the basic platform and the specialized direction.' The class hours of basic public courses generally accounts for one-third of the total hours, and the cumulative total hours are approximately one academic year. Professional skills courses generally account for two-thirds of the total class hours, and the total number of class hours of work practice is approximately one academic year. Elective courses should be set up in the teaching plan and the proportion of the class hours should account for no less than 10% of the total hours."[10]

In 2000, MOE promulgated *Opinions of MOE on Reinforcing the Cultivation of Higher Vocational and Technical Students* (No. 2 [2000] from the Department of Higher Education, MOE). This document is included two subject areas: *Principles and Opinions on Formulating Professional Teaching Plans for Higher Vocational and Technical Education* and *Key Points of Teaching Management for Higher Vocational Schools, Junior Colleges and Adult Higher Colleges.* Both have basically standardized the formulation of student training programs and the management of teaching in higher vocational colleges. *Principles and Opinions on Formulating Professional Teaching Plans for Higher Vocational and Technical Education* requires that we when are formulating training programs for higher vocational students they should be practicable and targeted, reinforce the cultivation of practical ability and implement the concept of "combining work-study programs." It specifically provides that the basic study duration for higher vocational and technical specialties is two to three years and the study duration of non-full-time specialties shall be appropriately extended. "The total in-class hours of three-year specialties are generally 1,600–1,800 hours; the total in-class hours of two-year specialties are generally 1,100–1,200 hours." "The class hours for practical teaching of three-year specialties is generally no less than 40% of the total hours of pedagogical practices. The practical teaching of the two-year program is generally no less than 30% of the total hours of pedagogical practices."[11] *Key Points of Teaching Management for Higher Vocational Schools, Junior Colleges and Adult Higher Colleges* stipulates: "Basic teaching management of higher vocational and technical colleges generally includes teaching plan management, teaching operation management, teaching quality management and evaluation, teacher team management, teaching infrastructure management such as laboratories, training bases and textbooks." It also provides that the general procedure for formulating a teaching plan includes: "learn and apprehend the spirit of relevant primary documents; extensively investigate the demands of the social labor market; organize school experts and social employers to discuss training objectives, basic specifications, knowledge, capacity and competence structures; the educational administration department of each school shall propose implementation guidelines and requirements for the formulation of the school's teaching plans; the teaching plans shall be directed and formulated by each department, examined and deliberated by the school teaching work (academic) committee, and issued for execution after being checked and signed by the principal in charge."[12]

## 2.2. Special Construction Project

A special construction project refers to a project that specifically aims at the construction of a certain aspect of the curriculum, such as the professional teaching standards and curriculum standards development projects. These kinds of construction projects are advantageous in that we can easily and significantly promote curriculum construction in specific areas. This is because there are relatively clear and definite construction goals.

1. Construction of a specialized curriculum

Construction of a specialized curriculum includes three elements: specialized teaching standards and curriculum standards construction, teaching materials construction and curriculum resources construction. Specialized courses are quite complicated, and there are great differences between local courses and college courses. As a result, in terms of the management of vocational courses, there hasn't been any rigid distinction on curriculum construction authority at the national, local, and school levels. The first two types of construction are carried out at the three levels simultaneously. As for curriculum resources construction, it calls for huge input, so the specific tasks that are undertaken by vocational schools and the construction actions are mainly carried out with support from MOE. Therefore, it is still incorporated into the national level.

① Development of specialized teaching standards and curriculum standards

Development of specialized teaching standards and curriculum standards in specialized curriculum construction began in Shanghai, and the concept of specialized teaching standards was first proposed by Shanghai authorities. In 2004, Shanghai authorities issued *Action Plan for Deepening the Curriculum Materials Reform of Secondary Vocational Education in Shanghai (2004–2007)* (No. 21(2004) from the Department of Vocational and Adult Education, Shanghai Municipal Education Commission), and proposed: "Optimize specialized teaching and develop teaching standards for 50 specialties such as vehicle operation and maintenance, in order to achieve the integration of 'double certificates', namely, the academic certificate and job qualification certificate."[13] By 2013, a total of 66 specialized teaching standards (including 996 course standards) had been accomplished, covering 192 kinds of job qualification certificates. 792 enterprise experts and 873 teachers were directly involved in the reform, covering all vocational schools in Shanghai. This was a pioneering action in the construction of national vocational curriculum construction, and has exerted a far-reaching influence. Many provinces and cities, such as Jiangsu, Zhejiang, Shandong, and Guangdong, have been inspired by the Shanghai initiatives and tried to organize similar development of local specialized teaching standards.

In 2012, MOE Promulgated *Opinions of the General Office of MOE on Formulating Specialized Teaching Standards for Secondary Vocational Schools* (No. 5 [2012] from the Department of Vocational and Adult Education, MOE), and initiated the development of specialized standards for secondary vocational schools at the national level. The document stipulates that the specialized teaching standards mainly include the following elements: specialty names, admission requirements, basic academic structure, training objectives, occupational scope, student specifications, main continuing specialties, curriculum structure, curriculum settings and requirements, teaching schedules, teaching implementation, teaching assessment, practical training and practice environment, specialized teachers, and so on.[14] Afterwards, we not only formulated specialized teaching standards for secondary vocational education, but also for higher vocational education; moreover, we further developed specialized teaching standards for the interconnection of secondary and higher vocational education. In 2012 and 2014, MOE published teaching standards for 410 higher vocational specialties and 230 secondary vocational specialties in total. During 2012–2014, the Shanghai Municipal Education Commission was entrusted by MOE to develop 52 specialized teaching standards linking up with international standards.

Guided by the development of specialized teaching standards in government departments, vocational schools spontaneously developed specialized teaching standards. However, they did not base the standards on identical development techniques. Some developed specialized teaching standards according to the learning area courses in Germany, while some developed specialized teaching standards according to the project-based curriculum model I designed.

② Teaching materials development

New curriculum models and curriculum standards need to be put into practice in teaching and supported by quality teaching materials. The curriculum reform during this period brought an upsurge in developing teaching materials. In developing teaching materials for specialized courses, publishers have actively played a dominant role. They often published a textbook with more than a dozen or even dozens of versions. Various school-based teaching textbooks emerged one after another. In order to improve the quality of teaching materials, MOE has been endeavoring to oversee the development of teaching materials. For example, *Several Opinions of MOE on Comprehensively Improving the Teaching Quality of Higher Vocational Education* (No. 16 [2006] from the Department of Higher Education, MOE) proposed the reinforcing of the construction of teaching materials and focus on about 3,000 kinds of national planning materials. *Several Opinions of MOE on Further Deepening Teaching Innovation of Secondary Vocational Education* (No. 8 [2008] from the Department of Vocational and Adult Education, MOE) was promulgated in 2008 and proposed establishing and perfecting textbook compilation, selection and validation mechanisms and to select 2000 kinds of high-quality textbooks.

③ Curriculum resources development

Curriculum implementation calls for the support of teaching resources. Developing an educational resource base was an important measure for MOE to implement curriculum construction during this period. The development of special curriculum resources was carried out in higher vocational schools, and the development of curriculum resources for secondary vocational schools was implemented on the basis of comprehensive projects such as demonstration schools' construction and high-quality curriculum construction.

In 2010, MOE released the *Notice on the 2010 Project Application of the Specialized Teaching Resources Database for Higher Vocational Education* (No. 129 [2010] letter from the Department of Higher Education, MOE), and proposed: "Select such specialties as CNC technology, vehicle inspection and maintenance, road and bridge engineering technology which are closely related to national industrial planning and social and economic development and extensively distributed, build and promote the use of sharing specialized teaching resources databases that represent the national level and symbolizes the characteristics of higher vocational education, lead the reform of specialized teaching models and teaching methods in higher vocational schools nationwide and improve the overall quality of student training and capacity to serve the society of higher vocational education." "In 2010, we initiated 11 specialized teaching resources database construction projects as CNC technology, vehicle inspection and maintenance, road and bridge engineering technology, applied electronic technology, mold design and manufacturing, architectural engineering technology, applied chemical technology, logistics management, accounting, nursing, ophthalmology and optometry technology."[15] Since then, we have set up specialized teaching resources database projects several times. For example, MOE issued the *Notice of MOE on Determining the Set Up of the 2014 Construction Projects of Specialized Teaching Resources Database for Vocational Education* (No. 10 [2014] letter from the Department of Vocational and Adult Education, MOE) in 2014, and established 14 resource database projects such as "horticultural techniques."

Since the actual effect of the teaching resources database construction failed to adequately achieve the anticipated goals, MOE began to change the style of project management. That is, from setting up projects to identifying good projects. The *Notice on Doing Well in Related Work to the Specialized Teaching Resources Database for Vocational Education in 2016* (No. 61 [2016] letter from the Department of Vocational and Adult Education, MOE) proposed: "From 2016, we shall organize vocational education specialized teaching resources database projects according to 'independent construction, overall planning at the provincial level, tapping into the database, well-aligned support, acceptance of monitoring, and continuous updating', and select national resources database alternatives from provincial resources database projects that have been constructed or are under construction."[16]

1. Construction of basic cultural curriculum

In 2001, MOE released *Opinions on Comprehensively Promoting Quality-Oriented Education and Deepening the Teaching Reform of Secondary Vocational Education* (No. 1 [2000] from the Department of Vocational and Adult Education, MOE), and proposed: "The state shall organize the development and compilation of basic cultural curriculum standards and textbooks with the characteristics and requirements of secondary vocational education." "Local education administrative departments shall, according to local conditions, adopt effective measures to enhance the supervision and inspection of teaching guidance and teaching quality of the basic cultural curriculum for secondary vocational schools."[17] However, this work has not been finished till now and the standards for the first batch of secondary vocational basic culture curriculum have not been officially promulgated yet, which demonstrates the difficulty of this work.

Before MOE officially promulgated basic cultural curriculum standards, some provinces and cities, such as Jiangsu and Shanghai, had compiled local basic cultural curriculum standards according to teaching needs. In 2004, Shanghai authorities released the *Action Plan for Deepening the Curriculum Materials Reform of Secondary Vocational Education in Shanghai (2004–2007)* (No. 21 [2004] from the Department of Vocational and Adult Education, Shanghai Municipal Education

Commission) and proposed: "Optimize moral education curriculum and the basic cultural curriculum, develop curriculum standards for 6 subjects such as Chinese, compile relevant demonstration materials, and actively implement stratified teaching."[18] Local education administrative departments organized to develop basic cultural curriculum standards. Some were authorized by MOE, while others were not. However, in terms of meeting the needs of practice, developing curriculum standards required for local teaching needs before the official release of the basic cultural curriculum standards by MOE, are of positive significance to the teaching of a standardized basic cultural curriculum.

2. Construction of implementation conditions

During this period, in order to improve training conditions and better cultivate students' occupational abilities, the state, local governments and vocational schools have heavily contributed to setting curriculum implementation conditions and concentrated on constructing training bases. Because of the large number of construction projects, it is difficult for me to thoroughly summarize and provide statistics. Here I can just enumerate some examples. For example, in 2005, the *Decision of the State Council on Vigorously Developing Vocational Education* (No. 35 [2005] from the State Council) proposed: "Pay high attention to practice and practical training, consistently implement plans for vocational training base construction, and establish 2,000 vocational training bases with a complete range of specialty categories, highly equipped and sharing high-quality resources in key specialized fields."[19] Because of the huge input in training base construction, government departments have adopted the idea of building public training bases so as to improve the service efficiency of training bases. For example, the Shanghai Municipal Education Commission has constructed a large number of open training centers based on vocational schools and is at present also collaboratively establishing corporate training centers with enterprises. The former Shanghai Municipal Human Resources and Social Security Bureau have established public training bases; the higher education zone of Changzhou city, Jiangsu province has also established public training bases. The construction of public training bases has significantly improved the training conditions for vocational education but the shared goal has never been achieved.

3. Comprehensive construction projects

In addition to the above-mentioned special projects, vocational curriculum construction also includes some comprehensive projects. The most important ones are demonstration schools' construction, high-quality curriculum construction, brand specialties construction, and so on. These projects are not clearly targeted at curriculum construction, and usually most curriculum construction is incorporated into the scope of the project. For example, high-quality curriculum construction must include the development of curriculum standards and curriculum resources. These projects were the focus of curriculum construction during this period and due importance should be attached to them. However, it is precisely because curriculum construction is not clearly targeted at specific content and is always inseparable from those listed above that it has also in practice caused much duplicated construction.

Both higher vocational and secondary vocational schools have implemented demonstration schools' construction and many local education administrative departments have followed MOE recommendations to implement local demonstrative schools' construction projects. Therefore, the construction of a model school was carried out at both MOE and the local levels. *Opinions on Implementing the Construction Plan of National Demonstrative Higher Vocational Colleges and Accelerating the Reform and Development of Higher Vocational Education* (No. 14 [2006] from the Department of Higher Education, MOE) proposed: "Construct about 4,000 high-quality professional core courses, 1500 kinds of specific teaching materials and teaching courseware … … Concentrate on the industrial fields that are specially supported by the state, develop and popularize shared teaching resources databases and provide high-quality services for students' autonomous learning; set up public service platforms by use of modern information tools and provide technical support for the sharing of high-quality teaching resources."[20] The construction of demonstration secondary vocational schools has basically followed the construction model for higher vocational schools.

The requirement for high-quality curriculum construction was first proposed in *Decision of the State Council on Vigorously Developing Vocational Education* (No. 35 [2005] from the State Council) in 2005. The document requires: "Strive to promote the construction of high-quality specialties, high-quality curriculum and teaching materials."[21] In 2006, MOE issued *Several Opinions of MOE on Comprehensively Improving the Teaching Quality of Higher Vocational Education* (No. 16 [2006] from the Department of Higher Education, MOE), and established a plan for the construction of a high-quality vocational curriculum: "Establish curriculum standards that highlight occupational competence cultivation, standardize the basic requirements of curriculum teaching, improve the quality of curriculum teaching. During the '11th Five-Year Plan' period, the state will initiate the construction of 1,000 high-quality courses that combine work and study and encourage local governments and schools to enhance curriculum construction."[22] In 2008, MOE issued *Several Opinions of MOE on Further Deepening Teaching*

*Innovation in Secondary Vocational Education* (No. 8 [2008] from the Department of Vocational and Adult Education, MOE), and put forward a plan for appraising and selecting 1,000 high-quality courses. High-quality curriculum construction shall be carried out at the local and school level.

In addition, there were also many different kinds of key specialties construction and brand specialties construction projects during this period. Since curriculum construction was also the core of specialty construction, these projects have also become an important support for the construction of the vocational curriculum.

The above is just a summary of the important curriculum construction actions during this period. In fact, various curriculum construction actions were carried out during this period, and they are so complicated that I can't summarize them comprehensively. For example, setting up elective courses and giving students the power to choose courses; implementing stratified teaching to adapt the courses to students at different learning levels, etc. All these were important curriculum construction actions during this period.

## 3. Features and Problems of Curriculum Construction at the Scientific Stage

We have achieved obvious and notable success in curriculum construction during this period. This is reflected in: 1. In terms of the breadth of curriculum construction, a wide range of schools have participated in curriculum construction and most vocational schools have implemented curriculum construction action. In economically developed areas, curriculum construction has even become the core of the majority of vocational schools during this period; 2. In terms of the depth of curriculum construction, we have fundamentally shaken the foundations of the traditional "three-stage" vocational curriculum model in such aspects as curriculum setting, curriculum content and teaching methods. For example, curriculum content has become much more practicable; the projects have become the compilation model adopted in the development of most textbooks; the proportion of practical teaching has greatly increased and the competency-based curriculum model has been more clearly reflected in the curriculum system.

On the one hand, this progress has benefited from the unparalleled attention paid to curriculum construction and various curriculum construction projects that have come one after another. On the other hand, they have benefited from the significant breakthroughs in curriculum construction theory and development techniques during this period. Without breakthroughs in the basic concepts of the vocational curriculum, people would still be tied up in the disputes of the 1990s and unable to build complete confidence in the competency-based curriculum model, and thus cannot go deeply into curriculum construction along this direction pathway. Without detailed design in curriculum development techniques, the majority of teachers won't obtain clear operation methods of curriculum construction; they will still remain confused about the methods and unable to carry out substantial curriculum development. These are the features of curriculum construction during this period, which can be summarized by "diversified" and "scientific."

However, this does not necessarily mean that curriculum construction during this period was perfect. On the contrary, there were many problems. If we compare it with the economic development process in China, it was probably equivalent to the economic development of China in the 1990s. Even in developed regions, it just reached the level at the beginning of the 21st century. To sum up, high-quality projects existed in parts of China, but the overall curriculum quality was not high. For example, Shanghai accomplished 66 specialized teaching standards and Shanghai was entrusted by MOE to develop 52 international specialized teaching standards. All these specialized teaching standards were developed by use of rigorous methods and the development results were of high standard. Besides that, there were also some high-quality textbooks produced. However, most curriculum development results were relatively rough in quality. For example, high-quality curriculum and curriculum resources databases have been blamed for their rough quality and low utilization rate, which remained challenging tasks to front line teachers. Due to the lack of textbooks that well match curriculum content and are well compiled, self-compiled teaching materials prevailed in vocational schools. Competency-based curriculum was superficially reflected in the curriculum. Its influence was more reflected in emphasis on the cultivation of students' occupational abilities in the curriculum, but it did not reach the level of the Western countries where courses are strictly organized according to ability.

In order to solve the above problems, we should not only better master the competency-based curriculum concepts and development techniques and improve the quality of curriculum development results, but also rethink the strategies for pushing vocational curriculum construction at the new historical stage.

## Part 3 Specialized Teaching Standards Construction Is the Foundation of Modern Vocational Education

There are two reasons for the dilemma faced by the above in vocational curriculum construction. First, the lack of top-level design and systematic planning for curriculum construction projects and the serious duplication of construction not only wastes lots of manpower and financial resources, but also affects the deepening of curriculum construction. Second, there is no distinction between curriculum construction actions at the national, local, and vocational school levels. That is, we don't distinguish which tasks shall be resolved by the state, which shall be resolved by local education administrative departments, and which shall be resolved by vocational schools. Vocational colleges have assumed many tasks that they cannot afford, which inevitably affects the quality of curriculum construction results. Developing national vocational specialized teaching standards is an important strategy to get rid of this dilemma, which should be the core mission for future vocational curriculum construction in China.

## 1. The Significance of Developing National Specialized Teaching Standards

We should understand the significance of developing national specialized teaching standards at the level of "modern vocational education construction." China has established the construction goal of "modern vocational education," and national specialized teaching standards are the basis of modern vocational education. This is because the entire vocational education system keeps operating effectively on the basis of specialized teaching standards. They are extremely important strategic significance to such aspects as standardizing the teaching of vocational schools, comprehensively improving teaching quality and deepening the reform of student training models: 1. They are the foundation for vocational schools to regulate teaching. As the basis of national specialized teaching standards, curriculum settings and teaching requirements of vocational schools shall have common basic norms; 2. They are the basis for comprehensively improving teaching quality. Developing national specialized teaching standards will help to swiftly improve the construction level of curriculum in vocational schools, solve redundant courses, and promote the connection in a variety of ways; 3. They are basis for deepening the reform of student training models. How to truly meet enterprises' requirements is the main theme of the reform of vocational student training models, and this reform is difficult to be implemented without national specialized teaching standards; 4. They are the basis for improving educational appropriations and the efficiency of teaching resources. With specialized teaching standards, we will find the right direction to use educational appropriations and teaching resources. Therefore, the construction level of specialized teaching standards significantly symbolizes the modernization level of vocational education in a country or region. This is the key element that modern vocational education construction must grasp.

## 2. The Overall Situation of the Construction of Specialized Teaching Standards in Developed Countries

Strictly speaking, there is no concept of specialized teaching standards in foreign countries. However, if we have the core function of specialized teaching standards as the overall description and regulation of the content of vocational education, then we will find prevailing texts with a similar function and nature internationally. Moreover, the standardized construction of the teaching content of vocational education has been a common trend for the development of vocational education in western developed countries since the 1990s, such as the development of the National Vocational Qualification System (NVQ) in Britain, the development of learning area curriculum in Germany and the development of teaching content standards in each state of the U.S.A.

The NVQ in UK is an attempt to construct vocational specialized teaching standards at the national level, as vocational qualifications must be expressed by curriculum modules. Using this approach, while establishing the vocational qualification system, we should also establish a national specialized teaching standards system in vocation education.

Germany has the most mature specialized teaching standards, and the already well-established *Vocational Training Regulations* sets out the specialized teaching standards for corporate training in the "dual system." On May 9, 1996, KMK promulgated the new *Guidelines for the Framework and Teaching Plan of Occupational Specialized Education in Vocational Schools* so as to develop a learning curriculum. This has perfected the specialized teaching standards in the "dual system," and its development has facilitated the establishment of a complete standard teaching system in Germany.

The construction of a vocational teaching standard system in the U.S. dates from the boom of standards construction in the 1980s. After the release of *A Nation at Risk*, each state began to develop standards for academic curriculum content one after another. Although secondary vocational education in the U.S. has a different historical context and federal legal basis from academic education, its teaching standards were equally valued at the time. This process was strongly promoted by *American Choice: High Skills or Low Wages*, an important report in 1990. This report held the view that the lack of explicit vocational education standards in the U.S.A. was one of the main factors hindering the development of a highly skilled workforce. The *Carl D. Perkins Act II*, was promulgated in 1990, and it explicitly required each state to develop a vocational teaching standards system and implement a test of achievement level. Propelled by a series of acts, a total of 31 states had established secondary vocational education teaching standards at the state level by the end of 2006. As for other states, some were under construction and some already had local standards. The research showed that the implementation of teaching standards did not reduce but greatly improved students' choice of vocational courses.

Comparatively, China started late in this field and has lagged behind western developed countries for almost 20 years. Therefore, it is a very pressing task to establish vocational teaching standards.

## 3. Key Technical Issues in Developing National Specialized Teaching Standards

In fact, the national-level construction of a vocational education curriculum has always been the central task of MOE. In 2012, MOE initiated formulation of specialized teaching standards for secondary vocational schools; it announced the teaching standards for the first batch of 95 secondary vocational specialties in 2014, and then announced the teaching standards for the second batch of 135 secondary vocational specialties in 2015. In 2010, MOE initiated the development of specialized teaching standards for higher vocational schools and announced the teaching standards for the first batch of 410 specialties, which were approved in 2012. In 2016, MOE launched and completed 15 pilot projects on teaching standards development to interconnect secondary and higher vocational education. The release of these specialized teaching standards filled the gap in vocational teaching standards in China and marked the end of an era when China had no student training standards to follow in vocational schools. Of course, the development of national specialized teaching standards is a process of gradual exploration and improvement and the development techniques are still continually improving ... The concept of specialized teaching standards originates from Shanghai. However, it should be noticed that Shanghai is just a region and a relatively small area. The development of national specialized teaching standards will be up against a problem that Shanghai did not encounter. This problem is how to solve the contradiction between unifying of the country's standards and the diversity and flexibility of the many schools.

There are two common tactics to solving this contradiction: 1. National specialized teaching standards only give a summary description of content. However, long-term practice shows that most vocational schools are not capable of embodying the description standards according to their particular school-operating features. The tactic results in a plethora of materials without practical value; 2. National specialized teaching standards are only in charge of developing core courses, and other courses are developed by vocational schools themselves. However, the reality is different as vocational schools have different specialized core courses, and the courses developed by vocational colleges themselves are very poor in quality. Learning from the experience of other countries, we have the following effective strategies for solving this problem: 1. Develop according to main specialties rather than specialties; 2. Develop according to modules rather than courses. It is necessary to establish the boundaries between the specialties of the main categories and form a module library with the main specialty categories as the basic categories.

Developing consistent standards according to the basic categories of the main specialty categories enables vocational schools to freely choose specialty orientation; developing according to the basic module unit enables vocational schools to freely choose curriculum settings. The core thought is to distinguish national-level specialized teaching standards from those at the school level in terms of functional orientation. In the past, national-level curriculum development was restricted to specialty and curriculum and specialized teaching standards were not completely distinguished from student training programs in terms of functional orientation. Thus curriculum development made no essential distinction from vocational schools' curriculum development and even confined the course of vocational curriculum construction instead.

This means that national specialized teaching standards are not significantly distinct from Shanghai's specialized teaching standards. The specialized teaching standards adopted by Shanghai are student training programs in essence, and national specialized teaching standards should be the basis for vocational schools to formulate student training programs. The distinctions between the two are: 1. Student training programs are developed by taking specialties as the basic categories, while specialized teaching standards are developed by taking the main specialty categories as the basic categories. For example, the specialized teaching standards in Ohio are divided into 16 main categories. The development of specialized teaching standards aims to decentralize the authority of precisely setting targets of specialized student training to school-operating entities of vocational education, so that they can adjust their specialty orientation according to the requirements of the labor market and form their own specialized characteristics. 2. Student training programs are required to describe training objectives and student specifications, while specialized teaching standards are not. What specialized teaching standards need to describe is a concept superordinate than training objectives and student specifications. That is, learners' career paths and occupation capacity requirements. 3. The course content in training programs is presented according to the basic course unit, and the course content in specialized teaching standards should be presented according to the basic module unit. A module is a component of the course and the course is composed of integrated modules. 4. Training programs highlight the regulation of implementing specific requirements for student training, while specialized teaching standards should highlight the requirements for school-operating entities to formulate student training programs, especially highlight the requirement for integrating modules into the curriculum.

The development of national specialized teaching standards in China should start at a high point and exert its historical influence. In terms of development techniques, we are fully confident reaching and even transcending the level of developed countries in some respects: 1. Adequately reflect the core competence of technical and skilled professionals in contemporary society. 2. Deepen the development of occupational capacities. Occupational capacity analysis on the basis of occupation descriptions is a basic approach for most countries to establish national specialized teaching standards.

## Notes

1 Vocational and Technical Education: 20 Years of Review and Witnessing, 1999.
2 CPC Central Committee: Decision of the CPC Central Committee on the Reform of the Education System, 1985.
3 State Council: Decision of the State Council on Vigorously Developing Vocational and Technical Education, 1991.
4 MOE: Several Plans for the Two-Year Teaching Arrangements of Engineering Specialties in Secondary Specialized Schools, 1979.
5 MOE: Regulations Concerning the Work of Full-Time Secondary Specialized Schools, 1979.
6 Former State Education Commission: Opinions on Formulating Teaching Plans for (Three-Year) Vocational Senior High Schools, 1990.
7 MOE: Several Opinions of MOE on Further Deepening the Teaching Innovation of Secondary Vocational Education, 2008.
8 MOE: Opinions on Curriculum Setting and Teaching Arrangement of Moral Education in Secondary Vocational Schools, 2001.
9 MOE: Several Opinions of MOE on Further Deepening the Teaching Innovation of Secondary Vocational Education, 2008.
10 MOE: Principles and Opinions of MOE on Formulating Teaching Plans for Secondary Vocational Schools, 2009.
11 MOE: Principles and Opinions on Formulating Professional Teaching Plans for Higher Vocational and Technical Education, 2002.
12 MOE: Key Points for Teaching Management for Higher Vocational Schools, Junior Colleges and Adult Higher Colleges, 2002.
13 Shanghai Municipal Education Commission: Action Plan for Deepening the Curriculum Materials Reform of Secondary Vocational Education in Shanghai (2004–2007), 2004.
14 MOE: Opinions of the General Office of MOE on Formulating Specialized Teaching Standards for Secondary Vocational Schools, 2012.

15 MOE: Notice on the 2010 Project Application of the Specialized Teaching Resources Database for Higher Vocational Education, 2010.
16 MOE: Notice on Doing Well in Related Work to the Specialized Teaching Resources Database for Vocational Education in 2016, 2016.
17 MOE: Opinions on Comprehensively Promoting Quality-Oriented Education and Deepening the Teaching Reform of Secondary Vocational Education, 2000.
18 Shanghai Municipal Education Commission: Action Plan for Deepening the Curriculum Materials Reform of Secondary Vocational Education in Shanghai (2004–2007), 2004.
19 State Council: Decision of the State Council on Vigorously Developing Vocational Education, 2005.
20 MOE, MOF: Opinions on Implementing the Construction Plan of National Demonstrative Higher Vocational Colleges and Accelerating the Reform and Development of Higher Vocational Education, 2006.
21 State Council: Decision of the State Council on Vigorously Developing Vocational Education, 2005.
22 MOE: Several Opinions of MOE on Comprehensively Improving the Teaching Quality of Higher Vocational Education, 2006.
23 Xu Han: A Comparative Study of Chinese and German Secondary Vocational Curriculum Reform, China Social Sciences Press, 2015.

CHAPTER EIGHT

# Building a Training System That Meets the Requirements for Teacher Specialization

A basic principle in pedagogy is: the quality of all education lies in the quality of the teachers. The same is true of vocational education. With the gradual improvement and development of the vocational education system, education administrative departments at all levels have been endeavoring to know how to cultivate high-quality teachers. Compared with other kinds of education, vocational teachers' cultivation is more sophisticated. The main reasons are twofold: First, the source of vocational teachers is not as simple as that of other types of education and vocational teachers cannot be completely trained by universities. In addition to university graduates, it also requires a large number of technical experts from enterprises. Second, the ability structure of vocational teachers is more complicated. Vocational teachers need to be equipped with not only professional theoretical knowledge, but also hands-on abilities. In order to solve the two problems, education administrations at all levels have, over the past four decades since reform and opening-up, implemented diversified investigations into training vocational teachers, gathered lots of experience, and left much space worth exploring.

## Part 1 The Serious Shortage of Teachers Was a Conspicuous Impediment in Developing Vocational Education at the Initial Stage after Reform and Opening-Up

After reform and opening-up, secondary vocational schools gradually reappeared but were still confronted with extreme difficulties in faculty development.

In 1985, the *Decision of the CPC Central Committee on the Reform of the Education System* acutely pointed out: "The severe shortage of teachers is an extensive impediment faced by the current secondary vocational and technical education." This timely and significant document also indicated the approaches needed to recruit vocational teachers: "Schools operated by each unit and department must rely primarily on their own strength to solve the problem of professional technical teachers. They can recruit external teachers and science technicians as part-time teachers, and also invite professional technicians and skillful craftsmen for skills teaching. A number of vocational and technical normal schools need to be established and all relevant colleges and universities as well as research institutions should undertake the mission of training vocational and technical teachers, so as to guarantee stable sources of professional teachers. Secondary vocational and technical education is primarily in the charge of local governments. For those schools operated by various central departments, local governments should also coordinate and cooperate with them."[1]

In 1986, the State Education Commission (now MOE), SDPC (now NDRC), SETC (now MOFCOM) and the Ministry of Labor and Personnel (now MOHRSS) jointly convened the first national conference on vocational and technical education after reform and opening-up. *Several Opinions on Strengthening Faculty Development in Vocational and Technical Schools*, which was approved at the conference, described the status of vocational teachers at that time as follows: "In recent years, as vocational and technical schools have developed on a large scale, faculty deficiency and low quality are becoming acute: specialized course teachers in vocational middle schools are in critical shortage and have no stable source; secondary specialized schools have changed to recruit junior high school graduates and they need to replenish a large number of culture course teachers in the future; professional teachers are outmoded in their knowledge and need to be updated urgently; teachers in technical training schools are generally insufficient. This situation is far from meeting teaching requirements, and timely and effective measures must be taken to establish and improve the training system for vocational and technical teachers, focus on solving the problem of teacher cultivation and training, and implement the goals proposed in the *Decision of the CPC Central Committee on the Reform of the Education System*."[2]

In 1989, *Opinions of the Ministry of Labour on Reinforcing Vocational and Technical Training and Faculty Development* (No. 1 [1989] from the Ministry of Labour on teacher training) described faculty deficiency of vocational schools and training centers subordinated to the Ministry of Labor (now MOHRSS) at that time as follows: "At present, problems such as the insufficient quantity, low quality and unreasonable structure of vocational and technical training of teachers (especially production practice instructors) are serious. More than 50% vacancies exist nationwide of production practice instructors in technical training schools. Among the existing practice instructors, only 10% have college degrees or above; less than 15% are first-grade practice instructors; only 3% are senior practice instructors. Among the culture and technology theory course teachers, those with a bachelor's degree or above and working as lecturers each account for about 30%, and senior lecturers account for less than 5%; enterprises have more than 200,000 full-time corporate staff training teachers, most of whom are culture and technology theory course teachers and can't adapt to the requirements for job training; there are more than 1,600 career training centers, with only 1,500 full-time teachers."[3]

Therefore, vocational education documents have consistently concentrated on increasing the number of vocational teachers and improving their degree and skill levels in the 1980s and 1990s. For example, the *Decision of the State Council on Vigorously Developing Vocational and Technical Education* (No. 55 [1991] from the State Council) required: "In accordance with the principle of integrating and cultivating full-time and part-time training, we should endeavor to solve, through multiple channels, the issues of sourcing vocational and technical teachers, especially technical teachers." In 2002, *Opinions of the General Office of MOE on Enhancing Faculty Development in Higher Vocational (Higher Technical) Colleges and Universities* (No. 5 [2002] from the Department of Higher Education, MOE) put forward the following goals for faculty development in higher vocational (higher technical) colleges and universities: "Build a team of full-time and part-time teachers with noble virtues, innovative teaching ideas, strong reforming consciousness, high teaching levels and great practical abilities."[4]

After decades of construction, the overall situation of vocational teachers has improved a lot. Statistically, the number of full-time teachers in secondary specialized schools and vocational high schools at the end of 1996 throughout the country was 204,300 and 268,500 respectively, an increase of 9,559 and 13,600 over those in 1985.[5] The absolute increase number is small, but faculty development during a period cannot be evaluated by the absolute increase in numbers only. This is because it also involved the problems associated with the replacement of old for new teachers. Furthermore, teacher recruitment is subject to teacher competence and qualifications. From 1997 to 2016, the number of teachers in the three types of schools changed significantly, increasing from 716,000 in 1997 to 839,600 in 2016, with an absolute increase number of more than 100,000; it reached 902,900 in 2009 at the peak. The total number of teachers has fluctuated greatly during this period, ranging widely from 700,000 to 900,000. The fluctuation was mainly a result of the changes in the number of vocational schools and enrollments. In terms of the changes in the number of schools, it's partly because some schools have been abolished, mainly technical schools; partly because some have been upgraded to higher vocational schools. For example, the number of teachers declined sharply during 2000–2004, when higher vocational education developed on a large scale. If excluding the teachers in those schools that were upgraded to higher vocational ones, the number of teachers in many secondary vocational schools actually increased during this period. The recruitment of large numbers of new teachers has brought great demand for teacher training. Moreover, the rate of qualified academic backgrounds among teachers also tended to fluctuate during this period and basically stabilized at around 70% after 2014. However, one change we need to note is that the student-teacher ratio declined from 32.59 in 1997 to 19.81 in 2016, which basically met the requirements by MOE for the student-teacher ratio for secondary vocational education. The greater change was the significant improvement of teachers' specialization level. That is, the proportion of specialized course teachers who received specialized course training increased dramatically. At the preliminary stage of the establishment of vocational high schools, many culture course teachers "changed their professions" to work as specialized course teachers. This was a prominent problem confronted by faculty development at that time.

Higher vocational education developed relatively late. However, the number of higher vocational colleges has since grown rapidly under the guidance of the popularization policy of higher education and accordingly the number of teachers also increased rapidly. It increased from 237,654 in 2004 to 466,934 in 2016, which almost doubled and exceeded by more than half the number of secondary vocational teachers. As a kind of vocational education at the higher education level, higher vocational education has begun to play a dominant role in China's vocational education system.

Table 8.1 The number of full-time teachers, the student-teacher ratio and the number of academically qualified full-time teachers in secondary vocational education[1]

| Year | The Number of Full-Time Teachers (Ten Thousand) | The Student-Teacher Ratio[2] | The Number of Academically Qualified Full-Time Teachers [3] (%) |
|---|---|---|---|
| 1997 | 71.60 | 32.59 | 66.77 |
| 1998 | 76.07 | 33.95 | 69.49 |
| 1999 | 76.11 | 33.79 | 71.49 |
| 2000 | 71.79 | 33.80 | 72.86 |
| 2001 | 67.14 | 34.17 | 73.86 |
| 2002 | 65.34 | 38.46 | 74.00 |
| 2003 | 68.60 | 42.97 | 54.30 |
| 2004 | 70.85 | 47.23 | 55.74 |
| 2005 | 74.98 | 23.00 | 56.40 |
| 2006 | 79.91 | 22.65 | 57.80 |
| 2007 | 85.89 | 23.95 | 58.44 |
| 2008 | 89.49 | 23.76 | 59.54 |
| 2009 | 90.29 | 26.05 | 61.40 |
| 2010 | 86.74 | 26.37 | 65.38 |
| 2011 | 88.19 | 25.01 | 66.74 |
| 2012 | 88.10 | 24.19 | 67.51 |
| 2013 | 86.79 | 22.97 | 67.75 |
| 2014 | 85.84 | 21.34 | 69.05 |
| 2015 | 84.41 | 20.47 | 69.66 |
| 2016 | 83.96 | 19.81 | 69.57 |

(Data source: *Educational Statistics Yearbook of China*, National Statistics Bulletin on Education Career Development; being processed)

Notes: (1) Secondary vocational education includes general secondary specialized schools, vocational high schools, technical training schools, and adult secondary specialized schools.
(2) The student-teacher ratio of secondary vocational education does not involve the data from technical training schools.
(3) The proportion of full-time teachers qualified with an academic background refers to the percentage of full-time teachers who have the minimum academic qualifications specified by the state accounts for the total number at a certain level of education. The minimum academic qualifications for teachers at all levels shall be governed by related provisions in *Teachers Law of the People's Republic of China*. In order to become a qualified teacher in senior high school, secondary specialized school, technical training school and a qualified culture course and specialized course teacher in vocational high school, they should have a bachelor's degree in an advanced normal university or other undergraduate college degree or above.
(4) The data from 1997 to 2002 refers to full-time teachers in secondary specialized schools who were academically qualified.

(*Continued*)

Table 8.2 The number of higher vocational teachers during the period 2004–2016

| Year | 2004 | 2005 | 2006 | 2007 | 2008 | 2009 | 2010 | 2011 | 2012 | 2013 | 2014 | 2015 | 2016 |
|---|---|---|---|---|---|---|---|---|---|---|---|---|---|
| The number of teachers | 237,654 | 267,855 | 316,299 | 354,817 | 377,137 | 395,016 | 404,098 | 412,624 | 423,381 | 436,561 | 438,300 | 454,576 | 466,934 |

(Data source: from relevant data in Educational Statistics Yearbook of China)

## Part 2 Developing Multiple Approaches to Cultivate Vocational Teachers

Vocational schools need teachers, then how can they obtain the teachers they need? Since reform and opening-up, vocational education circles have made great efforts to develop approaches for cultivating vocational teachers, and successively implemented a number of important investigations. This process constitutes the main method for the development of vocational teacher cultivation over the past four decades.

### 1. Investigations of Models of Vocational and Technical Teacher Education

Vocational and technical teacher education is the earliest model that was investigated by people to cultivate vocational teachers. As envisaged in the *Decision of the CPC Central Committee on the Reform of the Education System*, we can cultivate vocational teachers by drawing lessons from the model through which general teacher education cultivates primary and secondary school teachers. There are two ways to do this: one is to independently establish vocational and technical education colleges and the other is to set up vocational and technical normal schools on the basis of existing colleges.

Figure 8.1 The Gate of Tianjin University of Technology and Education

Table 8.3 Independent vocational and technical normal colleges in China during 1979–1988

| Serial Number | School Names | Cities and Provinces | Superior Department in Charge | Founding Year |
|---|---|---|---|---|
| 1 | Tianjin Technician Normal College (now Tianjin University of Technology and Education) | Tianjin | The Ministry of Labour | 1979 |
| 2 | Jilin Technician Normal College (now Jilin Engineering Normal University) | Changchun City in Jilin Province | Jilin Provincial Education Commission | 1979 |
| 3 | Hebei Vocational and Technical Normal College (now Hebei Normal University College of Career Technology) | Shijiazhuang City in Hebei Province | The Labour Bureau of Hebei Province | 1984 |
| 4 | Changzhou Technician Normal College (now Jiangsu University of Technology) | Changzhou City in Jiangsu Province | Jiangsu Provincial Education Commission | 1985 |
| 5 | Anhui Agricultural Technology Normal College (now Anhui Science and Technology University) | Fengyang County in Anhui Province | Anhui Provincial Education Commission | 1985 |
| 6 | Hebei Agricultural Technology Normal College (now Hebei Normal University of Science and Technology) | Changli County in Hebei Province | Hebei Provincial Education Commission | 1985 |
| 7 | Shanghai Technician Normal College (now Shanghai Normal University) | Shanghai | Shanghai Municipal Education Commission | 1985 |
| 8 | Nanchang Vocational and Technical Normal College (now Jiangxi Science and Technology Normal University) | Nanchang City in Jiangxi Province | Jiangxi Provincial Education Commission | 1987 |

Table 8.3 Continued

| Serial Number | School Names | Cities and Provinces | Superior Department in Charge | Founding Year |
|---|---|---|---|---|
| 9 | Henan Vocational and Technical Normal College (now Henan Institute of Science and Technology) | Xinxiang City in Henan Province | Henan Provincial Education Commission | 1987 |
| 10 | Zhejiang Rural Normal Specialised Postsecondary College (now Zhejiang Wanli University) | Ningbo City in Zhejiang Province | Zhejiang Provincial Education Commission | 1984 |
| 11 | Shanxi Vocational and Technical Normal Specialised Postsecondary College (now Shanxi Normal University) | Linfen City in Shanxi Province | Shanxi Provincial Education Commission | 1988 |

The first independent vocational and technical normal college was established in 1979. In order to solve the demands for teachers in technical training schools after the end of the "Cultural Revolution," SDPC and MOE jointly submitted a report to the State Council on January 10 1979: *Request for Instructions on the Additional Establishment of Four Normal Colleges for Technician Education* (No. 9 [1979] from SDPC and the State Labor Bureau). Thirteen leaders from the State Council including the State Council Premier Hua Guofeng as well as Deng Xiaoping, Li Xiannian, and Xu Xiangqian read the request and approved the establishment of four additional normal colleges for technician education, namely Tianjin Technician Normal College, Jilin Technician Normal College, Shandong Technician Normal College, and Henan Technician Normal College. Only two schools actually enrolled students afterwards, namely Tianjin Technician Normal College (now Tianjin University of Technology and Education) and Jilin Technician Normal College (now Jilin Engineering Normal University). The former began enrolling students in 1980, whereas the latter began in 1979.

From 1979 to 1988, a total of 11 independent vocational and technical normal colleges were established in China.

By the year 2000, there were a total of eight independent vocational and technical normal colleges in China, as four vocational and technical normal colleges were merged into other institutions. That is, Shanghai Technician Normal College was merged into Shanghai Normal University in 1994; Hebei Vocational and Technical Normal College was merged into Hebei Normal University in 1996;

Shanxi Vocational and Technical Normal Specialized Postsecondary College was merged into Shanxi Normal University in 1999; Zhejiang Rural Normal Specialised Postsecondary College was merged into Zhejiang Wanli Vocational and Technical College in 1999 in the same year; the former Institute For Nationalities was reorganized into Guangdong Polytechnic Normal University in 1998.

These independent vocational and technical normal colleges put a high value on investigating the problem of how to cultivate top-class vocational education teachers, especially those with practical skills. In order to overcome this issue, these schools not only established skills training centers, but also recruited students from secondary vocational schools. Therefore, the students they cultivated were well received by vocational schools.

The other approach was to set up vocational and technical normal colleges within the existing universities. In the late 1980s and early 1990s, the State Education Commission (now MOE) of PRC successively approved eight universities, including Tianjin University, Zhejiang University, Hebei Normal University College of Career Technology, Tongji University, Southeast University, Xi'an Jiaotong University, Hunan Agricultural University, and Sichuan University, to establish vocational and technical normal colleges or rural vocational teacher training centers to cultivate vocational faculty by relying on the tremendous strength of well-established universities. Today, the vocational and technical normal colleges in some universities still maintain and operate well, while some have been abolished. In addition to these eight universities, some local universities also established vocational and technical normal colleges, such as the Vocational and Technical Education College in Guangxi Normal University and Yunnan Normal University.

Both of the two approaches for implementing vocational and technical teacher education have their own advantages and disadvantages. The advantages of independently-established vocational and technical normal colleges are as follows: 1. It's easier to embody the principles of teacher cultivation in terms of the preferred training model. This is because these kinds of vocational and technical normal colleges are completely independent school-operating entities, and feature independent investigation of teacher training models and freedom of implementing reform of training models under the premise of impartial external evaluation. 2. Since the whole school aims to cultivate teachers, it can satisfy the demand for vocational schools teachers to a large extent whether in terms of diversified specialty setting or the number of teachers. If a province can really operate an independent vocational and technical normal college well, based upon some universities and establish some vocational and technical normal colleges according to specialty demands, it should well meet the demand for vocational schools teachers in that province. As for its weakness, it lies in vocational colleges not needing a very large number of professional teachers and specialty settings of vocational schools varying with the demands of the labor market. As a result, they are easily affected by the development of vocational schools and their graduates will have difficulties in job hunting.

Vocational and technical normal colleges that are established on the basis of universities also has its advantages, mainly manifest in the following ways: 1. It can improve the quality of student training by virtue of the university's specialty advantages; 2. It's relatively small in school-operating scale and not susceptible to changes in the number of teachers required by vocational schools, thus it is easy to continue to develop. Its weaknesses are also quite evident: 1. Due to its late development, it is in an unfavorable position in competition with the various specialties of the universities and is difficult to win over the resources required for development. 2. The universities have established its systems such as academic standards and training standards over a long time; these systems have reflected the requirements of its existing specialties and they are unlikely to be adjusted according to the special requirements and principles of specialty development and training in vocational and technical normal colleges. Therefore, its development tends to be very limited, and it's difficult to genuinely implement specialty construction and student training in accordance with the principles of vocational education.

Actually, the two development approaches of vocational and technical normal colleges complement each other. However, from the perspective of school operation practice, it is a more successful approach to establish vocational and technical normal colleges and cultivate teachers in well-established universities. This is because, up to now, most of the independently-established vocational and technical normal colleges have changed their names; some have completely changed school-operating directions; some have retained the function of vocational teacher training, though, this function has already weakened a lot. According to some researchers, among the 110,000 full-time students in the eight vocational and technical normal colleges in 2013, teacher-training majors only accounted for a very low proportion; the proportion was even less than 10% in some colleges.[6] For vocational and technical normal colleges established in universities, they were generally confronted with difficulties in school operation, though, the overall operation was normal.

To analyze the reasons, the proximate cause is that school authorities of independent vocational and technical normal colleges lack an in-depth understanding of the special status of these special colleges in higher education. The change of school-operating directions of vocational and technical normal colleges is a decision made by school authorities willfully despite the strong disagreement of teachers. They are prejudiced against vocational education, and do not want to explore how to operate vocational and technical normal colleges. All these factors contribute to misunderstandings about school-operations and qualities. Therefore, they inevitably encounter setbacks in operating schools, which in turn gives them reasons to change their school-operating directions. In addition to the subjective factors of human beings, there are also some objective reasons: 1. The school-operating model offers freedom for the re-selection of the school-operating direction. The training model of independently-established vocational and technical normal colleges is "professional education + teacher education," and the school-operating system of these colleges inherently determines that they have two choices in school-operating orientation. In other words, they can either continue to stick to the training model of "professional education + teacher education" so as to cultivate vocational teachers, or persist in teacher education to become a kind of pure professional education. Under these circumstances, which kind of school-operating model to choose by this kind of college shall depend largely on the perception of its leaders. As for the vocational and technical normal colleges affiliated to universities, their training model is also "professional education + teacher education." However, they compete with other specialties within the college, so they can only choose either to keep on adhering to training vocational teachers, or stop school operations. They cannot convert to purely professional education because relevant colleges and departments already existed. As a consequence, leaders and teachers can only insist on the functional orientation of teacher training. 2. The unfavorable school-operating position is difficult to change in the long run. Most of the independent vocational and technical normal colleges are established upon the original poor school-operating conditions; the state and local governments have invested little in such institutions except for Tianjin University of Technology and Education, and hardly promoted any substantively preferential policies; the society also has prejudice against "professional technology": all these factors lead to the generally unfavorable school-operating position of these kinds of schools, and they hope to break through the dilemma by changing school-operating directions.

Despite the great difficulties in practice, the *Decision of the State Council on Accelerating the Development of Modern Vocational Education* in 2014 still proposed to enforce the construction of vocational and technical normal colleges.

## 2. Investigation of Teacher Training Models of Vocational and Technical Education

Vocational and technical teacher education can only provide a very limited number of teachers. Vocational education is different from general education. The differences lie in that general education has a few subjects and facilitates continuing education in those subjects; all its courses can find corresponding subjects in universities, so they can easily establish a match with university specialties. As for vocational education, it has a great variety of specialties and it is very difficult to set up specialties that can meet the demands for such a diversity of teachers; moreover, specialties in many vocational schools cannot find corresponding specialties in universities, because these specialties are not suitable to be set at the university level, such as hairdressing and beauty and cooking. Statistics show that the eight vocational and technical normal colleges only cover 23.7% of the specialties in secondary vocational schools.[7] Now vocational colleges cannot recruit the required teachers from the vocational and technical normal colleges, so they have to employ teachers through other approaches, such as graduates of non-vocational and technical normal colleges and enterprise technologists. This leads to a big problem with the quality of vocational teachers, that is, a large number of vocational school teachers who are trained in specialized education and teaching. MOE has realized this problem and initiated the vocational school in-service teacher training program. This is another approach for exploring the cultivation of vocational teachers.

### 2.1 Establishing National Key Vocational Teacher Training Bases

Construction of national key vocational teacher training bases is the primary measure for the establishment of a vocational teacher training system. In 1998, MOE proposed in the *Action Plan for Education Rejuvenation for the 21st Century*: "Focus on constructing 50 training bases for vocational teachers and practice instructors on the basis of general higher education institutions and higher vocational and technical colleges. Local authorities should also get behind the construction of vocational teacher training bases."[8] In July 1999, the General Office of MOE promulgated the *Notice on Organizing and Recommending National Key Vocational Teacher Training Bases*, which officially initiated the construction of teacher training bases. In 1999, 2000, and 2001, MOE selected 20, 24, and 8 national key teacher training bases, respectively, in 52 universities, junior colleges, and secondary technical training schools separately. On March 5, 2001, MOE announced the *Notice of MOE on Adjusting Some National Key Vocational Teacher Training Bases* (No. 1[2001] letter from the Department of Vocational and Adult Education, MOE): "Absorb Ocean University of Qingdao (now Ocean University of China), AMBF (now Wuxi Machinery and Electron Higher Vocational and Technical School), Shandong-Bavaria Vocational Teacher Training Center, Hubei Beer School (i.e., BTA, a secondary school in Hubei Light Industry Technology Institute), amalgamate them with Pingdu Vocational Education Center, Changzhou Technician Normal College, Shandong Engineering College (now Shandong University of Technology) and Hubei University of Technology respectively, and jointly integrate into four bases: Ocean University of Qingdao—Pingdu Vocational Education Center, Changzhou Technician Normal College—AMBF, Shandong Engineering College—Shandong-Bavaria Vocational teacher training Center, Hubei University of Technology—Hubei Beer School."[9] After this, the total number of bases was still 52 by 2001, but the number of schools was expanded to 56. Since then, MOE has continued to expand the number of bases and changed the name "Training Base" to "Education and Training Base." In 2003, MOE approved Huazhong University of Science and Technology and JiMei University to become National Key Vocational Teacher Training Bases; in 2007, Tsinghua University and Beijing Institute of Technology were approved to be National Key Vocational Teacher Education and Training Bases; in 2012, MOE approved 33 units including Tianjin Vocational Institute to be National Key Vocational Teacher Education and Training Bases, and built a total of 101 National Key Vocational Teacher Education and Training Bases.[10]

Figure 8.2 The National Key Vocational Teacher Training Base in the East China Normal University

National Key Vocational Teacher Education and Training Bases played a positive role for local places. While constructing National Key Vocational Teacher Education and Training Bases, a total of over 300 local Vocational Teacher Education and Training Bases had been built by 2012,[11] and basically formed a flexible and open vocational teacher training system with national bases as the head and provincial bases as the main body.

At the same time in 2009, the General Office of MOHRSS issued *Notice on the Publication of the First Batch of Education and Training Bases for Technical School Teachers Nationwide*, and approved 21 technical colleges, including Xi'an

Technician College, to become the first batch of training bases for technical school teachers nationwide.

### 2.2. The Introduction of the Quality Improvement Plan for Vocational School Teachers

On December 26, 2006, MOE and MOF issued *Opinions of MOE and MOF on Implementing the Quality Improvement Plan for Secondary Vocational School Teachers* (No. 13 [2006] from the Department of Vocational and Adult Education, MOE), and determined to carry out the development of large scale of teacher training upon bases. This document proposed: "By 2010, we will train 150,000 professional backbone teachers for secondary vocational schools (including technical schools with distinct school-operating features and excellent records of achievement). Among these teachers, central finance will focus on supporting training 30,000 teachers and provincial finance will support training 120,000 teachers, in order to optimize the competence structure of teachers and improve the teaching standards of vocational education; help National Key Vocational Teacher Education and Training Bases and National Vocational Professional Teacher Training Model Units to develop 80 professional teacher education and training schemes, courses and textbooks so as to adapt to the requirements for the training of vocational teachers." The training supported by Central Finance is called "State-level Training for professional backbone teachers,"[12] and the training supported by provincial finance is called "Province-level Training for professional backbone teachers." Moreover, this plan also attaches great importance to teacher training abroad and proposes: "During 2007–2010, MOE and MOF shall select 250 teachers with excellent academic records of achievement from the State-level Training to study abroad for a month or two every year, concentrate on learning advanced vocational education and teaching concepts and teaching methods of specialized courses from abroad and cultivate a number of high-level experts in vocational education teaching."[13]

On November 8, 2011, MOE and MOF issued *Opinions of MOE and MOF on Implementing the Quality Improvement Plan for Vocational School Teachers* (No. 14 [2011] from the Department of Vocational and Adult Education, MOE), and proposed a plan for a new round of vocational teacher training: "During 2011–2015, 450,000 professional backbone teachers of vocational schools will be organized to participate in the training. Central Finance will focus on supporting training 100,000 teachers and provincial finance will focus on training 350,000, with the aim of improving teachers' educating and teaching levels, especially their practical teaching ability and curriculum design and development; support 20,000 young secondary vocational school teachers to join in enterprise practice, so as to improve their industrial, cultural, literacy and professional skills and levels; support vocational schools to establish part-time teacher posts and optimize the personnel structure of vocational school teachers; support national vocational teacher bases to establish 300 specialties for vocational teachers, develop training standards, training schemes, core curriculum and featured teaching materials for 100 undergraduate specialties of vocational teachers, enhance the training conditions and infrastructure development of the bases and improve the educational and training systems that are adapted to the demands for specialized teachers."[14]

Compared with the *Plan* in 2006, this *Plan* not only enlarges the number of teachers trained from 150,000 to 450,000, but also extends the training objects from secondary vocational school teachers to higher vocational college teachers, and highlighting enterprise practice training. More importantly, it also proposes the construction project for vocational teacher education and training systems: "During the period, 2012–2014, support national vocational teacher bases to set up 300 specialties for vocational teacher education and training and improve the training conditions of the vocational teacher bases. This project gives consideration to the layout of both specialties and regions, highlights the supporting focus, gives priority to the specialties that are related to modern agriculture, advanced manufacturing and modern service industries, to the bases that have achieved remarkable and effective results in vocational teachers teaching, and to the bases in western and minority areas with relatively unfavorable education and training conditions."

On October 28, 2016, MOE and MOF continued to issue *Opinions of MOE and MOF on Implementing the Quality Improvement Plan for Vocational School Teachers (2017–2020)* (No. 10 [2016] on teachers), and continued to propose a plan for another new round of vocational teacher training: "During the period 2017–2020, vocational school teachers and headmasters will be organized to participate in state-level training according to hierarchical classification, in order to encourage local authorities to implement a five-year training program for all headmasters and teachers in a planned and progressive manner and improve teachers' 'double quality' and headmasters' school-operating and governing ability; support research and studies as well as collaborative innovation of teachers in secondary vocational schools, higher vocational schools and application-oriented colleges, and establish a group of model teams for innovating professional skills of secondary and higher vocational school teachers; promote the mutual exchange and cooperation between teachers and enterprise staff, establish a standardized mechanism for teachers to join in enterprise practice and enterprise experts to work as part-time teachers, effectively improve the overall quality and construction level of vocational school teachers through setting an example, in innovation mechanisms, preferential promotion and taking a point to lead the whole, in order to accelerate the establishment of a full-time and part-time professional 'double-quality' teaching teams with noble virtues, high qualities, excellent craftsmanship and reasonable structure."[15]

The three plans maintain good continuity in time. Compared with the previous two plans, the plan in 2016 has important changes in the following respects in addition to subtle changes such as extending the objectives to teachers of application-oriented universities and headmasters of vocational schools: 1. It does not propose the explicit number of training targets; neither does the *Administrative Measures about the Quality Improvement Plan for Vocational School Teachers* issued by MOE in 2017. Now that quantitative requirements are not clearly stated, we think the number of training objectives can be defined according to demand and actual training abilities. 2. Delegate the training tasks more to local governments and propose the implementation principle of "taking the central government as the leader and local governments as the main body." 3. Put emphasis on classification training, and set up four training programs including leadership research and studies of specialty leaders, professional skills training of "double-quality" teachers, follow-up visiting and learning of excellent young teachers, and special study of leading principals in terms of model training for vocational school teachers; as for the synergistic improvement of the quality of teachers in secondary and higher vocational schools, it established three training programs, including the synergistic research and study on connecting specialty teachers in secondary and higher vocational schools, the passing-down and innovation of teachers' techniques and skills in urgently needed fields and the development of backbone training experts; in terms of the two-way exchange and cooperation between schools and enterprise, it has established two training programs: sending teachers to enterprise practice and setting up special posts for part-time teachers, which has made the training much more targeted. 4. Attach special importance to teachers' practical training, that is, to focus on improving not only their theoretical level but also their practice ability and enhancing the training effects. This can be seen from the designed training programs.

### 2.3. Planning for Teachers' Practicing Ability Enhancement

For vocational teachers, one of the most important aspects of their knowledge and ability structure is to understand enterprises and enhance their practice ability. On February 16, 1998, the State Education Commission (now MOE) issued *Principles and Opinions on Deepening the Teaching Reform of Vocational Education for the 21st Century* (No. 1 [1998] from the Department of Vocational Education, MOE). This document puts forward the training requirements for "double-quality" teachers.

That is, to cultivate teachers who can not only teach theories but also instruct students in practical operation. For this purpose, the document proposes: "It's necessary to take measures such as arranging teachers to be placed in enterprises and public institutions for internship and training, in order to acquaint cultural course teachers with professional knowledge, make specialized course teachers grasp professional skills and improve the practice ability of most teachers, especially young and middle-aged teachers."[16] It highlights the idea of organizing teachers to enter enterprises for internship, and this idea has subsequently been continued in relevant documents. For example, the *Decision of the State Council on Vigorously Promoting Vocational Education Reform and Development* (No. 16 [2002] from the State Council) also proposes: "Teachers need be arranged to go to enterprises and public institutions for professional practice and inspection in a planned manner, so as to improve their professional standards."[17]

In order to offer teachers a platform for enterprise internship, MOE initiated the plan for establishing teacher training centers in enterprises. In March 2001, MOE issued the *Notice on the Publication of the First Batch of National Model Units of Professional Skills Training for Vocational Teachers Nationwide* (No. 3 [2001] letter from the Department of Vocational and Adult Education, MOE) and determined that six units will become national model units of professional skills training for vocational teachers, including Shanghai Baosteel Group Corporation, the Haier Group, Sichuan Changhong Electric Co., Ltd., China FAW Group Corporation, Dongfeng Motor Corporation, and Suzhou Industrial Park Institute of Vocational Technology (SIPIVT). Later, Beijing Tourism Group (BTG) and Wuhan Huazhong Numerical Control Co., Ltd. were also included.

The purpose of establishing national model units of professional skills training for vocational teachers was to cooperate with National Key Vocational Teacher Training Bases in their work at that time. What's more, the cultivation of teachers' practicing ability has always been one of the training components in the quality enhancement plan for vocational school teachers. Although practical ability is very important for vocational teachers, a large number of new teachers recruited by vocational schools are the current year's graduates from universities and colleges. This creates growing pressure when confronted with the practical ability training of vocational teachers and the training for teachers' practical enhancement increasingly important.

In November 2005, the State Council issued the *Decision of the State Council on Vigorously Developing Vocational Education* (No. 35 [2005] from the State Council), which requires "implementing the quality enhancement plan for vocational school teachers; local finance at all levels should continue to support the construction of vocational teacher training bases and teacher training. To establish a system for vocational teachers to go to enterprises for practice, and professional teachers must go for practice in enterprises or to front-line production service for two months every other year."[18]

On September 28, 2006, MOE issued *Opinions on Establishing a System for Secondary Vocational School Teachers to Practice in Enterprises* (No. 11 [2006] from the Department of Vocational and Adult Education, MOE), which explicitly proposed the requirement for establishing an enterprise practice system for vocational school teachers. It also set out: "Local education administrative department should combine specialty settings of local vocational schools, coordinate relevant industry segments, select a number of backbone enterprises which show strong representation in the industry, have high technological level and good staff training foundations, value and support the development of vocational education, as the key bases for vocational school teachers to join in enterprise practice. Secondary vocational schools should actively strive for support from enterprises, rely fully on enterprises that cooperate with schools, expand the content and forms of school-enterprise cooperation and establish stable channels for teachers to go for practice in enterprises."[19] Guided by this document, the construction of teacher-enterprise practice bases has become an important part of establishing a training system for vocational teachers.

In July 2015, MOE issued *Opinions on Deepening the Teaching Reform of Vocational Education and Comprehensively Enhancing the Quality of Teacher Training*, and proposed "establishing a number of teacher education and training bases and teacher-enterprise practice bases, and energetically exploring a high-level model of training 'double-quality' teachers." It also requested "implementing a five-year training system for all teachers, implementing the system of practice prior to teaching and regular practice among new teachers, and cultivating a number of "coach-type" teaching masters and specialty leaders."[20]

In October 2015, MOE issued the *Action Plan for Innovation and Development of Higher Vocational Education (2015–2018)* (referred to as the *Action Plan*), and specifically proposed "concentrating on enhancing professional teaching ability and practical hands-on ability, and improve the training and continuing education system for full-time teachers in junior colleges and higher vocational schools. Encourage high-level universities and large and medium enterprises to jointly build 'double-quality' teacher education and training bases, explore the training model of 'Academic Education + Enterprise Training'; perfect the training mechanism of letting young teachers learn from experienced teachers; establish a system of teacher training in rotation; professional teachers should take part in enterprise practice and the accumulated time should be no less than six months every five years. Enhance the ability of vocational and technical normal schools to cultivate vocational teachers."[21]

In May 2016, MOE and another seven departments issued the *Provisions on Enterprise Practice for Vocational School Teachers*, which stipulates: "Specialized course teachers (including practice instructors) of vocational schools must go for practice in enterprises or front-line of production and service every 5 years and the accumulated time should be no less than 6 months according to their specialty features. New teachers without enterprise work experience should go for practice first and then work as teachers. Teachers of public elementary courses should also regularly investigate, research and study in enterprises." It also proposes that "national and provincial education administrative departments should cooperate with the competent authorities of the industry, select a number of open and public model teacher-enterprise practice bases on the basis of existing resources, guide vocational schools to integrate internal and external enterprise resources to build productive teacher-enterprise practice bases at school level, gradually establish and perfect the teacher-enterprise practice system."[22]

By 2011, "the number of teacher-enterprise practice units should reach 100, and the provincial bases and enterprise practice units should further optimize the layout and highlight the features."[23] By 2012, we should establish a total of 400 enterprise practice units for vocational teachers.[24]

## 3. Investigation of the Academic Education of Vocational Teachers

So-called academic education here refers to education to a master's degree or above. The construction of a vocational school teacher training system not only needs to guarantee the supply of undergraduate teachers through developing vocational and technical normal education, but also need to improve teachers' educating and teaching ability and professional practice ability through developing the teacher in-service training system; At the same time, it's also confronted with the problem of cultivating teachers with higher academic qualifications. In order to build a highly qualified teaching team, vocational schools need a large number of teachers with a master's degree or even a doctor degree. For this purpose, MOE has made a lot of effort to provide approaches for improving teachers' degrees.

In May 2000, MOE and the Academic Degree Commission of the State Council jointly issued *Notice on the Work of Encouraging In-Service Secondary Vocational School Teachers for Further Study for Their Master's Degree* (No. 5 [2000] from the Department of Vocational and Adult Education, MOE). The document pointed out: Since reform and opening-up, the degree level of secondary vocational teachers has been significantly improved, with 67.62% having a bachelor degree or above, an increase of 21.22% over 1984; 37.42% of teachers in vocational high schools have bachelor degree or above, an increase of 18.12% over

1985. The number of teachers with a master's degree is significantly smaller than that of ordinary high school teachers. There is a big gap compared with the requirement that 10% of full-time teachers and headmasters engaged in high school education should have a master's degree by 2010. On this basis, the document put forward: During the period 2000–2005, an average of about 1,000 secondary vocational school in-service teachers shall be enrolled for the further study for master's degrees every year.[25] Teachers will eventually receive an academic master's degree without postgraduate qualifications. The document regulates that the candidate should be under 40 years old, which makes it impossible for teachers over 40 years to obtain a master's degree through this approach. On March 16, 2001, MOE and the Office of the Academic Degree Commission of the State Council jointly issued *Notice on Establishing an Expert Steering Group for the Work of Encouraging In-Service Secondary Vocational School Teachers for Further Study for Their Master's Degree in China* (No. 26 [2001] letter from the Department of Vocational and Adult Education, MOE), and established an expert working group to specifically instruct the implementation of this work.

In 2005, the enrollment plan was expanded to 2,375 students. According to statistics, the number of enrolling units for in-service secondary vocational school teachers was 33 in 2009, with 46 enrollment specialties and for 1,945 students to be enrolled; the enrollments were further expanded. In the past decade since the start of this work, 9,100 students have been enrolled; 6,600 have graduated; over 95% of the graduates have returned to work in vocational schools and become the backbone of teaching and specialty leaders. In 2012, the number of colleges and universities that implemented enrollment and cultivation reached 32, and the number of enrolled students reached 2,300, which greatly contributed to the improvement of the degree level of teachers.[26]

In-service secondary vocational teachers' study for master's degree adopts the training model of being admitted by passing a separate test and then eventually obtaining an academic degree. This provides a large number of secondary vocational teachers with a suitable aptitude to study for a master's degree. The reason is that it adopts a separate test to make it easier for secondary vocational teachers to succeed and gain entry to study a degree-granting program; this approach also plays a crucial role in enhancing the incentive of secondary vocational teachers to do further study. Teachers who eventually obtain an academic degree will do so as the whole training process is carried out in accordance with academic requirements, which is not the case for secondary vocational teachers.

On December 24, 2011, MOE issued *Opinions on Further Improving the Cultivation and Training System for Vocational Teachers* (No. 16 [2011] from the Department of Vocational and Adult Education, MOE), and continued to emphasize that "education administrative departments at all levels must support the vocational teacher training bases and schools that are accredited to award master's and doctor's degrees to expand the training scale of vocational teachers to postgraduate level and improve the training quality."[27] On September 6, 2012, MOE, NDRC and MOF issued *Opinions on Deepening the Reform of Teacher Education* (No. 13[2012] on teachers), and proposed "expanding the enrollments of education for master's and doctor's degrees, and cultivate high-level teachers for elementary and secondary schools and secondary vocational schools."[28] Postgraduate teachers are urgently demanded by vocational schools, especially higher vocational colleges. They are in urgent demand of a large number of graduates with a doctor's degree to enrich the teaching group and better embody the advanced school-operating level of higher vocational education. However, the targets proposed in this document encountered great difficulties in implementation.

In the current academic degree system in China, master's and doctor's degrees include two categories, namely academic degrees and professional degrees. It's almost impossible to expand the enrollments for academic degrees: 1. The above documents do not explicitly define the number of students that can to be enrolled by vocational and technical education master's and doctor's degree programs at the operational level. However, within the university, the enrollments in vocational programs are not listed separately and the enrollment number that can be allocated depends on the allocation rules of the university depending on where the specialties are; 2. Even if there were more enrollments, vocational and technical programs still confront the problem of a serious shortage of tutors. The number of tutors directly restricts the enrollment of graduate students. In terms of professional degrees, under the direction of degree system reform in China, the master's degree program for in-service secondary vocational teachers began to stop enrollments in 2014, and changed to cultivate master's degree teachers and administrators through a Master of Education (M.Ed.). In 2016, the entrance exam for M.Ed. began to be unified with that for an academic degree and the entrance exam became much more difficult. This reform has brought two major difficulties to improving the proportion of vocational school teachers with master's degrees: 1. It's difficult to cultivate masters of education in the field of vocational and technical education; what's worse is that the cultivation of enterprise practicing ability is of great difficulty in implementation and the cultivation model is still at the exploratory stage. As a result, full-time enrollments are generally small; 2. Although the system still allows secondary vocational teachers to have equal access to the entrance exam for M.Ed., the exam has become much harder. This renders most teachers with abundant practical experience unable to obtain further opportunities to learn. Professional doctorates in education provide a special path for vocational school leaders and teachers to obtain a doctoral degree. In December 2008, the 26th conference of the Academic Degree Commission of the State Council deliberated and approved the *Establishment Scheme of Professional Doctorate in Education* and determined to set up professional doctorates in education. The *Scheme* stipulates: Professional doctorates in education aim to cultivate and create interdisciplinary, profession-oriented and high-level specialized graduates in education, teaching and education management. Professional doctorates in education only enroll elementary and secondary school teachers and various categories of school administrators at all levels who have a master's degree, over 5 years of full-time working experience in education and related fields, and who have achieved considerable success. However, while enrolling doctoral students in education, it is impossible to separately list the enrolled number of students in vocational education specialties. Therefore, it completely lacks transparency and sense to increase the proportion of vocational teachers with doctoral degrees through this approach.

So it seems a more realistic way to improve the proportion of vocational teachers with master's and doctor's degree by recruiting teachers from various specialties, and then cultivating them with vocational education knowledge and skills.

## Part 3 Cultivating a Model Selection and System Construction for Vocational Teachers

The above summarizes three important approaches to the vocational teacher education and training system in China since reform and opening-up. Among the three approaches, degree education shows a steady and orderly developing trend. This is because the degree education system is relatively standardized in itself, and does not have very large numbers in training. What needs to be analyzed are two different approaches: vocational and technical teacher education and in-service teacher training. Since the implementation of the teacher quality enhancement plan, the approach of in-service teacher training can be said to have played the most important role in the training of vocational teachers. A large number of teachers have been trained through this approach over these years and many teachers have also obtained opportunities for training abroad. While making these achievements, however, we have also encountered many chaotic situations. Perhaps this is because *Opinions of MOE and MOF on Implementing the Quality Improvement Plan for Vocational School Teachers (2017–2020)* in 2016 does not specify an explicit number of places for teacher training. So, at this stage, analysis of the essence of the "chaos" will give us greater visibility into the future developing direction.

## 1. Major Problems Confronted by Vocational Teachers

### 1.1. How to Establish the Connection between Vocational and Technical Teacher Education and In-Service Teacher Training

The "chaos" first manifests in that the training objectives are not classified; teachers with different foundations are put together for training, which makes the training much less targeted, and makes it difficult for teachers with a weak educational theoretical base to truly understand the training content and impossible for teachers with a good educational theoretical base to get targeted improvement on the basis of broadly based and generalized knowledge. To solve this problem, on the one hand, it's necessary to divide the training objectives into new teachers, backbone teachers, specialty leaders, and teaching masters, and provide them with different training content according to the training requirements of different types of teachers; on the other hand, it's necessary to establish a bridge between vocational and technical teacher education and in-service teacher training. The latter is more important because it involves the issue of system building.

As mentioned above, China's vocational teacher training includes two approaches, namely, vocational and technical teacher education and in-service teacher training, so we have two kinds of teachers with different foundations when training in-service teachers. The first kind are teachers who graduated from vocational and technical normal universities and have received systematic vocational and technical education theory and teaching practice training while studying there; the others are teachers who did not graduate from normal universities and those who are enterprise technicians. The two sources of teachers are advantageous in that they have a solid specialized foundation, or strong practical operating ability. The greatest weakness lies in their lack of the most basic teacher education. The educational concepts and teaching skills of some teachers are formed only based on their daily experience and are seriously defective. This problem is more serious in vocational schools. For example, some teachers are unskilled in basic explanation and this makes students incapable of understanding what they teach. For the teachers from these two sources, it's necessary to design separate training content for them. However, the current vocational teacher training system fails to take this into consideration, thus leading to the "chaos."

The American vocational teacher training system has fully taken this into account in terms of system design, and established a very standardized practice model. The U.S. vocational teacher training is completely carried out on the basis of how a teacher obtains a qualification license. Graduates who have studied relevant courses in university can directly obtain temporary teacher licenses: this is referred to as the traditional path. Teachers recruited through other paths, especially those from enterprises, must get through the training and identification before they can obtain temporary teacher licenses: this is called the alternative path and requires them to acquire knowledge and skills equivalent to those taught in university through alternative means. Therefore, the process of teachers from the alternative path is more complicated than those from the traditional path before formally undertaking course teaching tasks. The acquisition of a temporary teacher license makes teachers from the two paths eventually reach the same starting point in terms of system design.

How America designs its vocational teacher training system is of enlightening significance to us. China's teacher license is not graded but one-off, so teachers often lack the impetus to participate in training and keep on with specialty development. Without doubt, we have a professional title system to stimulate teachers' professional development. However, the title system is encouraging while the teacher license system is limiting and the two are essentially different in function. Without teacher license grading, it will be difficult to establish a connection between the two sources of teachers in the system. This is because it is impossible to precisely match the capacity requirements and difficult to solve targeted problems in training without a more meticulous distinction of the level of teacher professional development.

### 1.2. How to Distinguish the Functions of Different Levels of Vocational Teacher Training Bases

Vocational teacher training bases include two levels at the state level and the province level. This brings about the question of how to distinguish the training objectives and content between the two levels. Relevant documents distinguish the functions of the two in this way: with the national base as the head and the provincial base as the main body. But this distinction is very vague. What is the "head"? What is the "main body"? Does the main body mean to assume more training tasks and the head mean to play a role model for training? Or should they be understood in other ways? The document does not give a specific description, so this distinction fails to play a definite role of turning theory into practice.

The failure of clearly distinguishing the training functions of state-level and province-level training bases has brought a notable problem in practice. That is, teachers who have participated in province-level training will continue to be sent to participate in state-level training, and teachers who have accomplished state-level training will still be sent to participate in province-level training, and the training at the two levels often overlaps in content. This is the second important manifestation of the "chaos." In other words, duplicating training is very serious. Some teachers often listen to the same lecture given by the same expert several times, which not only considerably reduces the efficiency of training but also impacts the sustainable development of teachers' ability.

If we want to distinguish the functions between state-level and province-level training bases, it's crucial for us to distinguish teachers' professional level. This problem can be effectively solved by defining teachers' professional level and then docking the professional level with the training level. For example, the training of specialty leaders, backbone teachers and below can be undertaken by province-level training bases and the training of teaching masters can be assumed by state-level training bases. Certainly, there is still a level of training below the province, namely, the training organized by vocational schools themselves, usually referred to as school-based training. The training at this level should rate its function as a kind of specific training according to schools' specific needs. The distinction of training functions will also give rise to differences in training models.

### 1.3. How to Solve the Problem That Teachers Are Repeatedly Sent to Participate in Training

The third manifestation of the "chaos" is that many teachers constantly participate in various training, while some have never participated in any standardized training, especially teacher culture courses in vocational schools. The reasons for this problem are complex, including: 1. Human factors. For example, some vocational schools consider participation in training as a kind of welfare and have a specific purpose in opportunity allocation; some vocational schools think of arranging teachers to participate in training as a kind of burden and always send those teachers who have small amount of work and easily abide by work assignment to participate in training. 2. Economic factors. Some vocational schools are well funded for school operations and have a large amount of funds for teacher training. Sometimes, they will repeatedly send teachers to participate in training so as to spend the funds, while some schools face tight outlay for school operations and have very few opportunities to send teachers to participate in training.

However, in addition to the contingency factors above, there are some necessary reasons inherent in the system. The solution to the problems caused by the above contingency factors is also bound up with system design. This system still means to scientifically design a hierarchical professional license system according to the professional ability development stage of teachers. With this system, every teacher can have an explicit learning module at different stages of professional ability development, so that we can judge teachers' training needs according to the deficient modules and fundamentally solve the above problems. China is a country with a large number of vocational teachers. Without this system, China will have great difficulty guaranteeing the effective operation of teacher training, and teacher training will become a tool for some institutions to gain economic profits and play a very limited role on the development of teachers' professional competency.

### 1.4. How to Remedy the Conflict between Teachers' Participation in Training and Normal Teaching Work in Schools

Another manifestation of the "chaos" is that the in-service training often severely disturbs the teaching sequence in vocational schools, thus making some schools feel resentful toward "state-level training" and "province-level training" programs. Teaching training often takes a long period of time on a large scale and schools are unlikely able to implement all teacher training during the summer or winter vacation; moreover, teacher training often requires many practical activities and some practical activities cannot be carried out during vacations. As a result, many "state-level training" and "province-level training" programs are arranged in normal teaching hours. This will inevitably give rise to the conflict between teacher training and normal school teaching. If this conflict fails to be resolved, teacher training will have difficulty sustaining its development. The best solution to this problem is to let teachers flexibly choose their time for training according to their teaching plan.

This target is completely achievable. For example, the American vocational teacher license system stipulates the learning modules and these modules can be accomplished within 4–5 years, which provides teachers plenty of options to choose from. Furthermore, its teaching is usually implemented in the evening, which can help to stagger teachers' daytime working hours and minimize the impact of training on teaching. For teachers who live far away, they set up a centralized remote teaching place. This shows that the key strategies to achieve this target include both system design and specific arrangements for teacher training. For example, if we don't distinguish the functions of teaching training at state-level and province-level, and a large number of teachers participate in state-level training for the purpose of obtaining basic teaching ability, then this problem will be difficult to resolve. This is because the locations of state-level training are often far away from the schools where they work and the long distance makes them unable to flexibly arrange their training time. If this kind of training is undertaken by provincial or even municipal training bases, then the problem can be easily settled.

## 2. Key Strategies for the Establishment of a Vocational Teacher Training System

The above is some analysis of the problems that occurred with the implementation of the two plans for the quality enhancement of teachers and some resolution strategies proposed accordingly. However, all these strategies lead to one path. That is, to establish a vocational education teacher training system in order to make vocational teacher training evolve from project to system.

As a matter of fact, the concept of a "vocational education teacher training system" has constantly appeared in released files. *Opinions on Further Improving the Cultivation and Training System for Vocational Teachers* issued by MOE in 2011 (No. 16 [2011] from the Department of Vocational and Adult Education, MOE) also put forward: "In recent years, great progress has been made in cultivating and training vocational teachers; the teacher cultivating and training system has taken initial shape; the cultivating and training system has been basically formed and the quality of cultivating and training has been continuously improved. From a general view, however, system establishment is still a vulnerable link in cultivating and training teachers and involves such problems as defective systems, unclear features and inappropriate implementation, which makes it unable to adapt well to the imperative requirements for reinforcing the development of vocational teachers in the new era. Therefore, we must take it as an important and urgent mission to improve the teacher cultivating and training systems, strengthen the leadership of organizations, enhance overall planning, accelerate reform and innovation, and make great efforts to create a new dimension for the development of vocational teachers."[29] Although the document pointedly stressed the problems in the system, it still made the important judgment that "the system has taken initial shape." More importantly, this judgment was made in 2011.

However, "the system has taken initial shape" mentioned here only indicates the perfection of cultivating and training institutions rather than creating clear-cut assignment of responsibility and internal relations among these institutions. Whereas, the latter is much more important and intricate for the establishment of a vocational teacher training system. The system establishment involves two essential issues.

### 2.1. Choice of Training Model for Vocational Teachers

In order to establish a training system for vocational teachers, we must first choose which path to take. That is, which path will China's vocational education teacher training mainly rely on, vocational and technological teacher education or in-service teacher training. The general view is that both paths need to be taken. Therefore, recent important documents continue to stress the necessity of reinforcing vocational and technical teacher education. For example, *Planning for Modern Vocational Education System Establishment (2014–2020)* released in 2014 (No. 6 [2014] from MOE) keeps on proposing to "reinforce the construction of vocational and technical normal schools"[30] (while it's very necessary to increase investment in existing vocational and technical schools, the problem addressed here is path selection). A well-established vocational teacher training system must choose one from the two as the dominant path because they are incompatible with each other. If vocational and technical teacher education is chosen as the main path, then there is no need to design the in-service teacher training system very rigorously; if in-service teacher training is taken the main path, then vocational and technical teacher education can mainly focus on specialties with high theoretical requirements.

From the international perspective, both Germany and the U.S. have well-established vocational education teacher training systems, but their models are completely different from each other. Germany adopts the model of vocational and technical teacher education, while the U.S. adopts the model of in-service teacher training. The comparison between the two models is shown in Table 8.4. It can be found that the two models are similar in that both consist of three basic components, namely, a university education course, teacher ability training, and working as a teacher. The difference lies in how they deal with the relationship between the three components. The German model arranges the three components in a straight line, while the American model arranges the three components in parallel. The German model's advantage is that it can concentrate on "pre-service teachers," but this model costs a lot and requires the establishment of vast teacher training institutions. As for the U.S. model, it juxtaposes the three components and cultivates teachers by taking full advantage of the resources in the schools where the teachers work, which can greatly save educational costs.

Table 8.4 Comparison of the vocational teacher training modes between Germany and the U.S.

| The mode of German vocational teacher training | | |
|---|---|---|
| University education course | Teacher ability training | Working as a teacher |

| The mode of American vocational teacher training |
|---|
| University education course |
| Teacher competence training |
| Work as a teacher |

Which model should China choose for its vocational teacher training? Practice shows that pre-service teacher training developed in times of great hardship; it has been gradually shrinking in scale, and the number of teachers trained only accounts for an insignificant proportion in the total number of vocational teachers. As vocational and technical teacher education has failed to provide adequate sources of teachers for vocational education, vocational education has no choice but to recruit teachers from various universities or all walks of life and then train these teachers by means of in-service education. This is the reality confronted by China's vocational teacher training in terms of path selection.

Compared with the model of pre-service teacher training, post-service teacher training has other advantages, including: 1. Good training effect. Since the model of post-service teacher training targets in-service teachers who already have some practical teaching experience and are assuming school teaching tasks, it will be easy for them to understand education theory and become greatly interested in it. The opposite is true for college and university students. This contrast can be easily observed in the practice of teacher training; 2. No waste of education. The model of post-service teacher training targets in-service teachers. They are highly targeted and the training effect is readily apparent. If pre-service teacher training fails to ensure that the students who have been trained can work as teachers, then this kind of training will be nothing but a waste.

### 2.2. Establishment of a Licensing System Based on Vocational Teachers' Competency Standards

From the above analysis, we can see that the establishment of a vocational teacher training system with in-service teachers as the subject relies on the establishment of a licensing system based on the standards of vocational teachers' competence. The U.S. sets a good model for us on this issue.

In China, relevant documents have attached great importance to the development of vocational teachers' competency standards. On August 20, 2012, the State Council issued *Opinions on Strengthening the Improvement of Teachers* (No. 41 [2012] from the State Council), which was the first document issued by the State Council specifically for teachers. The document proposes: "Perfect the teachers' professional development standard system. Introduce professional standards for teachers in kindergartens, primary schools, secondary schools, vocational schools, colleges and universities and special education schools according to the characteristics of various types of education at each level, and take these standards as an important basis for such work as teacher cultivation, access, training and evaluation. Formulate professional standards and qualifications for kindergarten principals, general primary and secondary school headmasters, and secondary vocational school principals, and improve the professional level of these principals (headmasters). Formulate approval standards for education theory specialties, carry out professional accreditation and evaluation, standardize the management of education theory specialties, and establish a quality evaluation system for teacher cultivation."[31] Here, it proposes the requirements not only for developing professional standards for vocational teachers, but also for developing professional standards and qualifications for vocational school principals. In order to implement the requirements proposed by the State Council in this document, MOE, NDRC, and MOF promulgated *Opinions on Deepening the Reform of Teacher Education* (No. 13 [2012] on teachers) on September 6, 2012, and wrote the requirements for establishing professional standards for vocational school teachers into the file.

On September 20, 2013, MOE issued *Professional Standards for Secondary Vocational School Teachers (Trial)* (No. 12 [2013] on teachers). Its release is a solution to the problem of establishing vocational teacher profession standards from scratch in China. However, objectively, our standards still fall far behind those of other countries such as the United States. The development of teacher profession standards is highly professional. Only by basing ourselves upon teaching practice, systematically sorting out theoretical education, and teaching knowledge required by teachers according to the demands of teacher cultivation and evaluation, can we successfully develop standards that really count.

## Notes

1 CPC Central Committee: Decision of the CPC Central Committee on the Reform of the Education System, 1985.
2 State Education Commission (now MOE): Several Opinions on Strengthening Faculty Development in Vocational and Technical Schools, 1986.
3 Ministry of Labour (now MOHRSS): Opinions of the Ministry of Labour on Reinforcing Vocational and Technical Training and Faculty Development, 1989.
4 MOE: Opinions of the General Office of MOE on Enhancing Faculty Development in Higher Vocational (Higher Technical) Colleges and Universities, 2002.
5 Editorial Department of Educational Statistics Yearbook of China: Educational Statistics Yearbook of China, People's Education Press, 1996.
6 Sun Cuixiang: Training of Vocational Teachers: A Problem that Needs Immediate Attention, Vocational & Technical Education Forum, No. 25, 2013.
7 Cao Ye: On the History and Realistic Choice of Teacher Training in Vocational and Technical Education in China, Education and Vocation, No.6, 2010.
8 MOE: Action Plan for Education Rejuvenation for the 21st Century, 1998.
9 MOE: Notice of MOE on Adjusting Some National Key Vocational Teacher Training Bases, 1998.

10 Editorial Department of Educational Statistics Yearbook of China: Educational Statistics Yearbook of China, People's Education Press, p. 280, 2012.
11 Same as the above footnote.
12 MOE, MOF: Opinions of MOE and MOF on Implementing the Quality Improvement Plan for Secondary Vocational School Teachers, 2006.
13 Same as the above footnote.
14 MOE, MOF: Opinions of MOE and MOF on Implementing the Quality Improvement Plan for Vocational School Teachers, 2011.
15 MOE, MOF: Opinions of MOE and MOF on Implementing the Quality Improvement Plan for Vocational School Teachers (2017–2020), 2016.
16 State Education Commission (now MOE): Principles and Opinions on Deepening the Teaching Reform of Vocational Education for the 21st Century, 1998.
17 State Council: Decision of the State Council on Vigorously Promoting Vocational Education Reform and Development, 2002.
18 State Council: Decision of the State Council on Vigorously Developing Vocational Education, 2005.
19 MOE: Opinions on Establishing a System for Secondary Vocational School Teachers to Practice in Enterprises, 2006.
20 MOE: Opinions on Deepening the Teaching Reform of Vocational Education and Comprehensively Enhancing the Quality of Talent Training, 2015.
21 MOE: Action Plan for Innovation and Development of Higher Vocational Education (2015–2018), 2015.
22 MOE: Provisions on Enterprise Practice for Vocational School Teachers, 2016.
23 MOE: Opinions of MOE on Strengthening Faculty Development of Secondary Vocational Schools during the '12th Five-Year' Period, 2011.
24 The Editorial Department of Educational Statistics Yearbook of China: Educational Statistics Yearbook of China, People's Education Press, p. 280, 2012.
25 MOE: Notice on the Work of Encouraging In-Service Secondary Vocational School Teachers for Their Further Study of Master Degree, 2000.
26 The Editorial Department of Educational Statistics Yearbook of China: Educational Statistics Yearbook of China, People's Education Press, p. 280, 2012.
27 MOE: Opinions on Further Improving the Cultivation and Training System for Vocational Teachers, 2011.
28 MOE, NDRC and MOF: Opinions on Deepening the Reform of Teacher Education, 2012.
29 MOE: Opinions on Further Improving the Cultivation and Training System for Vocational Teachers, 2011.
30 MOE: Planning for Modern Vocational Education System Establishment (2014–2020), 2014.
31 State Council: Opinions of the State Council on Strengthening the Improvement of Teachers, 2012.

CHAPTER NINE

# Developing a Modern Apprenticeship System to Cultivate Great Craftsmens

In 2014, MOE issued *Opinions of MOE on the Pilot Work of Modern Apprenticeship* (No. 9 [2014] from the Department of Vocational and Adult Education, MOE), which initiated the course of further deepening the student training models for vocational education in China. What I will talk about in this chapter is different from those in the previous chapters: since the launch of this reform by MOE, the modern apprenticeship pilot has only existed for about three years, and we have few successful cases to learn from and gain practical experience to summarize. As China has no developed theoretical research on modern apprenticeship, its modern apprenticeship system is still comparatively shallow in practice, and most vocational schools are still perplexed about how to implement modern apprenticeships. In this context, theoretical analysis on the motivations for modern apprenticeships in China and the problems that urgently need to be solved in practice will help promote the reform of modern apprenticeships smoothly.

Figure 9.1 A Korean vehicle repairing teacher is teaching practical training

# Part 1 The Background for Developing Modern Apprenticeships in China

A modern apprenticeship is an exotic concept, which has different expressions abroad. For example, it's called modern apprenticeships in Britain and new apprenticeships in Australia. In 1996, Britain launched the modern apprenticeship reform program. Soon afterwards this concept spread rapidly and became a hot topic in academic research and vocational education reform worldwide, including some developing countries such as South Africa and Indonesia. In addition to these countries, some other countries also implemented modern apprenticeships successfully, but they just do not directly adopt the concept of modern apprenticeships, such as in Germany and Switzerland. The student cultivating method in their dual system is a modern apprenticeship system. Our concept of a modern apprenticeship stems from Britain, but we also need to pay close attention to Germany in terms of implementation. Our previous research on German training models for vocational education mainly concentrated on its dual system, but it is just a system. Only by closely studying the master-apprentice-based training method in the dual system can we have a deeper understanding of the training model in Germany.

## 1. Two Purposes for Developing Modern Apprenticeship in Western Countries

Apprenticeships are a training model that covers a wide range of practices. For example, systematic learning as an apprentice for 7–8 years can be considered as an apprenticeship, and corporate training for its new staff for six months to one year can also be called an apprenticeship. The difference not only lies in the length of learning time, but also the purpose. For example, Britain, Australia, and Germany implement modern apprenticeships for different purposes, and an analysis of their differences will help us find a clear purpose for China to implement modern apprenticeships and design an appropriate path for implementation.

The main purpose for Britain and Australia to develop modern apprenticeships is to enrich the youth's work experience and promote their employment. This is because the high youth unemployment rate has always been a significant social problem that perplexes these countries, and numerous studies have shown that it's closely associated with their lack of work experience. The statements by M. Axmann and C. Hofmann from the International Labour Organization (ILO) thoroughly represent this policy orientation: "The reason why the resurgence of interest in apprenticeship receives a response at the trilateral meeting of ILO is that the youth unemployment rate is lower in countries with apprenticeships. The discussion has repeatedly stressed that apprenticeship is an effective means for youth to connect schools with the work world, because it allows them to get work experience while receiving technical and professional training."[1]

However, Germany implements modern apprenticeship for a more far-reaching purpose. That is, to cultivate craftsmen with exquisite skills. Germany has found the special value that modern apprenticeships have in cultivating technical and skilled experts required by modern industries, well maintained the traditional apprenticeship form in modern vocational education systems by means of the dual system, and nicely integrated it with school vocational education. There's no doubt that the great achievements of German industry benefit from this talent training model.

Internationally, from traditional handicraft industry to modern industry, apprenticeships have undergone a "U"-type development process in cultivating technical and skilled workers, as shown in Figure 9.2. Before the industrial revolution, an apprenticeship was the principal way to teach skills, and it has gone through two stages, namely, the traditional apprenticeship system and the guild apprenticeship system. The difference between the two lies in that masters are free to recruit and cultivate apprentices in traditional apprenticeship, while in the guild apprenticeship this process is carried out under the restrictions of guilds. After the industrial revolution, guild apprenticeships in most countries disappeared with the collapse of guilds, except for a few countries such as Germany. The preserved apprenticeships either returned to the previous folk status, or became enterprise apprenticeships that were only used by enterprises for cultivating new unskilled staff. During this period, the main route for most countries to acquire traditional skills was school vocational education. In the late 1990s, as mentioned above, the apprenticeship model was influenced by Britain and Australia and again gradually became the dominant way of skills acquisition under the support of national policies.

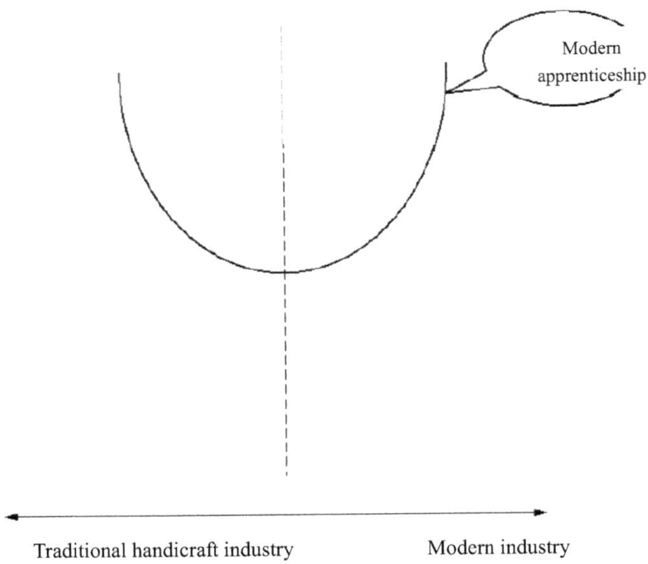


Figure 9.2 The relationship between industrial form and apprenticeship development

Different purposes for implementing modern apprenticeships directly affect how the practice framework is designed, such as the length of the apprenticeship, the requirements for the level of masters, which are all related to this. The reason why the modern apprenticeship is preserved or revived in both Germany and other countries is that people have increasingly recognized the fact that the study of professional theoretical knowledge is undeniably important for cultivating technical and skilled expertise required by modern industries, but empirical learning under the guidance of masters also plays an important role. The study of gradually building experiential knowledge, work knowledge, and practical knowledge since the 1980s is a significant epistemological basis for the revitalization of apprenticeship systems.

However, with the advent of intelligent technology, will apprenticeships still be valuable in cultivating technical and skilled experts? Rauner responded as follows: "Professional knowledge is the prerequisite of understanding and mastering the tasks in work."[2] "Professional knowledge" is the core concept for us to study the knowledge structure of technical and skilled expertise given the prevailing modern industrial background. The current intelligent machine revolution will not change this trend. Intelligent manufacturing will become nothing without a solid industrial foundation. This is the primary reason why intelligent manufacturing does not make any breakthroughs in the United States, which has an advanced software industry, but in Germany which has well-developed manufacturing industry. This kind of knowledge is complex in internal structure and diverse in external relations, and thus it must be mastered through apprenticeship training.

## 2. The Transforming Process of China's Training Model of Vocational Talent

Since the founding of new China, apprenticeships have evolved through three development stages: 1. From the beginning of the founding of new China to reform and opening-up. During this period, China implemented a planned economy, and apprenticeships were the primary way for enterprises to train new staff and the major route for people to acquire skills under this economic model. 2. From reform and opening-up to the launch of modern apprenticeship reform. It was not only a period when China's economic model shifted from a planned economy to a market economy, but also a crucial period when qualitative changes took place in the scale and structure of China's industries. During this period, China mainly cultivated technical and skilled workers through school vocational education; apprenticeship training was completely marginalized and existed informally: it was just a supplementary way for people to acquire skills. 3. From the launch of modern apprenticeship reform to now: As a time-honored training model of skilled workers, apprenticeships have regained people's attention and assumed a completely new form by being integrated with school vocational education.

Specifically, from the founding of new China to reform and opening-up, corporate apprenticeship had been the major method of cultivating technical and skilled workers in China. "By 1963, the new apprenticeship system has been gradually established in the whole of industry and everywhere, and subsequently became the method that cultivates backup technical workers on the largest scale and with the largest numbers."[3] Moreover, the work-study model that emerged in the 1950s was very similar to the German dual system. Of course, this kind of apprenticeship was lacking in school education (even if it was a work-study model, technical schools within enterprises were still involved in school operation; this is a great distinction from today's vocational schools that are separate from enterprises). This system involved many problems in effective student training; however, it was successful in terms of apprenticeship training. Its success was closely associated with the implementation of a completely planned economy and the overall absence of market mechanisms from the economic field at that time.

After reform and opening-up, China's corporate apprenticeship system suffered a total collapse, which not only related to the implementation of the market economy but also to the model of training technical and skilled experts. The increasingly improving level of corporate technology required technical and skilled workers, not only to master operating skills, but also to be equipped with deeper cultural knowledge and more systematic theoretical knowledge of professional technology. The task of cultivating this kind of knowledge cannot be undertaken by corporate apprenticeship models. As a result, corporate apprenticeships were abandoned as people thought of it as a backward training model for technical and skilled training at that time. Instead, people preferred a kind of school vocational education that could provide plenty of theoretical courses and are more scientific and rigorous training methods. After developing for more than three decades, school vocational education has undergone many twists and turns and suffered a lot of criticism, but it has satisfied the huge demand for technical and skilled labor during the economic boom period in China.

From this school-operating practice, people have noticed the obvious advantages of vocational education in cultivating technical and skilled talent. At the same time, they have also discovered a shortcoming, that is, the students are easily separated from the actual needs of enterprises. Therefore, people have been trying hard to remedy this deficiency by deepening school-enterprise cooperation and reinforcing business internships. Although the promotion process of school-enterprise cooperation is not perfect, the technical and skilled students who are trained through this system can basically meet the needs of industrial development. In the past, Chinese enterprises were still relatively low in their technical level, and they mainly adopted general technology. Enterprises could make employees basically adapt to their work as long as they offered some induction training on the basis of school training. However, with the all-around upgrading of China's enterprise technology and the urgent demand for technological innovation in the future industrial development, technical skills training through school vocational education has exposed its fundamental deficiencies.

The essential problem of school vocational education is that it can only teach students general knowledge and skills and can't make students acquire the special knowledge and skills required for the position no matter how curriculum is reformed and how teachers are cultivated. However, the latter accounts for a growing proportion in the development of modern enterprise technology. The latter determines the technical level of an enterprise, because the former is easy to obtain through school education and various means of communication while the acquisition of the latter must rely on experts who master the skills. We used to have a misconception that people should mainly master scientific and theoretical knowledge in the era of knowledge-driven economy. However, with the progress of knowledge theory research, people find that professional knowledge is more important and the mastery of this knowledge requires the combination of theory and experience in the era of a knowledge-driven economy. The same applies to technological innovation. Technological innovation is not a simple process of applying scientific theory. It requires technical and skilled experts, even generations of people, to concentrate on a certain technical matter for a long time on the basis of mastering scientific theories, in order to achieve a great breakthroughs.

The cultivation of students' professional qualities is another problem that is hard for school vocational education to solve. Industrial upgrading requires higher levels of technical and skilled experts. This kind of expertise is not only characterized by high levels of technical ability and skills but also high levels of professionalism. Furthermore, enterprises generally believe that professional quality outweighs technical ability and skill level. Of course, we cannot negate the significance of technical ability and skill level, but in many cases, professional quality becomes an important factor that affects the level of products and services. This element is exactly what Chinese technical and skilled workers lack at present. Confronted with the urgent demand of economic development for product quality improvement, China vigorously advocates enhancing the "craftsmanship spirit."

Premier of the State Council Li Keqiang put forward the following requirements in the *Report on the Work of the Government at the Fourth Session of the 12th National People's Congress of the People's Republic of China*: "We will move faster to bring domestic quality and safety standards in line with international standards, and to establish a system for making producers pay punitive compensation for failing to meet product quality standards. We will also encourage enterprises to use flexible and custom-tailored production processes and foster a craftsmanship spirit of striving for the best, so that more types of products, products of a higher quality, and brand products will be made."[4] *Talent Development Planning in the Manufacturing Industry* (No. 9 [2016] from the Department of Vocational and Adult Education, MOE) put forward the implementing idea: "We will advocate the industrial spirit with craftsmanship spirit as the core, introduce relevant instructions on promoting the development of industrial culture, forge an excellent industrial culture and enhance the soft power of China's industry. Manufacturing enterprises should take the craftsmanship spirit of making perfection the goal as an important part of employees' continuing education, and enhance employees' knowledge and understanding about professional ideas, professional duties and the professional mission."[5] Under the advocacy of the central government, how to cultivate the craftsmanship spirit has become a hot issue that is widely discussed in society. The cultivation of the craftsmanship spirit is a complicated project, and apprenticeships have unique place in it. If we let master craftsmen teach apprentices the craftsmanship spirit, it will not only be more practical in content but also more easily accepted by apprentices.

The demands of China's industrial upgrading for new technical and skilled personnel compels us to comprehensively consider the existing training model of school vocational education: while continuing to maintain the advantages of the model of training students through school vocational education, we should also rebuild the master-apprentice relationship within enterprises, comprehensively restore apprenticeships, and effectively integrate the two; only by doing so can we possibly meet the demands of the future industrial development for technical and skilled professionals in China.

## 3. The Purpose of Developing a Modern Apprenticeship System in China

The main purpose of developing a modern apprenticeship system in China is to meet the demands of industrial development for high-level technical and skilled professionals. In this sense, modern apprenticeship reform is considered to be the deepening of the reform of vocational education and the training model in the new era, that is, from the establishment of school-enterprise cooperation mechanisms to the establishment of master-apprentice relationships, thus creating work-based learning founded on master-apprentice relationships.

Promoting youth employment is also one of the purposes for China to establish modern apprenticeships, but it is not the primary one. This is because China may have some young people who need to have work experience for their employment, but we do not have the problem of the high youth unemployment rate that exists in other countries. The shortage of technical and skilled workers is an overall situation that China's labor employment faces at present. This is true not only for high-skilled professionals but also for ordinary skilled workers. Enterprises generally feel it is difficult to recruit workers. Even if they are recruited, it is difficult for them to retain them for long. Technical and skilled workers have a high employee turnover rate in employment. In the employment model of technical and skilled workers, work experience does not constitute a prerequisite for their employment. This is because in order to recruit employees, enterprises often only attach importance to whether employees have good basic qualities rather than whether they have plenty of work experience. In order to adapt the recruited employees to their jobs quickly, enterprises often actively provide on-the-job skills training for them, regardless of where they are from, vocational schools or the general community. This kind of training is implemented in the form of apprenticeships. This is also one of the important reasons why many Chinese enterprises lack motivation to cooperate with vocational schools. They don't need to worry about the impact of "noncooperation" on their employees' working competence because they already have special skills training plans in place for new employees.

Germany's modern apprenticeship system can be used as a model for our country. The main purpose of developing modern apprenticeships in China should be positioned to achieve the mission of China's vocational education at present. In other words, it should aim to provide technical and skilled workers with requisite skills for industrial upgrading, and provide technical and skilled professionals capable of technical research and development of technological innovation. People who have successfully researched and implemented modern apprenticeships in China share the same feelings on this point. They deeply understand that "the improvement of enterprises' enthusiasm to participate requires meeting their demands for a high-quality technical and skilled workforce."[6] After more than 30 years of extensive development, China's industry has now entered the phase of comprehensive industrial upgrading. For the current level of economic development, the factor-driven economic development model has begun to become ineffective. In order to get rid of the trap of middle-developed countries and reach the developed level, we must shift our economic development to the innovation-driven mode. With the proposed concept of German Industry 4.0, China has also initiated its intelligent process of industrial development. The speed of this process is much faster than our expectation. This is the basic direction of China's current economic development and the basic strategy determined by the government. The successful implementation of this economic development model does not mean we no longer need technical and skilled workers. Instead, we need technical and skilled professionals who have requisite skills and an innovative spirit more than ever. In this sense, it can be said that China has implemented an innovative modern apprenticeship development strategy compared with other countries.

## Part 2 Key Issues in Implementing Modern Apprenticeship in China

At present, modern apprenticeship pilot programs are being widely carried out in China. The pilots include two levels: vocational school level and regional level. MOE has issued a list of pilot schools and regions, and many vocational colleges are also spontaneously carrying out modern apprenticeship experiments. Some schools' spontaneous projects are even deeper than those issued by MOE, such as Hangzhou Vocational & Technical College. In order to get better acquainted with the modern apprenticeship in Western countries, MOE, local education administrative departments, and vocational schools have also organized administrators and teachers to study how modern apprenticeship is implemented in countries such as Britain and Switzerland. However, after short trials, many vocational schools began to feel perplexed about modern apprenticeships in general. Some know nothing about the core components and essential factors of modern apprenticeships, so they don't know where to start establishing modern apprenticeships; others have begun to feel suspicious about whether modern apprenticeships are possible to implement in China after encountering obstacles. Therefore, it's necessary to make a theoretical analysis on the key issues in implementing modern apprenticeships.

## 1. How to Understand the Essence of Modern Apprenticeship Systems

What is the modern apprenticeship system? It's generally acknowledged that a modern apprenticeship system is a kind of vocational education system that integrates traditional apprentice training with modern school education. This is a definition that is relatively well understood so far. However, with the deepening of practice, many new problems have emerged. For example, is it really necessary to base modern apprenticeships upon school-enterprise cooperation? Some vocational schools get around enterprises and directly bring industry masters into the classrooms that are established in vocational schools. They train students according to the master-apprentice training model, and completely achieve the effect of the apprenticeship training model. Can this training model be called a modern apprenticeship? As another example, some vocational schools have set up specialties based on traditional crafts, and these specialties have always adopted a master-apprentice training model. Can this training model be called a modern apprenticeship? If so, is modernity is reflected in what ways? In this regard, it's necessary to make a more profound analysis on the implications of modern apprenticeships. The following four are the essential aspects of a modern apprenticeship system:

### 1.1. Modern Apprenticeships Are an Approach to Learning Technical Practice Competence Based on a Solid Master-Apprentice Relationship

A modern apprenticeship must be an apprenticeship first. The study of technical practice ability based on a solid master-apprentice relationship is the most fundamental component of modern apprenticeships. Modern apprenticeships are not simply school-enterprise cooperation. It is just one of the important preconditions for the establishment of modern apprenticeships rather than necessarily an essential condition. Modern apprenticeships are proposed to solve the extensive study of technical practice competence, which is caused by the lack of a profound corporate master-apprentice relationship based on the availability of various vocational education and training models. Therefore, only a training model that systematically teaches technical practical ability on the basis of a firm master-apprentice relationship can be called a modern apprenticeship. Moreover, a training approach with a loose and short-term master-apprentice relationship cannot be referred to as a modern apprenticeship either. Apprenticeships must specify how long the master-apprentice relationship lasts, how close the relationship is, and whether it plays a crucial role in apprentices' study of technical practice competence.

### 1.2. Modern Apprenticeship Is an Apprenticeship That Aims to Cultivate Technical and Skilled Professionals for Modern Industry and the Service Industry

At present, the definition of modern apprenticeships is generalized. In other words, all apprenticeships that exist in the current society and are oriented toward traditional industries and involve vocational schools are called modern apprenticeships, such as an apprenticeship in ceramics making. It's certainly that all apprenticeships that exist in contemporary society are branded as "modern" in a broader sense, and they are indeed different from traditional apprenticeships when such apprenticeships involved vocational schools. However, we must notice that the topic of modern apprenticeships is proposed to be the training model in modern industry and the service industry. This is because traditional industries have no argument about the adoption of apprenticeships in training. However, it is not the same for modern industry and the service industry. One of the important reasons why apprenticeships have decayed in many countries since the industrial revolution is that technical and skilled workers in new industries are required to be equipped with universal scientific knowledge and standardized skills. This kind of knowledge and skills are better acquired through school vocational education. The reason why modern apprenticeships are proposed is that people have realized empirical knowledge that still accounts for a large proportion in the knowledge and ability structure of technical and skilled workers in modern industry and the service industry. Therefore, the second important requirement of modern apprenticeships is to establish a master-apprentice-based training model for the cultivation of a technical and skilled workforce in modern industry and the service industry.

### 1.3. A Modern Apprenticeship System Is a Training Model That Integrates New Master-Apprentice Learning Approaches with School Vocational Education

Apprenticeships have irreplaceable advantages in the cultivation of a technical and skilled workforce. It particularly plays a very prominent role in transmitting technological know-how and cultivating technological innovative ability. However, this kind of vocational education training also has obvious disadvantages: 1. The instructional methods used by masters in traditional apprenticeship are very time-worn, and even without a clear method. It all depends on the understanding of apprentices themselves; the training is very inefficient, and sometimes abnormal personal bondage will be involved; 2. The weaknesses are very conspicuous in the transmission of theoretical knowledge and the training of basic skills. For example, it's no doubt that masters will teach their apprentices theoretical knowledge. However, modern technology requires employees to master theoretical knowledge, which can only be satisfied through systematic cultural courses and technical theory courses. Moreover, this mission can only be undertaken by modern school education. Another example is basic skills training. This kind of training will be much more efficient if it's implemented by courses at schools. In order to cultivate the technical knowledge and skills required by modern industry and the service industry, we need to reform the instructional methods used by masters and integrate more modern pedagogical knowledge into it on the one hand; we also need to effectively combine apprenticeships with school education on the other hand. Only by doing so can we revitalize the traditional apprenticeship and take full advantage of the technical skills training.

### 1.4. Modern Apprenticeships Are a Kind of Technical and Skills Training System with Modern Vocational Education as the Basis

The fourth feature of modern apprenticeships is that it is a training model existing in modern vocational education. Common apprenticeships, including folk apprenticeships and corporate apprenticeships, only serve the technical skills required by masters or enterprises themselves. One of the prominent problems of this training system is that it's very narrow and limited in its content. Apprentices can only learn the skills that their masters have for their occupations. This will not only affect their job-hopping but also make it impossible for them to possess the innovative ability of learning a variety of important techniques. Therefore, modern apprenticeships must be clearly distinguished from the customized training models. If an apprenticeship only meets a company's temporary needs for technical and skilled workers, then this modern apprenticeship is not humanized and won't last for long. In order to solve this problem, we need to establish the training content of modern apprenticeships based on public professional teaching standards, and take them as the basis for us to evaluate and identify the training results. In this way, modern apprenticeships can break away from the narrow apprenticeships of individual enterprises and make it a social training system for technical and skilled workers.

## 2. What Kind of Modern Apprenticeships Should China Develop?

What is the practice model for China's modern apprenticeships? What kind of modern apprenticeships should China develop? According to the above analysis, we can design the structure of China's modern apprenticeships, as shown in Figure 9.3. This is the ideal state of modern apprenticeship training in China, and it can be considered as the development target of China's modern apprenticeships.

Modern apprenticeships are a deeply connected combination of an apprentice training sequence and a school training sequence. The first is the apprentice training sequence. According to different goals and orientations of training, the complete apprentice training sequence can be divided into four levels that proceed from simple to complex: folk apprenticeships, apprentice training that aims to promote youth employment, apprentice training that aims to acquire high-level technological expertise, and apprentice training that aims to achieve technological innovation. Folk apprenticeship exists widely in individual economies and the micro-economy, and it aims to train traditional manual skills or simple operating skills. In terms of apprentice training that aims to promote youth employment, it refers to the skills training offered by enterprises of a certain scale for their new employees for the purpose of making them qualified for the basic requirements of the job. Apprenticeship training at this level is mainly done by enterprises themselves, and some more complex technical training may require the involvement of secondary vocational schools. As for apprentice training that aims to acquire high-level technological competence, it is longer in training process, more rigorous in organization, and more complex in training content. It aims to train technical and skilled experts with high-level skills and meet the demands of enterprises for highly skilled professionals. Apprenticeship training at this level requires integration with secondary vocational education and specialized higher vocational education. Apprentice training that aims to achieve technological innovation is a kind of apprenticeship at a higher-level that targets at enabling technical and skilled professionals to attain innovative ability. This level of apprenticeship requires a combination of specialized higher vocational education and technology-applied undergraduate education. It's more complicated apprentice training and needs to be completely implemented within enterprises.

Another important sequence of modern apprenticeship is the school training sequence. It covers three levels: secondary vocational education, specialist higher vocational education, and technology-applied undergraduate education. The three levels of vocational education are all required by modern apprenticeships. However, they correspond to different levels of apprenticeships, and thus have different training targets. In the current vocational education system in China, secondary vocational education and specialized higher vocational education are comparatively well perfected. China has required the newly promoted undergraduate colleges and universities to transform their school-operating orientation into technology-applied undergraduate education, but this kind of higher education is still a concept and has no successful transformation cases, and the transformation will be a very complicated process. Nevertheless, the establishment of a complete modern apprenticeship system in China can't be separated from technology-applied undergraduate education.

In Figure 9.3, only the overlapped parts of the two sequences can be called a modern apprenticeship. Other parts are not components of the national education system and cannot be included as modern apprenticeships.

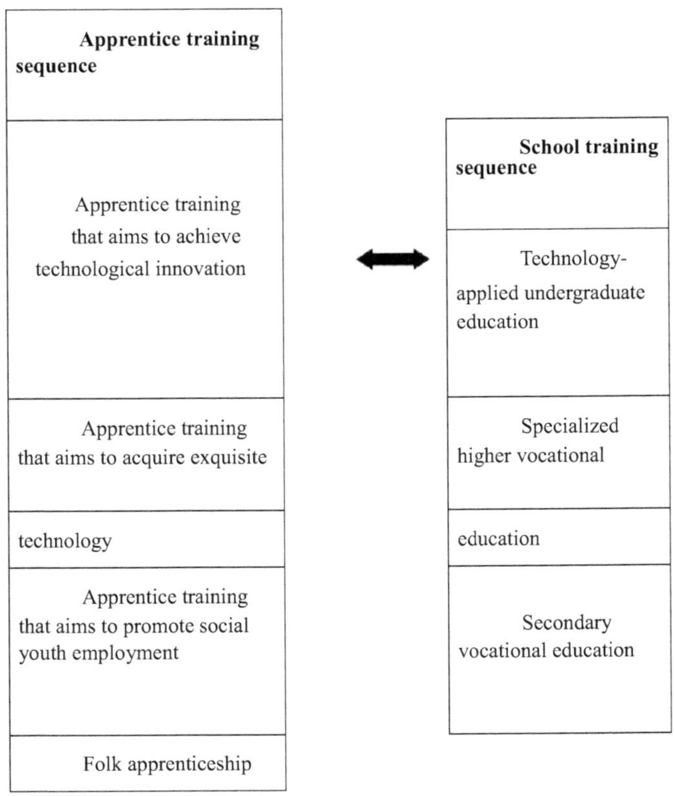


Figure 9.3 The structure of the modern apprenticeship system in China

## 3. What Kind of System Barriers Does China Face in Developing a Modern Apprenticeship System?

The modern apprenticeship structure designed above is just an ideal, and the realization of this ideal involves a very sophisticated system forming process.

### 3.1. We Must First Establish a Concept of Social System Formation in Order to Solve System Problems

China has introduced Germany's dual system since the 1980s. However, few have succeeded so far, and it tends to be more and more difficult. The core problem is that enterprises are not highly motivated to participate and it's difficult to establish a stabilized school-enterprise partnership for training. In the last 10 years, China has been trying hard to promote school-enterprise cooperation, and it has been the core content in almost all-important vocational education documents. However, only a few vocational schools have successfully implemented it through their own efforts, and not any substantial breakthroughs have been made in system establishment. Modern apprenticeships are a deeper model of training involving school-enterprise cooperation. Its implementation needs to take school-enterprise cooperation as the precondition and corporate master-apprentice relationship as the foundation at the same time. In this process, there is an additional role of the master to develop. From this, we can see the difficulty of its implementation.

In order to make modern apprenticeships truly become a normal vocational education training model in China, we must first realize that it needs a long time to establish a modern apprenticeship system. It is so complicated a system that we will surely achieve nothing if we're hurry to pursue success. The success of Germany's vocational education model is the result of a century of development, and this model has not occurred in other European countries. In addition, we need to establish a concept of social system construction. A social system is not subjectively designed but a result of various interactive social forces. This is Marx's historical materialism. However, we now seem to have totally forgotten this while formulating various policies. When developing vocational education, we always have many ideas, targets, and designs, and we seem to think we can develop vocational education into whatever we want it to be. It's a pity that we rarely intensively study the interaction of various social forces in system construction and make the best use of circumstances to bring forth a new system through appropriate governmental intervention. Practice has proved that this design pattern of development is absolutely ineffective and will lead to enormous waste of social resources.

### 3.2. Hyper-Liberal Labor Market Is the Crucial System Barrier to Modern Apprenticeship

From the perspective of the concept of social system construction, the most important social interaction mechanism that hinders the development of China's modern apprenticeship system is the interaction among enterprises, masters, and apprentices in the completely liberal labor market. In order to successfully establish a modern apprenticeship, we need to inspire the enthusiasm of enterprises, masters, and apprentices. It also requires enterprises' positive support, masters' serious teaching, and apprentices' diligent study. However, the completely liberal labor market will seriously weaken the enthusiasm of the three parties: 1. For enterprises, the experts they cultivate may not be able to be used by themselves. When they need experts, they can easily poach some from other enterprises without spending too much. Under these circumstances, enterprises will not actively participate in training technicians and skilled workers. 2. For masters, they can't guarantee their own positions and also have to worry that their apprentices could possibly compete with them in the completely liberal labor market. In such a system environment, masters will not seriously teach apprentices their technological know-how, let alone joint technological innovation. They will only teach apprentices some basic skills, which will make it difficult to realize the core objective of developing a modern apprenticeship system in China. 3. For apprentices, they will question whether they need to accumulate high-level skills because technical and skilled workers are highly mobile in the completely free labor market; moreover, they have two ways to accumulate highly developed skills, let alone achieve great technological innovations through persistent research.

Scholars usually divide the capitalist economic model into a coordinated market economy and a liberal market economy. The former is represented by Germany and Japan, and the latter is represented by the United States and Britain. Through the international comparison of the relationship between economic systems and vocational education systems in these countries, we can arrive at a significant conclusion: the degree of liberalization of the labor market is the crucial factor that determines whether apprenticeships will survive; if apprenticeships want to survive, it must include a factor that can coordinate the interests of all parties in the labor market and make the labor market more transparent and relatively stable. This is because information in the completely liberal labor market not only makes it hard to establish a credible commitment among all parties involved in the apprenticeship, but also to motivate their enthusiasm for participating in apprenticeships. Moreover, technical and skilled workers are so overly mobile that they have no way to accumulate innovative technological expertise. This is why Germany has retained apprenticeship so well while British apprenticeship system has made halting progress. The survival of Germany's apprenticeship is closely related to the *Handicraft Protection Act* issued in 1897. One of the important components of this *Act* is to endow the handicraft association the quasi-public power of skill qualification authentication and supervision, "thus establishing a modern model for reconciling diverse interests."[7] Britain lacks such a system and this always makes it hard to coordinate the contradictions among all parties, and thus makes the survival of the apprenticeship system difficult. Corporate apprenticeships have severely declined since the 1980s, which is strongly related to the overall shift of the economic model to a market-oriented economy.

### 3.3. A Coordinated Labor Market Is the Precondition to Establish a Modern Apprenticeship System in China

The establishment of a coordinated labor market is the crucial premise for the development of a modern apprenticeship system in China. We need to thoroughly research the relations among all stakeholders in the labor market, grasp the critical points of its roles, and then formulate relevant coordinated policies; otherwise, we can't break through the two limitations in the development of modern apprenticeships in China: 1. From pilot to system. Modern apprenticeships have achieved success in some pilot schools. However, local experience can't become the overall model without a systematic approach. It's exactly the same as making efforts to keep a street absolutely clean, but we can't keep a city clean without system construction. 2. From serving company itself to serving social demands for professionals. At present, the relatively successful pilot cases of modern apprenticeship all serve the social demands for highly skilled professionals. However, from the perspective of the country, modern apprenticeships should aim to meet the demands of the whole society for a highly skilled workforce. In order to achieve this, we must also rely on the construction of a system.

At present, from "basic" to "decisive" is an important direction for the adjustment of the role of the market in China's economic policies. This adjustment is based on the actual needs of China's economic development at present. It can contribute to enhancing the vitality of economic operations and bringing economic operations back more to its own principles. However, when we apply this policy into the labor market, we should see the negative effects on the cultivation of technical and skilled workers in China. Therefore, if we want to develop China's modern apprenticeship system in the current economic environment, we need to solve the most crucial issue, namely, how to rebuild master-apprentice relationship within enterprises under the conditions of a market-oriented economy. The experience of Germany and Japan tells us that this is perfectly possible. That's to say, we need to separate the product market from the labor market so that the product market can better unleash economic vitality in a liberal way. Meanwhile, we should establish an appropriate monitoring system and coordination mechanism in the labor market, so as to inspire all parties to get involved in skill formation. This is feasible in China, as China has corresponding system foundations. China implements the socialist market economy with Chinese characteristics. Although China emphasizes that the market should play a decisive role in economic operation, decisive does not mean absolute; control and coordination are the inherent elements of our economic model.

## 4. What Supporting Conditions Are Required for the Development of a Modern Apprenticeship System in China

Developing a modern apprenticeship system needs great reform of training models for China's vocational education. Its successful implementation requires not only the basic system premise of a coordinated labor market, but also other supporting conditions. The following three aspects are the most important of all:

### 4.1. A National System of Professional Teaching Standards and Certification Is the Foundation of a Modern Apprenticeship System

First of all, we should establish scientific and systematic professional teaching standards and a corresponding certification system that can identify how well apprentices are trained. The reason why Britain, Australia, and other countries can give great impetus to the establishment of modern apprenticeships after entering the 21st century is that they had finished establishing a national qualification framework in the 1990s.

A national system of professional teaching standards and certification is the foundation for the operation of vocational education. Without it, modern apprenticeships will encounter great difficulties in its implementation and even give rise to extremely serious problems: 1. The quality of apprentice training cannot be evaluated. This makes it impossible to protect the responsibilities that enterprises and masters have for their apprentices, and makes them readily consider their apprentices as a cheap labor force. This is the most prominent problem in previous apprenticeship systems. If this problem prevails, it may evolve into a political issue. At the same time, stealing state funds for training in the name of training apprentices is likely to happen if apprentice training is funded by the state. 2. It's hard to motivate masters' enthusiasm to teach their apprentices. If apprentice training lacks standards and is chaotic in its training circle, and apprentices finish their apprenticeship after being trained for a short period, masters will think apprentice training could be a threat to their position. This will severely affect their enthusiasm to teach apprentices and make it impossible to establish a good master-apprentice relationship. As a matter of fact, in modern corporate apprenticeships, contradictions can be found not only between apprentices and enterprises, but also between apprentices and masters. 3. Apprentices' enthusiasm can't be stimulated easily. This is because they have no idea about what goals they can strive for, and what kind of career development their endeavors can bring them in the future.

A national system of professional teaching standards and certification is still quite weak in China, and it's not strong enough to support the operation of a modern apprenticeship system. Although education authorities have enhanced the establishment of national professional teaching standards in recent years, the content has failed to completely break away from the previous framework of training programs and teaching syllabus, and has failed to establish a certification system that is compatible with these standards. Therefore, it's difficult to substantially work on professional competence training. Although labor authorities have developed national professional qualification standards and established a supporting certification system, the basic units established are "type of work" and "post." They are quite narrow in scope and can't be adopted as complete reference standards for training. Therefore, the "Dual Certifications" implemented in recent years usually integrates part of the certificate content into certain links to the training program, and thus makes it impossible to be directly carried out according to the requirements of professional qualification certificates. The two systems operate simultaneously but do not communicate with each other. This makes the training institutions of technical and skilled workers have no idea what to do. Therefore, it's necessary to establish a unified system of national professional teaching standards and certification. Moreover, this system must clearly differentiate the training standards of vocational schools and enterprises.

### 4.2. Perfecting the Enterprise-Master System Is an Important Guarantee for Modern Apprenticeships

The implementation of modern apprenticeships means that there will be two main bodies that undertake the task of training for students: vocational school teachers and corporate masters. Corporate masters shall assume the main responsibilities of skills training. It's just the same as the state has a stringent management system for teachers and provides an impeccable training system to continuously improve teachers' qualities. If we want to implement a modern apprenticeship system, we also need to set up a corporate-master system; specify the qualifications, responsibilities, powers, treatment, and training of masters; and establish a stable master team. This is because masters' ability level, moral character, and sense of responsibility are the crucial factors that affect talent development in modern apprenticeships. For example, Germany's dual system contains an ideal master system, which effectively guarantees the quality of its training. An ideal modern apprenticeship system requires the establishment of a rigorous master system that is as strict as the teacher system.

However, a master system is completely absent in Chinese enterprises at present. Master recruitment in pilot vocational schools for modern apprenticeship is only an act of the schools rather than the state. The establishment of master system will be a project that is extremely complex and extremely large in scale. Its complexity largely originates from the special identity of corporate technical experts. They are different from school teachers. For school teachers, teaching is their own work, but apprenticeship training is only an ancillary work for corporate technical experts. This will not only make technical experts lack the enthusiasm to serve as masters, but also make their management complicated.

### 4.3. A Smooth Education Path for Apprentices Is a Powerful Force for the Development of a Modern Apprenticeship System

Another important support condition that modern apprenticeships need is the design of apprentices' education path. The reason why this problem is proposed is that the current entrance examinations at different levels are extremely unfavorable for those who have highly developed technical skills but are not good at exam-oriented education. Few vocational schools do not set up separate classes and implement targeted education for students who are preparing for further education, because these students will have great difficulty entering their ideal universities if they don't do it this way. At present, entrance examinations for vocational school students concentrate on cultural knowledge and professional theories, and skills are not placed at a prominent position. How can such an examination system stimulate students' enthusiasm for skills accumulation? It's difficult for students who study at schools to be admitted to universities without being educated in specialized theoretical knowledge, let alone for those who spend much in apprentice training in enterprises. In some pilot schools, parents strongly object to their children's entry into pilot classes for modern apprenticeships. If an education brings no future to its students, then this kind of education will not be promising.

In order to solve this problem, we cannot depend on ideas and slogans only. Instead, we should also have a serious system design. That is, an explicit design of the education path for apprentices with the willingness to enter a higher school. We can design it from two aspects: 1. Reform the subjects and methods of the entrance examinations that target vocational school students, greatly realign examinations focusing on practical capacities and implement examinations mainly through practice, in order to provide more entrance opportunities for students with solid technical skills; 2. Establish special high-level qualifications for students who receive apprentice training. For example, the British modern apprenticeship pilot project established an authorized professional management degree for apprentices. The four-year degree was jointly developed by 40 employers, authorized management research institutes, and several universities, with the purpose of solving managers' lack of actual abilities.

## Notes

1 Akoojee, P. Gonon, U. Hauschildt, C. Hofmann. Apprenticeship in a globalized world: premises, promises and pitfalls. Co-organizers and cooperation partners of the INAP conference 2013 (17).
2 Zhiqun Zhao, Felix Rauner, Ursel Hauschildt. Assuring the acquisition of expertise: apprenticeship in the modern economy. Beijing: Foreign Language Teaching and Research Press, 2011: 23.
3 Wang Xing: The Social Construction of Skill Formation - A Sociology Approach to the Evolving Trajectory of the Apprentice in China Factories, Social Sciences Academic Press (China), 2014.
4 Li Keqiang: Report on the Work of the Government at the Fourth Session of the 12th National People's Congress of the People's Republic of China, 2016.
5 MOE: Talent Development Planning in the Manufacturing Industry, 2016.
6 Pan Jianfeng: Exploration of Modern Apprentice: A Comparatively Successful Case, Chinese Vocational and Technical Education, No. 5, 2016.
7 Kathleen Thelen: How Institutions Evolve - The Political Economy of Skills in Germany, Britain, the United States, and Japan, Shanghai People's Publishing House, 2010, p. 42.

CHAPTER TEN

# Constructing a Social System That Transforms Vocational Education from Grading to Classification

Vocational education circles have always pursued an equal status with general education; only by achieving an equal status with general education can vocational education fully exert its role in training a skilled workforce. Of course, few vocational education systems in major developed countries can genuinely be completely equal with general education, even in countries such as Germany, Japan, the United States, and Britain. However, it's necessary for China to bridge the gap between the two, otherwise, an unbalanced workforce structure will come into being. Reviewing the course of China's vocational education since reform and opening-up over the past four decades, we find that the overarching theme is to realize modernization and finally transform it from "grading" to "classification." In other words, we should try to build a vocational education system that contains all modernized elements and an ideal academic system, in order to gain its due position in the education system. Although the concept of a "modern vocational education system" was proposed in 2002, however, the aspiration can be traced back to the reform and opening-up period in the 1980s. The development of vocational education since reform and opening-up over the past four decades has presented a basically continuous process in this sense. The question is, even if all these are successfully built, can China's vocational education truly become equal with general education? Will people choose vocational education in a rational way? As the quality improves, vocational education will surely become more appealing to students. However, it will not fundamentally change the unequal status between vocational education and general education. The root of this problem lies in occupational inequality.

Figure 10.1 A foreign teacher is teaching students how to install pipelines

## Part 1 Guarantee the Economic Status and Social Benefits of Skilled Workers through System Change

Diversified demands for social occupations require diversified education, and thus people need to rationally select education types. Only when the selected education matches the individual's intellectual characteristics can his or her potential be maximized. People's choice of education types can be affected by various factors, such as individual's explicit understanding about his or her intellectual characteristics and interests, and rational planning for his or her career development. This depends on whether there is a well-established supportive career education, such as elite education. When people have access to plenty of opportunities for elite education, they will tend to be more rational about their choice of education types. The two aspects are what our current education system severely lacks. Due to the lack of well-established career education, people neither have appropriate occupational concepts about employment nor rational attitudes when choosing educational opportunities; due to scarce opportunities for elite education, people always hope to embark on the track of elite education when deciding what type of education to choose in education streaming. Both will affect people's attitudes toward vocational education.

In addition to the above factors, the most fundamental factor that hinders people's willingness to choose vocational education is that unfair treatment of technical and skilled workers still prevails in employment and career development in our society, namely, inequality among various occupations. People's choice of a specific school is determined by its education quality, while their choice of an education type is determined by the working environment (such as occupational status, wage, power, environmental comfort) and career development opportunities that education can bring. This is labor market grading. Labor economics divides the labor market into the primary labor market and the secondary labor market. The primary labor market is basically characterized by full-time posts with benefits, opportunities for promotion and certain job security. The secondary labor market is mainly characterized by low-paid and low-level jobs with few opportunities for promotion, over 40 working hours every week usually, little or no welfare, and high employee turnover rates.[1] Since the secondary labor market lacks opportunities for promotion, its employees have little chance to enter the primary labor market. Confronted with the two markets, how will people make their education choices?

When vocational education encounters development predicaments, people always think of the full swing toward secondary specialized schools and technical training schools in the 1980s and 1990s. In the 1980s, the best junior high school graduates preferred to choose secondary schools rather than key senior high schools. However, what made secondary specialized schools very popular at that time was not their high quality, but that their graduates could work in government departments, public institutions or state-owned enterprises, become cadres, and rural students could change their registered residence from "agricultural to non-agricultural" status. What a tempting prospect! In 1998, the state stopped assigning jobs for graduates of secondary specialized schools and junior colleges. At the same time, the expansion of higher education led to increasing numbers of university graduates. Graduates of secondary specialized schools became disadvantaged in academic qualification, and they were rapidly degraded to ordinary workers. As a result, secondary specialized schools completely became unappealing to students. As for graduates of technical training schools, although they could not become cadres, they could still work in state-owned enterprises, or at least in enterprises under collective ownership. This was also very tempting at that time. However, vocational high school graduates could not enjoy such "treatment," and this made it much more difficult to develop vocational high schools.

Skilled workers did not have equal opportunities for work environment and career development, which was manifested in the following ways: First, the dual worker system was implemented, and workers and cadres were artificially separated. The employment market used to be divided into the skilled workers market and the labor market. A senior fitter may have designed and manufactured over 40 work fixtures for the enterprise. However, the only reward he got was to be assigned to work in the technical room and no longer engage in physical labor every day. He could not enjoy any book and newspaper fees or duty allowances that engineers had, just because he was not a cadre. Second, skilled workers were generally at a lower wage level, far behind the wages of the management level; worse still, they did not enjoy stable wages and lacked the sense of economic security. The same wages of 8th-grade workers used to be almost the same as that of 2nd-grade professors before reform and opening-up. However, this has gone forever. Furthermore, the wages of most ordinary workers were so low that they could only maintain their basic life, and the gap could be a few dozens of times apart compared with corporate senior managers. Although most provinces and municipalities have introduced minimum wage standard systems now, the wage of workers in Shanghai is only RMB 2,300. Even these low wages could not be obtained by workers without working overtime, let alone any rest time. Wage arrears used to be so prevalent among workers that the then Premier Wen Jiabao of the State Council had to ask for wages for migrant workers in person. Third, the working environment of workshops is generally poor, such as poor sanitary and atmospheric conditions, imperfect safety facilities, brutal management, and failure to respect worker's personalities. Fourth, workers have very limited promotion opportunities within enterprises. There is not much difference between the wages of technicians who have worked for many years and new workers. In terms of duties, workers are basically unlikely to be promoted to management, as corporate managers are usually people with high academic qualifications. Fifth, skilled workers basically have no opportunities to be formally employed by public institutions, let alone civil servant jobs that people long for. This is because civil servants are recruited specifically from people with bachelor degrees or above.

The above only lists some issues. The cause of these problems is related to the fact that China has been developing socialist market economy for a very short period of time and has not established enough systems to protect laborers' rights and interests. At the same time, we should acknowledge that great progress have been made by government in establishing systems to protect labor rights and interests. For example, the labor contract signing system has been widely implemented among workers; work-related injuries have been generally resolved reasonably; wage arrears of migrant workers have basically disappeared, etc. However, these are just the basic aspects of labor rights and interests protection. In order to make vocational education more appealing, we should try our best to minimize the gap between workers and managers in terms of working environment and career development, and finally eliminate the boundary between the two. In this regard, a lot of government action has been taken. For example, after the lively discussion on reviewing the labor force, many state-level programs have been opened up to skilled workers; some local governments, such as Shenzhen, have made great efforts to realize policy fairness. In Shenzhen, a technician certificate enables people to obtain a registered permanent residence in the same way as an academic certificate does. This makes people highly motivated to obtain a technician certificate. All these are substantial reforms. However, these are just local reforms, and an overall system is still severely lacking. This problem has not been fundamentally solved. A huge gap still exists between workers and managers in terms of wage level, working environment, job security, promotion opportunity, social status, and opportunity for continuing education. The gap is so large so that some enterprises even have a feeling that "it's easy to find 10 doctors but tough to find an 8th-grade worker." There is even news that employers offer technicians an annual salary of over hundreds of thousands. Highly skilled talents are still in severe shortage.

Therefore, in order to make vocational education truly a valued type of education, we should continue to promote the establishment of a modern vocational education system, attract students by quality enhancement, and enable people to be more rational about their choices of education types by implementing career education and expanding elite education opportunities. Furthermore, the fundamental measure is to achieve occupational equality. That's to say, we should reform relevant labor and employment systems, improve the employment environment and career development space for technical and skilled workers, and build a favorable external system environment for the development of vocational education. This is the deeper topic for the future development of China's vocational education. Internationally, it can be seen that vocational education is highly attractive in only a few countries such as Switzerland, Germany, and Japan; vocational education has a low status in most countries and is difficult being equal to general education. In Germany, an increasing number of people prefer to choose research universities. The low status of vocational education is a problem prevailing in the world nowadays. What causes this difference among countries is the laborers' rights and interests protection system. The reason for the high status of vocational education in countries such as Switzerland is that vocational education can bring learners good conditions and employment opportunities; the reason why Japanese skilled workers are willing to devote themselves to technology is closely related to the fact that Japanese enterprises implement lifelong employment systems and provide workers with secure job opportunities.

China must strive to develop vocational education. The establishment of the strategic position of vocational education is an important achievement made by China in developing vocational education over the past 4 decades since reform and opening-up. This is a very insightful judgment. From the perspective of industrial development, the real economy must dominate China's industries in the future; the two international financial crises in the 21st century have strengthened our direction for its development, and high-tech industries must be supported by a large number of technical and skilled professionals who have received a modern vocational education. From the perspective of individual development, China is a big country with nearly 1.4 billion population, and it must direct its major population toward vocational and technical jobs in order to solve the problem of employment. What matters now is the misalignment between national strategic needs and individual career choices. It is the primary cause for the dilemma that vocational education faces in school operations, and the fundamental solution is to systematically improve the employment environment and career development opportunities for technical and skilled professionals.

## Part 2 Putting Reasonable Limits on the Freedom of Corporate Labor Recruitment under Market Economy Conditions

Only by reducing the differences among different occupations can we attract more people to learn and improve skills, and provide plenty of highly skilled workers for China's high-tech-based industrial development strategy. Industrial development must be accompanied by vocational development; otherwise, the industry will lack the talent foundation for its further development. Although China has made some progress in improving the working environment and career development opportunities, on the whole no substantial changes have been made yet. This can't be separated from the backward production technology of enterprises in China. Under these circumstances, there's no doubt that the production environment of factories will be poor and the labor values of skilled workers will be difficult to be fully demonstrated. The development of production technology is the corporeal foundation to realize occupational equality. We can see that the development of production technology is the most fundamental impetus that promotes vocational education to develop from traditional apprenticeships to modern vocational education in form, and develop from an education open to very few handicraft industry practitioners to the current education open for everyone in scale.

However, the development of production technology will not necessarily facilitate occupational development. This is because occupational development belongs to the development of production relations and its formation requires people's incentive to reform. This is one of the important disagreements between Marxist economics and classical economics. Classical economics insists on minimal government intervention in the market, and believes that the less the government intervenes, the more motivated the market will be and the easier it will be to achieve a balanced interaction among each market entity. Since the 1980s, the United States and Britain have adopted this idea in their economic development policies again and named it neoliberalism. Germany and Japan have adopted a coordinated market economy model. That is, government and social organizations such as industry associations need to positively coordinate corporate behaviors. Of course, some coordination is mandatory. The two economic policies have led to two different social forms. We can't completely make sure which model is superior at present. This is because factors affecting the level of economic development include not only production technology and production relations, but also plentiful raw materials, control over the international financial market, original research, etc. By relying on original research in information technology, the United States has obtained an important source for its sustained economic growth. However, one thing is for sure: the manufacturing industry in Japan and Germany has achieved successful development and their quality enjoys great prestige in the world; compared with them, the United States and Britain are far behind.

Now that the future industrial form determined by China is closer to that of Germany and Japan, it's necessary to learn from them and moderately restrict the freedom of the market. The core is to impose appropriate restrictions on the freedom of corporate labor recruitment, such as restrictions on corporate power of dismissal, on the gap between the wages of workers and corporate managers, on the production environment of factories, requirements for enterprises to establish a definite worker promotion system, and give equivalent rewards to those who have made significant contributions. As Mr. Yang Jintu profoundly pointed out: "If complete market behaviors lead to polarization, then the government should allocate more financial resources to vulnerable groups, and take regulation measures to hold back polarization."[2] Improvements in these aspects should be deepened from discussion on the disparities within the labor force and the promotion and reward of talented individuals to the establishment of inclusive systems. This is because, unlike product pricing, the improvement of the working environment is a result of market mechanisms rather than workers' struggles for power and the active role of government policies. Capitalists will not volunteer to change workers' employment environment, which is proven by the history of the improved employment situations in capitalist countries. According to Marx's view, a sweeping economic crisis will inevitably break out if workers' employment situation is freely regulated by the market. German workers have a higher position than Britain and the United States. This is not because their capitalists are more kind, but that their systems are different.

This shows the complementarity between the industrial structure and the employment system. In other words, this shows whether the industrial structure matches the employment system. The pillar of the U.S. economy is technological innovation and financial control. This kind of industrial model is not highly dependent on the technical levels of workers. What it needs is a very liberated employment environment, which can trigger innovation to the fullest. Therefore, the basic idea that supports the development of the U.S. economy is the highly liberated competition in the market. However, the industrial structure of Germany totally differs from that of the United States. High-end manufacturing is dominant in Germany's economic development. This kind of industrial form depends highly on the technical levels of workers, and as a result it needs to create an advantageous employment environment for workers and establish a well-organized vocational training system.

How to improve workers' employment situation through active policy measures is related to how China positions the market economy and considers the market entities (namely enterprises). This problem can be easily solved in the planned economic system, and China has indeed solved this problem very well under given historical circumstances. However, it can't be easily solved in the market economy system. This is because to what extent it can be solved is influenced by both the power of each market entity and the economic policies adopted, that's to say, to adopt a completely liberated market economy, or a restricted market economy. In terms of policy, China has determined the socialist market economy with Chinese characteristics as its economic model. Since China is still at the primary stage of socialism, it once had to put up with many unreasonable factors existing in the market economy. However, when China's economy reaches beyond the current level, we should put forth efforts to reform workers' employment environment. This is not only a matter related to workers, but also related to the long-term development of the industry.

It can be seen that China's market economy has developed a lot nowadays, and China should put efforts into the issue of how to position its future market economy. That is, whether to keep adopting a very loose market economy model, or choose a systematized market economy model and especially improve the systematized management of workers' employment environment according to the requirements of the nature of the socialist market economy. Germany performed very well during the European debt crisis, while excessive freethinking Britain and the United States made irrational in major choices. This makes people reconsider the importance of system restrictions. Essentially, China's socialist market economy determines that economic operations should reflect socialist system requirements as much as possible.

The fear is that implementing some restrictive policies on the freedom of market economy operations may affect the enthusiasm of enterprises. It's true that improving workers' employment environment through policies will increase enterprise costs. However, from the experience of German economic development, we can learn that improving workers' employment environment is conductive to inspiring their enthusiasm. This is very important for high-tech-based modern industries. Therefore, we should try to find the best balance point between the restriction and freedom of corporate behaviors when formulating policies. It's certain that the implementation of this policy not only depends on laws and regulations, but also on intermediate coordinating organizations, such as guilds, according to the experience of Germany. Such organizations can play a role that government cannot in improving workers' employment environment in many respects. However, intermediate coordinating organizations are still at a low level and extremely undeveloped in China's social governance structure. Therefore, we should actively render support and guidance for the development of such organizations and take it as one of the important components for transforming China's social governance models.

## Notes

1 Gray, K.C. & E.L. Herr. Workforce education: the basics [M]. Boston: Allyn and Bacon, 1998(76).

2 Yang Jintu: Analysis on the Policy Environment of Developing Vocational Education in China, Research in Educational Development, No. 9, 2005.

# References

## Chinese


1. Bi Jieli, Wang Lin: Survey and Analysis Report on Skilled Talent Training through School-Enterprise Cooperation (I), China Training, No.6, 2010.
2. MOF, MOE, MOHRSS: Guidance Opinions on Establishing and Perfecting the Average Allocation System for Secondary Vocational School Students by MOF, MOE and MOHRSS, 2015.
3. Cao Ye: On the History and Realistic Choice of Teacher Training in Vocational and Technical Education in China, Education and Vocation, No.6, 2010.
4. Chen Shida, He Peihua: On Job Hunting and Wages: The Latest Market Guidance Wage Levels in Zhejiang Province, Zhejiang University Press, 2009.
5. Large Country Economic Transformation Research Group: From a Big Country of Human Resources to a Manufacturing Powerhouse, Economic Science Press, 2012.
6. Da Hai: Interview with Chen Guang, Director of the Textbook Division, the Department of Vocational and Adult Education, MOE, on the Formulation and Management of the Specialty Catalogue of Secondary Vocational Schools: New Circumstances, New Principles and New Features, Vocational and Technical Education, No. 30, 2001.
7. Deng Zemin: The Specialty Catalogue for Secondary Vocational Schools, Chinese Vocational and Technical Education, No. 16, 2010.

8. Ding Dajian: The Shortage of Highly Skilled Talents and the Misalignment of Their Value Evaluation, Private Education Research, No. 4, 2004.
9. Dong Cuncai: Encyclopedia of China (on Education), Encyclopedia of China Publishing House, 1985.
10. Felix Rauner, Rupert Maclean: Handbook of Technical and Vocational Education and Training Research (Volume 1), Beijing Normal University Press, 2014.
11. National Bureau of Statistics: The Further Promotion of Supply-Side Structural Reform, the Speeding Up of Transformation and Upgrading—No. 10 of the Series of Economic and Social Development Achievements Since the 18th CPC National Congress, http: //www.stats.gov.cn/tjsj/sjjd/201707/t20170714_1513096.html.
12. Guo Tongxin: The Constant Promotion of Transformation and Upgrading, the Unceasing Enhancement of Development Momentum, People's Daily, April 27, 2017.
13. State Council: Report on Accelerating the Development of Higher Education, 1983.
14. State Council: Decision of the State Council on the Main Points of the Current Industrial Policies, 1989.
15. State Council: Decision of the State Council on Vigorously Developing Vocational and Technical Education, 1991.
16. State Council: Opinions of the State Council on the Implementation of "Outline of China's Education Reform and Development, 1994.
17. The State Education Committee: The Ninth Five-Year Plan for China's Educational Development and the Development Outline by 2010, 1996.
18. State Council: Decision of the CPC Central Committee and the State Council on Deepening Education Reform and Comprehensively Promoting Quality Education, 1999.
19. State Council: Decision of the State Council on Vigorously Promoting the Reform and Development of Vocational Education, 2002.
20. State Council: Decision of the State Council on Vigorously Developing Vocational Education, 2005.
21. State Council: Interim Provisions on Promoting the Industrial Structure Adjustment, 2005.
22. State Council: Main Points for the Work of the State Council in 2006, 2006.
23. State Council: Several Opinions of the State Council on Accelerating the Development of the Service Industry, 2007.
24. State Council: Main Points for the Work of the State Council in 2007, 2007.
25. State Council: Decision of the State Council on Accelerating the Fostering and Development of Strategic Emerging Industries, 2010.
26. Office of National Medium-and Long-Term Education Reform and Development Plan: Outline of the National Medium- and Long-Term Education Reform and Development Plan (2010–2020), 2010.
27. State Council: Industrial Transformation and Upgrading Plan (2011–2015), 2011.
28. State Council: The '12th Five-Year' Plan for the National Development of Strategic Emerging Industries, 2012.

29. State Council: Opinions of the State Council on Strengthening the Improvement of Teachers, 2012.
30. State Council: Decision of the State Council on Accelerating the Development of Modern Vocational Education, 2014.
31. State Council: Guiding Opinions of the State Council of the People's Republic of China, on Accelerating Development of Productive Service and Promoting Industrial Structure Adjustment and Upgrade, 2014.
32. State Council: The '13th Five-Year' National Science and Technology Innovation Plan, 2016.
33. State Council: The '13th Five-Year' Plan for China's Educational Development, 2017.
34. The National Education Inspection Team: The National Education Inspection Report: Focus on Secondary Vocational Education (Abstract), 2011.
35. National Bureau of Statistics: National Data, http://data.stats.gov.cn/easyquery.htm?cn=C01.
36. National Bureau of Statistics: China Statistical Yearbook (2016), http://www.stats.gov.cn/tjsj/ndsj/2016/indexch.htm.
37. Hangzhou Municipal People's Government: Several Opinions of Hangzhou Municipal People's Government on Promoting School-Enterprise Cooperation in Secondary Vocational Education, 2012.
38. Li Keqiang: Report on the Work of the Government at the Fourth Session of the 12th National People's Congress of the People's Republic of China, 2016.
39. He Yinglin, Song Xingchuan: Research on the Concept of Highly Skilled Talent, Vocational & Technical Education Forum, No.1, 2006.
40. MOE: Several Plans for the Two-Year Teaching Arrangements of Engineering Specialties in Secondary Specialized Schools, 1979.
41. MOE: Regulations Concerning the Work of Full-Time Secondary Specialized Schools, 1979.
42. MOE, MOHRSS (former State Labour Bureau): Report on the Structural Reform of Secondary Education, 1980.
43. MOE: Action Plan for Education Rejuvenation for the 21st Century, 1998.
44. MOE: Notice of MOE on Adjusting Some National Key Vocational Teacher Training Bases, 1998.
45. MOE: Opinions of the Trial Implementation on Developing Higher Vocational and Technical Education According to New Management Modes and Operational Mechanisms, 1999.
46. MOE: Standards Setting for Higher Vocational Schools (Provisional), 2000.
47. MOE: Notice on the Work of Encouraging In-Service Secondary Vocational School Teachers for Their Further Study of Master Degree, 2000.
48. MOE: Opinions on Comprehensively Promoting Quality-Oriented Education and Deepening the Teaching Reform of Secondary Vocational Education, 2000.
49. MOE: National Statistics Bulletin on Education Career Development 1999, 2000.

50. MOE: National Statistics Bulletin on Education Career Development 2000, 2001.
51. MOE: Opinions on Curriculum Setting and Teaching Arrangement of Moral Education in Secondary Vocational Schools, 2001.
52. MOE: Decision on Vigorously Promoting the Reform and Development of Vocational Education, 2002.
53. Seven departments including MOE: Several Opinions of Seven Departments including MOE on Further Enhancing Vocational Education, 2002.
54. MOE: Principles and Opinions on Formulating Professional Teaching Plans for Higher Vocational and Technical Education, 2002.
55. MOE: Key Points of Teaching Management for Higher Vocational Schools, Junior Colleges and Adult Higher Colleges, 2002.
56. MOE: Opinions of MOE on Reinforcing the Cultivation of Higher Vocational and Technical Talents, 2002.
57. MOE: Opinions of the General Office of MOE on Enhancing Faculty Development in Higher Vocational (Higher Technical) Colleges and Universities, 2002.
58. MOE: Some Opinions of MOE on Being Employment-Oriented and Deepening the Reform of Higher Vocational Education, 2004.
59. MOE: The Instructive Specialty Catalogue for Higher Vocational and Technical Education in Regular Colleges and Universities (Trial), 2004.
60. MOE: Action Plan for Education Rejuvenation in 2003–2007, 2004.
61. Seven departments including MOE: Several Opinions on Further Enhancing Vocational Education, 2004.
62. MOE: Opinions on Establishing a System for Secondary Vocational School Teachers to Practice in Enterprises, 2006.
63. MOE, MOF: Opinions on Implementing the Construction Plan of National Demonstrative Higher Vocational Colleges and Accelerating the Reform and Development of Higher Vocational Education, 2006.
64. MOE: Several Opinions of MOE on Comprehensively Improving the Teaching Quality of Higher Vocational Education, 2006.
65. MOE, MOF: Opinions of MOE and MOF on Implementing the Quality Improvement Plan for Secondary Vocational School Teachers, 2006.
66. MOE: Main Points for the Work of MOE in 2006, 2006.
67. MOE: Main Points for the Work of MOE in 2007, 2007.
68. MOE: Main Points for the Work of MOE in 2008, 2008.
69. MOE: Several Opinions of MOE on Further Deepening the Teaching Innovation of Secondary Vocational Education, 2008.
70. MOE: Main Points for the Work of MOE in 2009, 2009.
71. MOE: Principles and Opinions of MOE on Formulating Teaching Plans for Secondary Vocational Schools, 2009.

72. MOE: Notice of MOE on Printing and Distributing "The Specialty Catalogue of Secondary Vocational Schools (Revised in 2010)", 2010.
73. MOE: The Specialty Catalogue of Secondary Vocational Schools (Revised in 2010), 2010.
74. MOE: Notice on the 2010 Project Application of the Specialized Teaching Resources Database for Higher Vocational Education, 2010.
75. MOE: Notice on Supporting Higher Vocational Schools to Improve the Ability of Developing Professional Service Industries, 2011.
76. MOE: Instructions of MOE on Promoting the Coordinated Development between Secondary and Higher Vocational Education, 2011.
77. MOE: Opinions of MOE on Giving Full Play to the Guiding Role of Industries and Promoting the Reform and Development of Vocational Education, 2011.
78. MOE, MOF: Opinions of MOE and MOF on Implementing the Quality Improvement Plan for Vocational School Teachers, 2011.
79. MOE: Opinions of MOE on Strengthening Faculty Development of Secondary Vocational Schools during the '12th Five-Year' Period, 2011.
80. MOE: Opinions on Further Improving the Cultivation and Training System for Vocational Teachers, 2011.
81. MOE: Some Suggestions on the Overall Improvement of the Quality of Higher Education, 2012.
82. MOE: Opinions of the General Office of MOE on Formulating Specialized Teaching Standards for Secondary Vocational Schools, 2012.
83. MOE, NDRC and MOF: Opinions on Deepening the Reform of Teacher Education, 2012.
84. MOE: Instructions of MOE on Further Promoting Educational Reform and Cooperative Development in Yangtze River Delta, 2014.
85. Six departments including MOE: Planning for the Establishment of a Modern Vocational Education System (2014–2020), 2014,
86. MOE: Notice of MOE on Printing and Distributing the "Administrative Measures for Specialty Setup of Higher Vocational Education (Specialist)" and "The Specialty Catalogue of Higher Vocational Education (Specialist) in Regular Colleges and Universities (2015)", 2015.
87. MOE: Opinions on Deepening the Teaching Reform of Vocational Education and Comprehensively Enhancing the Quality of Talent Training, 2015.
88. MOE: Action Plan for Innovation and Development of Higher Vocational Education (2015–2018), 2015.
89. National Bureau of Statistics of China: National Statistics Bulletin on Education Career Development 2015, 2016.
90. MOE: Notice on Doing Well in Related Work to the Specialized Teaching Resources Database for Vocational Education in 2016, 2016.
91. MOE, MOF: Opinions of MOE and MOF on Implementing the Quality Improvement Plan for Vocational School Teachers (2017–2020), 2016.

92. MOE: Provisions on Enterprise Practice for Vocational School Teachers, 2016.
93. MOE: Talent Development Planning in the Manufacturing Industry, 2016.
94. MOE: Opinions of MOE on the Work of Setting Up Colleges and Universities during the 'Thirteenth Five-Year Plan' Period, 2017.
95. Reporter: Four out of Ten College Graduates Become Front-Line Technical Workers, Xinmin Evening News (Daily), March 15, 2005.
96. Jiang Xiaojuan: The Improvement and Upgrade of Industrial Structure: New Tasks in the New Stage, Finance & Trade Economics, No. 4, 2005.
97. Jin Yanming, Ye Yongyin: The Quiet Transformation of Talent Structure after "Human Substituted by Machines" in Dongguan, http://news.xinhuanet.com/city/2016-04/13/c_128891214.htm
98. Kathleen Thelen: How Institutions Evolve—The Political Economy of Skills in Germany, Britain, the United States, and Japan, Shanghai People's Publishing House, 2010.
99. Lang Qunxiu: Analysis on the Connotation of Highly Skilled Talent, Vocational and Technical Education, No. 22, 2006.
100. Ministry of Labour (now MOHRSS): Opinions of the Ministry of Labour on Reinforcing Vocational and Technical Training and Faculty Development, 1989.
101. Li Yuhong: Research on the Classification System of Vocational Education—On the Construction of Classification Standards for Marketing Vocational Education, China Fortune Press, 2012.
102. Lin Dan: The Illusion and Truth of the Distorted Educational Policies, Teaching and Administration, No. 6, 2004.
103. Lin Zhibo: Select Talents without Sticking to One pattern, People's Daily, Page 4, December 19, 2003.
104. Liu Xiyao: Report at the National Conference on Education (Abstract), 1978.
105. Liu Fonian: Review and Exploration—On Several Educational Theoretical Issues, East China Normal University Press, 1991.
106. Liu Li: Research on the Wage Incentive Mechanism of Technical and Skilled Talents in Iron and Steel Enterprises, China Business·Theoretical Research, No. 16, 2013.
107. Liu Chunsheng, Ma Zhenhua: Definition of Highly Skilled Talent, Communication of Vocational Education No. 3, 2006.
108. Luo Chuanyin: Perfect the Highly Skilled Talent Training System, China Personnel, October 25, 2010.
109. Ouyang Yuliang, Gao Zhimin, Wang Liangjian: An Overview of Research on Highly Skilled Talents, Vocational and Technical Education, No. 34, 2006.
110. Pan Manyuan: My View on the Orientation of Application-Oriented Undergraduate Colleges and Universities, Research in Education Development, No. 21, 2007.
111. Pan Haisheng, Wang Shibin, Long Deyi: Analysis on the Status and Influencing Factors of School-Enterprise Cooperation for China's Higher Vocational Education, Research in Higher Education of Engineering, No. 3, 2013.

112. Pan Jianfeng: Exploration of Modern Apprentice: A Comparatively Successful Case, Chinese Vocational and Technical Education, No. 5, 2016.
113. Cingta Query: The 181 Universities are a Step Ahead of Other Universities in Transforming Themselves into Application-Oriented Universities, http://www.360doc.com/content/16/0311/14/7592490_541311539.shtml.
114. The Talent Work Conference Brings Four Major Changes, Beijing Times, December 22, 2003.
115. Research Group "On Studying and Experimenting the Infiltrated 'Dual Enrollment, Dual Diploma' School-Operating Model of Vocational School and Ordinary School in Secondary Education" in Shanghai: Preliminary Exploration of the School-Operating Models of Comprehensive Senior High Schools, Vocational & Technical Education Forum, No.5, 1999.
116. Secretariat of Shanghai Vocational and Technical Education Forum: Basic Understanding of Several Issues about Vocational and Technical Education—Studies on Shanghai Vocational and Technical Education Forum for the Past Decade, Higher Education Press, 2005.
117. Shanghai Municipal Labour and Social Security Bureau (now Shanghai Municipal Human Resources and Social Security Bureau): Relevant Circumstances about Enhancing Vocational Training and Accelerating the Establishment of a Professional Skilled Talent Team in Shanghai, 2003.
118. Shanghai Municipal Education Commission: Action Plan for Deepening the Curriculum Materials Reform of Secondary Vocational Education in Shanghai (2004–2007), 2004.
119. Si Yingge: 114 Staffs are Hired as Worker Technicians and Offered High Salaries by Qianqiu Coal Mine, Trade Union Information, No. 14, 2011.
120. Shi Weiping, Xu Guoqing: Reflection and Exploration on the School-Operating Model of Urban Secondary Vocational Schools in China, Education Research, No. 12, 2000.
121. Song Fengjing: Skilled Talent Cultivation and Beijing's Economic Development, Hualing Press, 2005.
122. Sun Yuzhi: Modern Apprenticeship in Europe, China Labor and Social Security Publishing House, 2016.
123. Sun Cuixiang: Training of Vocational Teachers: A Problem that Needs Immediate Attention, Vocational & Technical Education Forum, No. 25, 2013.
124. Issuance of the Enforcement Regulations of the Highly Skilled Talent Plan Issued by Taicang City (County-Level), Suzhou Human Resources and Social Security Network, www.tcrcsc.com/news_18617.html
125. Tan Zhaopeng: Some Experience about Studying "Decision of the CPC Central Committee on Reform of the Education System", Educational Review, No. 4, 1985.
126. Wang Tongsan: Quantitative Economics in the 21st Century (Volume 3), Social Sciences Academic Press (China), 2003.

127. Wang Xing: The Social Construction of Skill Formation—A Sociology Approach to the Evolving Trajectory of the Apprentice in China Factories, Social Sciences Academic Press (China), 2014.
128. Wang Wenjin: Survey Report on School-Enterprise Cooperation in Enterprises, Chinese Vocational and Technical Education, No. 2, 2009.
129. Wang Yun, Zeng Zheng: Continuous Optimization and Upgrade of Industrial Structure is an Important Trait of the New Normal, Gmw.cn, http://news.xinhuanet.com/fortune/2016-01/05/c_128597450.htm
130. Anonymous: An Undercover PhD—Terrified by the Assembly Lines in the Workshops for 25 Days, http://club.china.com
131. Xu Han: A Comparative Study of Chinese and German Secondary Vocational Curriculum Reform, China Social Sciences Press, 2015.
132. Guo Yushi, Zhang Tianfei, etc., Notes about the "Decision of the CPC Central Committee on the Reform of the Education System", Journal of East China Normal University (Educational Sciences), 1985.
133. Chief editor Xue Ximin: Theory and Practice of Higher Vocational and Technical Education, Fudan University Press, 2000.
134. Yan Li: Seek for a Technician with an Annual Salary of RMB 500, 000, Xinmin Evening News (Daily), April 7, 2005.
135. Yan Xueyi: On Vocational and Technical Education, Shanghai Scientific and Technological Literature Press, 1999.
136. Yang Jintu: Major Changes in 30 Years—Overview of the Important Issues in Vocational Education in China in 1979–2008, Educational Science Publishing House, 2011.
137. Yang Jintu: Rise and Fall of Vocational Education and Replacement of Old and New Educational Thinking—A Hundred Years of Vocational Education Review, Research in Educational Development, No. 24, 2004.
138. Yang Jintu: Analysis on the Policy Environment of Developing Vocational Education in China, Research in Educational Development, No. 9, 2005.
139. Yang Jintu: Talent Concept and Vocational Education, Vocational and Technical Education, No.36, 2008.
140. Yang Jintu: Review of the Development History of Chinese Higher Vocational Education in the 20th Century, Vocational & Technical Education Forum, No. 13, 2017.
141. Yang Peiting: The Theory of Science and Technology, Zhejiang Education Publishing House, 1985.
142. Yin Weimin: Promote the Spirit of World Skills Competition and Enhance the Construction of Skilled Talents, Economic Daily, December 16, 2015.
143. Yin Ming: Handbook of Socialist Market Economy, Hehai University Press, 1993.
144. Yin Weimin, Wang Fang, Liu Keyong: Early Warning Report on the Goodness of Fit of the Specialty Structure of Vocational Schools with the Industrial Structure in Jiangsu Province (2016), Jiangsu Phoenix Education Publishing, Ltd, 2017.

145. State Education Commission (now MOE): Several Opinions on Strengthening Faculty Development in Vocational and Technical Schools, 1986.
146. State Education Commission (now MOE): Opinions on Formulating Teaching Plans for (Three-Year) Vocational Senior High Schools, 1990.
147. State Education Commission (now MOE): Notice of the State Education Commission on Promulgating "The Specialty Catalogue for Regular Secondary Specialized Schools", 1993.
148. State Education Commission (now MOE): Principles and Opinions on Deepening the Teaching Reform of Vocational Education for the 21st Century, 1998.
149. Vocational and Technical Education: 20 Years of Review and Witnessing, Vocational and Technical Education, 1999.
150. CPC Central Committee: Decision of the CPC Central Committee on the Reform of the Education System, 1985.
151. CPC Central Committee, State Council: Outline of China's Education Reform and Development, 1993.
152. The Nineteenth Session of the Eighth National People's Congress: Vocational Education Law of the People's Republic of China, 1996.
153. CPC Central Committee: Decision of the CPC Central Committee on Certain Major Issues Concerning the Reform and Development of State-Owned Enterprises, 1999.
154. The CPC Central Committee and the State Council: Decision of the CPC Central Committee and the State Council on Further Enhancing the Development of Human Resources, 2003.
155. The Financial and Economic Committee of the National People's Congress, NDRC: The 13th Five-Year Plan for Economic and Social Development of the People's Republic of China, 2016.
156. Edited by China Vocational Education Association: Collected Works of Huang Yanpei on Education, Shanghai Educational Publishing House, 1985.
157. China Association of Staff and Workers Education and Vocational Training: School-Enterprise Cooperation has Become a Normal Teaching Mode in Technical Training Schools—Research Report on the Cultivation of Chinese Technical Talents, Vocational and Technical Education, No. 30, 2009.
158. National Bureau of Statistics of China: National Statistics Bulletin on Education Career Development 1995, www.edu.cn/edu/tjsj/zhsj/jiao_yu_fa_zhan/200603/t20060323_11629.shtml
159. The Editorial Department of Educational Statistics Yearbook of China: Educational Statistics Yearbook of China, People's Education Press, 2012.
160. Zhang Xiaoming: Shanghai's Economic Development over the Past 3 Decades: A Giant Leap from Ten-Billion Level to Thousand-Billion Level, Wenhui Daily, December 30, 2008.
161. Zhu Yu, Gui Huizhen: Take Advantages of the East Wind to Set Sail Smoothly—Overview of National Talent Work, XINHUANET, December 19, 2003.

# Foreign


1. P. Gonon Akoojee, U. Hauschildt, C. Hofmann. Apprenticeship in a Globalized World: Premises, Promises and Pitfalls. Co-organisers and Cooperation Partners of the INAP Conference 2013.
2. BMB+F. Duale Berufausbildung an der Schwelle zum nächsten Jahrtausend. Herausforderungen bewältigen-voneinander lernen. Bericht der Konferenz zur Duale Berufsausbildung in Dänemark, Deutschland, Liechtenstein, Luxemburg, Nieserlande, Österreich, Schweiz. Bonn. 1999.
3. Bundensminiterium für Bildung und Forschung. Berufsbildungsbericht 2017. Bundesministerium für Bildung und Forschung (BMBF). Bonn 2017.
4. Christian Schmidt. Übergänge und Übergangssystem vor dem Hintergrund einer nachhaltigen Entwicklung des Berufsbildungssystem. In: Andreas Fischer/Dietmar Frommberger. Vielfalt an Übergängen in der beruflichen Bildung-Zwölf Ansichten. Schneider Verlag, 2013.
5. DIHK. Ausbildung 2015. Ergebinisse eine DIHK Online Unternehmensbefragung. Berlin 2015: 7.
6. Jörg Dräger/Clemens Wieland. Vorwort [R]//Dieter Euler. Das duale System in Deutschland-Vorbild für einen Transfer ins Ausland? Eine Studie im Auftrag der Bertelsmann Stiftung [R]. Gütersloh: Bertelsmann Stiftung, 2013.
7. Felix Rauner. Innovative Berufsbildung-von einem Versorgungs-zu einem Innovationsprojekt. In: Dorothea Piening/Felix Rauner. Innovative Berufsbildung㊁Auf die Attraktivität für Jugendliche und Unternehmen Kommt es an! Lit Verlag Berlin 2008.
8. K. C. Gray & E. L. Herr. Workforce Education: The Basics [M]. Boston: Allyn and Bacon, 1998.
9. Günter Walden, Ursula Beicht, Hermann Herget. Warum Betriebe (nicht) ausbilden, BWP 2002, (02).
10. J. S. Scott, M. Sarkees-Wircenski. Overview of Career and Technical Education [M]. USA: American Technical Publishers. 2008.
11. Rainer Gepperth. Grußworte und Referate vor dem Plenum. Symposium zur beruflichen Bildung 1994 Hangzhou.
12. B. R. Stewart & D. H. Bristow. Tech prep programs: the role and essential elements, in Journal of vocational and technical education, Volume 13, Number 2 (1997).
13. Thomas Sondermann & Beate Scheffler Berufsbildung 2020-Konsequenzen für die Weiterentwicklung des Berufskonzepts. Berufsbildung in Wissenschaft und Praxis. 2012.
14. Zhiqun Zhao, Felix Rauner, Ursel Hauschildt. Assuring the Acquisition of Expertise: Apprenticeship in the Modern Economy. Beijing: Foreign Language Teaching and Research Press. 2011.

www.ingramcontent.com/pod-product-compliance
Ingram Content Group UK Ltd.
Pitfield, Milton Keynes, MK11 3LW, UK
UKHW021827100926
8556IPUK00003B/196

9 781433 169304